Reforms, Reaction, Revolutions (1855–1932)

HISTORY OF RUSSIA

VOLUME THREE

HISTORY OF RUSSIA

Reforms, Reaction,

by **PAUL MILIUKOV,** *former professor at the University*

of Moscow, and **CHARLES SEIGNOBOS** *and*

L. EISENMANN, *professors at the University of Paris*

Translated by Charles Lam Markmann

FUNK & WAGNALLS

VOLUME THREE

Revolutions (1855–1932)

WITH THE COLLABORATION OF

CAMENA D'ALMEIDA, *professor at the University of Bordeaux;*
General G. DANILOV, *former Quartermaster General of the Russian Armies;* P. GRONSKY, *former professor at the Polytechnic Institute of Petrograd;* A. KIZEVETTER, *professor at the University of Prague, former professor at the University of Moscow;*
V. MYAKOTIN, *professor at the University of Sofia;* B. MIRKIN-GUETZEVITCH, *former professor at the University of Leningrad;*
and L. NIEDERLE, *honorary professor at the University of Prague*

NEW YORK

Contents

*The first five sections and the penultimate section of this part of the chapter were written by Professor Mirkin-Guetzevitch; the two others were written by Professor Miliukov.

*Professor Mirkin-Guetzevitch was responsible for all except the sections on The Construction of the Chinese-Eastern Railway and the Leasing of the Liao-Tung Peninsula, written by Professor Gronsky, and The Russian-Japanese War, written by General Danilov.

CHAPTER SEVEN

Nicholas II (1894–1917): The Reign Concluded
[PAUL MILIUKOV]

List of Maps

Reforms, Reaction, Revolution (1855–1932)

HISTORY OF RUSSIA

VOLUME THREE

CHAPTER 1

Alexander II (1855–1881)

I / THE END OF THE CRIMEAN WAR (1855–1856) AND THE EX-PECTATION OF REFORMS [B. MIRKIN-GUETZEVITCH]

The Austrian Ultimatum

The Crimean War was at its height when Alexander II became tsar. The Allies were occupying Russian soil and laying siege to Sebastopol; the Austrian army was ready to join them, and enemy squadrons in all Russian waters, whether in Europe or in the Far East, had the coast line within range of their guns.

Although the new tsar genuinely wanted peace, he had to carry on the war. Sebastopol fell on 27 August/8 September 1855 after a heroic defense, but the Russian army in the Crimea was able to evacuate the city and take up new positions outside it without pursuit by the Allies, who did not occupy the city until 30 August/11 September. In the Caucasus the Russians defeated the Turkish army of Anatolia and captured the fortress of Kars on 16/28 November 1855. On 28 December, acting in concert with England, Austria threatened to join the Allies if Alexander did not accept her ultimatum by January 17, 1856. This ultimatum stipulated that the Danubian principalities must be placed under a collective European protectorate; that the contracting parties must have the right of control of Danube navigation; that the Black Sea be neutralized; that the rights of Christians in the Ottoman Empire be recognized without prejudice to Turkey's independence and the sultan's sovereignty, and that the belligerents retain the right, when peace talks were initiated, to propose further conditions conformable to the peace of Europe. At first Alexander rejected this ultimatum, especially its final provision, the vagueness of which made him anxious. Then, after he had been reassured that this article was aimed only at the neutralization of the Åland Islands and the restoration of Kars to the Turks, and particularly after his uncle, King Friedrich Wilhelm IV of Prussia, had made it plain to him that all hope was lost and all resistance was futile, he summoned a special council to study the Austrian terms. Its chairman, Nesselrode, declared himself in favor of accepting them, and the other members painted so desperate a picture of the military and financial situation that it seemed impossible to continue the war. A few years later Alexander II was to accuse himself of having been a coward in these days of 1856.

The Congress of Paris (1856)

The success of his troops in the Caucasus made it possible for the tsar to accept Austria's terms on 4/16 January 1856 and to agree to an armistice and the initiation of peace negotiations. The Congress of Paris opened on February 25 under the chairmanship of Comte Walewski, Foreign Minister to Napoleon III. Russia's representative was Count Alexis Orlov, Austria's were Buol and Baron v. Hübner, England's were Lord Clarendon and Lord Cowley, Sardinia's was Conte di Cavour, and Turkey's were Ali Pasha and Fuad. Prussia was not permitted to participate until after the negotiations had begun. The treaty of peace was signed on March 30.

This treaty placed Turkey under the protection of all the European powers, which guaranteed her territorial integrity and independence (Article XVII). In the event of conflict between Turkey and any of the signatory powers, mediation would be compulsory (Article VIII). The protection of the Ottoman Empire's Christian subjects was entrusted to all the great European powers rather than to Russia alone, as had been the case before the war. The treaty recorded for posterity the sultan's voluntary agreement to the promulgation, in his name alone and by virtue of his sovereign rights, of a firman that would regularize the legal status of his Christian subjects (Article IX). It confirmed the Straits Convention of 1841 and neutralized the Black Sea, on the coasts of which neither Russia nor Turkey would any longer be permitted to maintain arsenals; under a special convention that was endorsed by the other powers they pledged themselves to keep only a limited number of light vessels in the Black Sea for coast-guard purposes (Articles X–XIV). The treaty also regulated navigation on the Danube and stripped Russia of a part of Bessarabia in order to incorporate it into Moldavia (Articles XX and XXI).

On April 15, 1856, under a treaty aimed against Russia, the guaranty of Turkey's territorial integrity was pledged by England, Austria, and France; it provided as well that any violation of the Treaty of Paris would be treated as a *casus belli*. Under a convention with France and England, Russia agreed to the neutralization of the Åland Islands. In Paris, Count Orlov gave Napoleon III oral assurance that reforms would be carried out in Poland, that the Catholic church would no longer be persecuted there, etc. For his part, Napoleon III promised not to raise the Polish question in the forthcoming Congress.

The Expectation of Reforms

The failure of the Crimean War was tantamount to a condemnation of the reign of Nicholas I. The defeat and the harsh terms of the Treaty of Paris were proof to the eyes of the whole world of the need for reforms within Russia.

During the lifetime of Nicholas I only a few political emigrants such as Nikolai Turgenyev and Alexander Herzen had dared openly and unmercifully to criticize the reactionary government and the military disaster. After the accession of Alexander II, the resentment of the general public, which had mounted during the final years of the previous reign, began to make itself evident. The advent of a new tsar gave rise to the hope of a political change. The death of Nicholas I was regarded as the end of that kind of governmental tutelage that extended over the entire country and burdened the whole organization of society. It was hoped that the new sovereign would inaugurate a new era in Russian history, that the despotic rule of Nicholas' police and the reactionary measures applied since 1848 would disappear, and that society would be able freely to voice its opinions. Nevertheless the Russian intellectuals, whom the oppressive rule of Nicholas had constrained to inaction, did not at first attempt to urge the new sovereign to embark on reforms, for they were convinced that he himself was about to take such an initiative. They contented themselves with a modest program, formulated by Nikolai Chernyshevsky in the *Sovremennik* in 1856: assistance to education, an increase in the number of teachers and pupils, the construction of railways, and the scientific exploitation of the country's economic resources. This last, unspecific clause was intended to imply the abolition of serfdom, on which no one dared to voice his views freely in public but the necessity of which was categorically stated in manuscript documents that were circulated in Moscow and Petersburg at the time. Emancipation was the fundamental problem to the intellectuals. They believed that it could entail the alteration of the entire political system: if the emancipation of the peasants was

also made the basis for the destruction of the bureaucratic system—
that is, the predominance of the nobility in local institutions—there
would be no choice, they said, but to reform the whole system as well.
They were so convinced that a liberal policy was at hand that they
enthusiastically greeted every government statement, even the most
meaningless. For example, when in the manifesto of 19/31 March
1856, which announced to Russia that the war had ended and
peace had been made, Alexander expressed the hope that with the
aid of Providence "the internal organization" of the country "would
be strengthened and improved, that justice and mercy would prevail
in the courts, that the desire to learn and to perform useful labor
would spread and grow everywhere, and that every man would enjoy
the fruits of his honest toil in peace under the protection of laws
affording equal justice to all," the intellectuals took these rather
vague pledges for references to the liberal principles of a new domestic
policy.

While the nation was expecting reforms, Alexander II recognized
their necessity and was preparing to put them into practice as soon
as the war ended.

II / THE PERIOD OF THE "GREAT REFORMS" [P. GRONSKY]

The Personality of Alexander II and His Political Apprenticeship

Alexander II is often presented by the official panegyrists as the
major inspiration and the prime mover of the "great reforms." His
biographers, like the memorialists of his own time, emphasize the
remarkable character of the Liberator Tsar. All of them portray
him as a man superior to his associates, striding with a firm step
down the road of reform. Nothing could be less accurate. The training that had been given to Alexander II had not prepared him to
play the part of the reformer.

Certainly his childhood and youth had benefited by the influence of
his tutors, Mörder and the famous poet, Vasily Zhukovsky. Both were
men of great culture, steeped in humanitarian ideals, and they had
succeeded in implanting worthy sentiments in the mind of their
young pupil. The whole secret of Mörder's influence on Alexander's
character, according to Zhukovsky, "lay in the gentle and beneficent
influence of a naturally noble soul." But neither of these men was
capable of preparing Alexander for his future task. Zhukovsky himself, though he had fostered the development of the young prince's

literary tastes, had been unable, because of the lack of a desire to do so and of clearly defined political ideas, to cultivate civic virtues in his pupil and to give him a definite idea of what Russia was and of everything that she needed.

Nevertheless, when he ascended the throne at the age of twenty-three, Alexander was already a man of experience. He was a man whose tastes, whose sympathies, and whose convictions had by now been shaped. His father had always striven to make a good soldier of him, as accustomed to handling weapons and commanding troops as he was inculcated with all the military science of his time. Much time and effort had been dedicated to his military education. He had become enthusiastically interested not only in strategy, military history, fortification, and tactics, but also in maneuvers and reviews. He had devoted the greater part of his time to them and had associated largely with palace guard officers. His father, who had always seized any occasion to bring the young man into the process of government, had often made him his deputy when he himself was traveling. Sent in 1848 to Vienna and Berlin, where he could observe for himself the growth of the revolutionary movement, Alexander had been invested with full powers to carry on diplomatic negotiations of great importance and delicate character. Appointed to head the military schools, he had punctiliously devoted himself to meeting their needs and improving their curricula and teaching systems. As he had grown more familiar with affairs of state, he had become a convinced upholder of his father's political system. When the news of the French revolution of 1848 spread through Petersburg and Nicholas issued his famous manifesto against the revolutionary tide in Europe, Alexander called together the officers of the guard and, by way of demonstrating their participation in the ideas set forth in the manifesto, he and they had organized a lively demonstration in honor of the tsar. It was not only with Alexander's approval but occasionally on his initiative, as in the case of the creation of the famous Buturlin Committee,* that his father had invoked certain reactionary measures. Alexander had also given evidence of a conservative conception of the peasant problem, and more than once, in the sessions of special commissions, he had championed the interests and the prerogatives of the landed proprietors. It was well known that he had not approved of Bibikov's system of inventories † and that it was as a result of his intervention in 1853 that this system had not been introduced into Lithuania. These things

*See Volume II, p. 278.
†See Volume II, p. 258.

explained the hope that was invested in him by much of the nobility.

While there was every ground to believe that he could carry on his father's work, the public began to become aware, during the Crimean War and especially after the signature of the Treaty of Paris, that he had made up his mind to reform the political system and to abolish serfdom. There could be no further doubt on this score after the famous address that he delivered in the spring of 1856 to the Moscow nobility, which was uneasy over his plans:

There are rumors that it is my intention to abolish serfdom. This is not correct, but this ill-founded hope has already given rise to a number of instances of refusal of obedience by peasants to landowners. You can freely state as much everywhere. Nonetheless I will not say that I am wholly opposed to such a measure. We are living in an age that will one day, perhaps, require that this be done. I believe that you are of the same opinion as I; hence it is preferable that such a move come from above rather than from below.

For the bitter experience of the war had opened his eyes. He had recognized that Russia's backward condition was the major reason for her political impotence and that, unless there were reforms, the revolution that he himself had seen in Europe in 1848 might break out one day in Russia and assume formidable dimensions. If, in spite of his conservative principles, he was prepared to bring about reforms and to abolish serfdom, it was in order to assure the peace and prosperity of his empire.

The Emancipation of the Serfs

From the time when the nobility had been relieved of the obligation of military service, the peasants, who knew that serfdom had been the consequence of that obligation, had been convinced that all the land was to be restored to them. Since the ukase of Peter III on the "liberties of the nobility," they had been waiting with certainty, and sometimes with impatience, for the tsar to set them free without depriving them of their land. There was hardly a moment when, in connection with the most varied events, the rumor of their imminent liberation did not run through the countrysides. Forever disappointed, they consistently ascribed the postponement of this reform to the scheming of the nobles, who were resisting the tsar's wishes and "evading" his ukases. That was why a partial solution of the peasant problem was impossible. Either it must be left as it was or it must be resolved completely. If Alexander made up his mind to attack it first, it was because, as long as serfdom continued to exist, it would be impossible even to contemplate the execution of the other necessary reforms to further the economic development of the country.

When Alexander declared in Moscow, to the amazement of everyone, even Lanskoi, his minister of the interior, that the nobility ought to give thought to the eventual abolition of serfdom, the nobles themselves were still far from ready to assume the initiative of this step. Lanskoi set about examining the problem with the help of A. Levshin, who was supposed to be an expert on the subject. But the nobles were in no hurry. They still believed that they could successfully pretend to know nothing at all about the matter. Since the censorship was still vigorously prohibiting any allusion to serfdom—the interdict was not to be lifted until the end of 1857—it was impossible to raise the question even in the press. No one knew what attitude to take or what was intended by the government, from which everyone was accustomed to receiving his opinions. Advocates of a radical solution—that is, the emancipation of the peasants and the redemption of their holdings from the landowners with the help of the state—prepared two proposals under the leadership of Professor Kavelin and a young official in the Ministry of the Interior, Nikolai Miliutin. The first was soon made public by Chernyshevsky in the *Sovremennik;* the second was presented to the tsar by Grand Duchess Yelena Pavlovna, who herself favored the liberation of the serfs. With the permission of Alexander, who was still waiting for the nobility to take the initiative of the reform, a "secret" commission was set up in January 1857 to study both proposals. Composed of partisans (I. I. Rostovtsev) and opponents (headed by Alexis Orlov) of emancipation, it did not push itself in the completion of its task, for the committee was convinced that its fate would be identical with that of all its predecessors under Nicholas. Then, in order to accelerate its labors, Alexander enlarged it by appointing his brother, Konstantin Nikolayevitch, who was well known for his liberal views. Toward the same end Konstantin suggested that the government's intentions be made public. On 18/30 August 1857 the commission rejected this suggestion, preferring gradually to assemble the documentation that it required. In the end the decisive step was taken. At the instigation of Nazimov, governor general of Vilna, the nobles of the Lithuanian provinces declared their readiness to pose the principle of the abolition of serfdom, provided that the landowners retain all their holdings. Alexander now had the pretext for which he had been waiting in order to accomplish his reform. On 20 November/2 December 1857 a rescript called on the nobles of the Lithuanian provinces in three governments to elect committees assigned to the examination of methods of emancipation on the basis of two mandatory principles: the right of the emancipated peasant to buy his *usadebnaya osyedlost*—the plot of land on which he had his "domicile": hut and outbuildings—within a specified time (this was Levshin's idea), and, pending his ability to purchase it, his right of enjoyment of a parcel of land adequate to supply his needs and enable him to pay his taxes. This was not really a radical reform, but, in comparison to the Lithuanian nobles' proposals, it was a major forward step.

Initially the rescript was circulated among the nobility of the other provinces as a secret document, but then it was made public. Soon it came to the knowledge of the peasants. The nobles resigned themselves to asking for the creation of committees similar to those in the Lithuanian governments, because they were afraid of disorders and also because in the majority they feared that they might be forced to accept the terms of emancipation laid down for the Lithuanian landowners.

For there was in fact no identity of interests between the landowners of the northern Russian provinces, which were not very fertile but were, rather, industrial, and those of the southern provinces, where agriculture was the major source of wealth.

Most often the northern nobleman, since there was not enough profit in it, did not directly exploit his land. He preferred to subject his serfs to tribute proportioned not only to the production of their land holdings but also to their incomes from the various trades that they practiced outside the village. This was why he placed less value on his land than on his ownership of the peasant's person, through which he was enabled to exploit the man's special knowledge and vocational aptitude. Hence the northern nobleman's first thought was to give the land to the peasants but make them pay the highest possible price for their own personal freedom. But, lest the demand that the serfs pay the cost of their own emancipation arouse public anger, the nobility took an oblique approach by demanding the same price in the guise of indemnification for the loss of the peasant's "domicile," or, as the proposal was later modified, for the first *desyatin* of redeemed land.

While the price of land was much higher in the south, the great wheat-producing area, than in the north, the value of the serf's labor, at best modest in its return, diminished proportionately to the intensification of agriculture and its expansion into production for the market and for export—as the transition, in other words, from a housekeeping to a mercantile economy progressed. Side by side with serf labor there was an increasing use of free, wage-earning workers, because the latter were more productive. In many regions, in fact, land inhabited by serfs commanded a lower price than unoccupied land. Hence the rescript subjected the southern gentry to only a single immediate sacrifice—his agreement to the peasant's right of redemption of his "domicile"—for the peasants would still be bound to their villages and could always provide their former owners with a cheap source of labor. True, the rescript also provided that the peasants should have in addition the "temporary" enjoyment—until they were in a position to purchase—of specified areas of land; but the southern nobility hoped to obtain a construction of the adjective that would mean a rather brief period at the expiration of which the land would revert to the nobleman's ownership and the peasant would be nothing but a landless proletarian. That was why they were more inclined to accept the rescript.

A reconciliation of the interests of the southern landowners with those of the northerners was impossible. The southerners were prepared to free their serfs but wanted to hold onto their land. The northerners, who were interested only in the serf's personal labor, were quite willing to turn over their lands at once, provided they were heavily indemnified therefor. The government would not countenance either side's position. It was fully aware of the danger represented by the enfranchisement of the peasants without land; moreover, it feared that it would be compelled to contribute to the redemption of the land, a burden that, in the light of the financial situation, would be too onerous for the state. Its hesitations gave the nobles the opportunity to try to make their respective theories prevail. This they undertook at once, chiefly in the government committees, which harshly criticized the rescript and attempted to deform its purpose through arbitrary interpretations. If, then, the government did not wish to lose control of the execution of the reform, it would obviously have to evolve a more detailed plan.

Two proposals were presented to it: one by Baron Rosen, the other by the committee of the Tver government. Rosen's project, which advanced the interests of the southern nobility, provided that the peasants would obtain only a temporary use of the land, which would then be restored to its original owners, who would also preserve their rights to police their own estates. The second project, the brain child of A. M. Unkovsky, one of the members of the Tver committee, stipulated on the contrary that the land would be bought in by the peasants. It was approved by the "rural section" created on 4/16 March 1858 in the Ministry of the Interior, which included the two prime experts in the subject, Nikolai Miliutin and Yakov Solovyev, both of whom favored the purchase of the land. The final choice between the two proposals, which were so diametrically opposite, lay chiefly with I. I. Rostovtsev, a member of the secret or "principal" committee. A thoroughly honest official enjoying the complete confidence of the tsar and well disposed toward the peasants, but lacking in knowledge, Rostovtsev took a leave of absence in the summer of 1858 in order to study all the accumulated documentation from the perspective of leisure abroad. He became convinced that, if peasant agitation was to be avoided, it was essential to eliminate the dangerous notion of "temporary obligation"—that is, the grant of land use for a limited time—in favor of immediate purchase. He wrote four letters to this effect to Alexander, who ordered him to present their essential matter to the principal committee as soon as he returned to Russia. This committee took them under study in December 1858 and made them the basis of the official governmental program. In the interim, the tsar journeyed to various cities in Russia and exhorted the nobility to lend its closest collaboration to the reform; in fact, he criticized the Moscow nobles for their delays and vacillation. In addition, a ukase of 20 June/2 July 1858, which produced a tremendous impression, had placed all the land belonging to the crown's estates at the entire disposal of the peasants and had granted them civil equality before the courts and in all business transactions.

While the government's intentions were clear at the beginning of 1859, those of the committees established at the end of 1858 in almost all the governments of Russia, and composed of noblemen, were still an unknown quantity. There was a broad diversity of views, but there could be no doubt that the great majority was opposed to the government's plan. The members of the committees were convinced that they could discuss their own proposals on an equal footing in Petersburg with the officials of the Ministry of the Interior, whom they accused of fostering Socialism, nurturing subversive intentions, living in a vacuum, and knowing nothing of the conditions of real life; and the nobles were confident that by adducing their own experience they could confound the enemy. At the same time, the nobility, which was the "ruling class," was increasingly permeated by the idea that there should be something to counterbalance the emancipation of the peasants: by way of compensation it demanded not only the retention of its police powers but also political rights and representation in the central institutions.

It was to be cruelly disillusioned. In March 1859, under the com-

bined chairmanship of Rostovtsev, the principal committee was augmented by drafting commissions assigned to examine the proposals
submitted by the committees of the various governments. These
drafting commissions were subdivided into four subgroups: administrative, economic, legal, and financial. Miliutin staffed them with a
number of his friends who shared his ideas, such as Piotr Semenov
and the two Slavophiles, Georgi Samarin and Prince Cherkassky,
but numerous dangerous opponents of radical emancipation, such as
Rosen, were also appointed to them. Had the delegates of the individual governments' committees been permitted to take part in their
deliberations, it is more than likely that the opponents of the reform
would have enjoyed a majority. In order to guard against this risk,
Miliutin maneuvered a decision that the delegations of these committees would include both majority and minority representatives,
that these delegations would have neither voting rights nor even
consultative functions in the drafting commissions, and that they
would be invited merely to provide elaborations of their respective proposals, individually. In actuality their testimony was not even preserved in the records of the commissions' proceedings; their projects
were only partly examined, and this, as a rule, in their absence. This
was the extent of the hearing given, without any profit for them, to
the delegations of the committees of the twenty-one governments that
had been the first to complete their labors. As a result of this procedure, the drafting commissions could definitively reject those
proposals that called for the restitution of the land to its owners at
the end of a stated period of "temporary obligation," which was usually eight to twelve years; in addition they were in a position to
rebuff the nobles' aspirations to become the "chiefs" of the emancipated rural communities; at the same time the commissions could
increase the size of the peasants' parcels while at the same time
lowering the purchase price, contrary to the hopes of the owners.
The delegates' anger was not moderate. In vain they demanded permission to have their proposals discussed in plenary sessions and to
present their conclusions to the tsar; they were authorized only to
hold "private meetings" and they returned to their estates in a fury
of resentment.*

*It was this resentment that must be considered the source of the many proposals
for constitutional reform that were prepared between 1859 and 1864 by the assemblies of the nobility, in which liberals and conservatives closed ranks in shared
indignation at the tyranny of the "bureaucracy" of Petersburg. In all this the
radicals preferred to see only the aspirations of the aristocracy. Nonetheless some

After the delegates had gone, the drafting commissions proceeded with the refinement of their own projects. But Rostovtsev, their chairman, died on 6/18 February 1860, and his successor, Count Victor N. Panin, the minister of justice, was an outright enemy of the reform. Although the tsar told Grand Duchess Yelena Pavlovna, who was stunned by the appointment of Panin, that "Panin's convictions come down to the precise execution of his orders," the appointment nonetheless had a deleterious effect on the reform. The delegates of the last governments' committees, the "second convocation," arrived in Petersburg in the hope of being able to launch a new assault on the radical members of the drafting commissions. Anything but resigned to accepting the principle of compulsory land redemption, they sent a letter to Panin on 24 March/5 April demanding that the period of land tenure to be accorded to the peasants be reduced, that the personal emancipation of the serfs be postponed until the expiration of this tenure, and that peasants and their owners be required to reach voluntary accords, on the basis of the law of supply and demand, as was proper between owners of land in fee simple and completely free and independent citizens of the rural community under no further collective bond. Panin defended their stand. In the drafting commissions he stubbornly insisted that "enjoyment in perpetuity" of the land could not be granted to the peasants without infringement of the landlords' property rights, and he declared his adherence to the untrammeled preservation of the great landowners' police power on their properties. There was soon a personal conflict between him and Miliutin. The tsar himself was clearly inclined to believe, as Rostovtsev had pointed out to him not long before his death, that the drafting commissions were "weighting the scales" too far in favor of the peasants and that some concessions must be made to the landowners. It was with this in mind that he ordered the termination of the drafting commissions' operations on 10/22 October 1860; thanking the commissioners for their cooperation, he added that "perhaps it will still be necessary to change many things."

The principal committee, to which the voluminous archives of the drafting commissions were submitted, labored for two months under the leadership of Grand Duke Konstantin Nikolayevitch, who had replaced Orlov. Behind the chairman stood the four champions of

---

of the propositions put forward by these assemblies were truly democratic and some of the criticisms that they made were beyond challenge: for example, the creation of the zemstvo was inspired by the principles of autonomy and decentralization that they wanted to initiate in order wholly to reorganize local institutions.

the reform, but against them they had five opponents, including Panin, who persisted in upholding the landowners' right to absolute property and police powers. The tsar demanded that Konstantin reach an agreement with Panin. By way of compromise the grand duke agreed to reduce the size of the parcels to be acquired by the peasants. This proposal won the support of the majority and on 14/26 January 1861 the principal committee adjourned. Thus the nobles had succeeded in cutting down the amount of land that they would have to yield to the peasants. Where, for instance, in six governments in which the serfs worked six million *desyatini*, the drafting commissions had proposed that only 825,000 be left to the nobles and that 5.161 million be turned over to the peasants,* Panin and the principal committee managed to reduce the peasants' share to 4.794 million and to raise the nobles' to something over a million *desyatini*. Actually, since not all the lands owned by the nobility were under cultivation by the peasants, the nobles in these six governments retained ten million *desyatini;* in other words, they gave up only about a third of their real holdings.

The plan had finally to go before the Imperial Council. In its first meeting the tsar told the councilors that he considered "the task of the emancipation of the peasants a vital question for Russia on which the growth of her energies and her power depends," and, "because further delay can be injurious to the state," he insisted that the program be completed by mid-February, before spring sowing began in the fields. Since the majority in the Council almost always opposed the drafting commissions' proposals—occasionally by as many as thirty-five votes to eight—he had to intervene personally in order to gain their adoption. Nevertheless he approved a further reduction in the maximum area of the peasants' parcels in many regions. He also allowed the Council, at the instance of Prince Gagarin, to come to another decision prejudicial to the peasants by granting the incumbent owner the right to convey the quarter of a normal plot to his former serf without payment. This was what was called "the beggar's share."

On 19 February/3 March 1861 the "statute of the peasants liberated from serfdom" was given the force of law, and, in order to mark this historic date, the tsar issued a solemn manifesto that had been written for him by Metropolitan Filaret. The "general statute" established the legal status of the emancipated peasants, the bases of

---

*The committees of these six governments, on the other hand, had suggested that only three of the six million *desyatini* be ceded to the serfs and that the other half be retained by the nobles.

their administrative organization, and the regulations governing their purchases of land. A series of "local regulations," taking cognizance of varying local situations, determined the economic conditions of enfranchisement in the different parts of the country—Great Russia, Little Russia, and White Russia—in the Polish and Lithuanian provinces, in the Caucasus, and in Bessarabia. House serfs were emancipated as of right, without compensation, two years after the publication of the statute. The others could not immediately enforce the mandatory right of redeeming their land; instead, they were merely authorized to enter into agreements with the landowners for purchase within twenty years—this was the so-called period of "temporary obligation." They received personal freedom and parcels of land for which they had to pay a specified rental subject to review during this same twenty-year period. The landowners' police power was transferred to the "local commune,"* which was made autonomous and was composed of peasants who had been owned by the same proprietor and lived in the same village. The parcels of land and the rental payments were apportioned among the members of the rural community on the basis of the size of each family and in conformity to established custom. A number of communes together formed a canton (*volost*). Each canton was endowed with a peasant court, the members of which were elected annually by the cantonal assembly; they would render judgments on the basis of traditional law and their jurisdiction would extend to all civil matters in which the money value of the issue did not exceed a hundred rubles, as well as to all offenses punishable by penalties not exceeding one week of imprisonment, six days of enforced public labor, and fines of three rubles. The elected village authorities were subject to the "cantonal chiefs" † and the "cantonal directorates";‡ although their posts were elective, they amounted in fact to nothing more than district police agents, and this was hardly compatible with true autonomy. Representatives of all other classes were excluded from the administrative units represented by the "rural communes" and the cantons; hence the canton was specifically peasant. In addition, by reason of the survival of the agrarian community, the mir, the peasants were still subject to a collective bond for the payment of taxes, and the passport system assured the effectiveness of this. The peasant class was no longer enslaved, but it was still subject to forced labor, and as a result of this inequity it was still differentiated from the privileged caste of the nobility.

*Selskoye obshchestvo, the peasant administrative communes.
†Volostnoi starshina.
‡Volostnoye pravlenye.

In principle, the local regulations gave each peasant a plot equivalent to what he had cultivated before his emancipation; but in practice this parcel could be reduced or enlarged, because the regulations established maximum and minimum areas for each region. For this purpose Russia was divided into three zones—the black soil, or fertile land; the nonfertile land; and the steppes—and these were subdivided into sixteen "categories." The size of the peasant's parcel varied from three to four and a half *desyatini* in the first zone, from three to eight in the second, and from six and a half to twelve in the third. The rental due for a whole parcel was set at nine rubles per "soul" in the nonfertile and industrial regions and the fertile zone, where the forced-labor system had prevailed, and at eight rubles in the rest. The total purchase price of the land depended on the rental rate and the area involved. Inasmuch as half the rental (four rubles) was in any case mandatory for the first *desyatin*, the smaller the plot, therefore, the higher its price. In such case, rather than make such a purchase, many peasants preferred to take for nothing their "beggar's share," or quarter; and this was especially true of those regions where the soil was the most productive and the most costly: in other words, the south. Since the peasants there could find no other source of income apart from farming, the inadequacy of this "beggar's share" naturally forced them into extremely arduous toil and into complete dependence on the nearest large landowner.

This solution of the peasant question, favorable as it was to the interests of the nobles, did not fulfill either the desires of the peasants or the hopes of democratic circles. Slavophiles like Samarin and Cherkassky, Occidentalists like Katkov and Kavelin, Socialists like Herzen and Chernyshevsky, all had been unanimous at first in their enthusiastic reception of the idea of emancipation. Herzen, who termed Alexander "the heir of December 14," had paid tribute to him in 1857: "Thou hast conquered, Galilean who toilest with us for a greater future." Even the intransigent Chernyshevsky had written in 1856: "Our monarch loves his people and his people loves him, and the abolition of serfdom crowns the age of Alexander with the world's greatest glory." Herzen in his famous *Kolokol (The Bell)* and Chernyshevsky in his articles in *Sovremennik (The Contemporary)* had labored unstintingly for the cession of all their land to the peasants without indemnification. Hence they were deeply disappointed. Chernyshevsky expressed Herzen's thought as well when, at the end of 1858, he wrote: "I am ashamed when I remember my premature confidence." As for the peasants themselves, they felt that they had been given only a sham "freedom" instead of the "complete freedom" that they had expected. They accused the great landowners of having once again "got round" the tsar's ukase. The agrarian disorders that had entirely ceased during the whole period when the reform was in preparation began again in many places immediately after the publication of the manifesto of 19 February/3 March 1861. The repression of them by military detachments, especially in the case of the rising of the village of Bedna in the government of Penza, which was led by a certain Anton Petrov, made a profound impression on public opinion and contributed to the creation of the first revolutionary movement in intellectual circles.

Since the redemption of the land was dependent on voluntary agreements between peasants and owners, it dragged out for twenty years, until 1881, when it was made compulsory for the one and a half million peasants who had not opted for it during the period of "temporary obligation." Yet, in spite of what might have been expected, it was the landowners who called for its acceleration soon after the publication of the manifesto, and, during the first ten years, it was opted for in 70 per cent of the landed estates. This had to do with the difficulties that the tensions between owners and peasants created for the nobles in the exploitation of their land and especially with the owners' increasing need to pay their debts. In fact, at the time of the emancipation, 70 per cent of the serfs were mortgaged to the state lending institutions, and these debts had to be paid out of the purchase price of the land. Of the 588 million rubles that were paid by peasants for nobles' lands between 1861 and 1871, 262 millions went directly to the mortgagees. Furthermore, because of the depreciation of the special bonds* that the state issued to the nobles in order to help the peasants complete their purchases, they actually received not 326 but 230 million rubles. Naturally the position of the nobles was still one of constriction. In 1865 they resumed borrowing from the new land-mortgage banks. By 1870 the total of their debts had reached 250 million rubles; ten years later it was 400 million and in 1890 it exceeded 600 million.

The nobility, the majority of which was still a caste of "servitors of the tsar" rather than one of rural landowners, looked on land only as a source of income. Burdened by debt, left almost without livestock after the emancipation, and lacking the resources to obtain the paid labor required for the exploitation of its properties, it could not even hold onto what was left to it of the land to which it had clung so tenaciously before the emancipation. The nobles willingly rented land to

*This was the form taken by the state's financial collaboration in the execution of the scheme.

the peasants, who, allotted inadequate parcels by the
were compelled to look for more land and therefor
their former lords regardless of cost. By the most
mates, the peasants were leasing a minimum of twenty-five million
desyatini in 1880. Since they had been given thirty-three million at the
time of emancipation, they had almost doubled the total area of the
land that they were working. Not only did they rent land; they bought
it. Of the approximately fifty-nine million *desyatini* that they sowed
between 1880 and 1890—while the nonpeasant landowners were not
working more than nine million, or barely 13 per cent of the total—
the peasants owned more than forty-seven million in fee and were rent-
ing barely twelve million. This was because the nobles were more and
more often divesting themselves of their land, which they could no
longer cultivate or which was covered with mortgages. The average
number of *desyatini* sold per year rose from 517,000 between 1859 and
1875 to 741,000 in 1879, 775,000 in 1890, and, about 1900, a million;
in 1905, under the first revolution, more than seven and a half million
desyatini of land owned by nobles were to be put on sale. In the beginning it was mainly speculators—merchants and industrialists—who
bought the nobles' great estates. First they drained them of everything
possible, cutting down the trees, exhausting the soil, selling the buildings, the equipment, and the livestock; then, when the estates had
been wrecked and looted, they were parceled out and sold at outra-
geous prices to the peasants. The total area of estates owned by the
nobility, including tilled and fallow land and woods, diminished from
decade to decade: it fell from 87.181 million *desyatini* in 1862 to
80.735 million in 1872, to 71.295 million in 1882, to 62.935 million in
1892, to 53.178 million in 1902, and to 43.205 million in 1911. Thus in
the fifty years that followed the emancipation of the serfs the nobility
lost more than half of the land that it had owned.

The peasants owned by the landed gentry, who totaled twenty-two
million "souls" of the male sex at the time of the emancipation, constituted less than half of the peasant mass. In addition there were the
so-called appanage peasants, who belonged to the administration of
the imperial palaces and totaled nine hundred thousand, and the state
peasants,* of whom there were almost as many as the gentry's. The

*Since the time of Peter the Great, who had gathered these peasants into a single
group and subjected them to a uniform tax, this category had included: (1) the
peasants of northern Russia, formerly free, who had not been turned over to the
lords because they were so remote from the administrative centers; (2) the inhabitants of the former fortified border region of the south, small holders registered
as peasants and called *odnodvoretsi* (owners of one "fire"); (3) the indigenous

appanage peasants also had to redeem their lands after their liberation, but they were afforded more favorable terms: purchase was obligatory for them at once, and they received maximum parcels. In 1861 the state peasants were in a better situation than the serfs of private owners. Through the forethought of Kiselev (1837–1856), minister under Nicholas I, they had already been provided with larger plots— eight *desyatini* in the provinces where land was scarce and almost fifteen in the richer provinces—and their payments were better proportioned to the actual product of their labors. Kiselev's successor, Muravyev, who was a believer in serfdom, tried without success to drag down their situation to that of the privately owned peasants. Their basic organization was entrusted to Miliutin after the emancipation and a ukase of 1866 ratified their old privileges.

In sum, the worst-provided-for peasants after the emancipation were those of the private landowners. According to Professor Khodsky's statistics, 13 per cent of them—as against 60 per cent of the state peasants—were well endowed with land, 43.5 per cent—as against 35 per cent—were adequately supplied, and 42 per cent—as against 13 per cent—did not have enough. It was this last group that was to suffer especially from the agricultural crisis at the end of the nineteenth century. The small size of plots and the excessive levels of taxation and rentals would in the end create a dangerous set of conditions for the public safety.

The Reform of Local Government; the Creation and the Function of the Zemstvo

By eliminating the police powers of the landed proprietors over the peasants, the emancipation of the serfs made it necessary to reorganize the whole system of local government.

The principal committee appointed to develop the emancipation program took cognizance of this fact in 1859. The minister of the interior created a special commission to work out this reorganization under Miliutin, who at once drafted a memorandum setting forth his views on the basic principles of administrative and economic organization. He considered it essential, in the reformation of the criminal and secret police, to modify the local administration, which was fragmented among numerous committees and often exercised police

---

tribes of eastern Russia, formerly subject to a special tax (*yasak*). Because of the land-use payments exacted by the Treasury at the rate of so much per "soul," individual ownership had been converted into communal ownership among these populations during the eighteenth and nineteenth centuries.

power, to invest its economic control with greater unity and independence, and to establish the degree to which each group in the society would participate in this control. His memorandum was approved by Alexander II and on 25 March/6 April 1859 an imperial ordinance stated the principles that were to govern the organization of a new system of local government.

The committees of the various governments sent their reorganization proposals to the principal committee and the drafting commissions. One of these proposals, the earliest in point of date, had been adopted by the committee of the Tver government, which had completed its study on 5/18 February 1859. The work of A. M. Unkovsky, marshal of the nobility of Tver and a delegate to the drafting commissions, it was based on the principles of the absolute separation of powers, decentralization, and self-government.* It provided for an independent judiciary and public trials in which juries would be mandatory. At the head of each district it placed the marshal of the nobility, but it provided for his election by a district assembly in which all classes, and not the nobility alone, would be represented. The base of local government was set on the canton, as a territorial division representing all residents without distinction as to class. The canton was made the repository of all the rights formerly held by the noble landed proprietors over the serfs, and cantonal officials were to be elected by a general assembly.

This and the other government committees' proposals were referred to the commission headed by Miliutin. This body lost no time in agreeing on police reform. But its debates were protracted when it attacked the question of creating a new body: the provincial assembly, or zemstvo.† The conflict arose between those who favored domination by the nobility in local government and those who backed the equal participation of all classes in provincial self-government. In 1861 this commission's liberal chairman, Miliutin, was supplanted by the new minister of the interior, P. A. Valuev. This was a major victory for the conservatives. Valuev, who championed the privileges of the nobility, was determined to give that class as dominant a place as possible in the zemstvo, to make the zemstvo subject to governmental control, and to reduce its function to the purely economic. The plan for which he won the commission's approval and that he submitted to the Imperial Council was dominated by two concerns: to render the provincial institutions purely formal and to make them wholly dependent

*In English in the original.—Translator.

†From *zemlya*, "the country." The zemstvo was the equivalent of the German *Landtag* (or of the American state legislature—Translator).

on the nobility.* A number of the imperial councilors—Baron Korf, Bakhtin, Kovalevsky, Prince Suvorov, Miliutin, Reitern, and others— were devastating in their criticisms of him and his proposal. They condemned it on the ground that it was not a real system of local self-government, and they sought to rescue the zemstvo from excessive supervision by the state and from domination by the nobility. In particular Korf criticized all the provisions that tended to weaken the function of the zemstvo in local administration. Although the Imperial Council made some amendments to the proposal, it nevertheless retained many of its provisions. Hence the zemstvo statute, which the tsar ratified on 1/13 January 1864, was an unfinished reform, a compromise that, even as it proclaimed the principle of self-government, subordinated the zemstvo to the governmental agents, denied it all means of enforcement, and restricted its jurisdiction.

Two kinds of zemstvo were created: the district zemstvo and the government zemstvo. They were not part of the governmental agency of local administration and they were subject to "the rules of the common law, exactly like private organizations and private individuals." Their task was to make it possible for representatives of all classes to take part in the management of local affairs.

The members of the district zemstvo were elected for three-year terms. Their electors were not divided into colleges based on social class, because this criterion seemed incompatible with the nature of the zemstvo, which was essentially to defend the general economic interests of its district and not those of one or another social class: they were divided into three distinct categories on the basis of property qualifications by virtue of the principle that "participation in the control of local affairs ought to be proportioned to the extent of each participant's economic interests"—in a word, the size of land holdings and the worth of other property.

The first category of voters embraced all owners of land without regard to their social class. First there were the large landowners, who met the qualification of possession of a minimum equivalent to fifty peasant parcels—in practice the rate of poll tax varied from one government to another with the value and the productivity of the land: from one hundred fifty to eight hundred *desyatini;* on the average it

---

*He proposed that the property qualification of the suffrage for noble landowners be less than half that for commoners who owned land, and, in order to guarantee the predominance of landowners over peasants, he further proposed that the landowners should have one representative in the district zemstvo for every three thousand peasant land holdings while the peasants themselves should have one representative for every six thousand holdings.

was two hundred fifty to three hundred. Next came the small land-owners who had one-twelfth of the minimum—that is, twelve to fifteen *desyatini*—but who, however, did not enjoy direct suffrage: they were represented by electoral delegates whom they chose in primary assemblies; they were entitled to a number of delegates equal to the number of times the poll-tax minimum was represented in the total number of *desyatini* owned by all small holders who attended the primary assembly's meetings. This first category of voters also included the owners of buildings, apart from land, provided that they were assessed for tax purposes at a minimum of 15,000 rubles.

The second category of voters, which was more numerous than that of the landowners, was composed of city residents: (1) registered merchants equipped with licenses to do business; (2) owners of industrial establishments with an annual volume of business of at least 6000 rubles; (3) owners of buildings worth at least 3000 rubles in cities of more than ten thousand population, at least 1000 rubles in towns of two thousand population, and at least 500 rubles in all others. The poll tax for city voters, then, depending on the size of their towns, was five, fifteen, or thirty times lower than that of the landowners in their districts.

The third category of voters was the peasants, grouped in rural communes (*selskoye obshchestvo*). They were subject to no property qualification. Every head of a family was eligible to vote in the election of their delegates, which was conducted in three steps. In each canton all the heads of families in the rural communes voted for the cantonal assembly, the organ of peasant self-government. These assemblies elected an electoral college in their turn, and it was this college that finally elected the deputies to the zemstvo.

The zemstvo met in regular and special sessions in the district capital. As a matter of right its president was always the district marshal of the nobility, so that automatically it was under the tutelage of that class. Its total membership was fixed by law. No single one of the social groups represented in it—landowners, city dwellers, or peasants—could have an absolute majority and thus thwart the others. For the 33 governments to which the statute of 1864 was applicable there were in all 13,024 zemstvo delegates: 6204 were elected by the landowners, 1649 by the city voters, and 5171 by the peasants. While the landowners thus had the largest single representation, they could not assume a decisive part without the alliance of one of the two other groups.

As viewed in the intentions of the law, the zemstvo was not supposed to be a class institution. Although the principle of the separation of the voters into three categories was purely fiscal, nevertheless in reality two of the three categories—the landowners and the peasants—represented specific social classes, at least for a number of years. In effect, immediately after the 1861 reform, the private ownership of land that had hitherto, apart from rare exceptions, been the privilege of the nobility remained almost wholly in the hands of the nobles. Hence the representatives of the landowners were initially almost without exception the representatives of the nobility. This situation changed gradually as noblemen's estates were sold to merchants and peasants, but it was to be fifteen years before the results of this slow development were to become apparent. As for the peasants' delegates, it was the intention of the law that they should represent not the small rural landowner but the peasant class. The organs of peasant self-government—that is, the cantonal assemblies that elected them—rather markedly retained the character of class institutions in practice. Access to the peasant community, the mir, was very difficult, and the head of a family who ceased to be a member of it lost not only the right of collective ownership of land but at the same time that of participation in the operations of peasant self-government.

The government zemstvo managed the affairs of each government as a whole. It was composed of representatives from each district zemstvo, elected from among its members, and it was headed by the marshal of the nobility of the government.

The sessions of the zemstvo were relatively short. They were limited to laying down the broad outlines of its work, to examining and voting on budgetary projects, to establishing programs of action for coming years. In order to carry out its decisions it appointed to three-year terms—the same as its own—permanent district or government delegations made up of a chairman and at least two members. The choice of the chairman was subject to ratification by the administrative authority: the minister of the interior for the government zemstvo and the governor for the district zemstvo; rejected candidates had to be replaced through new elections. No approval was needed for the members of the delegations, whose election could be held only after the chairmen had been confirmed. The permanent delegations were empowered to hire the staffs and experts required for the management of the various aspects of the regional economy. Since the organization of public education and public health required a large number of teachers and physicians, the number of specialists needed increased in direct proportion to the growth of the activity of the zemstvo. Its jurisdiction was quite broad. It covered, for instance, the management of capital investments and land, public health and education, the movement and maintenance of food supplies, agricultural development, highways, and local financial obligations. But this jurisdiction was not absolute. According to the intentions of the 1864 statute it was purely economic. While the zemstvo concerned itself especially with medical assistance and public education, it did so only within the limitations defined by the law and particularly in their economic aspects. The agencies of the national government continued to operate side by side with it in many branches of regional administration. Hence it was only a supplement to the overall imperial administration. Furthermore, it had no administrative power properly so called, because, contrary to the views insisted on by Baron Korf, its deliberations had no enforceability. In order to have its decisions carried out or even to collect local taxes, it had to have resort, in the absence of special agents of its own, to the ordinary police, who were under the orders of the governor. It was only after 1873 that a number of successive decrees granted the zemstvo the right to promulgate decrees having the force of law, especially in order to take health and similar measures in cases of emergency.

If the autonomy that the statute of 1864 intended to accord to the zemstvo within the limited domain of its powers proved to be restricted, it was above all because the zemstvo lacked the means of exercising this autonomy in reality. In this field, in actuality, it enjoyed a rather visible independence of the representatives of the central government, especially the governors. The minister of the interior and the governor could oppose certain of its decisions, as well as the acts of its permanent delegations, if they were manifestly contrary to law. In certain cases, furthermore, for fundamental reasons they could refuse to approve the decisions taken by the zemstvo. But, if these decisions, vetoed for whatever reason, were reaffirmed by the zemstvo, to which they were sent back, they became final. All that the minister of the interior or the governor could then do on his own responsibility was to suspend the execution of them and inform the Senate, which was the highest legislative body.

What was the effect of this administrative reform on life in the provinces and the countryside? In spite of all its flaws, the statute of 1864 was of outstanding importance in the history of Russia because it summoned the entire population to direct its own local interests. It made it possible for local energies to be consolidated and organized. It fostered a number of economic undertakings and made possible the creation of educational and social enterprises.

The task on which the zemstvo embarked was completely new. The past had nothing to contribute that might assist it in its apprenticeship. It had to break its own path, to surmount many obstacles, some of them external, some inherent in its task. In practice it encountered the permanent opposition of the government, which was in a constant state of alarm at its tendency to expand its activity. Furthermore, the zemstvo found itself at the head of a remarkably ignorant population, and it lacked the necessary personnel to cope with its onerous and multiple obligations. Fortunately the Russian intelligentsia was to contribute heavily to the ranks of the experts who were essential to it, contributing to the social purposes of the zemstvo all its knowledge and its zealous desire to serve the people. By joining their efforts, the zemstvo and the intellectuals succeeded in creating elementary schools, clinics, and a host of other useful public services. The activities of the zemstvo, varying as they did from one government and even from one district to another, were especially important in Moscow, Tver, Chernigov, and, in the beginning, Petersburg.

Before the reforms of Alexander II public health services might be said to have been nonexistent in Russia. As for education, which was entrusted to district or government committees of social assistance charged, as agents of the national government, with providing for the spiritual needs of the population, it was so scanty in the provinces, and particularly in rural areas, that in 1856 there were at the most only 8000 elementary schools in the entire empire, including 6088 in European Russia, 1753 in the Baltic provinces, and 312 in Siberia. In these two fields, then, the nation had virtually to start from nothing.

Initially in each of the thirty-three governments of European Russia in which it had been inaugurated the zemstvo was handicapped by the lack of funds. It had inherited a local budget that antedated its own creation and assets that belonged to the committees of social welfare. But on what was garnered in the form of local receipts it had to rely for the costs of numerous mandatory outlays. For several years, in the majority of instances, the zemstvo had to resign itself to the fact that half of its budget was taken up by these obligations, especially the salaries of a vast army of employees of the national government and the maintenance and improvement of administrative quarters. Although its available resources were at first relatively modest, it made every effort to perform its social tasks, which it regarded as its major functions.

Every attention was given to popular education. When, by 1880, the number of schools in the whole empire had already risen to 22,770, most were the obligation of the zemstvo. Little by little the zemstvo school progressed to the first rank in the school system, and when the teacher appeared in the village it was the advent of a vanguard of progress. The earliest teachers were confronted with a delicate problem: the creation of a new kind of provincial school, the secular. In order to make a reality of this school, the purpose of which was not only to teach the peasants' children to read and write but also to guarantee them a full elementary education, it was necessary to battle the ignorance of the peasant class, which was still illiterate almost everywhere, the opposition of certain landowners irrevocably committed to serfdom, the distrust of the cities, and also the tyranny of the national government, which regarded the teachers as dangerous propagandists of democratic notions. But they were filled with the desire to be of use to the people, and their ideals gave them the courage and the strength to endure all the rigors of their apostolate. They swiftly earned the reputation of indefatigable and selfless workers—and in the beginning their reward was worse than modest.

The zemstvo did more than give the rural areas free elementary schools; it also provided them, even in their most remote outposts, with physicians, agronomists, engineers who devoted themselves to improving the welfare of the rural population. The zemstvo provided the intellectuals in the liberal professions with the means of working in and for the country. Through these experts, the peasants, who had known no one but their landlords and the agents of the government, soon learned to appreciate the worth of a proper scientific training. For the first time they made contact with the intelligentsia, which, because of its dedication, won their respect and their affection.

Following the basic thought of its creator, furthermore, the zemstvo brought to reality the equality of all citizens before the law. Nobles, city men, and peasants worked together in the zemstvo on a footing of parity: yesterday's slave, the peasant, sat in the same hall and shared the same rights with his former owner. The zemstvo also developed into an outstanding school in civic growth. Its executive agencies, the permanent delegations whose members it chose and required to account for their work, not only fostered the closer association of the representatives of the three separate social categories but also made it possible for the more capable delegates of all three groups of voters to take part in the management of local affairs. The zemstvo was the training ground for a great number of remarkable workers, those new men who, at once landowners and administrators, were motivated only by the desire to elevate the general condition of their native regions, public men gifted with genuine administrative experience and accustomed to the public and critical discussion of the measures to be taken and the means of their application. In the districts and the governments the zemstvo became the center of social life and the focus of public and press interest. Its social accomplishments, which were especially important in certain governments, did not everywhere assume the same character. In the governments of the central regions the zemstvo tended to concentrate above all on public education; in those of the east (Vyatka and Perm) it devoted itself to providing economic assistance to the population. But everywhere, because of the zemstvo, provincial Russia was completely altered. By 1880 she had wholly emerged from the torpor in which she had vegetated before 1864.

Not every zemstvo was satisfied with regional autonomy. In certain governments they aspired to what they called the "coronation of the work"—that is, the establishment of constitutional government in Russia.

The proposal to limit the tsar's legislative power through an elected Representative Assembly had been put forward already by the assemblies of the nobles. As early as 1855, in a memorandum *On the Domestic Situation in Russia*, submitted to the tsar through the intercession of Count Bludov, Konstantin Aksakov had insisted on the necessity of convoking a *Zemsky Sobor*. While the emancipation of the peasants was under study, the idea of convening a Representative Assembly had been spreading among the committees of the nobility. A delegate of the majority of the Simbirsk nobles' committee, Shidlovsky, had stated in a letter that had been conveyed to Alexander that "the nobility is the most reliable natural pillar of the throne and the nation," and he had suggested that delegates be assembled under the personal chairmanship of the tsar in order finally to resolve the problem of the emancipation of the serfs. From another source, the chamberlain, N. P. Bezobrazov, through the good offices of Timashev, chief of the constabulary corps, had sent the tsar a memorandum entitled *On the Importance of the Russian Nobility and the Place That It Ought to Hold in Political Life*, in which he had proposed the calling of a Consultative Assembly of delegates of the nobility of the various governments and deputies of the committees of those governments in order to discuss the general problems of interest to the state and above all to debate the peasant reform. Propaganda for constitutional reform had been especially intense after the publication of the manifesto of 19 February/3 March 1861. At that time it had aroused some response in the press, and in many government assemblies favorable reactions had been expressed by noblemen. In a meeting on 1/13 February 1862, by a vote of 109 to 19, the nobility of Tver had openly stated that "the convocation of the delegates of all Russia in the sole means of achieving a satisfactory solution of the problems that the regulation of 19 February/3 March has posed but not resolved." During the special session of the Petersburg nobility, Platonov, marshal of the nobility of the district of Tsarskoye Selo, had read a paper *On the Necessity of Convoking the Delegates of All Russia.*

It is necessary [he had stated] to set up a barrier to the tyranny of the officials of government, to allow the voice of the people to be heard regularly by the throne without either distortion or delay, and to fuse all the parts of the empire into a stable political entity. The only means of achieving this is the institution of a Representative Assembly of the whole population, a Duma of the empire that will keep the tsar informed and will debate proposals for laws and major governmental measures before their ratification by the sovereign. Without such national representation, the state itself incurs the risk of perishing in a future that is not distant.

While it had not followed Platonov, whose proposal it had laid over for its regular meeting in December 1862, the Petersburg nobility had nevertheless sustained its interest in the constitutional question. Then the Moscow nobility had sent the tsar a petition demanding the public disclosure of the budget, freedom of the press, and the convocation of a Duma composed of delegates of all classes of the population and given the task of preparing a project for reform, the sessions to be held in Moscow. Alexander II himself had seemed to favor the idea of establishing a constitution. During a conversation with Miliutin in August 1863, he had declared that he had no aversion to the constitutional system and that he could not grant it to the Poles, who had rebelled against him, without also bestowing it on his loyal subjects, the Russians. When the Diet of Finland was inaugurated in 1863 he said in his speech from the throne that "liberal institutions, far from being a threat, are a guaranty of order and progress."

The creation of the zemstvo encouraged the advocates of a constitution. If public opinion was so warmly receptive to the statute of 1/13 January 1864, it was precisely because it regarded the establishment of regional autonomy as a virtual augury of future national representation. In February 1864 Prince Dolgoruky wrote in the magazine *Listok* (*The Leaf*) that "the zemstvo is rich in fruitful promise that it will be a broad and solid foundation for the future constitutional system." The address of the Moscow nobility to the tsar, adopted on 11/23 January 1865 by 270 votes to 36, concluded with this appeal: "Sire, crown the political structure that you have founded with the convocation of a General Assembly of delegates of all Russia to deliberate on the general interests of the empire." By entering the zemstvo, in which it occupied a preponderant place, the nobility had contributed its political thinking, and the zemstvo succeeded the assembly of the nobility as the champion of constitutional concepts. The zemstvo of the Petersburg government, under the chairmanship of Platonov, was the most fervent. In December 1865 it resolved to request the creation of a central zemstvo headquarters to carry out the functions of common interest that applied to the local administrations, and one of the delegates, Count A. P. Shuvalov, declared in a much applauded speech that this creation should be "the inevitable consequence of the general will and the natural evolution of the autonomy of the zemstvo." During its next session, in November 1866, after the promulgation of the law of 21 November/3 December that substantially restricted the rights of the zemstvo in levying taxes and aroused many protests, the Petersburg zemstvo made its position still clearer on the necessity for national representation. Discussion of the report in which its permanent delegation had analyzed the effect of the new law on zemstvo budgets was marked by sharp debate, during which the question of a central representative body was raised again. On the instance of Count Shuvalov, the assembly asked that questions dealing with regional taxation be resolved jointly by the government and a "Russian zemstvo" composed of representatives from each district and government zemstvo. This request brought down the anger of the central government on the Petersburg zemstvo, and it was dissolved. The chairman and the members of its permanent delegation were unseated; Kruse, the chairman, was sent to Orenburg; the delegates who had taken an active part in the discussion of the "Russian zemstvo" were deported on administrative order; Senator Luboshchinsky was ordered to resign because of the speech that he had made; and Count Shuvalov was instructed to remove himself from the country— he went to Paris. After these summary measures the constitutionalist campaign was not mentioned again in any zemstvo until about 1875.

Not all the advocates of this movement were liberals. Some of them were noblemen, landowners opposed to the emancipation of the serfs, who were looking to the establishment of a constitutional system as a means of consolidating their caste privileges. If they wanted a constitutional charter, it was one for the nobility exclusively; if they thought in terms of an elected assembly, it was an assembly of representatives of the nobility. If they sought to limit the power of the sovereign, it was only in order to cut off his liberal activities. In almost every zemstvo, on the other hand, the tendencies were democratic; what was sought there was the election of representatives of the nation by the whole population without regard to class. When, after Karakozov's attempt to assassinate him, Alexander gave up the furtherance of liberal reforms and hurled himself into reactionism, the partisans of an aristocratic constitution left the camp of the opposition for that of the supporters of the government in the hope of being able to paralyze the execution of the "great reforms" already achieved. But the liberals, who were the zemstvo majorities, were merely waiting for the appropriate moment to demand a constitution on the western model that would guarantee the right of suffrage to all social classes.

The Reform of Municipal Government: Municipal Autonomy

In the majority of instances the municipal bodies established by Catherine II in 1785 had demonstrated their inefficacy because of their complicated machinery, their lack of independence of the central government, and, above all, the denial of the power to levy taxes, without which it was impossible to expect them to be able to govern their cities well. L. A. Perovsky, minister of the interior under Nicholas I, had assigned the task of finding means of remedying their impotence to Miliutin, the future collaborator of Alexander II during "the era of the great reforms." Miliutin was at that time a very new official in the ministry. His work and that of such other eminent personalities as Georgi Samarin and Ivan Aksakov, whom he had conscripted as his assistants, had led only to the issuance of a new municipal regulation for Petersburg, which Nicholas I had ratified on 13/25 February 1846. This was an attempt to create more flexible municipal institutions that would be better adapted to the needs of the moment.

Although it did not include the power to levy taxes, it aroused the envy of the other cities. From the outset of the "movement of liberation," therefore, many of them sought to be included in its benefits. In 1863 it was extended to Moscow and Odessa. But, under simultaneous pressure from the cities and the assemblies of the nobility, the government decided, with the imperial ordinance of 1862, to embark on a general urban reform on the model of Petersburg's self-government. At the request of the minister of the interior, commissions composed of all categories of municipal electors were brought into being in every city and charged with formulating their views on the reform. With the help of these 509 commissions and, above all, of documentation assembled in western Europe, the minister drafted a legislative proposal that was submitted for review in 1864 to Baron Korf, director general of the codification section. With his comments annexed, it was then transmitted to the Imperial Council in 1866. But the Council tabled it under the influence of the tide of reaction that had grown very strong in higher circles after the failure of Karakozov's attempt to assassinate Alexander II. The proposal was not resubmitted to the Imperial Council until 1869 by the new minister of the interior, Timashev. On the pretext that it had not first been studied in the ministry in the presence of the cities' representatives, the Council returned it to Timashev. The mayors of Petersburg, Moscow, and six provincial cities worked together—rather unharmoniously—on its revision. In the end the new law on cities, approved by the Imperial Council, was promulgated in 1870.

Its two essential principles were those of the zemstvo statute of 1864: participation by all social classes in government and the creation of property qualifications for the suffrage. In decided contrast to the earlier 1846 law, all residents of cities, regardless of their social category, were eligible to vote provided that they possessed real property subject to municipal tax, industrial or commercial enterprises, or licences as merchants, industrialists, or commercial employees of the first class. While the poll tax was very low—the payment of a minimal tax on the operation of a business or the ownership of property—the result was most inequitable. The voters of each city were divided into three colleges on the basis of the amount of taxes that they paid, in such a fashion that the total of the taxes paid by the members of any one college should equal one-third of what was paid by all the voters together. Thus the first college comprised the biggest taxpayers, the upper middle class; the second college, which, naturally, was larger, embraced the owners of moderate property; the third and largest college included all the rest of the taxpayers. Each college was entitled to the same number of representatives in the municipal duma. The minimum voting age was twenty-five; women were not permitted to vote directly, but they could give their proxies to qualified male voters. Voters who were away at election time could not vote by proxy or absentee ballot. No one could cast more than two votes, one of which was his own and the other of which was that of the person for whom he acted as proxy.

The municipal duma was elected for a four-year term, and the size of its membership, in proportion to the number of eligible voters, varied between 30 and 72 except in the two capitals: in Petersburg it was 250 and in Moscow it was 180. The duma was free to elect the members of its executive organism, which was called the bureau and was headed by the mayor. Only the nominations of the mayor, his colleagues, and his deputies* had to be approved by the minister of the

---

*Zamestitel, or deputy empowered to take the mayor's place in his absence.

interior. There was an exception for Petersburg and Moscow, whose mayors, instead of being elected by the duma, were appointed by the tsar from a list of two candidates presented by each duma. The mayor was the presiding officer of both the bureau and the duma. This assimilation of administrative and executive functions had been instituted on the demand of the mayors who had taken part in the revision of the draft law for city government in 1869. Its purpose was to increase the importance and the power of the mayor by preventing the duma, which was a permanent assembly, from hobbling the executive authority by constant challenge and question, and from meddling in the management of current administrative business. Thus the mayor, as the general manager, was responsible for the city's government and economy, answerable to an assembly of which he himself was the head. This innovation evoked sharp criticism from the press and public opinion, and it led to frequent conflicts in the cities. Another characteristic made an even more radical distinction between the municipal duma and the zemstvo: the duma could be convened at any time in case of need to work with its executive bureau, and hence it was a permanent body. Primarily the reason for this permanence lay in the inherent conditions of city life, but it was to be explained as well by the relative ease of assembling a body whose members all lived in the same city, whereas factors of distance made it impossible for the zemstvo to meet frequently. In addition the municipal duma had the right to elect not only its bureau but also special committees to direct various branches of the municipal government. The heads of some of these committees played very influential parts.

What was the municipality's power after the law of 1870? It extended to the management of the city's territory and finances, improvement and beautification, the assurance of civilian supplies, public health, assistance to the needy and other charitable activities, public safety (fire and other emergencies), the expansion of public education and local commerce, and the construction and upkeep of theaters and other public facilities. The municipality had the status of a legal person and it could buy and sell property, seek loans, sign contracts, and initiate litigation. It had also the right to submit requests to the central government for the fulfillment of local needs. It could issue binding decrees, but only in matters of health and the improvement and beautification of the city, and without any means by which to supervise the execution of its orders, which was the business of the national police force. In addition—and this was a distinct advance over the 1846 law—it had the power to levy taxes on its residents, but only by way of their real and business property—that is, houses, land, fixtures

annexed to the realty within buildings, licences for the operation of
business or industry, including all kinds of small shops, inns, restau-
rants, rental vehicles and horses, privately owned vehicles and horses,
and, though only in the two capitals, the quarters occupied by gam-
bling clubs and industrial enterprises, as well as peddling. Under such
restrictions, the city's resources were the more inadequate in the light
of its heavy obligations to the state. A large part of the municipal
budget, especially in the years immediately after the reform, was allocated to the expenses of the national government: for instance, the
maintenance of quarters for its local branches and for the police.
These "mandatory" charges on the budget were especially burdensome to smaller cities, whose budgets were extremely modest.

The autonomy of the city was not total. Like the zemstvo, the duma
was limited to "taking part" in the management of local affairs, because
the government intended to place both bodies, like the provincial assemblies, under the control of the state bureaucracy. Within the limits
of its powers the city was independent. The governor could merely
verify the legality of what was done by the duma and its bureau; in the
event of conflict, the decision was made by a newly created body, a
kind of administrative tribunal instituted in each government and
called the Council of Municipal Affairs. Its decisions could be appealed
by either side to the Senate, which sat as a court of last resort. But
there were certain measures that the duma could not put into practice
without the approval of the central government. It had to obtain
ratification for all legislation concerning the regulation and policing
of urban commerce, the collection of municipal taxes, major bond
issues, every initial conveyance of municipally owned land that also
included a right of absolute enjoyment or transfer of title, the improvement of such land with buildings that might impede the free movement of pedestrian and vehicular traffic, and the imposition of tolls on
land and water travel.

The law of 1870 met the needs of the Russian cities that were beginning to be industrialized and to become large commercial centers, as
the zemstvo, established six years earlier, had met the needs of the
governments and districts. But one of the major defects in the 1870
law, which was not shared by that of 1864 on the zemstvo, was the
three-class electoral system. This procedure, which was totally foreign
to Russian urban tradition and which none of the urban committees
of 1863 had anticipated, had been borrowed from Prussia by the
Petersburg bureaucrats. It led to immoderate domination by the rich
upper middle class. Often the first college had fewer members than
representatives. In Petersburg it contained not more than two hundred

of the city's total of eighteen thousand voters. The plutocratic character of this system was so blatant that even the highly reactionary law of 1892 could not keep it alive any longer.

The development of the cities was heavily influenced by the 1870 law. The rich, large cities in particular made great advances, but many smaller cities as well succeeded in accomplishing things both useful and well managed. Russian city officials gave careful study to municipal organization in western Europe and profited by foreign experience. In the large centers, particularly in Petersburg and Moscow, they established a whole host of city services on a broad scale. They organized municipal agencies or granted concessions to private companies for the scientific maintenance of the water supply, highway upkeep, street paving, lighting, and the construction of slaughterhouses. For them, as for the zemstvo, the two dominating interests were public schooling and health. They were responsible for the complete transformation of the hospital services, which had hitherto been the responsibility of the central government; the number of hospitals was increased and their operation was much improved. There was a similar increase in the number of schools, quarters for which were easier to find in the cities than in rural areas. Although it did not rise as high as in the zemstvo, the municipal budgetary allocation to education became steadily larger. The rise was very rapid between 1870 and 1880: 1500 per cent in Chernigov, 700 per cent in Kiev. Educational activity was especially great in both capitals. Most frequently the city entrusted the task of developing the schools to a committee whose members it appointed. As in the countryside, these committees were rich in energetic, exceptional men who were dedicated to the management of their cities, and inestimable contributions were made by the staffs of physicians, teachers, statisticians, and experts and assistants of all kinds whom they had to recruit. If at the end of the reign of Alexander II the cities of Russia were beginning to stir out of the deep stupor into which they had been plunged under the reign of Nicholas I, it was certainly the result of the municipal autonomy inaugurated by the law of 1870.

Judicial Reforms

Though it might not have been directly provoked by the abolition of serfdom, like the reform of the provincial administration, the reform of the judiciary was at least precipitated by it. It was urgently required for a variety of reasons. First of all, the abrogation of the landowner's right of property in the peasants destroyed the whole foundation of the local judicial system that had rested since the time of Catherine II on the principle of the separateness of social classes and the predominance of the nobility. Moreover, the diversity of tribunals was a further source of confusion. Since Catherine II there had been special courts for each class, and since the beginning of the nineteenth century the free peasants had had courts in which the presiding judge was a nobleman and the associate judges were peasants. But it was extremely difficult to state precisely the boundaries of each of these jurisdictions. And the rendering of justice was mottled with many vices that aroused criticisms as harsh as they were deserved. Delays inherent in procedure were extreme, and litigation was interminable. In criminal cases the accused spent years in prison before they came to trial and again before their fates were finally settled. Preliminary hearings and trials themselves were all in writing, in the secrecy of the court clerks' offices. The accused in a criminal case or the parties to a civil suit never knew how or why a decision had been arrived at. The rule of adversary procedure being completely unknown, the criminal defendant had no one to speak for him and the profession of the lawyer did not exist. Investigations were conducted according to a system of formal proofs, which inevitably imposed prior restraints on the investigators' freedom of decision and often led to the conviction of innocent men. The courts, which were under the supervision of the government, were often under pressure from it as well; while the governor had no right to intervene in procedure, he was empowered to approve or disapprove the decisions of a whole series of courts. Since no certification of professional qualification was required of anyone in the judicial system, its members were often unequal to their obligations and very frequently incapable of understanding the matters on which they were sitting in judgment.

All these defects were so glaring that even under Nicholas I a special commission for their correction had been created under the chairmanship of Count Bludov, director of the codification section after 1850. While the peasant reform was under study, some committees of governments had declared their advocacy of a broad reform in the judiciary. The Tver committee, for example, headed by A. M. Unkovsky, had proposed the adoption of a strict separation of judicial and administrative powers, full publicity for all trials, oral debate and testimony, adversary procedure, and juries. As for Count Bludov, who was proceeding with his revisions of procedure, he had considerably broadened his task and in 1860 he had drafted proposed Codes of Civil and Criminal Procedure that included the abolition of the class courts, full press coverage of judicial process, oral testimony, and adversary pleadings. Once the emancipation of the peasants had been accomplished, the advocates of a radical reform of the judiciary system resolved to accelerate it. In the autumn of 1861, V. N. Butkov, secretary of state, submitted to the tsar a report on the divergencies that were revealed in the various proposals from Bludov and that made it impossible for the Chancellory of the State to present them to the Imperial Council, and Butkov emphasized the need to define the principles of a reform. Alexander II approved this and ordered the Chancellory to draft such bases; Count Bludov, who was more than seventy-five years old in 1861, was left with nothing but the general supervision of the work. In the Chancellory, where the actual task of evolving the reform had been placed in his hands, Butkov had as his principal collaborator S. I. Zarudny. Formerly a student in the School of Mathematics of the University of Kharkov, Zarudny had begun his governmental career in the Ministry of Justice. Having made a thorough study of Russian law and foreign juridical literature, he had quickly become known as a remarkable expert in his field. In 1857 Butkov had offered him the post of Assistant Secretary of State to the Imperial Council. In 1858 he had been sent abroad to study the legal systems of various western countries, a fact that explained the influence of the best European models on his reform. Charged with preparing draft laws, he had been the major inspiration of the work accomplished in the Chancellory of the State under Butkov's direction, with the collaboration of many eminent jurists such as Podyedonostsev, Knirim, Kvist, Utin, Stoyanovsky, Rovinsky, and Butskovsky.

Zarudny and his associates began by defining the principles to be applied: equality for all persons before the law without regard to class, separation of the judicial and administrative powers, permanent tenure of judges, the creation of an independent bar, public reports of trials, oral testimony, adversary procedure, and the use of the jury. Examined and approved by the Imperial Council, these principles were ratified by the emperor on 29 September/11 October 1862. Eleven months later, in the autumn of 1863, thanks to the energy of Zarudny and his collaborators, who had accomplished a mountainous task, the drafts for the new statute on the judiciary and the argumentation on their behalf were presented to the Imperial Council for its study. Accepted by Minister of Justice D. N. Zamyatnin, and his deputy, Stoyanovsky, they were then approved by the Council and on 20 November/2 December 1864 they were promulgated by the tsar.

After having examined these proposals [the imperial ukase declared] we have found them to be in entire conformity with our desire to create in

Russia a system of justice that will be swift, equitable, merciful, and equal for all our subjects; to augment the power of the courts; to guarantee them the independence that should be theirs, and in general to strengthen the people's respect for law, which is indispensable to the public welfare and which should be the constant concern of each and every man from the highest to the lowest in the social order.

The statute of 20 November/2 December 1864 changed the entire judicial system from top to bottom. It marked a date in the history of the Russian courts.

First of all the statute guaranteed the independence of the courts and the public knowledge of their work. The permanency of tenure granted to all judges fortified them against any governmental pressure and assured the swift and impartial application of the law. By sharply distinguishing between administrative and judicial functions, it prevented interference by government in judicial procedure. By introducing oral testimony, it made it possible for the court to have direct communication with witnesses, accused men, and parties to civil actions; it also made it possible for the conduct of the courts to be subject to the scrutiny of public opinion, especially in that public hearings were made the rule and that closed sessions were possible only in exceptional cases and then only through special judicial decision. By introducing the adversary principle, it made it possible to bring out all the circumstances of every case, to champion orally and publicly the interests of criminal defendants and civil litigants, and as a consequence to have the representation of counsel; henceforth the law would be a profession in its own right.

Furthermore, the statute established the equality of all men before the law. It eliminated the class courts and replaced them—except in the case of justices of the peace—by three kinds of tribunals: local courts, courts of appeal, and the supreme judicial division of the Senate.

Finally—and this is the essential point—it instituted the jury system in Russia, as well as the election of justices of the peace. During the period in which the reform was being drafted, some experts, including the famous jurist Spasovitch, had expressed the fear that, because of the ignorance of the mass of the population, the introduction of the jury system might be premature. Its adoption had been won only as a result of the dedicated zeal of Rovinsky and Zarudny. A juror's eligibility was determined by his ability to read and write, a minimum age of twenty-five and a maximum age of seventy, and residence of at least two months in the jurisdiction. There were also conditions to be met: the prospective juror must own land worth at least one-twentieth of the value stipulated for zemstvo electors or, if he lived in a city, real property assessed for tax purposes at 500 to 2000 rubles, varying with the size of the city; or else he must be the recipient of rents or other fixed income ranging, again with the size of the city, from 400 to 1000 rubles a year. Panels of prospective jurors, prepared in advance by special commissions, were presented to the presiding judge of the district court, and from these lists the court selected the jurors who would hear each case. There were twelve jurors, plus two alternates, one of whom would be called if necessary to replace one of the twelve; the jurors would decide the guilt or innocence of criminal defendants and were allowed to take extenuating circumstances into consideration. Hence they played a decisive part. Since they were representative of local society as a whole, the justice that they dispensed was entitled to be called popular or public justice.

This was also true of the lowest local courts, those of the justices of the peace, whose jurisdiction was limited to misdemeanors and petty civil matters. The inauguration of this system was in fact a courageous extension of the principle of an elected judiciary. It was the belief of the men who prepared the statute that the justice of the peace should be a man of good general reputation and, in order that he have a more intimate bond with the population, a resident of the area in which he sat, and that he should be able to provide the entire local population, without regard to class distinctions, with a recognized tribunal for the settlement of minor cases. That was why the justices of the peace were made elective and their election was put into the hands of the new organisms of provincial self-government, whose powers extended to all social classes. Thus the lot of local justice was closely bound with that of the zemstvo. It was the district zemstvo—in the capitals, the municipal duma—that elected these justices. They were required to have completed at least secondary schooling and to own land or buildings worth 15,000 rubles in rural areas, 6000 in the two capitals, and 3000 in all other cities. At the same time the district zemstvo had the right to elect a justice who did not meet the property qualifications, provided that it was unanimous in doing so. The justice's term ran for three years; his election had to be approved by the first department of the Senate. His decisions could be appealed to a conference of justices of the peace in the district, meeting in the district capital, which chose its own president and which, hierarchically, was answerable only to the Senate's supreme judicial division.

The judges of the other courts—district courts, courts of appeal, and the Senate's supreme judicial division—were appointed by the government. A great number of them was required. In view of the high qualifications that the Senate required of them, it was impossible to find them quickly. Furthermore it was in the government's best interest to select them only with the utmost prudence, because, once appointed, they could be removed only in the specific circumstances provided by law. That was why it was decided, at the suggestion of Zamyatnin, the minister of justice, even while steps were being initiated for the training of a new magistracy, that the new courts should be set up only gradually. The first were established in 1866 in the Petersburg and Moscow jurisdictions. In order to fill all the judicial posts, including those of investigating magistrates and senators of the supreme judicial division, it had been necessary to find almost four hundred qualified men. Zamyatnin managed to do this by recruiting them among the younger functionaries of the old courts, who as a rule proved equal to their responsibilities and were able to adapt themselves quickly to the new system of judicial procedure.

The new courts aroused widespread interest and won general respect. With the other reforms of the same period, they represented one of the foundations of the new civil order.

Reforms in Public Education

At the start of the reign of Alexander II, the elementary school was as good as nonexistent. The number of secondary schools was inadequate, and members of the lower social classes found access to them extremely difficult. The universities, which were subject to permanent government control, had lost all autonomy.

The government's new political orientation made it possible to remedy the decay of public education. All the various ministers of public education during the "era of the great reforms"—Norov (1855–1858), Kovalevsky (1858–1861), Golovnin (1861–1866)—displayed remarkable activity in its reformation.

Norov began by eliminating all the curbs and restrictions imposed on educational institutions at the end of the reign of Nicholas I. The ministry regained its former independence; its general control of the schools and its Scientific Committee were reinstituted, the school districts were liberated from the control of the governors general, and many regulations infringing on the freedom of instruction were abrogated. The universities returned to their normal way of life and the abolition of the famous committee of 2/14 April 1848, known as the Buturlin Committee, made it possible to ease the harsh rule of the censor.

E. P. Kovalevsky dedicated himself to the preparation of the reforms. After he had drafted a proposal in 1859 for a new censorship control, in 1860 he published a draft statute for elementary and secondary schooling.

But it was A. V. Golovnin who, after the brief interruption of the reactionary tenure of Count Putyatin as minister (from June to December of 1861), achieved the most effective work. He belonged to that circle of instructed and enlightened individuals grouped round Grand Duke Konstantin Pavlovitch, whose intimate he was and whose complete confidence he enjoyed. During the more than four years of Golovnin's ministry, his activity was evident in every branch of its administration. He reformed the central organization of the ministry and the censorship. In 1864 he issued a new statute for the Gymnasia and new regulations for elementary schools, followed in 1865 by a new university statute. In addition he initiated many less important reforms. What was unusual was the publicity that he gave to the reforms that were under study; the public was kept informed of the labors of the Ministry of Public Education and of the measures on which it was working; the press and other public institutions were enabled to take part in discussion of the minister's plans.

The establishment of elementary schools was envisaged as early as 1861. By imperial order a special committee was created to develop a plan for the organization of elementary instruction and to submit it to the "principal committee" charged with the preparation of the peasant reform. At the same time, the drafting commissions were looking into the problem of rural elementary schools. The minister of the interior invited the committees of the governments to submit their views, but only eight of them responded. The special commission in the Ministry of Public Education declared that it was impossible to make the establishment of elementary schools compulsory and that the task of inaugurating them must be left to the peasant communities, assisted by government subsidy. At the same time the Holy Synod too was examining the problem of elementary schooling and putting forward its pretension to the control of public education. It protested against the concentration of elementary schooling in the Ministry of Public Education and it insisted that in public elementary schools the clergy be given "the natural preponderance that is its due." Golovnin challenged such pretensions, and the imperial decree of 18/30 January 1862 left the Holy Synod in control only of those schools that had been founded by the clergy, while all the others were brought under the Ministry.

At the beginning of 1863 Golovnin presented the following proposal:

1. there would be two categories of elementary schools, the normal or "model" schools organized by the Ministry, and those founded by private groups or individuals; the organization and curriculum of these schools could be varied according to local conditions;
2. they would be placed under the control of local school boards composed of representatives of the various administrations;
3. education would not be compulsory;
4. in regions whose languages were other than Great Russian, instruction would initially be given in the local language and only later in Russia.

Baron Korf, whose part in the creation of the zemstvo we have already noted, thereupon pointed out to Golovnin that the assemblies of the nobility of the Petersburg and Nizhni-Novgorod governments had requested that elementary schooling be made a function of the newly created zemstvo. Korf himself shared this view, stating that the proposed school boards, which were bureaucratic organisms having no relation to the facts of life, could not properly govern elementary schooling and that it would be more logical to put it into the hands of the new autonomous provincial assemblies. The conservative members of the Imperial Council put forward a number of objections to participation by the zemstvo in public education. Ultimately the regulations approved by the tsar in 1864 authorized the zemstvo to concern itself with elementary schooling on the same footing as the other public institutions and private individuals. At the same time it limited the authority of the zemstvo in educational affairs to financial management of the schools, entrusting the control of the teaching itself to the school boards of the governments and districts. A government school board was headed by the diocesan bishop and composed of the governor, the director of elementary schools, and two members elected by the zemstvo. In practice, the heads of many of these boards were elected from among the members of the zemstvo.

As a result of the 1864 regulation the zemstvo succeeded in creating a special type of elementary school, the secular school, which became a normal or "model" primary school and which provided instruction for the great mass of the population: that is, the peasants. These schools made it possible for popular education to make great strides, thanks to the efforts of exceptional organizers such as Ushinsky, Vodovozov, P. A. Korsakov, and Baron M. A. Korf, among many others.

Of the 22,770 elementary schools that, as we have seen, already existed in European Russia in 1880, 17,782 were either entirely maintained by a zemstvo or supported by the peasant communities with its help. In sum, until the end of the reign of Alexander II, zemstvo and peasant community were responsible for the establishment of a thousand new schools a year on the average.

Against the secular school of the zemstvo the religious school directed by the Holy Synod and subsidized by the state made every effort to compete successfully. But, in spite of the state's financial help, the parochial schools could not match the rational organization of the secular schools. Even under the reactionary ministry of Count Tolstoi, who, as we shall see, bestowed his special solicitude on them, their number declined, while their rivals multiplied and improved.

In 1855 secondary education was in a better position than elementary education. Unquestionably the number of such schools was limited, but young people who wanted to enjoy secondary schooling were in a position to choose between the Gymnasia and the private institutions—"boarding schools" and "institutes"—created especially for the nobility. Moreover, in fact, the Gymnasia, like the private schools, were reserved for the children of the nobility. Children from other social classes, with the exception, however, of those of serfs and domestics,* could enter them only by producing a certificate from their corporation attesting that they no longer belonged to it.

The new statute on secondary education that Golovnin issued in 1864 proclaimed the absolute equality of all students in this domain: "Children of all classes in society, without distinction of class or religion, shall receive their education in Gymnasia and Progymnasia." In order to be eligible for admission to a secondary school, it was sufficient to pass the entrance examination. The statute of 1864 marked a great advance. The number of Gymnasia and the financial assistance given to them mounted steadily. In conformity with the new programs, three kinds of Gymnasia were set up: one with Latin and Greek, one with Latin alone, and a "real" one—like the German *Realschule*—without any ancient languages. Each was governed by a director, an inspector, and a pedagogical council with broadened jurisdiction. The teachers' economic situation was improved. The Ministry also concerned itself with furthering the publication of textbooks that met the requirements of modern education. It awarded prizes for the best

*See Volume II, p. 265.

textbooks in mathematics, natural sciences, modern languages, and jurisprudence. In addition it encouraged the translation of outstanding foreign textbooks.

For higher education the last years of the reign of Nicholas I had been a period of oppression and persecution. Norov, the first minister of public education under Alexander II, reinstated the statute of 1835, and the subjects stricken from the curriculum were again allowed to be taught. Furthermore, the universities regained the right to elect their own rectors.

After the troubles that broke out among the students about 1860, thought began to be given to a radical reform of the universities. Golovnin took it in hand. He had the staff of his Ministry draw up a proposed statute that he submitted to all the university councils, to a number of leading citizens, and, in French and German translations, to many foreign experts. This step was warmly applauded by the press and the public. The views expressed by the newspapers, the leaders, and the institutions that he consulted were published in a two-volume collection. After it had been examined by the Scientific Committee of the Ministry of Public Education and by the Imperial Council, the draft statute was approved by the tsar on 1/13 June 1863.

It guaranteed the autonomy of the universities. Each was headed by a rector, elected for a four-year term from among the regular professors, and there was an administrative council composed of all regular and special professors. The university council had a very broad jurisdiction that extended over both scholastic and administrative matters. It dealt with all major questions. Free of all outside interference, it made the decisions on methods of teaching, the training of candidates for the various chairs, the granting of scientific degrees, and the awards of prizes and medals; it approved the decisions of the university tribunal and the budget. Certain of its decisions, nevertheless, required the ratification of the trustee of the school district: these included the election of honorary members, the choice of *Dozenten* and lecturers, the appointment of other staff and of members of the university tribunal, and the selection of *Privatdozenten*.* Furthermore, elections and resignations of rectors, vice rectors and professors, the division of schools into sections, divisions and combinations of professorships, the designation of compulsory courses, and the decisions on doctoral candidacies had all to be submitted for approval to the Ministry.

*The *Dozent* (these titles were taken from the German) was an instructor in charge of a course; the *Privatdozent* was an assistant instructor.

The university tribunal was a new institution. This was a court that sat in judgment on the students, but only for disciplinary charges. Its three members, one of whom had to be a professor of law, were chosen by the university council; the professor of law was its presiding judge. Supervision of students was entrusted by the council to a vice rector, elected among the professors for three years, or to an inspector chosen outside the teaching corps for an indefinite term.

The organization of teaching itself was the business of the various schools, whose professors met under the presidency of a dean elected for three years. The *Dozenten,* the *Privatdozenten* and the lecturers could be invited to join these school councils and take part in deliberations, without voting rights. Vacant professorial chairs were ordinarily given to candidates proposed by the schools or by the university council, on a simple majority vote, but they could be conferred through competition, and also the minister had the right to appoint the candidate whom he preferred. In order to prevent a future lack of scholars qualified to sustain higher education and train new generations of young experts, outstanding students who had completed their studies were given fellowships that would enable them to continue their university work. Similarly there was much encouragement of scientific missions abroad, which were regarded as one of the best ways of training future professors.

Thanks to the statute of 1863, higher education attained parity with its purpose. The professors were the masters of the universities and labored for the growth of knowledge while they watched over the progress of their students. Russian scholarship developed rapidly. There can be no question that the period between 1863 and 1880 was the most brilliant in the history of the Russian universities.

Military Reforms and the Establishment of Compulsory Service

Whereas these reforms had been evolved by liberals but executed by conservatives, and even by opponents of all reform, the reform of the military had the good fortune to be put into practice by its author, General D. A. Miliutin, who was minister of war from 1861 to 1881. That it was possible to bring it to a successful conclusion was the result of the energy and perseverance of Miliutin and the trust that Alexander II reposed in him. In spite of the fact that he was a member of the military and had spent his entire life in the Russian army—D. A. Miliutin was a brother of N. Miliutin, one of the great artisans of the peasant reform and one of the active members of the select group that met frequently at the home of Grand Duchess Yelena Pavlovna—the general was a man of culture, with an extremely wide range of knowledge, who thoroughly understood the necessity of giving officers a decent education as well as a thorough professional training. As a young artillery officer in the guard he had written a number of works on mathematical and military subjects. In the beginning of 1840 he had served in the Caucasus, taking part in the mountain fighting and returning home wounded. In 1845 he was made a professor at the War Academy, and, during the fifteen years of his teaching career, he published a number of learned works, the most famous of which is devoted to Suvorov's 1799 campaign. After his appointment as minister of war he kept up his ties of friendship with many men in scientific and literary circles, notably Professors Kavelin and Korsh. He himself was keenly interested in the social movement and his military reform bore the impress of the liberal, egalitarian thinking of the age.

Before 1874 the term of military service was twenty-five years. Being a soldier meant exclusion from civilian life and separation from one's family for a quarter of a century—a desolating prospect from which men sought to flee by any possible means. The service itself, which was obligatory only for the *podatnye* (peasants and lower urban classes) was, furthermore, extremely cruel in itself. Discipline under Nicholas I, thoroughly impregnated with the Prussian concepts of blind obedience, was appallingly harsh; corporal punishment was used frequently and took many and sometimes extremely savage forms: the knout, the whip, the bludgeon, the cat-of-nine-tails, the rod.

Miliutin's first step was to reduce the term of military service from twenty-five to sixteen years; his next was to abolish the more brutal physical punishments. He revised the Military Criminal Code, lessening its penalties, and the army's criminal procedure, introducing some of the rules adopted in the general judicial reform of 1864.

He devoted himself as well, with special assiduity, to the transformation of the military academies that trained the future officers. These schools—the cadet corps—were profoundly hostile to anything that had a civilian taint, to any system of studies that was not exclusively military; the courses in their curricula were taught in most summary fashion; the main concern was military bearing and practice. Miliutin replaced these academies with military Gymnasia organized on the model of the civilian secondary schools, with the addition of special military training. The graduate of the military Gymnasium then went on to the officer-candidate school that would fit him for his particular branch of the service: engineers, artillery, cavalry, or infantry. This reform provided Russia with new nuclei of officers far better prepared for the performance of their delicate functions; instead of growing up in the climate of a military caste, they were given scientific training adapted to the various specialties of the army.

But Miliutin's most important accomplishment was the reform of recruitment and the establishment of equality in military service. The statute of 1/13 January 1874 provided that all young men must enter military service at the age of twenty. At the same time, it stipulated three categories of exemptions, which were universally applicable to all social classes. The first included men who were their families' only sons or grandsons, as well as sons who were supporting their younger brothers and sisters; the second consisted of young men with brothers under the age of eighteen; and the third embraced those who already had brothers in service, even if their families also contained other sons capable of working. Apart from these exempt categories, all conscripts were called up each year in a sequence determined by lot until each area had fulfilled its quota. If a given district was unable to provide enough recruits to meet its quota, the members of the exempt categories were then subject to conscription by lot—first the third category, then the second; men in the first category of exemptions could be drafted only through imperial rescript.

Thus chosen by lot, the conscripts served six years on active duty; they were then kept on reserve status for nine years; thereafter they entered the territorial militia, in which they remained until the age of forty. The term of active service, however, was susceptible of reduction in accordance with the conscript's educational background: it could be cut to six months for university men, to two years for graduates of secondary schools, and to three years for those who had completed the courses in the district schools or the upper elementary schools. Young men who volunteered before being called up could win further reductions in their tours of duty: the university men to three months and the secondary-school graduates to six months.

The military statute of 1874 was one of the most important of the reforms carried out under Alexander II. It democratized the Russian army, and it replaced the obsolete model of a professional army, in which soldiers drawn from the lower classes alone were sacrificed to the state, with a popular army created on the model of the modern army composed of all citizens without exception.

ᴄAlexander II (1855–1881):
The Reign Continued

·+◄▪▦▪►+·

I / "FATHERS AND SONS" [P A U L   M I L I U K O V]

It is a matter of common knowledge that in Russia ideas changed from one generation to another more radically than in western Europe, where civilization was older and more stable. But even in Russia it would be difficult to find two generations more opposite to each other than those of the 1840s and the 1860s.

The Formation of a Democratic Class in the Liberal Professions

While the men of the 1830s and 1840s deserved the qualification of "idealists" that has generally been ascribed to them, those who started life between 1860 and 1880 were called "realists." This difference attests first of all to a change in intellectual influence: that of Schelling and Hegel was succeeded by that of the radical Hegelians (Feuerbach), the materialists (Büchner, Moleschott, Vogt), and the English empiricists and naturalists (Mill, Spencer, Darwin, etc.). But the difference derived above all from the drastic change in the life of society that followed the emancipation of the peasants. That was the beginning of a genuinely new era in Russian history. The old ruling class, the nobility, was moving rapidly into decadence. The reforms of Alexander II gave everyone broader access to the liberal professions, to which the nobles had increasingly turned once they had stopped believing that they were obligated or naturally destined to military or government service. The activities of the press created the career of journalism; the reforms in the courts and their procedure inaugurated the judicial and legal professions; the establishment of the zemstvo entailed the creation of a host of positions for physicians, teachers, agronomists, statisticians, etc. Thus a class of the liberal professions came into being and, for the first time, gave the society a foundation stone for democracy. The social environment of this new class, its education, its way of living, its manner of dress and behavior in public, even its language—for, since the time of Elizabeth and Catherine II, the nobles considered themselves under an obligation to know and speak foreign languages—were far different from those of the young noblemen, surrounded since childhood by an army of unpaid servants and assured of attaining, in the fullness of time, to the highest posts in the army, the administration, or the government itself. The ideas of this new class, naturally, were also different. In intellectual circles, where he was a new arrival, the "commoner" brought with him, in the felicitous phrase of the critic, Mikhaïlovsky, who was at this time launching his career as a writer, the feeling of "outraged honor" and looked for his revenge to an arrogant and coarse attitude toward the representatives of the former "lords." Among the latter the most that was audible was the voice of an "uneasy conscience," of the "noble penitent," to quote Mikhaïlovsky again.

"Fathers and Sons"—the New Revolutionary Youth

These two types—the "son," the commoner; and the "father," the "noble penitent"—were masterfully portrayed in a famous novel, *Fathers and Sons* (1861), whose author himself, Ivan Turgenyev, a contemporary of Herzen and Bakunin, was a representative of the generation of the 1840s. The hero of the younger generation, Bazarov, symbolized "the victory of democracy over aristocracy." Turgenyev in fact described him by a term that was not new but that gained currency at this time—*nihilist*—on which the enemies of the younger generation and of democracy soon seized in order to give it an almost pejorative connotation. But Turgenyev strove for impartiality: he depicted at once the virtues and the faults of the "son" (Bazarov) and of the "father" (Kirsanov). Later he was to explain that, "if Bazarov is called a *nihilist*, it is *revolutionary* that is meant"—indeed, it was just at the time of the novel's publication that the first revolutionary current stirred among the Russian youth, particularly, as we shall see, among the students. N. Chernyshevsky, the most influential and the most important of the new generation's spokesman, said of this type of the revolutionary in 1863:

He was most recently born, and he is multiplying rapidly; he is a sign of the times and will disappear with his times—that is, soon. A half-dozen years ago these people were still unknown; three years ago they were de-

spised; a few years hence everyone will beseech them with the cry "Save us!"*
A few more years later, perhaps only a few months, they will be condemned,
hooted, jeered, shoved off the stage. . . . They will go off under a torrent
of imprecations, proud and modest, rough and good, as they have always
been . . .

That brilliant representative of the old civilization, Herzen, gave the
young quite a different reception. First of all he reproached them for
their lack of originality and their forgetfulness of their predecessors,
who, like himself at the beginning of the 1840s, had been fired with
enthusiasm by Feuerbach's ideas on the emancipation of the individual. And he saw nothing but a pose in their attitude, accusing them of
artificially exaggerating the contrast to those who had gone before
them:

You seek to avenge yourselves [he told them]; you want to tell us: "You
elders are hypocrites, we are cynics; you, in your utterances, were irreproachable in your morality, and we will be scoundrels; you were deferential to
your superiors and brutal to your subordinates, and we will be brutal to
everyone; you saluted but did not respect, and we will jostle and not apolo-
gize. Your idea of dignity consisted in courtesy and conventional honor; we
will find our honor in trampling on all the conventions and scorning all the
points of honor."

In sum Herzen refused to consider these young men the representatives
of true democracy: "Their vulgarity, elevated to the rank of a system,
has nothing in common with the artless rudeness of the peasant, who
does not offend us. . . . They have remained strangers to the people.
In every one of their acts and their words we instinctively recognize
the backstairs, the barracks, the office, or the seminary." On this point
Bakunin, Herzen's friend and close collaborator, held another view.
He wrote in 1867 to Herzen:

The young generation has a mass of faults, but it is a most natural phenomenon. The old morality, based on religious and patriarchal traditions and social
hierarchy, has crumbled irreparably; the new morality is still far from having
been created. Only a radical revolution in the social system will be capable of
bringing it into being. The young are seeking it, but they have not yet found
it; hence their hesitations and their contradictions. . . . But none of this
ought to close our eyes to their important virtues—I should say, even, their
lofty virtues. Their passion for equality, for work, justice, freedom, and reason
. . . is real and sincere. That is what has sent dozens of them to death and
hundreds of them to Siberia. . . . Don't turn into an old man, Herzen, and

*This was an allusion to the revolution expected by Chernyshevsky and his asso-
ciates.

don't damn the young; criticize them when they're wrong, but bow to their honest effort and their aspirations, their achievements and their sacrifices.

But already the generations were beginning to be divided. Herzen, Turgenyev, and their friends did not follow Bakunin. While he, as we shall see, never lost the fullness of his faith in either, they turned skeptical of both Socialism and revolution.

The New Mentors of the Young

What really then was that generation that was called *nihilist* and that called itself *revolutionary* and *realist?* The new guides for the young, in Herzen's stead, were Chernyshevsky, Dobrolyubov, and Pisarev, born, respectively, in 1828, 1836, and 1841. The first two came from ecclesiastical backgrounds and were thus indeed "commoners." At the literary evenings given by Pantsev, a wealthy patron of the arts, Chernyshevsky shocked the elegant Turgenyev with his plebeian manners and his coarse dress and food,* as well as with the assurance and the lack of respect with which this barely fledged student interrupted the learned arguments and the witty anecdotes of the famous writer. Dobrolyubov possessed a rigidity that astounded even his friends.

A strange thing [he noted in his diary]: a few days ago I felt in myself a possibility of falling in love, and yesterday I was suddenly taken with the desire to learn to dance, but I hope to be able to keep myself from being invaded by this kind of thing. If I want to accomplish something, I ought not to allow myself to be lulled or to make concessions to society, but, rather, keep my distance from it and "feed on my own bile."

These "bilious" men, as Herzen had labeled them, who professed a supreme contempt for the "useless men" of the old noble generations, for all their culture and their "esthetic" conceptions, were bearing a new evangel of destruction and emancipation. Pisarev, although he had received the usual education of a young nobleman, was the most acrid and intransigent of all three in his negation of the past. It was he who always found the most cutting and audacious phrases, those that spread across the world as the catchwords of "nihilism." This "noble penitent" made Bazarov his ideal. In this fictional hero he saw a man who "recognizes no rule, no moral law, no principle above or outside himself, who has no lofty end in view, who hardly thinks, and who, with all that and in spite of all that, possesses enormous powers." He made his own summation of the program of the "thinking realist": "Whatever can be broken must be broken; only what can withstand

*The gracious host, a friend of Nekrassov, used to prepare special dishes for him.

the attack is good; the rest, shattered into a thousand bits, is nothing but useless junk. In any case, strike out right and left. That will do no harm." With the zeal of the converted, the "nihilists," following Feuerbach, undertook the "rehabilitation of the flesh," and they launched a war to the death against all the survivals of the "gloomy reign" of the Russian Middle Ages in religion, politics, morality, philosophy, and the sciences. If these champions of destruction did not evolve a positive doctrine—that would be the task of their successors, Lavrov and Mikhaïlovsky—it was because they lived in a period of transition and lacked sufficient time. Chernyshevsky, who initiated his literary career in 1855 with his university thesis against esthetics, was exiled to Siberia in 1864 on the charge of having written a revolutionary proclamation. For several decades the censorship forbade even the mention of his name in the press. Dobrolyubov, who succeeded him as the literary critic of *Sovremennik*, died late in 1860, crushed by unceasing toil and cruelly harsh living conditions. Pisarev, the youngest of the three, became a regular contributor to *Russkoye Slovo* (*The Russian Word*) in 1860; in the summer of 1868, while swimming in the sea, he drowned—he was not yet twenty-seven. It was in prison, where he had spent the four years 1862–1865, that he wrote his finest articles.

What above all makes Chernyshevsky of interest is not his works of literary criticism but the attempt that he made in his *Notes on Mill* to be the first to provide a basis for that Russian version of agrarian Socialism that was later to be called *narodnitchestvo* (Populism). We have already discussed the part that he played in the preparation of the peasant reform. His participation in the first attempts at a revolutionary organization in Russia, as well as his contacts with the first secret society, *Zemlya i Volya* (Land and Liberty), from 1861 to 1863, are beyond question. But it was his novel of 1863, *What Is to Be Done?*, that had undeniably the most influence on the young. In it he demonstrated the application of "nihilism" to life in a series of characters: the rigid moralist, Rakhmetov, who sleeps on nails; the utilitarians and theoreticians of self-interest, Lopukhov and Kirsanov; the zealot of a social Utopia, Vera Pavlovna, dreaming her dreams out of Fourier. The philosophy and the logic of these characters was summed up in an amusing sentence by Vladimir Solovyev: "Man is descended from the monkey, so let us give our souls for the salvation of our friends." And this was how the adepts of the new religion preached materialism.

Dobrolyubov, who was less the theoretician, expanded and advanced Chernyshevsky's doctrine by applying it to a number of problems essential to the conduct of life. For him literary criticism was merely the pretext for explaining in his own fashion the types described by novelists and for thus answering the questions and the doubts that troubled the young. "I progressed from the abstract law of equity," he admitted, "to a more real principle, the good of mankind; in the end I reduced all my arguments to a single phrase: man and his happiness." The man whom he had in mind was "true man, man in flesh and blood, with his real ideas on the external world and not idea imagined out of sheer fiction." From this we may deduce that, as he explained in one of his verses, he wanted "actions instead of words." "Words" had been the portion of the men of the 1840s; it behooved his contemporaries to supplant empty words with "acts." To the devil with "the sublime aspirations of the soul" that were not translated into facts, and to the devil not only with "passive, impersonal, and limited" people but also with "strong, proud, energetic characters" who allowed themselves to drift into inaction and become of no use on earth. "It is better to endure a shipwreck than to subside into the mud"—that was Dobrolyubov's creed, and it inflamed his young readers.

Pisarev began his literary career after the young had felt the first magic of "action"—in this instance, popular education in its most accessible form, Sunday schools and reading rooms—had clashed head-on with the fierce opposition of the government. Initially efforts to raise the level of the education of the masses had been favorably received and had gained, indeed, the assistance of the Ministries of Public Education and the Interior. The example of Kiev, where a number of Sunday schools had been opened in 1859, had been followed by many other cities. Prosperous individuals had supplied the required funds, artists had organized concerts, and the government had provided the premises without charge. Teachers, students, officers, and clerics had actively worked together in the venture. What were the reasons behind so much zeal? The Sunday schools were supposed to "serve as the instruments for the popularization of liberal ideas in the mass of the people"; propagandists looked on them as "the seeds of the future transformation of the established order." Thus there had grown up a kind of secret society, "without specified forms, without registered members, but held together by the identity of the aims in view," and it was from just this group that Land and Liberty had emerged in 1861. The government had at once been perturbed. In January 1861 it had inaugurated a special supervision over the schools and installed a priest in each of them "in order that nothing contrary to the verities of the Orthodox

religion and the demands of morality might be tolerated in them."
In June 1862 the government had declared in a statement that, in
spite of everything, the schools of Petersburg were teaching "a
doctrine whose purpose was to unsettle faith, to propagate Socialist
theories on property, and to incite to rebellion against the authorities." Thereupon an imperial decree had closed all the Sunday
schools and reading rooms set up for the people. This was the reason
for the individual position taken by Pisarev. In his doctrine matters
of exclusively individualist inspiration were substituted for those of a
social character. His publication, *Russkoye Slovo*, proclaimed the
preeminence of "individualism" over the "Socialism" that was
preached by *Sovremennik*. As for himself, he was a vigorous pro-
ponent of "self-interest" and carried all the "nihilist" doctrines to the
extreme. He denied the validity of any common rule, any general ideal,
because "no oculist can prescribe the same glasses for all his patients."
His ideas led to the threshold of the subjectivism of the ancient
sophists. True, he added: "If I reject the common ideal, that in no
way means that I deny that the improvement of each individual is
essential," and this was the point on which he thrust all the emphasis of his preaching. He went on from there to reestablish little
by little the "common ideal" of public activity. In his view, when
Bazarov, the type of the revolutionary, had accomplished "the complete emancipation of his personality," there would still be another
problem for him to resolve: the liberation of other personalities, of
"thinking realists," of all who would dedicate themselves to "labor,"
not for their own pleasure but for the "good" of society and of "the
hungry and the naked." These "hungry" could not take care of
themselves. The "working class" was a mere "passive material" on
which the friends of mankind would long have to "work." That
was why it was necessary "to leave the cellars* and turn to the phenomena of intellectual labor," the sole reality. In other words, the
intellectuals must be made ready for the future. This was apparently
the "practical" application of a doctrine that had obviously taken
cognizance of the absolute incapacity shown by the scattered representatives of the cultivated class in their attempt to arouse the
"cellars." The acquisition of scientific knowledge and its popularization in one's own circle—this was the ultimate conclusion of Pisarev's
theory, and this was to be the major task of the student organizations
at the end of the 1860s. "The destiny of the people will be decided
not in the elementary schools but in the universities."

Podpolye, or "underground rooms"—meaning, here, action, secret organization.

The word *intellizhentsya* (the intellectuals), already used abroad by Herzen, was not yet to be found in Pisarev. To him the men of culture of the preceding generation were "esthetes," or "useless people," and those of his own generation were "thinking realists." The opponents of these "thinking realists" identified them by the name of "nihilists," in order to overwhelm them under the burden of what was incontestably exaggerated in the propaganda of Chernyshevsky, Dobrolyubov, and, in particular, Pisarev. Herzen, however, was aiming in his attacks only at some of the disciples of these masters, those whom he called "the Sobayevitches and the Nozdrevs of nihilism." It was not until much later that the generation of the 1860s was to be regarded in its entirety as the most typical manifestation of the Russian *intellizhentsya* in general. Historically this was an overgeneralized and imprecise use of both terms: "nihilist" and "intellectual." But it would be impossible to deny that the 1860s opened a new chapter in the history of the *intellizhentsya*, whose origins went back, if not to the age of Peter the Great, at least to that of Catherine II. These years, without question, set the new generation in opposition to its predecessors. They shaped a type of revolutionary that was to survive and evolve in a very slightly altered form.

II / THE BEGINNINGS OF THE REVOLUTIONARY MOVEMENT
[PAUL MILIUKOV]

Since the time of Catherine II there had been individuals and groups that had indeed laid down or attempted means of revolution against the autocracy. But it was only during the reign of Alexander II that the revolutionary movement in Russia began to acquire the character of an uninterrupted tradition that would be handed down from generation to generation and that would be made manifest in really revolutionary, and for the most part terroristic, actions.

The chief and, for a long time, the only protagonists of this movement were various groups of young people, in large part made up of students. From their foundation they set themselves the immediate goal of carrying revolutionary propaganda from the intellectual circles to the popular masses. Immediately they sought to reach the workers as well as the peasants. At the start their plan seemed utopian, because the people had hardly been made ready to adopt revolutionary ideas. Little by little, nevertheless, the more educated of the workers—and, later, of the peasants, from time to time—began to adhere to the movement. It was precisely this that distinguished the revolutionary movement under Alexander II from that of the previous period, which had gone hardly beyond the walls of literary drawing rooms and had limited itself to occasionally attempting to voice its ideas in the press in most carefully veiled form. The system of relative freedom established by Alexander II considerably facilitated the work of propaganda by word and deed. The formation of a class composed of the "liberal professions" created a kind of climate of good will and sympathy round the militants, whose ideas gained a response from it. Later the government's progressive abandonment of liberalism and the replacement of statesmen of liberal tendencies with conservatives frustrated the aspirations of the society by barring any hope of a peaceful solution, and thus it vastly increased the popularity of the idea of change by violence.

Since the end of the reign of Nicholas I new tendencies had appeared in addition to those of the Slavophiles and the Occidentalists. It would be impossible to associate these new trends with the old parties, because, on the one hand, they combined the Slavophile ideology with European aspirations and, on the other, they evidenced a radicalism that went remarkably beyond the program of the occidentalists: Socialist ideas had appeared, and Socialism had become preponderant among the intellectuals. At the outset of the reign of Alexander II, Socialists and liberals had still been united as a result of tradition and also because of their personal connections. But the radical press of the 1850s and the early 1860s, as we have seen, had already laid the groundwork for the schism. The year of the Polish insurrection, 1863, may be regarded as the date of the definitive division of Russian political currents into three major groups, each of which thereafter had its own individual history: conservatism, liberalism, and Socialism. During this bitter ordeal for liberalism and nationalism, the friends who until yesterday had been the amicable debaters of the drawing rooms of the 1830s and 1840s turned their backs on one another in order to join opposing camps. For a time some relations between the two camps did continue. But, with the entrance of the generation of the 1860s, which, in its freedom from the traditional ties, preached new doctrines, the conflict sharpened; it led to definitive opposition between political groups that, as a result of contradictions of a general nature but as well because of the social and political interests of which they became the advocates, grew increasingly alien to each other. In this regard too the reign of Alexander II marked the start of a social and political conflict that was not to be broken off again.

It is essential not to overlook these general conditions when one undertakes a close examination of the history of the revolutionary movement in Russia, and in particular the history of its beginnings between 1855 and 1877, before the initiation of terrorism.* It was divided into three periods: one of transition, from 1855 to 1863, the period of the first revolutionary ideology, which was marked by the divorce between Herzen and the revolutionary youth of the 1860s and by the growing influence of Bakunin; one of revolutionary organizations, from 1864 to 1873, the period of doctrinal conflicts among the representatives of Russian revolutionary currents abroad, and the preparation of the movement toward the people; and, between 1874 and 1877, the idyllic period of the "first crusade" to the people and, after the disillusion of that "crusade," the period of the systematic organization of revolution and conspiracy.

Early Revolutionary Ideology and the Decline of Herzen (1855–1863)

The spiritual father of the first revolutionary ideology was Alexander Herzen. In him, as, for that matter, in a great number of eminent intellectuals who were his contemporaries, the concepts of Slavophilism were much more closely allied with the newest Socialist doctrines than with the ideas of the liberals and Occidentalists. One conclusive proof of this marriage of ideas was Herzen's belief in the world-wide mission of the Russian people and especially of the Russian peasants, both predestined to establish Socialism. Well before the emancipation of the serfs, which was to arouse so much anticipation among the revolutionaries, he invested all his faith in the peasants, to whom he ascribed a specific mentality. In this he was in harmony with his friends in Moscow, the Slavophiles, because, for all his disapproval of the social order that they proposed as the ideal, he described as "good" the foundations on which they wished to erect it. In fact, for the early Slavophiles the specific character of the Russian popular "spirit" not only was incarnate in the Orthodox religion and Christian love but also expressed itself in the social forms that were peculiar to it—the absence of private property and the collective possession of land. This primitive form of agrarian collectivism, in the eyes of Herzen's contemporaries, was proof of the innate "communism" of the Russian people. It is hardly likely that Herzen had given any attention to *The Communist Manifesto* of Marx when it appeared in 1847. In contrast, he was strongly steeped in the thinking of Proudhon. Like the Frenchman, Herzen believed that the advent of Socialism would

*The inauguration of terrorism, which will be discussed below, represented the fourth period of the revolutionary movement.

be accomplished not through the operation of the political institutions of the state*—since these would have to be abolished at the same time as the state itself—but through the free play of purely economic relations among the individuals who constitute society. The basic principle of Proudhon's anarchism—namely, that a federation of free communes formed from below should take the place of constraints imposed from above—had made a deep impression on him. He believed it possible to reconcile his belief in the innate communism of the Russian peasants with the deepest significance of European Socialism. Was not the model for these free communes that should form federations to be found in the mir, that institution peculiar to Russia alone? If, as the Slavophiles insisted, the Russian people had never in its inmost heart accepted the Russian state but had always regarded all outside constraint as sin, was this not a negation of political institutions and law? It was here that the world mission of the Slavs was to be found; it was this that constituted that new "message" that they had to give to the universe; it was this that was the sign of the supremacy that they should exercise in the new era that was about to open for the world. Herzen found corroboration of this thought in the well-known parallel between modern times and the Roman Empire that was brought to his attention by the reading of a novel, *Arminius*. The Roman Empire had been destroyed by Christianity. Modern civilization would be destroyed by contemporary Christianity, which was Socialism. Like the Roman Empire, the modern world had grown old and exhausted. New "barbarians" must arise in order to enlighten humanity and save the world from ruin. They were the Slavs, and, in particular, the Russians. Europeans were paralyzed by the burden of their historical memories. The Russians were "independent" and free of the chains of history. "They have nothing to preserve"; while they "share in European critical thought, the aspirations of Europe are alien to them." In a word, Russia and especially the Russian people were revolutionaries and anarchists by nature.

This was the doctrine that so profoundly influenced the Russian

*Having gone to live abroad, Herzen was bitterly disappointed by the course taken by the 1848 revolution. Like Proudhon, he laid the responsibility for it on the French middle class, which had insisted on substituting a political for a social revolution. Moreover, the hostility of Russian intellectuals toward political institutions and parliamentary formalism had been to some degree a tradition since the insurrection of the Decembrists. The fact that, as we have seen, the landed nobility called for a constitutional reform after the emancipation of the serfs, in the hope of thus compensating for the loss of its social power by the acquisition of political power, further reinforced this hostility.

revolutionary movement. If it was correct, the problem of a "constitution" ceased to have any importance. In 1860, however, Herzen himself originated a petition to the tsar to demand a constitution. But what did he intend by it? His proposal called for the convocation of representatives of the communes, elected by the entire adult population. This assembly—which later generations were to call a Constituent Assembly—would have first of all to resolve not only the problem of the organization of property but also that of the organization of the autonomous local units, starting from the bottom—that is, from the commune. Undoubtedly Herzen was convinced that such an assembly would vote for the establishment of a new social order without going through the intermediate stage of political reforms or revolution. Only one condition was required in order to assure its complete success: its formal constitution and total freedom of decision. That was why the radical demands of the time were limited to freedom of the press, of propaganda, and of elections. The rest would come of itself: the pledge of that was the "communism" of the Russian peasants.

Only a little time later Herzen deeply repented of his petition, and Bakunin, who had also signed it, tried to explain that he had done so because he wanted to put Alexander II to the test. The revolutionaries could rely on no one but themselves, and the result of the peasant reform wholly justified their skepticism toward the public authorities. According to Herzen's doctrine, the peasants should act spontaneously and directly, without recourse to a Constituent Assembly. If they were indeed innate Socialists, then the task of the revolutionaries would be limited to destroying all the obstacles to the free manifestation of the popular will. Under such conditions the plebiscite on the elimination of the state and the creation of a federation of communes "from below" would so to speak force itself into being. This was the conclusion that Bakunin drew from Herzen's doctrine and that he set himself to propagating with all the energy of his impetuous, ardent spirit.

As a consequence of the enfranchisement of the serfs, the peasant entered the political arena as an independent factor for the first time; since, in addition, he could not be satisfied with the governmental solution of the agrarian question, the situation seemed propitious for revolution. The government itself was apprehensive of revolution and was expecting grave agrarian troubles when it issued the manifesto of 19 February/3 March 1861. But, when nothing serious ensued, the revolutionaries deferred their hopes to 1863, which was to mark the end of the transition period and the effective date of the emancipation law. The student groups, which Herzen himself, in his *Kolokol*, counseled to "go to the people," exploited this interval for the development of propaganda. In 1863 the young agitators initiated secret talks with the Polish revolutionaries who, in anticipation of disorders in Russia, were preparing an insurrection in their own country. Under Bakunin's influence, Herzen argued vigorously in his magazine for the Polish cause and even published an appeal to Russian officers not to fire on the rebels. Bakunin went further still. He helped to organize a Baltic expedition to transport arms to the Poles for use against Russia. In addition, at the same time as this venture, the revolutionaries conceived the project—apparently of major scope, but essentially infantile—of provoking a revolt in the Volga region, that classic theater of peasant and Cossack risings. They hoped, if not to win an unmistakable victory there, at least to draw off Russian forces toward the east when the Polish insurrection erupted. A number of Russian officers were dispatched to the Volga to distribute leaflets and a call to revolt. The material was distributed, but it did not produce the immediate response that the agitators anticipated. They were arrested, tried, and executed; the secret student groups were tracked down and their leaders were sent to Siberia.

The pathetic failure of all these efforts filled Herzen with bitterness and alienated the majority of his friends still in Russia and of his readers—overnight the circulation of *Kolokol* plunged from twenty-one hundred to five hundred copies. Furthermore, the first deportations and executions made a dramatic impression on public opinion, but not in the direction that the government expected. The young made heroes and martyrs of the first victims of the revolution. Instead of confining themselves to requesting the convocation of a Constituent Assembly, they adopted more radical political ideas that included resort to conspiracy. The leaders of the journalistic vanguard—Chernyshevksy, Mikhaïlov, Shelgunov—encouraged them. From abroad Bakunin fiercely defended these young men, ready for every sacrifice, against Herzen, who had lost his faith in success and had grasped the impossibility of revolution in Russia as she then was. The revolutionary movement entered on a new phase.

Revolutionary Student Groups and Preparations for Going to the People (1864–1873)

The old revolutionaries' reputations withered during this decade. New leaders arose. For the new troops that followed them and that were made up of the most ardent of the young, Herzen was too moderate, a mere straggler. Of all the men of the 1840s, Bakunin alone, who never lost contact with the young, retained all his popularity. He was still calling for immediate and violent revolution. He had found a disciple, who was to go far beyond him, in Netchayev, a student possessed of iron will and devoid of the least scruple in the choice of means. Netchayev preached the destruction of all state institutions and the abolition of all classes except that of the peasants. At the same time, the methods that he employed demonstrated such a lack of all concern of a moral nature that they merely discredited Bakunin with Marx and the leaders of the International that had just been founded. The system of intimidation that Netchayev used toward members of his own group brought about the assassination of one of them, Ivanov, on suspicion of having disobeyed Netchayev. This crime led to the discovery and dispersal of the group. Arrested by the Swiss authorities and turned over to the Russian government, Netchayev himself was imprisoned in the Fortress of Saints Peter and Paul. His fate abated the ardor of the students, who fell back into greater moderation and a better evaluation of the laws of evolution.

Herzen died in January 1870. But other exiles who had been able to elude the pursuits of the tsar's police were taking refuge in Europe. In March 1870, P. Lavrov, a professor in the Military Academy, arrived in Paris. He was a man of enormous leading and soon assumed the leadership of Russian evolutionary Socialism. Although he was more inclined to the scientific study of sociological problems, he yielded to the insistent pleas of the young and evolved a whole doctrine, that of Russian Populism. His *Historical Letters* became the gospel of the new generation. The guiding principle, which came closest to the aspirations of the young, was that the intellectuals had a "duty" to the people. Instead of the egocentric tenets of the nihilism of the 1860s, which preached individual perfection and, in general, the development of the personality, Populism taught abnegation and self-sacrifice for the good of the people. Inasmuch as the young generation wanted to embark on its task at once, without tarrying over lengthy special preparation for it, the question whether one should pursue one's studies became one of its favorite subjects of discussion. For a few years the center of these debates was Zürich. That city, too, was favored by a large number of girls from the best families, eager to follow the university courses from which they were barred in Russia and Germany. Many male students also lived there. According to Shishko, the historian of the revolutionary movement, Zürich had become the Mecca of Russian youth. In 1872 the debates in the city became more passionate than ever as a result of the arrival of the two leaders, Lavrov and Bakunin, each of whom defended his own ideas. Bakunin was still preaching his doctrine of immediate popular revolution. He exhorted the young to go to the people without further delay, not in order to "indoctrinate" the peasants but in order to incite immediate local revolts, which, in his vivid imagination, would assume the proportions of a general revolution. This "insurrectional" doctrine was often more welcome to the temperament of the young than the equilibrated and far too abstract thinking of Lavrov, who insisted on the necessity of continuing their university studies in order to be capable of instructing the people. The young split into Bakuninists, or "mutineers," who of course were the majority, and Lavrovites. Then a third leader, Tkachev, appeared in Zürich. A former member of the Netchayev group, he offered a doctrine that was too realistic to be popular. He taught that social revolution among and by the people was impossible, as recent experience had shown, and that preparing a social revolution for some indefinite future was a waste of time and a sacrifice of the propitious moment for revolution—it was still believed that the propitious moment provided by the emancipation of the serfs had not yet faded. There was only one possible solution: a political revolution made "from above" and without the concurrence of the popular masses. It was not, of course—for the intellectuals regarded proposals for political reforms only as expedients of the nobility and the middle class to "delude" the people with the bait of a "constitution"—a political reform that Tkachev had in mind, but rather a revolution: in other words, the seizure of power by a group of revolutionary conspirators under a highly centralized leadership; this was the road that Lenin was later to choose. The generations of the 1860s and 1870s, however, were too idealistic and romantic to be bewitched by such thinking. They devoutly believed in the innate Socialism of the Russian peasant and saw it as the guaranty of success for a revolution carried out from below as envisaged by Bakunin. Tkachev recruited only a few disciples.

Nevertheless, Bakuninists, Lavrovites, and Tkachevists were unanimous on one point: they must "go to the people." Whether it be in order to teach, or to learn, or to incite an uprising, it was essential to be among the people. The intellectuals had no other means of paying their "debt" and fulfilling their "obligations" to the people. The representatives of the "populist" literary school, which came into being at precisely this moment, were all out of the lower social classes. They were city men, seminarists, etc., who had come to know the Russian peasant well. They were the first to offer the enlightened public a real picture of the lower depths of the population in village and city alike. Sometimes the "singers of the people's sufferings," like Levitov and Reshetnikov, they depicted the people in a darkly realistic perspective; sometimes, like Nefedov and especially Zlatovratsky, they idealized the masses to the full extent of their own imaginations. It was of course this idealization that most impressed the young of Populist tendencies. "The people is communist"—this was the premise on which all revolutionary plans were founded. At the same time, in order to be able to mingle with the masses and overcome their suspicions and distrust, the propagandists regarded it as essential never to appear in the villages except when wearing village dress and speaking the language of the peasants. In order to prove their immediate usefulness to the peasants, they were urged to learn trades at which they could work in the villages.

Most opportunely for the young, who were chafing to hurl themselves into the struggle, a government decree of 1873 called on all young Russians studying in Switzerland to return to Russia. At once, and quite independently of the wishes of those concerned, the problem of continuing or interrupting university study was resolved, and in the negative. The young propagandists of both sexes went back to Russia in a body. They brought with them new energies for the revolutionary movement, which had been languishing since its setbacks in 1863 and above all since the individual terrorist action of Karakozov, a member of a student club, who had fired at Alexander II in 1866 and thus brought on a violent reaction by the government. The revolutionaries had gone into exile in order to elude the police; a ridiculous order by this same government brought them all home. After the ebb of the revolutionary tide, it was to be expected that there would be a new flood.

When the young emigrants returned to Russia, the road to the people had already been opened. A major contribution to this end had been made by a group of students led by Chaikovsky, who later gained a reputation in exile. Created at the end of the 1860 decade, and painfully influenced by the violent methods and amoral procedures of Netchayev, this group had adopted an unmistakably evolutionist and moralist position; as its principal goal it had chosen the education of the revolutionaries themselves before turning to the popular masses. With this in mind, it had prepared translations of Darwin, John Stuart Mill, Spencer, etc., and popularized books for the people, while at the same time publishing clandestine revolutionary pamphlets. It had even bought a printing plant in Switzerland and founded "autonomous clubs" in various Russian cities for the distribution of these works of popularization and propaganda. When Chaikovsky, soon seduced by religious mysticism and the idea of the "divinity of mankind," withdrew from the revolutionary movement and in the end emigrated to America, his group merged with that of Kravchinsky.* Finally another emigrant-to-be, Prince P. A. Kropotkin, a young officer who had just come back from a geographic expedition in Siberia, joined the organization in the spring of 1872. The members of these groups were organized into "communes": that is, a number of students set up housekeeping on a communal basis. According to Chaikovsky's testimony, this living in common brought them spiritually closer to one another and contributed to the elevation of the moral standards that governed their interrelations. That was why these associations were so especially closely knit, why they later facilitated the projects of conspirators, from which they barred all the young who were not members of these groups, who were not well known, or who did not conform to the principles of complete comradeship; thus the organization of plots was made easier while their discovery by the police was made more difficult. Among the numerous branches that the central group in Petersburg set up in the provinces through Chaikovsky's associates, many were of considerable size. A "commune" of intellectuals in Kiev, which was later to be described by the brilliant historian, Debagory-Mokryevitch, included among its members Catherine Breshko-Breshkovskaya, who in the future would be called the grandmother of the Russian revolution. One of the major members of the Odessa group was Felix Volkhovsky, the author of widely read works of popularization, who subsequently emigrated, established the Fund for the Free Russian Press, and published a magazine, *Free Russia*, in London. Other active groups were established in Kherson, Orel, Vyatka, Vologda, etc.

During the autumn and winter of 1873, under a joint agreement, these groups formed new ones especially designed to prepare the "crusade to the people." The idea of such a crusade was enthusiastically hailed by everyone—by those who had remained in Russia as well as by those who had just come home. According to an official report, thirty-seven of fifty-four governments were "infected" by the movement. Kravchinsky and Kropotkin have left excellent portrayals of the state of mind and the illusions of the young propagandists. In contrast to Netchayev's methods, these organizations imposed neither restrictions nor discipline apart from the moral rules that governed relations among their members. "The revolutionary party," they believed, should come into being spontaneously and arise out of the

*Kravchinsky, who was later a famous exile under the name of Stepnyak, published a series of celebrated works abroad: *Underground Russia*, a description of the revolutionary movement; *Russia Under the Tsars; King Stork and King Log*, etc.

heart of the popular masses. The movement was "a kind of revelation rather than propaganda," Kravchinsky said.

It is like a vigorous cry, uttered no one knows where, that resounds throughout the country and summons all those whose souls are not dead to serve the great cause of the salvation of the fatherland and of mankind. And all those whose souls are still alive will rise in anger against their past, hasten to answer the call, abandon birthplace, riches, honors, and family. They give themselves to the movement with that passionate enthusiasm, that ardent faith that recognizes no obstacles and reckons no sacrifices, and for which suffering and death are but goads as piercing as they are irresistible. They consist not only of that host of young people, many of whom in fact are of aristocratic families, who work fifteen hours a day in the factories and the workshops and the fields. . . . What is remarkable is the fact that the contagion has reached established men, men whose positions are secure— magistrates, physicians, officers . . .

This movement could not be regarded as political only. It was, rather, a kind of crusade; it had all the characteristics of religious movements.

The Launching and the Frustrations of the "Crusade to the People"
(1874–1877)

In the spring of 1874 the student groups suddenly stopped talking. The time for debate had passed; what we required was to start "work." Overcoats, boots, equipment for the workers were hastily assembled or made. Farewells were brief, replies were terse. Where are you going? To the Urals. On the Volga. Down south. To the Don. Heartfelt good wishes, vigorous hand-shakes. . . . Springtime was slipping by, the time had come. . . . And, like an electric current, the cry of *To the people!* ran through the young; sure of themselves, courageous, with neither weapons nor organization, they hurled themselves into the assault before the enemy's eyes.

There were almost two thousand of these young enthusiasts who, with virtually no preparation, took to the road for the "first crusade" to the people. The official report, prepared later by Count Pahlen, minister of the interior, corroborated Stepnyak's observation that they encountered strong sympathy and vigorous support among the educated class: "Many mature men in prominent positions not only were hostile to the government but even furnished effective assistance to the revolutionaries, as if they did not recognize that they were contributing to their own and society's destruction." Pahlen deplored "the lack of moral education" that was demonstrated by this class, its "lack of respect for religion, the family, the rights of the individual, and private property," as if the sympathies that it manifested for the propagandists were not unchallengeably the consequence of the violation of "the rights of the individual" by the government itself and of its refusal to grant the country a minimum of political freedom.

The behavior of the young revolutionaries was hardly revolutionary. Their clothes, which they thought were proletarian, their inability to speak the language of the people, their total ignorance of the conditions of village life immediately attracted attention to them. The police trailed their every step and within a few months was excellently equipped with information about the majority of them. At first the government did not know what attitude to adopt toward this new kind of crime. Finally it decided to put a first batch of 50 persons on trial, and then a second batch of 193, taken from the mass of those who had been arrested. For the first time there were public political trials, the sole purpose of which was to show society what perils threatened it. But these trials did not produce the effect that was expected of them. They acquainted the mass public with the fact of the existence of secret societies in Russia. Furthermore, the attitude of the accused, their spirit of abnegation and sacrifice, their idealism, the strength of their convictions, and their absolute lack of self-interest won them general sympathy. During the actual trials they took advantage of their freedom to testify not in order to present their own defense but to put the reactionary government itself on trial, and the newspapers were able to publish summaries of their speeches, which were printed in full by the clandestine press. Thus the accused openly voiced many thoughts that the average Russian shared but dared not express. The political trials made the revolution popular.

But the propagandists' disillusionment at the results of their "crusade" was shattering. Experience proved to them that they had been mistaken about the people's sentiments: not only did it not share their views or wish to hear them; but it also did not understand what they said. As long as they confined themselves to the land and criticized the landowners, they could still get a hearing from the peasants. But, as soon as they tried to explain Socialism, the methods of collective farming, etc., they could no longer hold the peasants' attention.* What was worse, they made themselves suspect in the peasants' eyes. Working the land in common meant to the peasants only the obligations of the days of serfdom, the payments, the forced labor, and the compulsory sowing that Nicholas I had attempted to enforce. Often the peasants themselves arrested the agitators and turned them over to the police.

*Stefanovitch did succeed in rallying a thousand peasants at Chigirin in 1877. But this success, which was the only important one, was gained only because the "rebels" invoked the name of the tsar and distributed a forged "Golden Charter" among the peasants. Such methods were officially condemned by the young.

The young leaders, however, did not stop at the mere recognition of the mistakes and the inadequacies of their methods; they were able to derive the necessary lesson from their failure. The peasants had been taken by surprise. It was now obvious that they must first be educated; instead of going to them dressed in masquerade in order "to give them a good democratic kick," the agitators must first live among them. The propagandists' speeches had not been understood and had seemed suspect. Hence it was necessary to begin not by oratory but by gaining the peasants' trust through the performance of useful services for them. In short, a labor of long duration and in the field required special measures in order to assure the coordination of all efforts. The agitators laid the blame for their failure on their lack of organization in large part. That was why in 1876 they formed an association that adopted the name of Land and Liberty *(Zemlya i Volya)*, already employed in 1860 and 1870. The idyllic period of the revolution was over, and real revolutionary activity was about to take its place. In 1877 the Populist propagandists would attempt their "second campaign" for the conquest of the people with new methods. A more bitter struggle with the agents of the government lay ahead for them. They would swiftly go over from peaceful propaganda to armed defense, and then to the terrorist acts that would gain universal notoriety for the mysterious "Central Committee."

III / REACTION AND THE TERRORIST REVOLUTIONARY MOVEMENT [PAUL MILIUKOV]

The terrorist revolutionary movement was a result of the reactionary policy that marked the end of the reign of Alexander II.

The Hesitations of Alexander II and the Contrast Between Internal and Economic Policies

Between 1861 and 1866 the policy of Alexander II revealed a strange mixture of liberalism and conservatism. The tsar's private thinking, as we have seen, bore no resemblance to the role of "emancipator" and reformer that he had assumed. As long as the enthusiasm aroused by the era of freedom that he had inaugurated endured, as long as he was surrounded by a group of men converted to reformist ideas, this contradiction was not apparent. But the preparation of the peasant reform brought to the surface the hesitations that characterized the reign of this well-meaning but irresolute tsar.

It was the defenders of serfdom, such as Count Panin, who succeeded

Rostovtsev as chairman of the "drafting commissions," to whom he assigned the task of putting the finishing touches to the plan for the emancipation of the peasants. It was the Imperial Council, headed by an avowed opponent of the peasant reform, Alexis Orlov, that he designated to examine the proposal. As soon as he had promulgated the act of emancipation he got rid of Nikolai Miliutin, who had devoted so much of his effort to the abolition of serfdom. At the head of the Ministry of State Domains, which was supposed to extend the benefits of the reform to the state peasants, he replaced the liberal, Kiselev, with the famous Muravyev, who in turn was succeeded by the reactionary, Zeleny. The disorders that broke out among the Petersburg students during the autumn of 1861 because of the appointment of conservatives to execute the measures taken by Kovalevsky, the liberal minister, frightened the tsar and drove him closer to his reactionary advisers. The epidemic of fires that raged in the capital in May 1862 and that was again, though without adequate evidence, ascribed to the same "red" elements, increased his apprehensions. Chernyshevsky, M. Mikhaïlov, and Serno Solovyevitch were exiled to Siberia without trial. The Sunday schools and public courses were banned. Rigid control was thereafter imposed on newspapers and magazines. The thousandth anniversary of the creation of the Russian state fell on September 7, 1862: some expected to see it celebrated by the grant of a constitution and others anticipated the proclamation of freedom of the press or of conscience, but no new reform was promulgated. On the contrary, repressive measures were adopted against the assemblies of the nobility that had carried on a campaign in favor of a constitution.

Events in Poland made no less dramatic an impression on the tsar and the government. At the start of his reign satisfaction seemed to prevail in Poland as elsewhere. In Poland all that was still awaited was an amnesty for the exiles and the grant of an "organic statute," the promise of which, first given by Nicholas I, had been reiterated by Alexander II to Napoleon III at the time of the conclusion of the Treaty of Paris. The tsar's lieutenants in Warsaw, who succeeded one another rapidly between 1860 and 1862, were not adequate to their duties. Prince Gorchakov, aged and ailing and weak in character, confined himself until his death in April 1861 to the preservation of external order. He was followed by four lieutenant generals in a single year: General Sukhozanet (who served twice), a man as ignorant as he was coarse; Count Lambert, who was a man of gentler character but comparable lack of education, and who besides was very seriously ill; and Count Lüders, a disciple of Nicholas I who was the enemy of everything civilized. It was not until June 1862 that Alexander II appointed Grand Duke Konstantin Nikolayevitch viceroy, with Marquis Vielopolsky, a great Polish patriot and a proved politician, as his deputy. This appointment came too late, because, under the influence of the emigration, a radical change had been made in Polish thinking during these two critical years. The moderate parties had given way to the radicals. Vielopolsky submitted conciliatory proposals that never emerged from the files of the administration in Petersburg. His function as mediator was a failure, and at the beginning of 1863 the insurrection exploded.

Although the young revolutionaries who took part in it had the support of Bakunin and the sympathy of Herzen, they were met by the hostility of the Russian liberals, who were driven into the arms of the "Slavophile" conservatives and nationalists by the insurrection. Katkov, the editor in chief of *Russky Vyestnik (The Russian Messenger)* and *Moskovskya Vyedomosti (The Moscow News)*, who until then had championed English democratic institutions, was the most glaring example of the abrupt about-face by the liberals. His nationalist articles wielded great influence, even in government circles. This was the first time that a Russian journalist had exerted any influence on the government. Unfortunately it was a most evil influence.

Encouraged by the reconciliation between some of the liberals and the Slavophiles, the government adopted a reactionary policy for the border provinces. It decided to subject Poland to the system of Russification that Nikolai Miliutin and Georgi Samarin had recommended for and applied to the western provinces, the northwest, Lithuania, White Russia, and the southwest Ukraine, where, after the end of the Polish insurrection, the government had launched a campaign against "Polishness" and Catholicism by assuming the defense of the non-Polish and non-Catholic elements. This policy, which was based on the lower social classes, had a democratic appearance in these areas, and this explained its ability to gain the approval of men like N. Miliutin and Samarin. But neither of them had ever dreamed of subjecting Poland herself to a policy conceived in terms of the western Russian provinces, which, transplanted to a totally Polish environment, was to assume a purely reactionary aspect and to be based exclusively on violence. This adaptation was the work of Prince Cherkassky, who succeeded N. Miliutin on the latter's death in 1866, having previously been his closest collaborator. The result of his revision was to make relations between Russians and Poles more and more strained, especially in the period that followed between 1870 and 1880. In the Ukraine, which since 1864 had been under the system of Russification already tested in the northwestern provinces, the government sought to prevent the use of the local language, Ukrainian. The Ukrainian nationalists had not yet become "separatists," although Katkov was already accusing them of this and waging his campaign against them on this pretext. But the necessity of emigrating, as M. Dragomanov was to do, in order to escape the harassments of the government, and the activities in which the emigrants engaged in Galicia made important contributions to the growth of the separatist sentiment in the Ukraine after 1875. The policy of Russification was inaugurated in the Baltic provinces and Finland too in 1864.

In Russia properly so called, however, Alexander II was showing himself to be increasingly progressive and was still continuing the reforms. In 1864 he created the zemstvo. In 1866 he inaugurated the new judicial organization, which was not extended to the western provinces, Lithuania, White Russia, or the Ukraine. In 1865 he abolished prior censorship of the press. In 1866 he took a highly favorable position toward a memorandum from Finance Minister Reitern, who pointed out to him that only timely reforms that granted the people peacefully what it was seeking to obtain by violence—that is, the abolition of obsolete political practices and deeply rooted abuses— were capable of preventing revolutions, and who made every effort to prove that the accomplishment of reforms was absolutely essential to the economic and financial consolidation of Russia. Alexander maintained the minister in favor* and allowed him to carry out a progressive economic and financial policy.

During his sixteen years in power, from 1862 to 1878, Reitern strove to transform that country of backward farmers, Russia, into an industrial nation. In particular he gave great attention to expediting the transport of grain, which represented the major part of Russia's exports, by establishing a railway network to link the great agricultural centers with the major land and sea outlets. When Alexander II came to the throne Russia had only 977 versts of railway lines, the chief of which were the Moscow-Petersburg and the Warsaw-Vienna routes. Reitern decided not only to link the fertile areas of the governments of the Volga basin, New Russia, and central Russia to a Baltic port by way of Moscow, but also to establish a connection between Moscow and the Black Sea. He granted the concession for this railway network to a group of capitalists headed by the French Crédit Mobilier under Péreire. This first concession did not produce good results, but for all that the government of Alexander II remained faithful to the concession system until the end of the reign: in 1881, of twenty-one thousand

*With Count Alexander Adlerberg, minister of the court; Gorchakov, foreign minister since 1856, and D. A. Miliutin, minister of war after 1862, Reitern was among the very few ministers who were able to retain the trust of Alexander II for many years.

versts of railway construction, 93 per cent belonged to private companies, whose obligations were reinforced by a government guaranty
of 5 per cent interest. It was between 1868 and 1875 that the growth of
the railway network was carried on most actively—over one hundred
thousand versts of track were laid during that period. The agricultural
areas were linked to the ports as well as to the Donets mineral basin.
For the first time the railways showed a profit. The price of wheat
rose substantially and the peasantry definitively emerged from the
ancient housekeeping economy to a mercantile economy. Between
1876 and 1880, probably as the result of the development of railways
as well as the reclamation of much land, grain exports—45 to 50
million poods a year at the end of the reign of Nicholas I, 69 million
immediately after the end of the Crimean War, and 76 million between
1861 and 1865—leaped enormously to the figure of 257 million poods.
Reitern also concerned himself largely with the organization of private
credit. He was not satisfied merely to reform the state bank; he encouraged the creation of private banks. That the majority of these
came into existence between 1863 and 1877 was the achievement of
his policy.

Thus, while domestic policy hesitated but tended to turn conserva-
tive and indeed reactionary, economic policy remained progressive.
This was a contrast that henceforth was always to be visible in
Russia.

Reaction

Karakozov, the student, tried to kill the tsar on 4/16 April 1866.
Thereafter Alexander II committed himself increasingly clearly to a
conservative policy. Reaction was especially strong in the domains of
the schools, the courts, and the press.

Although Karakozov, whose closest friends did not approve of the
idea of regicide, was totally alone in reaching the decision to make
his attempt, the tsar's reactionary advisers nonetheless inevitably tried
to place the responsibility for it on the entire young generation and
the policies of Golovnin, the liberal minister of public education.
The report of the special commission, headed by Count Muravyev,
that was appointed to investigate the Karakozov case condemned the
diffusion of revolutionary ideas among the young in the schools. Golovnin had to resign, and he was succeeded by his opponent, Count
D. A. Tolstoi. On 13/25 May 1866 an imperial rescript addressed to
Premier Paul P. Gagarin proclaimed that "the young should be reared
in the spirit of the truths of religion, respect for property, and the
observance of the basic principles of the social order." The rescript was

vehement in its attacks on the criticisms being poured out against the nobility, and it called on fathers of families to stand by the government in its educational endeavors. Tolstoi, who held his ministry from 1866 to 1880, dedicated all his effort to the application of this program, straining to destroy the reforms of his predecessors, or at least to dilute their effects.

At the very outset he sought to neutralize the influence of the zemstvo of elementary schooling. Afraid to move at once to alter the 1864 regulation, he began in 1869 by ordering the educational policies of the zemstvo to be placed under the supervision of special inspectors, who were made permanent members of the district school boards and thus were enabled to intervene in the selection of teachers and the organization of school courses, and to dismiss teachers whom they accused of acting against the government, religion, and morality and thus of doing harm to their pupils. Then, deciding that this system of inspection was inadequate, Tolstoi decided to reform the elementary-school system set up by Golovnin. His plan to transform the school boards into bureaucratic institutions directed by state inspectors was abruptly blocked by an unanticipated obstacle, the demands of the nobles, who succeeded in winning a hearing from the tsar; Tolstoi was thereupon ordered to turn over the direction of the schools to the representatives of the nobility. Therefore the new statute on public education (1874) made the marshals of the nobility the chairmen of the school boards of their respective districts and governments. The heads of the elementary schools remained permanent members of the boards, assigned to administrative duties, but they were subject to control and supervision by the marshal of the nobility of the government. The inspectors retained their functions in the district boards. In addition, Tolstoi, who at the same time was in charge of the affairs of the Orthodox church in his capacity as attorney general of the Holy Synod, as well as those of public education, threw the whole weight of his power behind the parochial schools run by the clergy. Not only did clerical influence invade public education, but the government preferred the church school to the secular, especially to the zemstvo school, which was a product of the spontaneous action of Russian society.

It was chiefly secondary education, in which the adolescents were exposed to the influences that shaped their characters and their ideas, that was the target of Tolstoi's "counter-reform." Part of the press agreed with the tsar and Tolstoi on the necessity of changing the curricula. Katkov and C. M. Leontyev, editors in chief respectively of *Russky Vyestnik (The Russian Messenger)* and *Moskovskya Vyedo-*

mosti (The Moscow News), were among the ardent advocates of this reactionism. Once a liberal and a partisan of the reforms, Katkov had made a turnabout under the influence of the growth of extremist ideas among the young and particularly, as we have seen, of the Polish insurrection of 1863. He had become the inspiration of the reactionary party that sought to dominate the tsar, to prevent new reforms, and to extirpate those that had already been achieved. Katkov and Leontyev accused the young of yielding to the spirit of nihilism and materialism, and he attributed this surrender to the poor organization of education and teaching in the secondary schools in particular; he called on the new minister of public education to halt the decadence of the schools with a firm hand and to restrain the young by forcing them to go to work and abandon politics. As for the curricula, he demanded the elimination of the natural sciences, which he regarded as harmful because they were conducive to materialism; a reduction in the study of history and literary history, and the use of the time thus gained for the more thorough study of ancient languages—not only Latin but also Greek, the knowledge of which he judged indispensable to Russians, since Russia was closer to Greek than to Roman civilization. Study of the languages and the literary masterpieces of antiquity, he reasoned, would give the young the habit of precise knowledge and would not foster idle speculation.

Tolstoi, like Katkov, looked on the classical languages and literature as a means of combatting the students' independence of mind, and, by concentrating their thinking and their imagination on classical culture, he hoped to divert their attention from what was going on around them. It was with this in mind that he conceived the entire reform of the secondary schools. On the basis of documents and reports supplied by the directors of the Gymnasia and the trustees of the school districts, he drafted a proposal that was studied first by a commission under Count Stroganov and then by a specially appointed committee of the Imperial Council; after thorough discussion, it was finally presented in 1871 to the Council's plenary assembly. There it met sharp opposition. A majority of twenty-nine members declared themselves against secondary education based on classical studies. These members especially criticized the article in the proposal that barred access to the universities to those young men who lacked the diploma of the classical Gymnasium. "It cannot be regarded as equitable," they asserted, "that entrance to the universities, those temples of science, should be forbidden to those young men who have studied the sciences in the highest sense of the word: namely, the positive sciences; or that the universities be open only to those who have studied the ancient, the dead languages." On the other hand a minority of eighteen members approved the proposal, and most particularly its prohibition that had so aroused the majority. Alexander II sided with the minority, and Tolstoi's draft became the new statute of Gymnasia and Progymnasia, promulgated by the tsar on 30 July/11 August 1871.

The Gymnasium became essentially a classical school. Its students started the study of Latin in their first year; they began Greek in the third year. Two hours daily were devoted to the study of ancient languages. On the other hand, the study of the natural sciences was abolished and that of history, literary history, and modern languages was reduced. The study of ancient languages was conducted with the major emphasis on grammar and the writing of themes. General culture was sacrificed to the thorough knowledge of Greek and Latin, and the students emerged from the Gymnasium as fine writers of compositions with only the most superficial knowledge of everything else. This was reflected in their intellectual development.

In order better to attain the political goal of the reform and divert the young from extreme political ideas, the exaggerated classicism of the curricula was reinforced by harsh discipline that was reminiscent of life in a garrison. The students had to learn to obey their superiors blindly and to carry out all their orders to the letter. The teaching councils were subordinated to the directors of the Gymnasia, whose prerogatives were broadened and who were given the duty of keeping the teachers under surveillance. In short, the Ministry was especially intent on uniformity in teaching and in the choice of textbooks. No book could be used without its prior approval. Thus school books that did not match the government's thinking were kept out of the secondary schools.

Although the "real" schools, which taught principally mathematics and drafting, survived side by side with the classical Gymnasia—their statute was approved by the tsar on 15/27 May 1872—their graduates were forbidden entrance to the universities and could continue their studies only in technical institutes of higher learning. Hence these schools were few, and the majority of the students preferred to attend the Gymnasia.

While the reform was being evolved and after its promulgation, vigorous but vain protests were made by enlightened opinion and the organs of the independent press—*Vyestnik Evropy (The European Messenger), Petersburgskya Novosti (The Petersburg News), Golos (The Voice)*. The minister was merely conforming to the tsar's own views, and he was the more attached to his classical system because he was interested far less in the instruction of the young than in the battle against their revolutionary tendencies.

He was no less unrelenting in his merciless campaign against the university statute of 1863. The disorders that broke out periodically among the students and that after 1870 were closely related to the advance of the revolutionary movement afforded him a continually renewable pretext for attacks on the autonomy of the universities. In 1868 he obtained the tsar's authorization to fill vacant professorships with candidates of his own choice, some of whom had previously failed to win the votes of their colleagues. In 1879 he issued instructions on the functions of the university inspectors that ran counter to the principles of the 1863 statute. While Katkov and Leontyev were the instigators of the secondary-school reform, it was Professor Lyubimov of the University of Moscow who became the minister's inspiration and counselor in the battle against university autonomy. In the wake of the press campaign that he had waged against it, Tolstoi decided to revise the 1863 statute. After the university disorders of 1874 a special committee composed of ministers on whom the various institutions of learning were dependent proclaimed the necessity of extending government control of education, introducing a rigorous disciplinary system into the universities, and regulating the admission of students in such a manner as to keep out the undesirables and the poor. In pursuance of this policy, a special commission headed by Delyanov, a member of the Imperial Council, was appointed in 1875 to investigate the state of the universities and prepare a proposal for their reform. Lyubimov, who was a member of this commission, and a colleague, Georgyevsky, visited the universities to conduct on-the-spot studies. The two inquisitors were very coolly received wherever they appeared; in fear of hostile demonstrations by the students, they dared not attend any of the actual lectures. The elected rectors of the universities were unanimous in their defense of the 1863 statute before the Delyanov Commission; in addition, the university councils waged a stubborn battle for the preservation of their autonomy. But Tolstoi could not be moved. In 1880 his new draft statute for the universities was submitted to the Imperial Council for its study. But his retirement took place soon afterward, and his policies were altered by his successors, Saburov and Baron Nikolai, so that the elimination of university autonomy was delayed until the reign of Alexander III (1884).

Reaction emerged in administration and the courts at the same time as in education. Contemporaneously with Tolstoi's appointment to succeed Golovnin, Prince V. A. Dolgoruky, the old head of the constabulary, was replaced by a young general who enjoyed great influence at court, Count P. A. Shuvalov. He, together with Minister of the Interior P. A. Timashev and General Zeleny, minister of domains, formed the very heart of the reactionism that pushed Alexander II into a policy of retrogression. On their advice, and in violation of both the letter and the spirit of the recent reforms, the powers of the governors were immediately enlarged. On Shuvalov's instigation the liberal Minister of Justice Zamyatnin, who had just carried out the reform of the courts, was replaced by Count Pahlen, a reactionary. Pahlen, who was totally ignorant of his new responsibilities, resolutely undertook to bring the magistracy under the control of the administration. Prosecutors were recruited among men who enjoyed governmental favor, and juries were scored for their excessive tendency to return verdicts of acquittal. Investigations of crimes against the state were carried out under a special system by the constabulary, and, beginning in 1871, defendants could be sentenced to exile by mere administrative order without trial by the appropriate court. In 1874 the penalties stipulated for political offenses were substantially increased and in 1878 such crimes were made the jurisdiction of military tribunals, which were to apply Article CCLXXIX of the Code of Military Justice—in short, the death penalty. Other measures were subsequently adopted in order to bring the legal profession to heel, for the reactionaries were perpetually angered by the continuation of adversary procedure.

Freedom of the press, too, gradually disappeared. As early as 1865, the provisional regulations, for all their pretense at abolishing prior censorship, had continued many of the restrictions: books, within a few days of their publication, had to be submitted to a censor who was empowered either to halt publication altogether or to require the partial or total elimination of a suspect passage. After 1866, because the courts had fallen into the habit of acquitting writers, the government stopped submitting press offenses to judicial process and resorted in large degree to measures of administrative restriction: refusal of the right to accept private advertisements, prohibition of the sale of individual issues, and, after two "warnings," temporary or permanent withdrawal of the right to publish. In 1873, in order to prevent press offenses, the minister of the interior was given the authority to forbid newspapers to mention major current issues; little by little he began to prepare an index of forbidden topics and to circulate it privately among the publishers of the newspapers.

The radical press, of course, was the first victim of this suppression. *Sovremennik (The Contemporary)* and *Russkoye Slovo (The Russian Word)*, which were the spokesmen for the tendencies that had been denounced in the imperial rescript addressed to Premier Gagarin, were suspended in 1866 by special order of the tsar. Even the Slavophile publications encountered major difficulties. Government orders compelled the suspension of publication of *Moskva (Moscow)* and of Ivan Aksakov's *Moskovityanin (The Muscovtie)* in 1867. The same fate befell *Vyest (The News)*, an aristocratic organ that championed serfdom. The fact that it was possible for *Vyestnik Evropy (The European Messenger)*, a liberal monthly review, to begin publication in 1866 was the result of its presentation as a historical magazine, and, when in 1868 it was converted into a political organ, it was able to survive only by the exercise of the utmost prudence. Although *Otechestvennya Zapiski (The Fatherland Annals)*, a Populist publication that took the place of *Sovremennik* in 1868, was dedicated by preference, in accordance with the basic spirit that had brought it into being, to social problems and avoided especially dangerous political issues such as that of a constitution, it was nonetheless the frequent victim of the censor's visitations. Liberal dailies—*Golos (The Voice)* in Petersburg and *Russkya Vyedomosti (The Russian News)* in Moscow—enjoyed a certain influence in the 1870s. In 1876 A. S. Suvorin established *Novoye Vremya (New Times)*, which at the start acquired the reputation of a liberal organ. Only Katkov's and Lyubimov's *Moskovskya Vyedomosti* and *Russky Vyestnik* and, later, Prince Meshchersky's *Grazhdanin (The Citizen)*, which had been the major opponents of the reforms of Alexander II, escaped the thunderbolts of the censor.

In the opposition press—which meant the whole press except for Katkov's publications and the semi-official *Syeverny Kuryer (Northern Courier)*—there was no choice but to have recourse to subterfuge of every variety in order to be able to publish not only radical and Socialist views but even liberal ideas. The consequence was the development of a kind of code language ("the language of Aesop"), which the educated public understood very clearly. This was why, as in the time of Nicholas I, literary criticism was still the major form of political literature. N. K. Mikhailovsky, who continued the independent dynasty of the Byelinskys, the Dobrolyubovs, the Pisarevs, the Chernyshevskys, was the intellectual master of the new generation. The works of Glyeb Uspensky, the most remarkable and the most gifted of the Populist literary men, not only analyzed the life of the urban lower middle class and the peasant world of the time with great penetration but also were propaganda novels. Among all the writers of this period, Saltykov-Shchedrin was set apart by the vigor and the originality of his talent. His *Gubernskye Otcherki (Provincial Sketches)*, which appeared in 1856–1857, presenting a gallery of provincial types of the period before the reforms of Alexander II, had already gained him a reputation. He was much given to satire, which lent itself with particular adaptability to the exigencies of the code language. The incomplete and imperfect execution of the reforms, the endless temporization by those in office, the mounting contradictions between liberal phrases and conservative thinking, the police measures, the new kinds of men whom the reforms were bringing into the bureaucracy, the press, and the bar—all these actors in public life and the psychology of the ruined nobility afforded him inexhaustible subjects for satire. His works were so saturated with allusions to the evils of his time that at times it is as difficult for the modern reader to find the clues as it is in the comedies of Aristophanes. To the readers who impatiently awaited each piece in the various issues of *The Fatherland Annals* and, after its suspension, in *The European Messenger*, the major attraction was precisely this subtlety of allusion, which concealed his true meanings from even the most suspicious censor.

As was to be expected, the eastern war of 1877–1878 filled public opinion with a high emotion of patriotism. But this sentiment backfired against the government when the public learned of all the corruption, the inadequacy of the army's supplies, and the Russian generals' military incompetence. Opinion was further angered by the disillusionments of the Congress of Berlin, which, after the peace of San Stefano, deprived Russia of the greater part of the fruits of her victories. The Slavophiles began to attack the government. Ivan Aksakov was banished from Moscow for having asserted at a public meeting of the Slavic Society that the "infamous news" arriving from Berlin "burned with shame and tortured the conscience" of the Russian people, which "is stirring and murmuring and growing more indignant . . . and is waiting for a solution from above." While it was certainly exaggeration to speak of the emotion of the Russian "people," there could be no doubt about the sentiments of enlightened opinion; but this was the result much more of the fact that the Bulgarian people, so totally unprepared for political life, had so easily been granted what the tsar would not concede to the Russian people: a constitution and national representation. The resentment was especially intense in liberal zemstvo circles. Although the government endeavored by all possible means to cut back their powers, the zemstvo meetings became the occasion for public declarations of a clearly political character, as, for that matter, did the press, the theater, scientific meetings, etc. A movement in favor of a constitution soon spread among the liberal members of the provincial assemblies.

Secret conferences for the discussion of current problems became frequent occurrences in southern Russia, in Kiev, and then in Kharkov. The government itself gave the liberals the opportunity to make their views known when, after a speech by the tsar in Moscow, it issued a public appeal to the nation in *The Government Messenger* to support it in its battle against the growth of the revolutionary movement. The constitutionalist group at once proposed to every zemstvo in which it had adherents that the government's appeal be answered with an address to the tsar. In the Chernigov zemstvo, I. I. Petrunkevitch made an especially sharp speech in which there was not a trace of equivocation. "To imagine that the use of force can ever stifle ideas, even anarchist ideas," he said, "reveals a total ignorance of the growth and propagation of thought. The battle against subversive ideas would be possible only if society possessed the appropriate weapons. These weapons are: speech, the press, freedom of thought, free knowledge," but they were not to be found in Russia. Russian public opinion did not exist because it had no means of expressing itself. What was lacking was a press that, without "fear of governmental harassment and with its concerns centered solely on the interests of society, its peaceful development, its vital needs, and the dangers that it might possibly face, would be able to arouse the feeling of independence, the instinct of preservation, and the desire to maintain the bases of the political system." After a denunciation of the distortions in the execution of the new laws and of the damage done to the education of the young by Count Tolstoi's classical system, Petrunkevitch called on the zemstvo "to acknowledge, with unspeakable sorrow, its impotence to take any kind of steps to counteract the evils." The zemstvo of the Tver government, in its petition, pointed out that "the tsar, solicitous of the welfare of the Bulgarian people, has given that nation real self-government"—the zemstvo was afraid to use the word *constitution*—"the inviolability of the rights of the individual, the independence of the courts, and the freedom of the press," and it expressed the hope of seeing the Russian people, "which with so much generosity has endured all the hardships of the war, benefited by the same advantages, which alone are capable of assuring it, in the tsar's phrase, of peaceful, progressive, and legal growth."

The government's response was a ban on the discussion of such matters in any zemstvo. Liberal members of these bodies, however, continued to meet. In 1879 they even attempted to initiate talks with the revolutionaries, who had already embarked on their terrorist activities. The liberals tried to persuade the revolutionaries to halt their violence until they themselves had sought to influence the government by peaceful means. But their impotence was too apparent, and what could be expected from their petitions to the tsar? Petrunkevitch, who had endeavored to pursue these negotiations, was arrested in April 1879 furthermore, and banished from the southern government of Chernigov to the remote northern government of Kostroma. Nevertheless, contact had been established between the liberal and revolutionary movements, which until then had had nothing to do with each other.

The Terrorist Revolutionary Movement

The failure of the "crusade to the people" had convinced the revolutionaries of the impossibility not only of fomenting an immediate rising but even more of carrying on the propaganda essential to the preparation of a social revolution. The desire to avenge their imprisoned or executed comrades and the necessity of creating an organization that would be able to combat the government impelled them to establish a clandestine organization far more powerful than their former scattered groups. A first effort in this direction, made in Moscow in 1876 by the Populist propagandists who wished to restrict themselves to peaceful procedures, was unsuccessful. A second effort, in Petersburg in the same year, was more fortunate. This was the work of revolutionary Populists, who formed an association under the much used name of Land and Liberty; it enlisted the survivors of the revolutionary cells under the leadership of the Natansons, husband and wife, and Alexander Mikhailov. It included a "central leadership"—later called "central committee"—divided into a number of sections: intellectuals, workers, peasants, and a "disorganization group." The purpose of the "central leadership" was to prepare for revolution through "organization" and "agitation." The "disorganization group" was intended to resort to armed force in its increasingly frequent clashes with the authorities. Its first public demonstration was held on 6/18 December 1876 near the Cathedral of Our Lady of Kazan. This demonstration, which had aroused great hopes, was rather small. A few workers joined it, the young demonstrators were dispersed without difficulty, and the leaders were arrested. They paid a high price for their work: some were deported, some were sentenced to five and even ten years at forced labor. Nevertheless, revolutionary activity in the cities continued to recruit more followers than did peaceful propaganda in the rural areas, and the work of "disorganization," to which the terrorist group was assigned, began to assume the preponderant rank.

One incident that made an exceptional impression on the public marked a new stage in the history of the revolutionary movement. One of the young men arrested in the demonstration outside the Cathedral of Our Lady of Kazan in Petersburg, Bogolyubov, was sentenced to fifteen years of forced labor. He refused to remove his cap in the presence of General Trepov, the capital's chief of police, who was visiting his prison. Trepov struck him and ordered that he be given a hundred lashes, even though political suspects were supposedly exempt from corporal punishment. The other prisoners, whose anger erupted in shouts and disorders, were also beaten by the police and the soldiers. These outrages came to public knowledge simultaneously with the disclosure of the abominable conditions in which the prisoners were being kept—Dicheskul, for example, who was locked into a dark cell filled with excrement and crawling with worms. Naturally the press was forbidden to report these facts, and an investigating commission appointed by the tsar found nothing wrong. Then young Vera Zassulitcha took it on herself to avenge the outraged public conscience. During General Trepov's normal appointment hours on 24 January/5 February 1878 she appeared at his office in the guise of a petitioner, and she wounded him dangerously with a revolver shot. Her trial was a tremendous sensation not only in Russia but abroad. Instead of defending her, Aleksandrov, her lawyer, pronounced a veritable indictment against the government as if it had been Trepov who was on trial. Miss Zassulitcha was acquitted. In spite of this the police were waiting to rearrest her, but a carriage was waiting outside the court, and, after a skirmish, the revolutionaries got her away from the police and helped her to cross the border. Land and Liberty assumed the responsibility for the attempted assassination and warned that it would pursue the struggle.

The period of the Terror was beginning. One of its first victims was General Mesentsev, chief of the constabulary corps, whom Stepnyak (Kravchinsky) forced on 4/10 August 1878 to expiate the execution of Kovalsky. Although the assassination was carried out in one of the busiest thoroughfares in Petersburg, Italy Street, everyone concerned got away. In southern Russia the revolutionaries were even more enthusiastic in their attitude toward terrorism. In fact it was the south where for the first time terrorists had been tried by military tribunals. These first defendants had been sentenced to death: Valery Osinsky, a young enthusiast; Lizogub, a millionnaire landowner who had not taken a personal part in the movement but who had turned over his entire fortune to the revolutionaries; Kovalsky, who had fired on police sent to search his house; and many more. On 9/21 February

1879 the revolutionaries gave their answer to the many executions and arrests carried out in Kiev, Odessa, and Kharkov: they assassinated the governor general of Kharkov, Prince Kropotkin, a cousin of the famous anarchist. On 1/13 March Mirsky tried without success to kill Mesentsev's successor, General Drenteln, who had signed a number of orders of arrest, search, and penal transportation. *Listok* (*The Leaf*), the publication of Land and Liberty, asserted that terror was for the revolutionaries not only a means of avenging their executed comrades or an instrument of legitimate defense, but also "the most effective weapon," the weapon that "compels the government to recognize the total impotence of the governmental system in the face of a danger whose source is invisible and unknown."

It was in this climate of general agitation, further aggravated by the arrests of liberal officials, that on 2/14 April 1879 the first of the systematic attacks on the tsar's person was made. While Alexander II was riding in his carriage, five shots were fired at him by a propagandist named Solovyev. All five missed. Solovyev, after gaining the approval of his comrades, had gone to Petersburg from Samara expressly to kill the tsar. Arrested where he stood, he was executed on 29 May/10 June.

His comrades had resolved to "carry on his work," but their plans were stubbornly opposed by others within the revolutionary movement. For some time the members of Land and Liberty had been split: some, like young Plekhanov, advocated propaganda, while others stood for terror. Their division having become acute, the most prominent of the revolutionaries met in a secret congress in Lipetsk, a watering place in the government of Voronezh, for a four-day discussion of the question of regicide, from 17/29 June to 21 June/3 July. In contradiction of their earlier statements, they resolved, mainly on the insistence of A. Zhelyabov, that terror should be not a weapon "of legitimate defense and vengeance" but a method "of active struggle for the political freedom of all and for the parliamentary system that is its sole guaranty." The resolution having been adopted, they went to the city of Voronezh for a meeting with the antiterrorists led by Plekhanov. He made a clear break with the terrorists, and the schism in the party was final. Neither of the new organizations retained the name of Land and Liberty. The partisans of terror, on their return to Petersburg in October, founded a new society, *Narodnaya Volya* ("The Will of the People"). Their opponents, who set social propaganda as their own major task, called their group *Cherny Peredyel* ("The Black [i.e., General] Portion"). The Will of the People, which was the more active of the two, naturally assumed the greater prominence. Plekhanov and his associates—Vera Zassulitcha, Stefanovitch, Deitch (Deutsch)—went abroad. There they laid the foundations for Russian Marxism and created what later became the Russian Social Democratic party, *Gruppa Osvobozhdenya Truda* ("Party of the Liberation of Labor"). It was The Will of the People from which the Russian Revolutionary Socialist party (the *narodniki*) was derived.

The "central executive committee" of The Will of the People began by issuing an appeal to the tsar that demanded political freedom and the parliamentary system. At the same time, on 26 August/7 September 1879, it decided that the target of its terrorists should be not the high officials and the governors general but the tsar himself if he refused to grant these essential demands. It was to take the committee one and a half years to accomplish its end. Numerous attempts, which testified to an abundance of energy and ingenuity on the part of the revolutionaries, were made before the success of 1/13 March 1881. The central committee, which included barely thirty members, managed to produce the illusion of a powerful, invisible organization, more redoubtable in the eyes of the government than all the other revolutionary associations had ever been. Furthermore it imbued the most diverse sectors of society with the liveliest hopes of imminent political changes. Everywhere, thanks to the impression that it had been able to create, it found not only sympathizers but even accomplices prepared to give it direct support. A climate of general sympathy enveloped each of its acts; this not only facilitated their preparation and execution but also made it possible to conceal the perpetrators from the vigilance of the police. An official of the Third Section itself—the political police—was a member of the revolutionary party and always gave his friends timely warnings of the searches and arrests that imperiled them. Firmly resolved to kill the tsar, the members of The Will of the People would not allow themselves to be discouraged by failures. The assassination attempts were repeated, always in the most unforeseen fashion. First the terrorists tried to blow up the train on which the tsar was supposed to return to Petersburg from the Crimea on 19 November/1 December 1879. They placed mines at a number of points along the route. One in particular was placed near Moscow, with amazing audacity, by Sofya Perovskaya, the daughter of the governor general of Petersburg himself. But some of the mines did not explode, and other damaged a train that was not the tsar's. Shortly afterward, on 5/17 February 1880, a new attack almost killed the tsar in his own residence in the Winter Palace. A carpenter, Khalturin, who was employed there, had offered his services to the central committee. He had evolved the idea of blowing up the tsar's dining room, which was two floors above the pantry. Zhelyabov had eagerly adopted this plan as an alternative in the event of the failure of the attack on the tsar's train. Little by little Khalturin had managed to assemble enough dynamite in the pantry to blow up both the intervening area, which was reserved to the palace guard, and the imperial dining room. He might have been able to lay in even more if, during the arrest of a revolutionary, the police had not found a map of the palace on which the tsar's dining room was marked with a cross. Closer supervision was put into effect over everyone who had access to the palace, and the transport of the dynamite was thus made more difficult. It was finally decided to act just as the tsar sat down to table. Khalturin lighted his fuses and went outside the palace in order to observe the results of his efforts. The explosion was frightful: it killed eleven soldiers, wounded fifty-six, and destroyed the imperial dining room. But the tsar himself was unhurt, thanks to a delay in the arrival of a distinguished guest, Prince Alexander v. Battenberg, who had kept Alexander II waiting a half-hour. He had barely crossed the threshold of the room when the explosion occurred, and he fled in fear. The proclamation issued by the central committee as a result of this failure declared that the struggle would be carried on "as long as the tsar refuses to turn over the task of organizing public life to a freely elected Constituent Assembly whose members hold the imperative mandate of their electors," that "the government has become an obstacle to the free development of the nation's life," and that, "as long as this first step toward the enfranchisement of the nation remains untaken," it would strive "by every means" to take that step itself.

The Truce in Terrorism and the "Dictatorship of the Heart"

How was the Terror to be combatted? Since the most severe methods proved futile, why not try to offer concessions in order to disarm, if not the revolutionaries, at least the liberal groups whose neutrality and sympathy were the major factor in the successes of the terrorists?

The tsar's own brother, Konstantin Nikolayevitch, was an advocate of liberal concessions. In the Marble Palace, which was his residence, he assembled leading men who, like Valuev, the minister, shared his views. Valuev had drafted a proposed constitution in November 1863, at the time when hope for the grant of a charter to Russia was particularly high. In it he envisaged the creation, in addition to the Imperial Council, of a special "Congress" composed of 150 to 177 elected "state delegates" and 30 to 35 delegates appointed by the tsar; this Congress would meet annually to deliberate on those matters that were submitted to it by the chairman of the Imperial Council, and it would send fourteen of its members and two of its vice chairmen as delegates to the plenary assembly of the Council, which would have the final word. The assassination attempt at the Winter Palace brought this project out of the oblivion in which it had been left since the beginning of reactionism. Grand Duke Konstantin Niko-layevitch, chairman of the Imperial Council, commissioned Secretary of State E. Perets to draft a new constitution that would "make it possible to take measures designed to calm minds overexcited by the government's vain attempts to repress revolt." Perets' draft provided for supplementing the Imperial Council with a "Consultative As-sembly" of forty-six delegates, which, "as a precautionary measure," he divided into various sections, each of which would concern itself "with different matters." They would come together only "temporarily, for a specified time," with an agenda clearly laid out in advance; the Imperial Council would make the decisions on the matters studied by the sections, and only the chairman of each section would be admitted to the Council's discussions. Even less liberal than the already modest proposal by Valuev, this production of Perets, as Grand Duke Konstantin endeavored to persuade the tsar, had "absolutely no political value, can in no way hamper the government, and offers no infringement of the sacred rights of autocracy."

But Grand Duke Konstantin and his associates had a bad reputa-tion for liberalism. Any program of concessions was bound to seem suspect if it came from them. If any was to win acceptance, it must be made to seem to concede nothing. This was the premise that was to be the guideline of the special commission appointed by the tsar after the Winter Palace explosion and charged with finding the means of eliminating the increasing revolutionary movement. A week before the explosion, Tsarevitch Alexander Alexandrovitch, discussing this same problem, had announced his opposition to any concession of a constitutional nature, which included Valuev's proposal. Three days after the attack, during a speech on 8/20 February 1880, he asserted that the root of the evil lay not in the inadequacy of police measures but in the lack of cohesion among the central institutions. The only truly effective measure that could claim support, then, was to subordi-nate all the ministries to one man who would be answerable to the tsar for the restoration of order. In other words, he called for the creation of a post that would fall somewhere between those of the prime minister in a homogeneous cabinet and a dictator. In support of his proposal for the institution of a "supreme commission of investigation" under the presidency of this new official, he invoked as precedents the similar commissions created in the wake of the fires of 1862 and the assassination attempt by Karakozov in 1866. This project, which was reactionary in its conception, was quickly approved, but it was to be put into execution in a liberal spirit. The very next day, during another speech, before the governors general, the tsar gave his approval to his heir's proposal. He established a special dictatorial organism, the Supreme Organization Commission, endowed it with extraordinary powers, and appointed as its head Count Loris-Melikov, governor general of Kharkov.

Loris-Melikov, the victor of Kars, though he was not a liberal, began with no preconceived ideas. He recognized that "sedition" could be countered only by granting satisfaction to the legitimate demands of the society and thus creating a vacuum round the revolutionaries. But he recognized as well that, if he offered a broad program of concessions at the very outset, he would inevitably come up against the resistance of the reactionary circles at court, and of the tsar in particular. Hence he decided to attack the major problem from the flank.

He began with the concentration of all powers in his own hands, just as the plan of the tsarevitch had suggested. The imperial ukase of 12/24 February 1880, which appointed him president of the Supreme Commission, at the same time placed under his command all the administrations that were charged with the security of the state, including the Third Section. Thus he combined the duties of the minister of the interior with those of the national chief of police. Without regard for the spirit of the judiciary reforms, he combined the courts with the police and had no hesitation in putting the police department under a former imperial attorney general, V. K. Pleve. Furthermore, far from relaxing them, he strengthened the repressive measures against members of the revolutionary movement. On the other hand, he made a great effort to appease the moderate liberals. He insisted on the dismissal of Count Tolstoi, who was known as "the strangler" of public education and whose name alone aroused universal hatred; he replaced Tolstoi with a liberal minister, Saburov. He devoted himself to the complete reerection of the zemstvo statute of 1864, which had been disfigured by all kinds of restrictions and mutilations. Instead of Greig, the incompetent and reactionary finance minister, he chose a liberal official who was a friend of N. Miliutin, A. A. Abaza. Abaza abolished the salt tax, the whole burden of which fell on the masses, and undertook a study looking toward the general revision of the entire fiscal system. Loris-Melikov approved the establishment of a large number of periodicals in which public opinion could freely express its views: for instance, *Strana (The Country)*, under L. Polonsky; *Poryadok (Order)*, under M. Stasyulevitch; *Russkaya Mysl (Russian Thought)*, a Moscow weekly; *Rus (Russia)*, the Slavophile organ of I. Aksakov, and *Zemstvo*, a very serious liberal journal published by the autonomous provincial administrations under the editorship of Skalon.

On 10/22 September 1880 he attempted to disclose to the press some of what he intended to do. He asked it especially "not to irritate minds in vain by insisting on the necessity of making the society a participant in the country's administration and legislation, either in the form of representative assemblies in the European style or in the guise of the ancient Russian *Zemsky Sobor.*" He let it be understood that, in the ruling circles, he was already under suspicion of intending to grant such demands and that this was the pretext for a campaign against him; he declared that he "had received no power" to accomplish such reforms and that, speaking for himself, he could "envisage nothing of the kind." His program for the next five to seven years was to reinforce the activity of the zemstvo within the limitations of its competence; to put an end to the violation of law by the police; to carry forward the decentralization of provincial government; to keep himself informed, through the help of special senatorial investigating commissions, of the needs and the wishes of the people; and, finally, to assure the press of freedom to discuss the actions of the government, with the single restriction that it "in no way incite minds with chimerical illusion." On the pretext that he no longer needed extraordinary powers in order to combat the spirit of "sedition," he obtained the abolition of the Supreme Commission, but he himself retained the functions of minister of the interior. Since he no longer had to concern himself with a heterogeneous and highly encumbering commission, he continued too to function as prime minister.

In actuality, aside from Mlodetsky's attempt to kill Loris-Melikov himself a few days after his appointment, which, moreover, was formally disavowed by the central committee, terrorist activity was suspended during 1880. This armistice might be explained in part by the attitude of expectancy that the revolutionaries and above all public opinion as a whole had adopted toward Loris-Melikov's plans. But it resulted chiefly from the vacuum that had been created in the ranks of the revolutionaries by the arrests and deportations ordered by the government, chiefly the arrest of Goldenberg, whose admissions had for the first time revealed the mystery of the central committee to the government.

While the revolutionaries' demands were to some degree utopian, Loris-Melikov's plans included no indication of real political concessions and in no way implied a constitutional system in the strict sense of the word. The government's policy, in spite of all the concessions granted until the beginning of 1881, was still the opposite not only of the revolutionaries' program but even of the liberals' requests. Loris-Melikov was well aware of the fact. Even when he was publicly declaring, before the representatives of the press, his opposition to any constitutional concession, he had allowed his actual thinking to show through in a private conversation with Perets: "I have taken a position," he told the author of the 1880 proposal, "against the aspirations of the constitutionalists, which at the present time are incapable of realization among us, but at the same time I completely share the conviction that it is necessary to listen to the views of sensible, practical men. The proposal might be feasible; only one must develop the most cautious and practical means of putting it into execution." Therefore, when at the beginning of 1881 he felt sufficiently sure of his strength with the tsar, he attempted another step toward meeting the aspirations of the public.

The opportunity for this was given to him by the termination of the labors of the senatorial investigating commissions that he had brought into being. As was to have been expected, the commissions had revealed glaring irregularities in the provinces: opposition by the administration to the zemstvo and the courts, the limitless and still mounting power of the governors general, contempt for legality. Loris-Melikov wanted to entrust provincial delegates with the duty of studying the results of the investigations and drawing conclusions from them in the form of draft laws. This was the procedure that had already been utilized when the "drafting commissions" had been called on to discuss the problem of the emancipation of the peasants before it was referred to the Imperial Council. In a report to the tsar on 28 January/9 February 1881, Loris-Melikov proposed as an initial step the convocation of two "preparatory commissions." The "administrative and economic commission" would be delegated to prepare general administrative reforms, such as the precise definition of the powers of the administration, the judiciary institutions, and the zemstvo; the evolution of zemstvo and municipal autonomy; the completion of the agrarian reform; means of preventing famine, etc. The "financial commission" would be charged with discussing financial reform. The draft laws prepared by both these commissions would then be transmitted to a consultative "general commission," which would combine the members of both original commissions and also experts elected by each zemstvo and municipality, two men for each; the zemstvo would in addition have the right to select its experts outside the ranks of its own members and among persons of recognized competence. After the draft laws had been debated by the "general commission," they would be presented to the Imperial Council, augmented by ten to fifteen elected provincial delegates. The minister, obviously, had no thought of establishing a regular representative institution; his sole intention was to associate the country's representatives with the preparation of a certain number of draft laws whose tenor had been determined in advance. The views of this consultative representation could in no way hamper the authority of the sole existing legislative authority, which was still the Imperial Council, an eminently bureaucratic body inasmuch as its membership included only an infinitesimal number of provincial delegates, and those had been carefully screened.

Even if it had been made public in time, so limited a proposal for reform would have found it most difficult to persuade the terrorist group to alter its tactics. But the whole discussion was cloaked in the densest mystery. Although Loris-Melikov admitted to himself that this was only the beginning of a reform inevitably destined to evolve into true national representation, he could not prevent himself from acknowledging that his modest effort was merely a very weak hothouse plant. "Let fresh shooting break out by some misfortune," he told Perets on 15/27 December 1880, "and I am done for; and my whole system will go up with me. We're going to retreat from the 'new times'—back perhaps to the Inquisition." He clearly foresaw what fate awaited his "dictatorship of the heart," as the public called the system that he had inaugurated. Events were to demonstrate the impossibility of succeeding by trickery in limiting the autocratic power, whose partisans would defend it with the utmost ferocity, even at the cost of their lives, whenever they became aware of the constitutional nature of concessions the necessity of which they could nevertheless not escape.

The Pursuit of the Tsar

Loris-Melikov's evolutionist system could not disarm the last survivors of the revolutionaries, who not only knew nothing of the clash of views that was taking place in the court but could not even suspect its importance. Precisely because the ranks of their central committee were being thinned and because part of public opinion was turning its back on them to devote itself ardently to the work of "civilization," as it was called in a contemporary expression, they decided to accelerate and redouble their efforts. The pursuit of the tsar began. In order not to fail in it, the terrorists committed all their forces to the task and planned a number of assassination attempts for the same day. They agreed to kill the tsar when he would be returning to the palace from his customary daily carriage ride. Death would lie in wait for him on every road that led to the palace. Trenches would be dug beneath Malaya-Sadovaya and Gorokhovaya Streets and mines would be placed in them. But, since this method did not seem certain, other conspirators, armed with bombs prepared by Kibaltchitch, the eminent chemist, would be stationed at various points along the route that the tsar would take. Toward the end of February, after the arrest of Zhelyabov, who was in charge of the plot, its general leadership was transferred to Sofya Perovskaya. The arrest of their chief induced the revolutionaries to accelerate the execution of their plan. The scheduled it for Sunday, 1/13 March, a day when it was the tsar's custom to pass the troops in review at the Mikhail cavalry school.

It was an irony of fate that, on the day that the revolutionaries had chosen for the tsar's death, he left the palace in the best of spirits. At last he had just given his approval to Loris-Melikov's proposal, and he was going to announce the news to Grand Duchess Catherine Mikhailovna. A cabinet meeting at which his decision would be converted into a legislative act was to be held three days later, on 4/16 March. The tsar's morganatic wife, Princess Yuryevskaya, begged him not to go through Malaya-Sadovaya Street, the dangerousness of which had been disclosed to her in anonymous letters. He took her advice, and, when he left the Mikhail Palace, he ordered his carriage to drive through Ekaterininskaya (Catherine) Street. Sofya Perovskaya at once directed her bomb throwers to shift their posts, and gave the final signal. The first bomb, hurled by Rysakov, destroyed the imperial carriage. Alexander II, who was still unharmed, stopped for a moment to look at the young conspirator and check the extent of the damage. Another conspirator, Grinevetsky, took advantage of this interval to hurl his bomb at the tsar's feet. Its explosion tore off the tsar's legs and killed Grinevetsky. Mortally wounded and rapidly losing blood, Alexander was taken to the Winter Palace, where he soon died without having regained consciousness.

This tragic end to a reign whose beginnings had been so brilliant was an ominous augury for Russia.

IV / EUROPEAN POLICY AND EXPANSION IN ASIA* [B.MIRKIN-GUETZEVITCH, PAUL MILIUKOV]

Since 1856 the basic objective of Russian diplomacy had been to obtain the revision of the Treaty of Paris. Since the internal conditions of the country did not permit her to launch a new European war, she had no choice but to fall back on diplomacy.

Prince Gorchakov, who directed foreign policy, was not a diplomat of the first rank. Intellectually he was the inferior of those illustrious statesmen—Bismarck, Cavour, Andrássy, and Napoleon III—who guided the destinies of Europe at the start of the second half of the nineteenth century. He developed a friendship with Bismarck during the latter's three years as Prussian ambassador in Petersburg. This friendship was of great importance to the orientation of Russian foreign policy, for Bismarck was at certain times to exert considerable influence over Gorchakov. Quite vain and self-infatuated, the Russian chancellor regarded himself as the rival of the Prussian minister, even when he contemplated European events only through the German's eyes. At the same time this friendship broadened Gorchakov's political horizon. He was capable of flexing to meet the exigencies of the modern world. Whereas the old Russian diplomacy, the heir of the traditions of the Holy Alliance, obsessed by the Polish problem, long associated with Austria in putting down national revolutions, could see nothing but a source of revolution in the very idea of nationality, Gorchakov understood that Russia, if she wished to regain her international prestige after the Crimean War, had to repudiate the methods of Nesselrode.

French-Russian Reconciliation

The friendly ties that Russia formed with Prussia after the Congress of Paris were not enough to set her free of the trammels that had been imposed on her by the Treaty of 1856. Therefore she resolved to enhance the French-Russian reconciliation that had been initiated during the Congress of Paris. On September 25, 1857 Alexander II and

*The first five sections and the penultimate section of this part of the chapter were written by Professor Mirkin-Guetzevitch; the two others were written by Professor Miliukov.

Napoleon III met in Stuttgart. They pledged each other mutual aid. The friendship of Alexander II was useful to the Italian policy of Napoleon III: Russia was a threat to Austria and compelled her to keep her troops on her eastern border at the most critical periods of the Italian campaign. In return, Napoleon III promised to help Russia in the Balkans, where, according to Gorchakov, she was prepared to make a reality of the national idea so dear to the French emperor. In the years that followed, it was the support of France to which Russia owed all her diplomatic successes in the Near East. French-Russian friendship facilitated the union of Moldavia with Wallachia. When the Turks stood in battle array to attack Montenegro, Napoleon III dispatched the French fleet to the Adriatic and Turkey had to bow to the wishes of Paris and Petersburg and accept the rectification of Montenegro's borders. In Serbia at the end of 1858, when Austria was preparing to send her troops to the aid of Prince Alexander Kara-georgevitch, an advocate of pro-Austrian and pro-Turkish policies who had been driven out by his own people, France vigorously supported the Russian government.

The Polish Problem and the French-Russian Rupture (1863)

This French-Russian alliance, which made it possible for Russia to gain a number of diplomatic victories over Austria and maintain her own prestige in the Balkans, was rent by the Polish question, which long divided Alexander II and Napoleon III.

In 1863 all Europe was passionately following and discussing the varying course of the Polish insurrection, the repressive steps taken by the Russian government, Muravyev's action, and the attitude of the Russian press. As in 1831, the events in Poland assumed an international importance in the eyes of European diplomats. Three countries—France, England, and Austria—made no secret of their sharp hostility toward Russia. France was influenced by her especially strong sympathy for Poland, which was shared not only by the Catholics, who were concerned over the Poles for religious reasons, and the Bonapartists, who made friendship for Poland virtually a dogma of their international conceptions, but also by the opposition parties, whose traditions impelled them to assist the Polish patriots in their resistance to the Russian government. Napoleon III was much embarrassed: the best interest of his foreign policy lay in close ties with Russia, but public opinion was imperative in its demand that the breveted defender of the principle of nationalities take the side of the Poles. In Austria's intervention there was no trace of the sentimental.

She wanted to put Russia into a difficult position and, above all, to break the friendship between France and Russia that had cost her so many frustrations in the Balkans. Similarly England had only one desire: to create a rift between France and Russia. While Austria was allowing an organization to be formed in Galicia to provide assistance to the insurgents, Napoleon was making a personal plea to Alexander II to restore the kingdom of Poland and make Grand Duke Konstantin its king. Alexander II replied with a categorical *no*.

This European meddling only strengthened the internal position of the Russian government, and Katkov's inflammatory articles further excited the nationalist passions of his readers. Besides, Russia was not isolated. Bismarck paraded his friendship for Russia and for Gorchakov. He offered them Prussia's help against the rebels and declared his readiness to send Prussian troops to the Vistula. On February 8, 1863 a Russian-Prussian convention was signed: Prussia pledged herself to back the Russians, and Russia's armies were authorized to cross the Prussian border in pursuit of the insurrectionists. On the urgings of his Foreign Minister Drouyn de Lhuys, Napoleon III lodged a vigorous protest. He charged that the mere fact of the Russian-Prussian convention had taken the Polish problem out of the domain of Russian internal policy and made it a matter of international concern. France sent a note to the Russian government on April 10. England and Austria associated themselves with it. England based her stand on the 1815 treaties of Vienna. Napoleon III, who could not decently invoke them, adduced the principle of nationalities and considerations of humanitarianism; he demanded that the Poles' rights be protected not only within the boundaries of the kingdom created by Alexander I but also in all the Polish provinces. The majority of the European powers, including the Holy See, adhered to the French note of April 10. Thus Russia found herself confronted by a European coalition. Napoleon III was already considering a plan for a military expedition in which all the members of the coalition would take part. This threat of war compelled Gorchakov to moderation. In his note of April 26 he asked France, Austria, and England to tell him what means they regarded as adequate for the pacification of Poland. In a note that reached him on June 17, the three powers gave him six recommendations: a complete amnesty; the establishment of national representation in conformance with the Charter of 1815; the admission of Poles to public employment; freedom of conscience and, above all, the abolition of all the restrictions imposed on the Catholic religion; recognition of Polish as the sole official language; and a return to normal conditions in military recruiting. In addition they proposed an international conference of all states that had signed the treaties of Vienna. In view of the discussion of the reform program, Napoleon III asked Austria and England on June 20 to commit themselves by treaty to the use of methods other than diplomatic negotiations if this should be required for the enforcement of their demands. This was tantamount to the proposal of a coalition against Russia. England and Austria, neither of which, at bottom, was particularly concerned with protecting the Poles, refused. Confident that the other powers did not share the belligerent intentions of France, Gorchakov and Bismarck regained assurance. On Bismarck's advice, Gorchakov proposed the idea of a conference of the three states among which Poland was divided. This proposal was rejected. England was insistent in wishing to undertake nothing on behalf of the Poles. Bismarck, who was leading Gorchakov, clearly recognized the weaknesses of Russia's adversaries. On September 7 a note from Gorchakov advised the powers that he regarded the diplomatic correspondence relative to the Polish insurrection as closed.

Irritated by this, the English government in its turn drafted a warning note; it declared that Russia had violated the treaty of Vienna and thereby lost her rights over Poland. But Bismarck persuaded Lord Palmerston that England had nothing to gain by raising this issue and that, if she withdrew her charge, he himself would make every effort to support her in the matter of the duchies. Palmerston ordered his note, which had already been sent, held up, and replaced it with another in which he assured Gorchakov of his entire "satisfaction." This reversal was a magnificent illustration of the lack of sincerity that was characteristic of the attitudes of the European powers, with the exception of France, in the Polish controversy. Bismarck, who was at that time the real strategist of the Russian maneuvers, was satisfied. Relations between France and Russia remained uneasy for a long time. The Russian nationalist press, with Katkov, regarded Prussia as Russia's only friend. Not only had the policy of Napoleon III produced no benefit for the Poles, but it had laid the foundation for the Russian-Prussian alliance against France in 1870.

The Denunciation of the Treaty of Paris and the Conference of London (1870–1871)

The Polish insurrection having been suppressed, the revision of the Treaty of Paris once more became Gorchakov's dominating concern. Inasmuch as he did not expect to obtain the consent of England, which was being made more and more inimical by Russia's successes in Asia, he decided to proceed without it. In his circular letter of August 20, 1866 he declared that, as a result of the basic change in the European political situation, Russia refused to consider herself bound by the restrictions imposed on her by the Treaty of Paris. "Our august master," he wrote (in French) , "has no intention of insisting on the general commitments of the treaties, which owed their validity only to the agreement subsisting among the great powers for enforcing their observance, and which today, because of the lack of this collective wish, have suffered too frequent and too severe infringements not to have been invalidated thereby."

The French-Prussian War provided him with the opportunity of attaining his ends. After Sadowa an Austrian-French alliance was possible and French diplomacy was straining to accomplish it. Bismarck feared it, because it would have compelled Prussia to fight against two enemies and on two fronts at the same time. But Alexander II came to his assistance by promising that, if Austria-Hungary attempted to cast off her neutrality, he would at once attack her. On July 23, 1870 Russia declared that she would remain neutral, but Gorchakov made a visit to Bismarck in Berlin, and Russia, now become *de facto* Prussia's ally, prevented Austria-Hungry from intervening. As the price for her support she was relying on the revision of the Treaty of Paris.

On September 26, 1870 Thiers was in Petersburg. He hoped that Russia would exert pressure on Prussia on behalf of France, and that above all Russia would help to obtain a twenty-five-day armistice. Gorchakov sought to bait the hook. Without swerving from his friendship with Bismarck, he had not lost sight of the revision of the Treaty of Paris, and he was working to build up backing against England, which he regarded as his chief adversary. He made vague promises to Thiers, whom he tried to turn against the English. Thiers, who was a sincere advocate of a French-Russian alliance—and who, as a historian, believed that such an alliance could have saved France earlier, in 1814—left Petersburg in total disillusion. After the capitulation of Metz, Gorchakov decided to move. At the end of October he notified Europe that, in view of the change in the political conditions that had prevailed at the signing of the Treaty of Paris, "His Imperial Majesty could no longer consider himself bound by the obligations of this treaty insofar as they restrict his rights of sovereignty in the Black Sea."*

In an extremely sharp reply England harshly criticized the doctrine

*The statement was written in French.

of public law enunciated by Gorchakov, and she vigorously protested against this unilateral violation of an international treaty. Certainly the justification alleged by Gorchakov was real. The French Empire, which had been a major factor in provoking the Crimean War, no longer existed; the Treaty of Paris had been violated by its other signatories: witness the occupation of Rome by French troops after Sedan. In this struggle among states and nations that led to the transformation of Europe, treaties really became nullities. The fact remained, nonetheless, that legally Gorchakov's thesis was indefensible: it was a negation of one of the fundamental concepts of international law.

Bismarck, who feared an Anglo-Russian war, suggested that a conference be held in London to discuss Gorchakov's statement. His proposal was accepted by England, which regarded it as an opportunity to bring Russia before a kind of international tribunal for having violated her commitments. The inauguration of the conference was delayed by the extremely delicate question of French participation. Paris was under siege. In order that a French delegate might go to London, the intervention and indeed the permission of the German command were required. But Bismarck, who did not wish the French-Prussian War to be brought up in London and who was trying to remain in confrontation with France alone, created all kinds of obstacles. As for Jules Favre of France, he did not want to leave Paris when the city was under siege and bombardment; he did not grasp the fact that at this critical moment of the war there was every advantage for France in attendance at an international conference. The conference began at last on January 17, 1871. On that first day it declared the inviolability of treaties (in French) : "The powers recognize that it is an essential principle of the law of peoples that no one of them can release itself from the obligations of a treaty or modify its provisions except through the consent of the contracting parties arrived at by amicable agreement." By arguing that *pacta sunt servanda* the Conference of London solemnly condemned the doctrine of the clause *rebus sic stantibus*. After having thus proclaimed its disapproval of Gorchakov's policy, the Conference concluded with the Convention of London of March 13. The articles in the Treaty of Paris that Russia no longer recognized were abrogated. The neutrality of the Black Sea was ended. Article II of the Convention, although it sustained the principle, laid down in 1856, of the closing of the Straits, authorized the sultan to open them in peace time to warships whenever he might deem this necessary "in order to safeguard the execution of the stipulations of the Treaty of Paris of March 30, 1856." This formula was more advantageous—though not much more—for Russia than the terms first proposed by Austria-Hungary, which recognized the right of passage through the Straits with the sultan's authorization only for the vessels of those powers "not bordering" on the coast. Brunnov, the Russian delegate, had not grasped the fact that the Austrian proposal was directed above all against Russia. The clause that was adopted, at least in its form, contained nothing offensive to the Russians. Although the Treaty of Paris had not been abrogated, although those provisions in it that were intended to protect Turkey against Russia and that were its major feature were retained, the Convention of London, because it abandoned the principle of the neutrality of the Black Sea, which was so humiliating for Russians, was nevertheless a success for Russia and an improvement in her international position.

The Alliance of the Three Emperors (1873)

A brief chill between Russia and Germany followed the Conference of London. First of all, Russia had expected Germany to support her more vigorously in the Conference than had been the fact; hence, although relations between Wilhelm I and Alexander II lost nothing of their intimacy and cordiality, the Russian diplomats complained of Bismarck's attitude. Moreover, Gorchakov was perturbed by the creation of the German Empire, the annexation of Alsace-Lorraine, and Germany's military might. The Polish problem was no longer in issue and Napoleon III had fallen; Russia was tending toward a reconciliation with France, as was shown by her efforts to protect France against the unremitting German menace.

But the tsar, alarmed by the gains of the social and revolutionary movements at home and by the frequency of political violence, was concerned more with the struggle against the revolution than with foreign policy. He was looking for an ally in that struggle. Bismarck promised his help; he committed himself even to support Russia in the east, although the friendly relations that he then enjoyed with Austria-Hungary were hardly in accord with such a pledge. In September 1872, Franz Josef, Wilhelm I, and Alexander II held a conference that culminated in 1873 in what was called the alliance of the three emperors. They came to agreement on three fundamental points: (1) mutual territorial guaranties and the recognition of the annexation of Alsace-Lorraine; (2) joint discussion of all problems relating to the question of the east; (3) common struggle against the revolutions that threatened all three monarchies.

But Bismarck was not a man to continue the diplomacy of the Holy Alliance. Germany's own interests concerned him far more than the repression of revolution in Russia. The alliance of the three emperors proved to be unworkable. As soon as it was concluded, Gorchakov had reassured the French ambassador in Berlin and had urged him to telegraph to Thiers that it did not contain any clauses directed against France. In 1875 the diplomatic help that he gave to France brought about its enfeeblement.

Russian Intervention in the French-German Quarrel of 1875

In the spring of 1875 Bismarck assumed a threatening posture toward France; German newspapers and especially the official press made warlike appeals. Bismarck accepted, or seemed to accept, under the pressure of the German General Staff, the necessity of a preventive war: France was recovering too quickly, she must be attacked without delay and struck hard before she became too powerful. But Russia and England, which were determined to preserve the peace, protested vigorously. Alexander II took the position of the defender of the peace of Europe and the arbiter of the conflict. He had been inspired to this attitude by Gorchakov, who aspired to play the leading part on the European stage. After a talk with Bismarck, who had been sorely vexed by his intervention, Gorchakov, in his haste to appear as the arbiter of Europe, proclaimed in a clumsily written circular letter that the peace of Europe and the tranquility of all peoples were now assured, thanks to the intervention of the Russian emperor. Bismarck had bowed before the opposition of England and Russia, but he did not forgive Gorchakov's stand. The complications in the Balkans gave him his chance for revenge.

The Russian-Turkish War and the Congress of Berlin (1877–1878)

Under the Treaty of Paris, Europe had taken Russia's place as the protector of the Christians in the Ottoman Empire and in the supervision of that realm. Turkey had been introduced into the concert of Europe and the text of the treaty itself had embodied new promises of reforms that the sultan had announced in the *Hatti Humayun* of 1856, as if to demonstrate that his continued presence in the concert of Europe depended in fact on their fulfillment. But there had been no clear definition of the extent and the modalities of joint action in the event that the sultan did not keep his promises and it was found necessary to intervene. In reality, since Europe had neither the wish to do so nor any community of views, her supervision and especially, as we shall see, England's part in the execution of this tutelage substantially delayed the solution of the Balkan problem and brought on a number of wars, the first of which was that of 1877–1878.

Immediately after the Treaty of Paris it became apparent that the sultan was not going to keep his new promises any more than he had done in the past and that the Ottoman Empire was not going to be Europeanized. The reports of foreign consuls and diplomatic representatives, English and other, proved that persecutions of the Christians were continuing. The massacres of Damascus and Djedda in 1860 impelled the English and French to occupy Syria—evidence that the powers had not abandoned their right of intervention. Gorchakov took the occasion to point out, in his notes of May 17 and August 17, 1860, that the situation of the other Christian provinces, especially Bosnia, Herzegovina, and Bulgaria, was no better and threatened to provoke dangerous conflicts. He proposed that the powers concert their plans if they did not want to be caught by surprise. But action was limited to the preparation of a purely formal protocol on Europe's right of supervision, and, in accord with Russia's desire, to the appointment of a commission to study the situation in the European provinces. Lebanon was given a constitution, and the insurrection of 1866–1867 in Crete brought about intervention by England. On this occasion Gorchakov renewed his earlier proposals, but without success.

Thenceforth, and especially after 1874, with the second prime ministry of Benjamin Disraeli (Lord Beaconsfield), English policy took a definitely anti-Russian and pro-Turkish turn. Although England too was being kept informed by her agents, she presented all news concerning the violences committed against the Christians by the Turks as Russian and Austrian-Hungarian inventions and she preferred to view the disorders that broke out in the Christian provinces merely as the result of Russian-Austrian plotting. She took no account of the national consciousness that was becoming more and more pronounced in the Christian countries of the Balkans. Between 1860 and 1870 the Bulgarians were struggling to detach their church, the symbol of their nationality, from the Greek church. In 1872 a Bulgarian national church (the Exarchate) was established with the support of the Turks. Serbia, which had been governed since 1860 by Prince Mikhail, backed the Bulgarian aspirations and dreamed of becoming the Slavic "Piedmont." Mikhail initiated talks with the young generation of Bulgarian patriots, for whom the independence of their church was no longer enough and who wanted political freedom. A Bulgarian revolutionary committee was already in existence in Bucharest, from where

it guided its "apostles"—one of whom, Levsky, was arrested and executed by the Turks in 1873—who were preparing for insurrection in
Bulgaria; everywhere, in northern Bulgaria, in the south (Rumelia),
and in Macedonia, the revolutionaries were carrying forward their
struggle on the territory of the Exarchate. The Serbs and the Montenegrins were uneasy over the fate of their brothers in Bosnia and
Herzegovina, "the cradle of Serbia." So it was not Russian "ambition"
but national aspirations that were the major factor in the insurrections
of 1875–1876.

The first of these erupted in Herzegovina in July 1875. It soon
spread into Bosnia. In August, when the Turkish garrisons totaled no
more than two thousand soldiers, there were already twenty thousand
insurgents. The European powers insisted that Serbia and Montenegro
remain neutral and limit themselves to dispatching six consuls for an
on-the-spot investigation in September. These consuls could see for
themselves that the Christians were really suffering, but they had no
authority to encourage them to rebel. While the Porte demanded above
all that the insurgents disarm and surrender completely, they made a
counter-demand for Europe's guaranty for the accomplishment of the
autonomist program that they had evolved.

When the insurrection did not abate over the winter but threatened
to become even more violent in the spring that followed, Russia,
Austria-Hungary, and Germany together looked for means of intervening. As usual, the Porte, in order to forestall European intervention, hastily issued the irade of October 2 and the firman of December
12 to renew its earlier pledges of reforms. In consequence of Austrian-
Russian-German negotiations, Russia left the lead to Austria-Hungary,
which was the country closest to the scene of action, and Andrássy
sent the Porte his famous note of December 30, 1875 (which was delivered on January 30, 1876). First pointing out that the old promises
had not been fulfilled, he outlined a program of religious, financial,
and agrarian reforms, and he proposed that the pashas' administration
be subject to the control of a "local assembly composed equally of
Christians and Moslems." England associated herself with this proposal, "on the request of the Porte itself," in order to emphasize that
this was not intervention "but merely friendly advice." The Porte
raised no obstacles to the acceptance of this "advice" and issued an
irade that was in direct contradiction of its behavior. Therefore the
insurgents maintained their attitude of distrust; they absolutely refused to lay down their arms and demanded that the supervision of
the reforms be entrusted to a special European commission, that the

Turkish troops withdraw into their forts, and that economic assistance be provided to refugees when they returned to their homes.

Hostilities were resumed in the spring with greater fury than ever. The assassination of the French and German consuls in Salonika on May 6 impelled the powers to more forceful action. Russia insisted that consideration be given to the demands of the rebels. England made the strange suggestion that territorial compensation be offered to Prince Nicholas of Montenegro, who was helping the insurgents. As a result of the talks among Alexander II, Bismarck, and Andrássy on May 11, a conference of the representatives of the great powers was held in Berlin at Bismarck's invitation. On May 15 the three imperial courts proposed that the other governments subscribe to a "memorandum of Berlin" drafted by Gorchakov two days earlier. This new document called on the Porte, in conformity with the insurgents' demands, to conclude a two-month armistice and to reach an understanding with them on the rehabilitation of the damaged churches and farms and the help that would be distributed among the victims of the rising by a mixed commission. It stipulated that the Christians, like the Mussulmans, should retain their weapons and that the Turkish troops should withdraw into their fortifications. The delegates of the powers would supervise the execution of the reforms and the return of the refugees to their homes. If, after two months, the powers had not succeeded in attaining their goals, the three imperial courts threatened recourse to measures more "efficacious" than diplomatic activity. Gorchakov then let it be understood that Russia would no longer restrain Serbia and Montenegro, which were ready to take up arms, that "the flame of insurrection would burn through Bulgaria, Epirus, Thessaly, and Albania," and that "the Christian countries of Europe, to which the voice of humanity will be conveyed by public opinion, will be compelled to intervene in order to halt the shedding of blood."

France and Italy immediately adhered to the memorandum, but England, whose Prime Minister Disraeli was made anxious by Russia's successes in central Asia and the prestige of the "white tsar," had just arranged a journey by the Prince of Wales to India and conferred the title of Empress of India on the Queen of England, officially refused on May 19 to be associated with it. Moreover, she advised Turkey not to agree to its conditions and promised the Porte her "moral support." But, though refusing to take part in a naval show of force by the powers, she found in the assassination of the consuls in Salonika a pretext for stationing and maintaining a squadron in the Bay of

Besika, at the entrance to the Dardanelles, and thus seemed to be acting in Turkey's interests. As for the Turks, they forestalled the intentions of the three emperors by a means that had become traditional in such cases and that was more effective than any promises of reforms: a palace revolution. On the instigation of Midhat Pasha, Sultan Abdul-Aziz was deposed by decision of the clergy and replaced on May 30 by Murad, a mere instrument of the victorious party. On June 9 Disraeli was able to inform Parliament with satisfaction that in the face of this overturn the powers had decided not to submit the memorandum of Berlin to the new government.

In the interim there had been the "Bulgarian massacres," which completely changed the attitude of the European powers, including England, toward Turkey. The British government having reproached it for its inability to put down the revolt by its own means, the Porte had augmented its regular troops in April with irregular detachments composed of bandits and criminals, the *bashibuzuki*. Early in May, when southern Bulgaria had risen, the Porte, without a thought to the inevitable consequences of their employment, had thrown them into action against the rebels. The population of Batak, which had been thoroughly disarmed and which had tried in vain to take refuge in its church, was exterminated to the last man between May 5 and 8, and the director of this achievement, Akhmed Aga, had been rewarded with the Order of Mejidia. Similar massacres had subsequently been carried out in other localities under the management of the governor of Bulgaria, Shefket Pasha. According to Baring, the British consul, the total number of victims was thirteen thousand. When *The Daily News* of London announced these atrocities on June 23, British public opinion, which thus far had been either uninterested or favorable to the Conservative government, was outraged. The government's optimistic statements and assurances had been cruelly disproved. On August 29 the foreign secretary, the Earl of Derby, was compelled to write to his ambassador in Constantinople, Sir George Elliot: "I find it necessary to convey to you, as a matter of information, that the impression made here by the events in Bulgaria has totally destroyed all sympathy for Turkey. This feeling is so powerful and so unanimous that Her Majesty's Government would find it a practical impossibility to intervene, even in the event that Russia should declare war on the Porte." A week later Gladstone, Disraeli's opponent, published his famous pamphlet on the Bulgarian atrocities. A short time later, in his speech in Blackheath, he reminded the powers that the Turkish provinces were not a prey that they could share out among themselves but in fact the property of their indigenous populations. What England and Russia could do, if they agreed to act jointly, the one at sea and the other on land, was to improve the situation of these populations without depriving the sultan of his sovereignty. Their alliance would make them invincible. "I do not delude myself," he added, "to the point of believing that Russia is devoid of all selfish interest, any more than any other state. But the humanitarian sympathy that has gripped her people at this moment is an almost instinctive pulse-beat. Why not act in all sincerity, in agreement with her, and why not restrain our irritations and our suspicions until such time as they may be justified by some action on her part and not by the memory of an old hatred?" But Disraeli did not share the public anger against the Turks. He contented himself with addressing a few admonitions to be Porte. In his speech in Aylesbury on September 20, he lashed out sharply against politicians who "take advantage of these fine sentiments to deprive the government, which is defending the vital interests of Great Britain, of the country's backing." This speech would have been enough, without confidential friendly counsel that gave the lie to public exhortations, to prove to the Turks that England's admonitions lacked sincerity.

Under such conditions the powers lost every means of control, and events took their own course. On July 1 the Serbs declared war against Turkey and a day later the Montenegrins emulated them. While the Montenegrins were successful in throwing back Turkish attacks in July and August, the Serbs, who were under the command of the Russian General Chernyayev and faced the major force of the enemy's army, could not defend their positions and held out only with great difficulty before Aleksinats, the key to the Morava Valley. On August 24 Prince Milan asked for mediation by the powers and on September 1, at his urging, Prince Nicholas of Montenegro did the same. On the same day England suggested to the Porte that a thirty-day armistice be called in order to discuss peace terms. In Europe and especially in Russia, which had sent many volunteers to enlist in the Serbian army, public opinion grew more and more impatient. On September 1 the Russian ambassador in London, Count Shuvalov, told the British foreign secretary that Russia had "decided inflexibly" to demand the immediate conclusion of an armistice but without allowing the Porte to present its own peace terms. Under Russian pressure, England proposed conditions, accepted by the other powers, to be imposed on the Porte: the maintenance of the *status quo* in Serbia, administrative reforms in Bosnia and Herzegovina, and guaranties against misgovernment in Bulgaria. Turkey had already sought to prevent this new intervention of the powers by fresh resort to a palace revolution. Sultan Murad was deposed on August 31 and replaced by his brother, Abdul-Hamid. On September 12 the new sultan formally refused an armistice and granted a mere "cease-fire" from September 17 until September 25, which he subsequently extended to October 2; on September 14 he laid down his terms for peace. This time England herself spoke out: she called the proposals of the Porte "unacceptable" and warned on September 25 that the rejection of the English terms would entail a declaration of war by Russia and that in such case England would find herself compelled "to abandon Turkey to her own resources."

Russia was not yet ready to make war, but she was thinking of a collective intervention by the powers against the Porte. On September 26 Gorchakov proposed to Disraeli that there be a simultaneous occupation of Bosnia and Herzegovina by Austria-Hungary, of Bulgaria by Russia, and of the Bosphorus by an inter-allied fleet, or, if England did not agree to this plan of action, that she restrict herself to the occupation of the Bosphorus, which would prevent the Turkish armies in Europe from receiving any reinforcement from Asia. On October 4 England rejected the Russian proposal but agreed to demand that Turkey suspend for a month the hostilities that had just been renewed on the Morava. To the utter amazement of Europe, the Porte countered with the suggestion of a six-month armistice. Although on the face of all the evidence the purpose of the Turkish offer was to avoid action by the powers, England hastened to accept it. But Russia put forth objections to it, and Bismarck backed Petersburg. England stood firm, and the negotiations dragged out until the time when the Serbs' military position had grown much worse. Toward the end of October the Morava army, which included the Russian volunteers, was thrown into complete rout by the Turks; Aleksinats was taken on October 31, Serbian territory was invaded, and the road to Belgrade lay open. New atrocities were to be feared; it was impossible to delay any longer. Alexander II, who was at the time in Livadia in the Crimea, resolved to act alone. On the day of the capture of Aleksinats he sent the Porte an ultimatum that called on it to agree within forty-eight hours to a six-month armistice. The Porte yielded. The tsar explained to the British ambassador that Europe's irresoluteness had forced him to move alone, that England's suspicions of Russia were without foundation, because he was not seeking conquests and believed that the occupation of Constantinople would be "a misfortune for Russia." He gave his word of honor that he did not want to take Constantinople and that, if necessity compelled him to it, he would confine himself to occupying only a part of Bulgaria until peace could be made and the safety of the Christian populations could be guaranteed. For the first time Russia proclaimed her determination to make war, even while stating the limitations that of her own accord she would impose on her military activity. But she was still hesitant to intervene alone, and she was still seeking to obtain Europe's pledge of joint action. Alexander II wanted a conference to be held that would prepare a plan for reforms in Bosnia, Herzegovina, and Bulgaria and that would establish the means of assuring its execution. In a note to the British government on November 3 Gorchakov elaborated the tsar's views and emphasized the fact that "the question of the east is a European and not a purely Russian question." The next day Lord Derby proposed that a conference be held in Constantinople that would take as the basis for its deliberations the English proposal of September, although under the express condition that the powers first recognize the independence and inviolability of the Ottoman Empire, renounce all territorial acquisition, and pledge that none of them would seek to exercise an exclusive influence in Turkey. On Russia's request it was decided that the Turkish representatives would not attend the preliminary sessions of this conference. As usual, England diluted the effect of her public proposal through confidential explanations to the Porte. Moreover, at the banquet for the Lord Mayor of London on November 10, Disraeli deemed it advisable to state that England was prepared for war and that her resources were inexhaustible. Alexander II answered him the very next day in the Hall of St. Georgi in the Kremlin: he declared openly, and before all Russia, that, if the Conference of Constantinople did not succeed in creating an alliance among the powers and genuinely assuring the improvement of the lives of the Christians in Turkey, he was "firmly resolved to act alone and that he was certain that all Russia would answer his call when this should be necessary and the honor of the country should require it." On November 15 Gorchakov informed the powers of the partial mobilization of the Russian army.

The preliminary sessions of the Conference, under the presidency of Count Ignatyev, opened on December 14 in the Russian embassy under the most favorable auspices. Lord Salisbury, the British delegate, had been given authority to recognize the powers' right of intervention but not to associate himself with their sanctions. On December 5 Bismarck had told the Reichstag that, in the event that the conference should fail and Russia should declare war, Germany would offer no opposition. Count Ignatyev was able to sketch, "on a Kiepert map," his proposal for a "Greater Bulgaria" embracing the whole population of the Balkan Peninsula that regarded itself as Bulgarian and recognized the supreme authority of the Exarchate—in other words, northern and southern Bulgaria, in both parts of the Balkans, and Macedonia. The prospect of occupying Bosnia and Herzegovina made Austria-Hungary support the reforms. Nine sessions were sufficient for the drafting of five proposals: a peace treaty with Serbia and Monte-negro, a basic system for Bosnia and Herzegovina, the organization of Bulgaria, and the creation of two international control commissions. On December 23 the official Conference began in the presence of the Turkish representatives, who had arrived equipped with a new dra-maturgy. In the midst of the session there were salvos of artillery, and Savfet Pasha, who was in the chair, rose and explained that a "great action" changing the form of government had just been carried out: "A constitution bestowed by His Majesty the Sultan on his empire has been made public and should mark the dawn of a new era of hap-piness and prosperity for the people." Once again the Porte was attempting to shunt the limited but real reforms demanded by the powers, this time by replacing them with a general constitution for the empire that was destined to remain a dead letter. Inasmuch as the Turkish delegates offered objections to each of the articles proposed by the representatives of the powers and accepted the whole only with the proviso that it be approved by their government, the Conference was adjourned until December 28.

On December 30, during their third session, the European delegates confirmed that their proposal had been approved by their respective governments, and they demanded an immediate response. They got it that evening. Eleven of the seventeen Eruopean conditions were re-jected, four were tabled for decision by future legislatures, and two were simply ignored. In the next session, on January 1, 1877, Lord Salisbury himself was constrained to acknowledge that this response was an affront to the dignity of the powers. After the session, he warned Grand Vizier Midhat that the Porte was playing a dangerous game, but in vain; he was arrogantly told in reply that the European conditions were incompatible with Turkey's dignity, independence, and territorial integrity. The Conference held its ninth and last session on January 20; it had accomplished nothing. In spite of the relaxation of its demands, the Turkish delegates stubbornly refused to accept the articles that would legalize Europe's right of intervention—that is, the creation of an international control commission and European ap-proval of the appointments of governors. Later Midhat Pasha ex-plained the reasons behind this obstinacy: "We know that, since the British Cabinet was in disagreement with Russia, it would sooner or later be unable to avoid, for all its declarations, intervening in the eastern question." In effect Disraeli's policy had culminated in the conversion of the eastern question into a duel between Russia and England. Even when he really intended to frighten the Porte, it was not the general intervention of Europe with which he threatened it, but war with Russia. But the value of this threat depended on Turkey's own estimate of Russian military strength. This estimate was remarkably low. Lord Salisbury was on sound ground when, explaining the failure of the Conference of Constantinople to the House of Lords, he identified as "one of the reasons for the unfortunate decision by the Turks their confidence that the Russian forces were broken, that the army was decimated by disease, that the mobilization had not succeeded . . ." Layard's memorandum, presented to the Porte on the eve of the war, in fact showed that some British diplomats confirmed the calculations of the Turks, who wanted to force the situation and "compel the Russians to declare war."

Whatever the case, this was the conclusion to which events led after the failure of the Conference of Constantinople. Russia, which had gone beyond the extreme limit on concessions that she had set for herself, did try again for joint diplomatic action by the powers. On January 19, 1877 Gorchakov asked them what measures they planned to adopt with respect to Turkey. England cited the recent changes within Turkey as the pretext for deferring a definitive reply. Midhat Pasha, having become useless after the comedy of the constitution, was deposed and banished. The new Turkish government urged the powers to "leave it in peace and to believe in the good faith of its intentions," an utterance that seemed insufficient even to England. On three more occasions—on February 19, 21, and 28—Shuvalov insisted in London that collective action be fixed on in order not to drive Russia into isolated action. Early in March the tsar sent Count Ignatyev to Berlin, Vienna, Paris, and London to explain that Russia could not demobilize her army before she had received some "tangible" concession and to present a proposal for a new "protocol" in which Europe's demands on Turkey would be reiterated. England replied by calling on Russia to disarm. On March 21 the Russian ambassadors went as far as to agree to this, always with the provision that Turkey disarm first, that peace be concluded with Montenegro—a treaty with Serbia had been signed on February 28—and that the Porte initiate actual reforms. They promised that, if these conditions were met, Russia would issue a "declaration" to announce that she was agreeing to disarm after negotiations to deal with demobilization had been held in Petersburg with a special Turkish emissary. On March 31, England, at the same time as the other powers, finally signed the "protocol of London," which was limited to a meaningless recapitulation of all the earlier negotiations and to a vague assurance that the powers would continue to parley together if the Porte again dashed their hopes. But on the same day England made it known that the protocol would be of no effect if disarmament were not carried out. On April 8, the Porte—which had recovered its courage after Elliot, the British ambassador, who had been recalled with the representatives of the other countries after the failure of the Conference, had been replaced in Constantinople by Layard—decided that there was no occasion to send an ambassador extraordinary to Petersburg unless Russia sent one to Constantinople at the same time. Then, next day, Turkey professed to see in the protocol nothing but an affront to her dignity and an infringement of her independence: rather than bow to this she would prefer to take the risk of war. The Russian response was not delayed. On April 19 Gorchakov issued a circular note to the powers, declaring that the protocol rejected by Turkey was the final expression of the collective will of Europe and the final attempt at conciliation, that it could no longer be hoped that the Porte would meet the conditions precedent to disarmament, that no choice remained but to seek through force what the powers had been unable to achieve through persuasion, and that, in order to take up this task and thus fulfill his duty to the interests of Russia while at the same time serving those of Europe, the tsar was ordering his troops to cross the Ottoman frontiers.

This time, unlike 1853, the powers did not hamper Russia in the "fulfillment of her duty," but they did make arrangements so that the effects of the new war would not damage their own interests. Under the treaty of Vienna of January 15, 1877, which clarified the secret convention of Reichstadt of June 1876, Austria-Hungary pledged her neutrality, but on condition that she herself might eventually occupy Bosnia and Herzegovina, that the powers retain the right to pronounce judgment on the results of the war, that Russia abstain from any territorial acquisition on the right bank of the Danube, in Rumania, and in Constantinople, that she renounce any explosive protectorate over Bulgaria and any unification of non-Slavic populations to Slavic provinces that might be liberated, and, finally, that Serbia not become a theater of military operations. On April 16 Rumania authorized the free passage of Russian troops toward the Danube, in return for the recognition of her complete independence—which she declared on May 22—and she in turn would join the war when the Turks shelled her cities and the sultan had deposed Prince Charles. As for England, she warned the Porte that she would give it no succor, but on May 6, as the price of her neutrality, she demanded that Russia exclude Egypt and the Suez Canal from the area of hostilities and renounce the occupation of Constantinople and any modification of the status of the Straits. Gorchakov accepted all these conditions by telegram, remarking at the same time that, if military operations required, it might be necessary temporarily to occupy Constantinople and that it would be necessary to settle the question of the Straits jointly.

Operations began simultaneously in the Balkans and Transcaucasia. On the Balkan front, three hundred thousand Russians faced the two hundred ninety-three thousand men who were available to Turkey at the start. In Transcaucasia there were two hundred thousand Russians against one hundred thousand Turks. On May 1 twenty thousand Montenegrins also joined the war and six thousand Bulgarians were added to the Russian army. Because of the spring floods on the Danube and the bad state of the roads, the Russians at first advanced quite slowly. Having begun their campaign on 12/24 April, they did not cross the river until 15/27–18/30 June. Since the Turks had massed the main body of their forces on the western and eastern parts of the river's course (at Viddin and in the "quadrilateral" *), the Russians crossed in the center, before Zimnitsa, without meeting much resistance. Since there were no major forces confronting them, they moved ahead rapidly and scored resounding successes during July. On 25 June/7 July they occupied the ancient capital of Bulgaria, Trnovo. Between 1/13 and 5/17 July, with relatively weak forces, General Gurko led a daring raid through the Balkans to penetrate into southern Bulgaria and dominate the Shipka defile by turning its flank; it fell into his hands on 7/19 July. This was when it became apparent that the offensive had been carried out with inadequate forces. The frightened Turks replaced their commander in chief, Abdul Kerim, with Mehemed Ali. At the same time General Osman Pasha, who recognized that it had been an error to divide the Turkish army into two corps, left Viddin, in front of which the Rumanians were passively sitting, and hastily occupied Plevna, a major tactical position on the Russians' flank. On instructions from the Russian commander in chief, Grand Duke Nikolai Nikolayevitch "the elder," General Krüdener ordered General Schilder-Schuldner to attack Plevna. Two bloody assaults against the city were launched on 8/20 and 18/30 July, and both were hurled back with heavy losses. In addition, General Gurko, who had been able to occupy Stara Zagora and Nova Zagora (in southern Bulgaria), also had to withdraw, as quickly as he had advanced, leaving to the mercies of the Turks the unhappy populations who had hailed his arrival. He retreated before Suleiman

*Formed by the strong points of Rustchuk, Silistria, Varna, and Shumla.

Pasha, who had hastily left the Montenegrin front—fortunately, this spared Montenegro from disaster. Gurko dug in in the Shipka defile. Threatened before and behind by Turkish forces that were still intact, the Russians had to halt and await reinforcements. Alexander, who was at the front, ordered the mobilization of the guard and the formation of four new corps, thus bringing the Russian army to five hundred fifty-four thousand men. In the second half of August the Turks went over to the offensive all along the line. Only General Radetsky's arrival at Shipka saved General Gurko's troops, under pressure from Suleiman. On 4/16 and 5/17 September the Turks tried again, but in vain, to capture the defile, which remained uncontestably in Russian hands. But a third attack on Plevna, carried out in the tsar's presence, failed on 30 August/11 September in spite of the courage of General Skobelev and the loss of sixteen thousand men—altogether the three attacks on Plevna cost the Russians twenty-six thousand men. Disraeli was exultant. Berlin counseled the Russians to retreat into winter quarters in Rumania. A council of war, attended by Alexander, decided to hold the positions in Bulgaria and the Balkans and to lay formal siege to Plevna after all communications with Sofia had been cut. The Russians, after a number of battles, succeeded in carrying out their plan toward the end of October. Osman Pasha's situation in Plevna was becoming desperate, especially after General Gurko had liberated the northern slopes of Etropol-Balkan on 12/24 November. Again the Turks removed their commander in chief. Suleiman replaced Mehemed Ali, but he could not cut Osman Pasha free. On 28 November/10 December Osman tried to break out and force a passage through to Viddin. He was thrown back and forced to surrender. Plevna had held out for one hundred forty-four days, until its food was exhausted; only famine had brought it to its knees, but it had halted the Russian drive. On 2/14 December Serbia entered the war again with an army of fifty thousand men. The Russian right wing was disengaged and the road to southern Bulgaria was opened.

On the Asian front operations followed an almost identical course. At first the Russians mounted a successful offensive from Aleksandropol against Kars and Erzerum, while on their right wing two corps advanced from Akhaltsykh on Ardahan and Batum and on their left wing one corps marched on Bayazid from Erivan. In the middle of May 1877 they captured Bayazid and Ardahan and began the blockade of Kars. At the same time, they endeavored to turn the mountain range of Saganly, which separates Kars from Erzerum and which was occupied by the center of Muktar Pasha's army, at either end. Fearing lest they be cut off from Erzerum, the Turks fell back, enticing their adversaries as far as Zivin, where, between 9/21 and 13/25 June, they turned about and gained a great victory. The Russians were forced to retreat everywhere and return within their own borders. They had been severely tried by painful marches, vigorous combat, and disease. Moreover, in the Caucasus they were at grips with a rising of the Abkhazians and the Daghestanis, fomented by the Turks. They had to put down this insurrection and reorganize their army. Fortunately for the Russians, the Turkish troops were in no better case, so that Muktar Pasha could not take the offensive. On 20 September/2 October the Russian army, which had received reinforcements and was under the command of Grand Duke Mikhail Nikolayevitch, launched a new campaign of broad scope. Muktar, who did not want to give up his positions between Aleksandropol and Kars, was encircled on 3/15 October by General Lazarev's troops and beaten by General Geyman. He withdrew precipitately behind the Saganly range as far as Erzerum, in the gorge of Deveboïnu, but there, on 22 October/4 November, he was thoroughly smashed by the Russians, who had followed in hot pursuit. This disaster threatened the resistance of Kars, whose garrison tried unsuccessfully to break out on this same day and which the Russians decided to take by storm. This exceptionally difficult operation was successfully carried out on 6–7/18–19 November: the garrison, seventeen thousand strong, surrendered. Thenceforth the Russians could devote themselves to the campaign's major goal, the siege of Erzerum. They were the masters of Armenia.

Disraeli was apprehensive at their victories on the two fronts. His anxiety mounted when, leaving the Balkans in the north, they rapidly advanced on Philippopoli, Adrianople, and Constantinople. On December 13, 1877 he reminded them that England could not in any circumstances permit even the temporary occupation of Constantinople. "If that occurs," he asserted, "the government will consider itself free to take the measures that it may deem necessary to the safeguarding of British interests." Fundamentally he wanted to force Russia to make concessions that had never previously been stated. On December 16 Gorchakov confirmed his earlier promise not to annex Constantinople, but he refused to impose any hobbles on Russia's operations as long as "a real and durable peace" had not been achieved, and he inquired what English interests could still be harmed by Russia after her adherence to England's previous demands. The reply did not reach him until January 12, 1878, after Turkey, through the good offices of England, had vainly sought to learn what peace terms were planned for her. The British reply did not mention Constantinople, but it forbade any operation in the Dardanelles and especially any dispatch of Russian troops to the peninsula of Gallipoli. On January 23, 1878, when it was learned that the Russians had struck out for Demotika and were threatening to cut off Gallipoli from the capital, England ordered Admiral Hornby to steam for Constantinople and "stand guard over the freedom of the Straits"; then, her fears having been proved premature, she recalled her fleet to the Bay of Bezika. During this time the Turkish plenipotentiaries, who could not bring themselves to sign the armistice conditions set by Grand Duke Nikolai Nikolayevitch, followed him from Kazanlyk, step by step. Finally, on 15/27 January, Alexander II ordered the grand duke to march on Constantinople if the armistice was not signed within three days. The Turks agreed on January 31. The conditions included the creation of an autonomous Bulgaria within her ethnic limits—that is, including Rumelia and Macedonia; the independence of Montenegro, Rumania, and Serbia; the autonomy of Bosnia and Herzegovina; the guaranty of Russian interests in the Straits, and territorial or financial indemnity. This was a goad to British apprehensions. Ambassador Layard telegraphed to London that these conditions "were tantamount to the destruction of the Ottoman Empire in Europe." Disraeli asked the House of Commons for 6 million pounds for war preparations and on February 8 he once more ordered the fleet to Constantinople on the pretext of assuring the safety of British subjects there in the event of disorders. On February 15 the British fleet was riding at anchor off the Princes Islands. Alexander retorted by ordering the occupation of Constantinople, but this order was not carried out because it did not reach the grand duke—and perhaps this delay was not the effect of chance alone—until the time when the British fleet, pursuant to new instructions from London, was leaving the Bosphorus. On March 3, in the little town of San Stefano, provisional peace terms ratified and clarified the armistice conditions.

England thereupon pointed out what was a foregone conclusion: that this peace that annulled the old treaties would have to be approved by a European congress. Austria-Hungary, furthermore, had already suggested Vienna and then Berlin as the site for the congress. An entire month was spent in negotiations on the extent to which the treaty of San Stefano could be revised. Since Russia rejected a complete revision from the very outset, the interested parties embarked on individual negotiations with her, during which Count Ignatyev made the tour of the European capitals. England was far less concerned with preserving Turkey's integrity than with weakening Russia's influence in the regions liberated by the Russian victories. That was why she insisted, in the secret Anglo-Russian accord of May 30, that the

"Greater Bulgaria" called for in the treaty of San Stefano be divided into three regions: Bulgaria properly so called, in the northern Balkans, which alone would become an independent principality; Rumelia, in the southern Balkans, which would be autonomous but would remain a Turkish province, and Macedonia, which would be purely and simply turned back to the sultan. Austria-Hungary, for her part, wanted payment of her price for neutrality, which had been promised to her in the secret Austrian-Russian treaty of January 1877: that is, the "occupation and administration" of Bosnia and Herzegovina. Unable to endure a new war, Russia was compelled to yield to the demands of the two powers, which, in return, agreed to allow her to keep her own basically rather modest conquests—Kars and Batum—and recover the part of Bessarabia that she had lost under the Treaty of Paris. Only Germany made no demands; therefore Berlin seemed the most suitable place for holding the congress, in which Bismarck expected to play his part as the "honest broker."

The Congress of Berlin, which lasted from June 13 to July 13, 1878, modified the treaty of San Stefano on the basis of the preliminary agreements reached by Russia with England and Austria-Hungary. Bismarck, who presided at the Congress, terrorized the Turkish delegates and refused to let the discussions stray from the issue. Whenever they threatened to do so, he flew into a rage, shouted, made scenes, and let it be understood that he had no time to concern himself with others' business. Under these conditions, the English, who had manipulated the cession of the island of Cyprus by Turkey in a secret treaty of June 4 under which, in return, they pledged to guarantee Turkey's possessions in Asia, found themselves in a difficult position to defend the interests of the Ottomans. Thus Disraeli had to agree to the occupation and administration of Bosnia and Herzegovina by Austria-Hungary, and indeed he threatened the representatives of the Porte with grave complications if they did not yield on this point. Russia, similarly, could not go back on her earlier consessions and was obliged to accept in particular the disappearance of "Greater Bulgaria." Bismarck did not wish a quarrel with Russia, and he was even inclined to do her minor favors, but he showed no indulgence for Gorchakov's vanity and openly preferred to deal with Count Shuvalov—on whom Gorchakov was prepared to throw the responsibility for the concessions—who considered it essential to ratify the promised concessions "if Russia wanted to avoid war."

Russian public opinion, which knew nothing of the secret agreements reached and the real dangers to which an inflexible stand would have exposed the country, accused the diplomats of having lost the spoils of a dearly won victory. Russians had regarded the war as a humanitarian undertaking. They were deeply disappointed when, through Europe's fault, they saw it end in the maintenance of an unstable situation and the creation of new sources of conflict in the Balkans. It was undeniable that Russia's gains bore no relation to her sacrifices, and it was undeniable too that, if in beginning the war she had merely pursued her traditional policy in the peninsula, this time her interests would have been in harmony not only with the contemporary world's sentiments of humanity and morality but also with the clearly understood interests of Europe as a whole.

Russian-German Alienation and the Isolation of Russia

Germany's attitude in the Congress of Berlin had grievously wounded all Russia, public opinion as well as diplomatic circles. In 1879 the only topic of conversation in Europe was the concentration of Russian troops and the inevitability of conflict between Russia and Germany. Alexander II retained his friendship for Wilhelm I, but he wrote to the Kaiser (in French) in August, complaining of Bismarck's policy toward Russia: "How explain this attitude among German diplomats, who are becoming more and more hostile to us in the east? . . . I feel that I ought to bring to your attention the unhappy consequences that this can provoke in our relations as good neighbors by embittering our two nations against each other . . . "

Bismarck, who was laboring to bring about the alliance between Germany and Austria-Hungary, replied to the tsar's accusations by showing Wilhelm I that Russia was hatching plots and that Alexander II had suggested a treaty of alliance to France—an allegation that French Foreign Minister William Waddington thought it necessary to deny officially on September 15, 1880. Bismarck insisted that the German alliance with Austria-Hungary, which was directed against Russia, be concluded as quickly as possible. But Wilhelm I hesitated. During his meeting with the tsar at Aleksandrovo at the beginning of September 1879, Alexander had urged him to renew their old friendship, and it was painful to the Kaiser to break with Russia. In order to force him to sign the treaty of alliance with Austria-Hungary, Bismarck had to threaten to resign.

During the last years of his reign Alexander II was obsessed by a single thought: the struggle against revolution. Living in unremitting fear of attacks on his person, he subordinated all his political concerns to this struggle. He wanted friendship with Germany because in 1880 that country made its laws against Socialists even harsher. On the other hand, he regarded republican France as nothing but a hotbed of revolutionary propaganda, and his anger was particularly hot when the French government refused to allow the extradition of Hartman, a Russian terrorist. When the tsar died on 1/13 March 1881, Russia was wholly isolated in Europe.

Russian Expansion in Central and Eastern Asia

It was during the reign of Alexander II that the long labor of colonization and military penetration was terminated and brought to completion, having slowly but surely carried the Russians to the sources of the two rivers flowing into the Sea of Aral: the Syr-Daria from the north and the Amu-Daria from the south. They advanced in two directions at the same time: from north to south by way of Siberia, across the territories of the three nomad Hordes of Kirghiz—the Small, the Great, and the Middle—which had already been subdued by them, and from west to east, from the eastern shore of the Caspian Sea into the heart of the steppes. It was chiefly the necessity of defending the settled Russian population against the incursions of the nomads that impelled them to thrust their outposts into the country of the Kirghizi and the Turkomans. Even religion could not unify these Mussulman tribes against the unbeliever, because, in order to arouse them to a holy war, as Vambéry, an expert on central Asia, so justly observed, there would also have had to be the prospect of good loot. In actuality these bellicose pillagers were incapable of uniting for their own joint defense. Therefore the Russian method of penetration was always the same. Since in every tribe there were always adventurers in search of arms and money with which to reinforce their power over the sedentary populations, the Russians began by dividing them, setting them against one another, and then backing each faction in regular rotation against its enemies. Then Russian troops would intervene, marking their path with a series of forts. Little by little, in this way, they changed from allies to lords and masters.

This slow and methodical penetration began somewhat before 1860 on the lower reaches of the Syr-Daria. Its objective was to establish, by means of a line of fortresses, a connection between two Russian outposts about 798 versts apart, Fort Perovsky and Vyernoye, and to set up supply bases as close to the garrisons as possible in order to avoid having to transport food across the steppe. On the pretext that the inhabitants of Kokan and Bokhara had attacked the Siberian border in 1860, Colonel Chernyayev seized Fort Tchimkent, in the very center of this region rich in wheat, in 1864. England was already perturbed, and Gorchakov had to allay her fears; in his note of 21 November/3 December 1864 he justified the Russian drive by adducing a state's need to defend its subjects and its civilization against the savage nomads of the frontier. Under the treaty of Tchugutchak, Russia obtained China's recognition of Russian possession of the Naryn basin (in northern Kokan), and, under an imperial ukase of 1865, the province of Turkestan was created. In June of the same year, Chernyayev took the occasion of an attack by the emir of Bokhara against the weakened Kokan to occupy Tashkent, the center of the region's communications routes. In May 1866, General Romanovsky, pushing forward, occupied Khodzhent on the lower part of the Syr-Daria. Mosaffer Ed-Din, the emir of Bokhara, exerted every effort, but in vain, to drive the Russians out of Kokan; finally, after a number of defeats, he recognized their conquests in 1867. In the same year the ukase of 11/23 elevated Turkestan to the rank of a government general, with Tashkent as its capital, and General Kaufman became its head. When the emir of Bokhara, not yet resigned to his defeat, began to plan a new campaign, Kaufman anticipated him. He marched on Samarkand and, when he had routed Mosaffer's troops, he occupied the city in May 1868. A rising by the inhabitants was savagely put down, and in the end Mosaffer signed a treaty that guaranteed the safety of the lives and property of Russian citizens, pledged safety for caravans, and reduced the taxes on commerce. When the local beys, who were vexed by these concessions, revolted against the emir, Kaufman defeated them too, and in 1870 he restored Mosaffer to power. Thereafter Bokhara remained definitively under Russian domination.

Grown more and more apprehensive, England, which thus far had restricted herself to simple warnings, demanded that Russia state the limits of her expansion. By common accord these were fixed at the border of Afghanistan, Kabul being included in the British sphere of influence and Bokhara in the Russian; the Atrek River was recognized as the Persian frontier. The Russian government thereupon dedicated itself to consolidating its influence in the territories that had been recognized as its. In 1869 it built Krasnovodsk and a whole series of forts along the eastern shore of the Caspian Sea. From there, by following the course of the Amu-Daria, it was possible to undertake a campaign against Khiva, the haven of the brigands whose incursions ceaselessly threatened the Russian possessions and who sold their prisoners as slaves. Ordered to set his captives free, Mohammed Rahim, the khan of the oasis, demanded recognition of his authority over the whole territory lying between the Syr-Daria and the Atrek. In 1873 Alexander II sent Count Peter Shuvalov to London to notify the

British Cabinet that he was compelled to occupy Khiva but that he had no intention of annexing it, and he decided to attack the khanate, which was surrounded by steppes that were difficult to traverse, from four sides at once. In spite of incredible hardships, glacial cold, snow, tropic heat, and clouds of burning sand, three of the four columns managed to cross the arid desert to the oasis of Khiva. On 29 May/ 10 June 1873 Khiva's gates were opened to them, and, under the treaty of 31 July/12 August, the khan acknowledged his vassalage to Russia, immediately set free his prisoners of all nationalities, ceded the right bank of the Amu-Daria to the Russians with exclusive rights of navigation on the river, exempted Russian goods from all taxes, and paid war reparations. All Turkestan was now in Russian hands, and the newly acquired regions were made into the transcaspian province.

In 1871 Russia took advantage of Yakub Bey's revolt against China to occupy Kuldja temporarily—it was returned to China, with the valley of the Ili, in 1879 under the convention of Livadia. In central Asia, on the other hand, Russia established definite gains. The Kokan region having risen against the khan because of his submission to the Russians, General Kaufman put down the revolt and entered the town of Kokan on 26 August/7 September 1875. The treaty of 25 September/ 7 October gave Russia the territories lying on the right bank of the upper part of the Syr-Daria. Subsequent to a new rebellion among the inhabitants, the region of Kokan, which had remained independent, was joined to the Russian possessions by the ukase of 20 February/3 March 1876. It became the province of Ferghana, and the khanate of Kokan went out of existence.

In 1878, by way of reply to England's hostile policy, General Stoletov was dispatched to Emir Shir Ali of Afghanistan. With his hatred of the English, the emir welcomed the Russian mission in great pomp. When he refused to receive Chamberlain, the British envoy, who was preparing to go to Kabul with a large military group, England declared war on him. The disappointments of this war were among the causes of Disraeli's fall in 1880. The second Gladstone government repudiated the policy of challenge toward Russia and, by evacuating Afghanistan, restored the "neutral zone" between the two powers' spheres of influence.

Russia complained of the forays by the Teke-Turkomans, which were not unrelated to British policy in the border areas of Afghanistan, for the Teke-Turkomans were trained and armed by British officers. To put an end to these raids, General Lazarev led an expedition in 1879 across 375 versts of sandy steppes into the very heart of the brigands' encampments. But he was met by fierce resistance and he was unable to capture the fort of Goek-Tepe, on the Persian border. In 1880 Russia warned Gladstone's government that she would be obliged to repeat the expedition. This was indeed done in that same year, after very careful preparation, under the command of General Skobelev. But it was not until the end of December, when he had received reinforcements led by General Kuropatkin, that Skobelev succeeded in approaching Goek-Tepe. Since the enemy was too brave and too numerous to be challenged in an immediate assault, he laid a regular siege to the fort. The defenders made numerous attempts to break out and it was not until 12/24 January 1881 that Goek-Tepe was captured, after a bloody battle. Skobelev won the good will of the vanquished through his generous distribution of relief. The raids ended, and Russian influence was assured in the transcaspian province as far as the borders of Persia and Afghanistan. Askhabad was occupied. This opened the way to Merv, but Russia reassured England with a pledge not to occupy that city.

In the Far East too the Russians continued their advance toward the Pacific Ocean. On 16/28 May 1858, under the convention of Aigun, China formally acknowledged their possession of the entire right bank of the Amur River, from the Argun to the Pacific, which in fact the Russians had already colonized. On 2/14 November 1860, under the treaty of Peking, China granted Russia a huge region on the right bank of the river, bounded by the Amur, the Ussuri, and the ocean, and this became the province of Ussuri. China granted the Russians the same commercial privileges enjoyed by citizens of the other powers, and in addition the privilege of opening banks within China and visiting the fairs of Urga and Kashgar. All these successes were gained by Russia without the expenditure of a single drop of blood. By voluntarily returning Kuldja in 1879 she avoided a war with China and gained a new extension of her commercial rights. On 12/24 February 1881 the convention of St. Petersburg opened new markets to Russia and granted her nationals the right to establish themselves anywhere in China.

The Russian possessions in the extreme northeast of Asia, finally, underwent some modifications. There was first the amputation of Alaska, separated from the Siberian continent by the Bering Sea; it was sold in 1867 to the United States for 7.2 million dollars—a modest price when one thinks of the lodes of gold that were later to be discovered in the region. On the other hand, Russia gained the Island of Sakhalin, ceded by Japan in 1875 in exchange for the northern islands of the Kurile Archipelago.

CHAPTER 3

Alexander III (1881–1894)

[V. MYAKOTIN]

I / THE TRIUMPH OF REACTION

The Personality of Alexander III

Alexander III was in the prime of life when he mounted the throne. The younger son of Alexander II, born in 1845, he had not become tsarevitch until 1865, when his elder brother, Nicholas, died of tuberculosis. As long as Nicholas was alive, it was he who was the object of all his parents' solicitude: they strove to give him as complete an education as possible. Alexander, regarded as a mere grand duke, and not overly endowed, was neglected; neither his education nor his moral training was a matter of special interest. But, when he became tsarevitch, a great effort was made to perfect and broaden his fields of knowledge: his teachers at this time included the famous historian Solovyev, and the distinguished expert in civil law K. P. Pobyedonostsev.

The teachings of these masters bore some fruit. Solovyev in particular succeeded in implanting a taste for Russian history in the tsarevitch; Pobyedonostsev, for his part, managed to gain a considerable ascendancy over him, and in a domain that had nothing in common with scholarship. But study as such hardly interested Alexander. He derived all the less profit from it because his attention was soon directed elsewhere. In 1866 he married Sophia-Frederika-Dagmar, daughter of King Christian IX of Denmark, who was called Marya Fyodorovna after her conversion to Orthodoxy. The family life to which he thereafter devoted himself did not lend itself especially to lessons, and they soon stopped. Somewhat later, on the other hand, the tsarevitch began to take an interest in the business of the state. During the Russian-Turkish War of 1877–1878 he commanded a quite large force of

troops, and, while he did not play an important part in military operations, he was excellently situated to observe the under side of war.
In the final years of his father's reign he attended the conferences at
which the major problems of domestic policy were discussed. Ministers began to pay attention to his views; Count Loris-Melikov himself,
although his own influence was so great in 1880, made a special effort
to obtain Alexander's approval for every plan that he prepared.

By the time of his accession, Alexander's character and opinions had
been definitely shaped. Modest and simple in his private life, a good
family man, he led a quiet life with his wife and children and a few
intimate friends. He punctiliously avoided all pomp and luxury. He
never changed his habits, and until his death he preferred small rooms
to the sumptuous apartments of the great palaces. But until the end of
his life he also accompanied this simplicity of life with a great brutality, which some interpreted as rectitude. Becoming tsar did not affect
his utter freedom in the choice of the words he used. His annotations
on the margins of the documents that were submitted to him were
studded with vulgarities not only on his subjects, including his own
ministers, but also on foreign ministers and sovereigns, and even, at
times, on his close relatives. This was not solely the fault of his lack of
self-control, which was the consequence of a poorly ordered education
and the lack of strength of character; it was also because he entertained the profound conviction that his rank as tsarevitch, and later
as tsar, gave him an absolutely exceptional position.

"Emperor Alexander III," Count Witte, one of his most ardent ad-
mirers, was to write later in his memoirs, "had an incontrovertibly
mediocre intelligence and wholly average endowments." Some of the
tsar's collaborators spoke even more unfavorably of him in their own
memoirs. In fact his intelligence was quite limited, and the belated
education that had been given to him had not been able to develop it
enough to broaden his horizon very much. Hence he naturally remained steeped in the ultra-monarchist ideas and convictions that were
the tradition of the Russian imperial house. He could not conceive of
any form of political organization other than absolute monarchy; the
slightest limitation on absolutism, in his eyes, was gravid with calam-
ity, and he was convinced that only simple-minded and improvident
men could fall into the error of accepting it. During his reign he read
a report from his minister in Tokyo, saying that the Japanese premier
had stated that the constitution proclaimed in his country met the
needs and the level of civilization of the Japanese people: Alexander
wrote in the margin: "Wretches, simpletons, idiots." He was incapable
of contemplating even the thought of similar "idiocy" in his own coun-

try; he saw no room in Russia for "disgusting liberalism"; autocracy, foreordained and protected by Providence, should remain unshakable in Russia. During his father's lifetime he was consciously reactionary. Pobyedonostsev, his former teacher, gained a great influence over him by flattering his authoritarian tendencies and persuading him that the reforms were undermining the traditional system in Russia, which was the only just order and the sole support of absolute power. "This man steeped in bigotry," as a contemporary wrote of Pobyedonostsev, "has a meddlesome character, a bilious humor, poor health; he is one of those men who demonstrated their avowed opposition to the progress and the reforms introduced into Russia under the reign of Alexander II." Under his influence the tsarevitch soon evidenced his open hostility to his father's political endeavors. In direct proportion to the growth of reformist action, the antagonism of the tsarevitch became more apparent. The establishment of some kind of equality, however incomplete it might be, among the various social classes, the expansion and democratization of education, the restrictions on censorship, the introduction of open and independent courts, all these reforms outraged him: the "*muzhik*," he said, ought to keep his place and especially not try at all to "thrust his nose into the schools." He described the press as "mangy" and the new courts as "revolutionary." Naturally he expressed the strongest opposition when Alexander II, on the initiative of his brother Konstantin, consulted a few men whom he trusted on a proposal for extending the rights of the assemblies of the nobility, the zemstvo, and the municipal councils and for convening a consultative assembly composed of delegates from each zemstvo and the municipal councils of the large cities. He argued that the delegates thus convened would be mere "yapping nuisances, lawyers . . ." who, far from backing the government, would only complicate its work. In vain Grand Duke Konstantin made him the concession of proposing a ban on the election of lawyers to the prospective assembly. "The crown prince," one of the members of the conference observed in his diary, "is clearly hostile to any basic modification of the *status quo* and regards any kind of constitutionalism as fatal."

While such opinions seemed at times to set the tsarevitch in opposition to his father, they were in harmony with the state of mind of a rather large part of the Russian nobility, which saw an affront to itself in the emancipation of the serfs and the other reforms and which dreamed of reerecting the old order more or less *in toto*. They were especially shared by the highest nobility, those persons closest to the imperial family. Little by little a whole party of noblemen came into being round the tsarevitch, sustaining and intensifying his conservative sentiments. His friends subjected the entire body of his father's reforms to acerbically incisive criticism and firmly asserted that an end must be put to these reforms that were justified by no real need of the country and that were dragging Russia out of her historic course and leading her to the abyss. They disguised their caste aspirations in the cloak of nationalist theories and speculations on the incompatibility between Russian and western civilizations. On the pretext of maintaining order they lusted for power; what they wanted was to return to the old, proved system of the alliance between the autocratic power and the nobility.

Alexander III, then, ascended the throne without either natural talents or broad political views. He was thoroughly convinced of the legitimacy of autocracy and of its salutary function. Authoritarian by nature, he was prepared to defend his sovereign power jealously. At the same time, he was ready to employ it for the reestablishment of a caste system and the consolidation of the privileges of the upper classes of society, primarily the nobility. He was resolved to continue with all the obstinacy that was characteristic of him along the road that he had chosen.

The Removal of the Regicides and the Decline of Terrorism

The militants of The Will of the People were firmly convinced that the assassination of Alexander II would be the trumpet of a popular insurrection, that their demands would be supported by the public, and that the government would be intimidated and compelled at least to make concessions if not to capitulate. That was why on 1/13 March, immediately after the assassination, the group's central executive committee issued an appeal to the people in the guise of a letter to the new tsar. It called for the establishment of a system of genuine political freedom and the convocation of a Constituent Assembly elected on the basis of a broadly democratic vote; in exchange, The Will of the People solemnly pledged itself, "in the name of the revolutionaries and before the nation and the entire world," to abandon all violence and to "work henceforth for the good of the people."

Contrary to its expectations, no attempt at a rising followed the death of Alexander II. The revolutionaries, virtually all of whose forces had been consumed during the period of terrorism and the majority of whose most active militants were arrested within twenty-four hours of the assassination, lacked leaders and staff; they themselves were too few in number to foment a revolt. Furthermore, the popular masses, on whose spontaneous upsurge they had counted, did not stir. Completely outside the political combat being waged by a fraction of the educated class, the masses did not always understand its significance; worse, in some instances they were even unaware of its existence. In spite of extremely harsh living conditions, the people was infinitely far from the state of ferment in which the revolutionaries liked to imagine it. In any case, if the masses were discontented, their target was not the imperial power; to them the tsar seemed rather to be a potential protector in their struggle to stay alive. Hence it was not the assassination of the tsar that could unleash the revolt of the peasant and worker masses, which were totally lacking in all organization. In some areas, in fact, the peasants saw the assassination as nothing but an act of vengeance by the nobility against the man who had set them free. The militants of The Will of the People were equally disillusioned by the reaction of the educated classes to the assassination of 1/13 March. The liberal groups were too loosely organized, they were too vulnerable to the reprisals of the government not to be afraid of compromising themselves by association with the revolutionaries. Hence the liberal movement that was expected by the revolutionaries had no breadth. It was confined to a few demonstrations, none of them well supported, on the part of one or another zemstvo or assembly of the nobility, which addressed petitions to the government calling on it to summon the delegates of the people and thus to take cognizance of the real needs and grievances of the nation. Although these petitions were drenched in fealty and moderation, and, unprecedented as they were, arrested the government's attention, they were no more able, if only because they were so few, than the similar requests made by rare individuals to make any deep impression.

The regicide had been vain. Not only was the revolutionary organization, which demanded the abolition of autocracy, totally cut off; it continued to grow rapidly weaker. Those of its leaders who had not been executed at the same time as the direct participants in the assassination, or sentenced to forced labor either for long terms or for life, had to flee abroad. By the beginning of 1883, only one member of the whole central executive committee of The Will of the People, so dreaded only yesterday, was still in Russia and free: Vera Gifner. Betrayed by a revolutionary who had sold out to the police, she herself was arrested a few months later. Those revolutionaries who had eluded the police tried to reorganize the central executive committee and the whole organization of The Will of the People. But German Lopatin, who with a few comrades had returned from exile for this express purpose, was soon arrested too; within a short time the police had succeeded in rounding up all the most active revolutionaries who were still seeking to extend the work of their predecessors. This time The Will of the People, which had succeeded in a few new assassinations of supporters of the autocracies, was smashed; it was never to rise again.

Its defeat brought about the cessation of the social and political movement. When it turned its back on terrorism, the nation, which lacked political experience and had been unable to create any organization apart from secret conspiratorial groups, abandoned politics at the same time. Terrorized and depressed by the savage reaction that was to rage throughout the country, the boldest minds would apply themselves henceforth to maintaining quiet lives in their own circles and restricting their activities to the purely intellectual. Without a protest they were to accept all the harassments to which the government would resort in order to accomplish its ideal of a "firm power." Only a few sudden outbursts of the spirit of revolt amid the general apathy would remind the country that the combat that had been broken off might one day be renewed. Thus, in 1887, seven conspirators planned to kill Alexander III. Six of them were students at the University of Petersburg; the seventh was a young man who had just completed his courses in the Ecclesiastical Academy. Having discovered their plot, the police allowed them to complete their preparations and did not arrest them until the very moment when, bombs in hand, they went out into the streets to lie in wait for the tsar to pass. They were tried and five of them were hanged; the two others were imprisoned in the fortress of Schlüsselburg. One of the hanged men was Ulyanov, whose brother, under the name of Vladimir Ilyitch Lenin, was to be the future founder of the Soviet state. But these men were alone. They had the support of no powerful organization, they had no ties with the old revolutionaries, and they did not hand on their mission to any followers.

The Conflict Between Loris-Melikov and Pobyedonostsev and the Victory of the Conservatives

The new government did not give a moment's consideration to the notion of yielding to the demands put forth by The Will of the People in its letter to the emperor. But what was government policy to be? Loris-Melikov considered it necessary to continue the system that he had established during the last months of the reign of Alexander II: on the one hand, the harshest repression of revolutionary activity; on the other, the execution of reforms capable at once of satisfying the urgent needs of the people and assuaging that part of enlightened opinion that, for all its sympathy with liberal thinking, did not favor a drastic change in the social and political order. Other members of the government, however, believed that Loris-Melikov was going too far down the dangerous road of liberal concessions and that the repressions of the revolutionaries, if they were to be effective and really to restore calm in the country, ought to be supplemented by a vigorous conservative—or, more accurately, reactionary—policy. These forces were headed by Pobyedonostsev, who had become attorney general of the Holy Synod not long before the death of Alexander II and thus a member of the Cabinet. Under the last tsar he had been content merely to withhold support from Loris-Melikov's policy. But from the very start of the new reign Pobyedonostsev launched open war on it.

Just before his death Alexander II had agreed to convene a special commission consisting of a certain number of delegates from the provincial assemblies in order to discuss various draft laws proposed by the government in advance of their submission to the Imperial Council. Loris-Melikov stood firm on the necessity of ratifying and announcing this decision without delay. Alexander III offered no opposition, but he preferred first to put the matter before a special committee composed of the ministers, the department chiefs of the Imperial Council, a few grand dukes, and old Count S. G. Stroganov, who had once been the first tutor of the children of Alexander II. The sessions of this committee, scheduled for 6/18 March, five days after the assassination, gave Loris-Melikov's antagonists the opportunity to wage an all-out attack against him. Count Stroganov opened the assault. He denounced the reform project as deadly, because, if it was adopted, "power would pass out of the hands of the absolute sovereign, who today is thoroughly indispensable to Russia, into the hands of a band of scoundrels who have no interest in the public welfare but think only of their own gains." Turning toward the tsar, he added: "This road leads directly to a constitution, which I want none of either for you or for Russia." Makov, minister of posts, voiced the same views: to him the proposal was nothing but "a curb on absolute power"; "its realization would drag Russia down into ruin . . . ; in the troubled times through which the nation is living today, there must be no thought but that of strengthening power and repressing revolt." As for Pobyedonostsev, he presented a remarkably pathetic oration. He too declared that the "drafting commission" proposed by Loris-Melikov would lead to a limitation on absolute power. "There is a desire to introduce a constitution into Russia," he cried, "or at least to take the first step in this direction. . . . Now what is a constitution? Western Europe offers us the answer to this question. The constitutions that prevail there serve as the instruments of every injustice, every plot. . . . The elected representatives never express the opinion of the people. And does someone want to ruin us, to destroy us by endowing us with this optical illusion of foreign origin with which we have no concern? Russia has been powerful thanks to her autocracy, thanks to the unbounded mutual trust and the close bonds that unite the people with its tsar. . . . Those who are called zemstvo delegates are merely driving a wedge between the tsar and the people." Through the misdoing of "frivolous babblers," he proceeded, Russian political life had turned off on to the wrong road. The serfs had been freed without any simultaneous creation of a strong authority, "without which the unlettered masses cannot function." In contrast, what had been done was to set up provincial and municipal institutions, idle "debating societies," and new judicial institutions, "haggling rooms for lawyers"; worst of all there was now freedom of the press, "the worst of all tongue-waggers," which "blames and criticizes the authorities." Now it was proposed, on foreign models, to establish "a supreme talk-shop," and that at the very time "when the mortal remains of the great-hearted tsar who was brought down by Russians in broad daylight have not even found their sepulcher."

In the ensuing debate, Loris-Melikov and Prime Minister Valuev, War Minister Miliutin, Finance Minister Abaza, Education Minister Saburov, Justice Minister Nabokov, State Controller Solsky, and Grand Duke Konstantin endeavored to prove that the proposal "contains not even the shadow of a constitution," that "the proposed drafting commission is merely a consultative organ that could not restrict government decision, and that its creation would be highly useful because it would give satisfaction to the great mass that has remained loyal and it would let the government know the needs of the people."

Loris-Melikov's proposal was neither rejected nor adopted; it was simply transmitted to a new commission. But the views of Alexander III had already taken shape. These views were unmistakably hostile to those ministers who had stood as the most resolute advocates of the plan. Pobyedonostsev set to with all his energies to reinforce these views in the tsar. He was totally successful. A few weeks later Alexander III wrote to him: "Today's meeting made a most painful impression on me. Loris, Miliutin, and Abaza are all positively pursuing the same policy and want to bring us in one way or another to representative government. But, as long as I remain unconvinced that Russia's happiness depends on it, obviously it is not going to happen. It is doubtful, furthermore, whether I shall ever be able to persuade my-

self of the usefulness of such a step; I am too certain that it is pernicious. . . . I am becoming more and more convinced that there is
nothing good to be expected from those ministers." While he was
turning his former pupil against Loris-Melikov and those ministers
who stood with him, Pobyedonostsev was no more sparing of the tsar's
uncle, Grand Duke Konstantin. He made the grand duke appear as
not only an advocate of limitations on absolute power but also a pre-
tender to the throne; Pobyedonostsev even offered the suspicion that
Konstantin had been involved in the revolutionary conspiracy that
had brought about the death of Alexander II, and in every way the
old tutor piled fuel on the fires of suspicion in the tsar's mind. In
addition he urgently counseled Alexander III to make a show of his
strong will in all circumstances, and he tried to demonstrate to the tsar
that society would not be restored to order "as long as the government
abstains from making its power clear through actions unmistakable
enough to leave no doubt in anyone's mind." He assured Alexander
that it was essential for him to present the people with a manifesto
devoid of "any ambiguity," and he volunteered to write it. Pobyedonostsev busied himself with the collection and transmission of private
letters and memoranda, all written by men who were striving to demonstrate the necessity of preserving the imperiled autocracy and to
portray Loris-Melikov as a man of fearsome ambitions who, led astray
by his liberal illusions, had been unable to protect the life of Alexander II. These innuendoes and counsels soon bore their fruit.

The ministers [Alexander III wrote to his brother Vladimir on 27 April/
9 May], are always promising me that they will adopt measures that will implement my manifesto, but, in view of the fact that I can never get any
decisive action out of them and that in the meantime minds persist in their
anxiety and many people anticipate something remarkable, I have decided to
turn to K. P. Pobyedonostsev and bid him to draft a proposed manifesto for
me. In this manifesto the course that I wish things to take will have to be
described in an unequivocal fashion, as well as my intention never to subscribe to any limitation on absolute power, which I regard as useful and
necessary for Russia.

None of the ministers had been told of the assignment conferred
on—more accurately, requested by—Pobyedonostsev. They learned of
it only after the manifesto had been finally approved and the decision
to issue it had been made. In it the sovereign expressed his trust in
"the force and justice of absolute power" and proclaimed his determination "to reinforce it and to protect it, for the good of the people,
against all attack." There could no longer be the least doubt of the
tsar's distrust of his chief counselors. Therefore, when the manifesto

was published on 29 April/11 May, Loris-Melikov, Miliutin, and Abaza resigned. Saburov, minister of public education, had already done so for other reasons; he had been replaced by Baron Nikolai. Alexander III was also expecting Grand Duke Konstantin to resign his post as admiral-general. But the grand duke had no intention of doing so; therefore his imperial nephew, who could not suffer his presence within the government, himself dismissed him. Pobyedonostsev had a victory to celebrate: the most competent of the liberal ministers at the end of the reign of Alexander II had been ousted from the new government.

The Last Resistance by the Liberals and the Work of Bunge and Ignatyev

The conservatives' victory was not yet complete. The selection of new ministers, in practice, did not depend entirely on the ideas and the wishes of Pobyedonostsev and his supporters. Count Ignatyev replaced Loris-Melikov as minister of the interior, and Bunge succeeded Abaza, whose under-secretary of state he had been, as minister of finance. Both men, like Baron Nikolai, who was in charge of education, were unwilling to repudiate all the policies of the preceding government. Certainly there was no further question of having elected delegates take part in the preparation of laws, but the reform plans conceived under Loris-Melikov with a view of improving the economic situation of the popular masses continued to occupy the attention of the new ministers, especially Bunge. He adopted a series of measures, some already elaborated by his predecessor, some of his own conception.

First of all he eased the tax burden on the peasants. Under conditions formulated by the government, he established the compulsory redemption of peasants' land in all cases in which this transaction had not yet been concluded through voluntary bargaining between the peasants and their former owners. Furthermore, since this procedure had already shown considerable profit for the state but the solvency of the peasant population had been substantially impaired, he made some reductions in the purchase price. For the same reasons, and for others of a legal nature as well, he also ordered the promulgation of a law for the reduction and, subsequently, the complete abolition of the head tax, which fell exclusively on the lower classes of society. At the same time, in order to counter the losses that this would impose on the Treasury, he immediately took another step that was hardly in accord with the principles of social justice. By requiring, in effect, that the obligation of buying their land be extended to the state peasants, he compelled them, in order to amortize their debts, to make annual payments to the Treasury, and these were a far heavier burden than the rental and use payments that the peasants had formerly had to make. Thus a large part of the fiscal burdens that had been removed from the peasant class as a whole fell back on a special category of peasants, who, it was true, often enjoyed a privileged economic position in comparison with their fellows. In addition to these partial modifications in the tax system, Bunge reduced the hitherto monopolistic part played by the police in the collection of taxes. He created a corps of tax inspectors whose double duty it was to supervise the collection of taxes and to examine the solvency of the taxpayers.

Simultaneously with his relaxation of the fiscal burdens on the majority of the peasants, he was seeking to assure them of stronger support from the state and to revive the rural economy. Since 1880 it had been apparent that the shortage of land resulting from the execution of the 1861 reform was, with the burden of taxation, a fundamental obstacle to any improvement in the situation of the peasants. The first remedy that was required was the enlargement of the area of peasant holdings. Bunge devoted himself to the solution of this problem. With Ignatyev's backing, he succeeded in bringing about the establishment of a State Peasant Bank, which would make loans to help the poorest peasants to acquire land and to which, initially, the state allocated an annual subsidy of 5 million rubles.

Bunge also dedicated great efforts to improving the workers' conditions of employment. Russian legislation had never, properly speaking, concerned itself with the matter and had made virtually no attempts at regulation. The internal organization of factories and workshops and the relations between employers and workers were the product of free negotiation between the parties, which in practice amounted to the imposition of the owners' tyrannies on their workers. To these there were no existing limits. In the government of Moscow in 1880, for example, the working day was rarely shorter than twelve hours; as a rule it was thirteen or thirteen and a half, and there were instances in which it ran as long as fifteen hours and even more; in the other industrial regions the fourteen- or fifteen-hour day was by no means a rare exception. Furthermore, there were no rules at all governing work by women and children, and both were abominably exploited by their employers. Moreover, many employers made it obligatory for their workers to buy all their needs from the special stores set up by the employers, whose prices had no ceilings and enabled the employers to make double or triple profits at the expense of the workers. Bunge sought to provide some legal protection at least for women and children employed in industry. A series of laws initiated in 1882 limited the length of the working day for them and established governmental control over their working conditions. The state-appointed factory inspectors who were assigned to supervise compliance with ministerial decrees and collect information on workers' living conditions.

This worker and peasant legislation was a mere palliative whose intrinsic inadequacy was emphasized by the deficiencies in its application. Legal protection was intended only for the labor of women and children, and the government appointed so few factory inspectors that in practice most industrial enterprises were exempt from all supervision. Similarly, the niggardly assets available to the Peasant Bank prevented it from engaging in operations of any great scope. Moreover, in the light of the economic circumstances of the impoverished peasants for whose benefit it had been established, the terms of its loans were too harsh. Within three years, consequently, there was a high total of unpaid arrearages, and the bank became apprehensive and began hastily to foreclose and sell off its debtors' holdings; then too it altered its policy and began to look for its borrowers among the peasants who were already more prosperous. The reduction in the peasants' tax burden, though it was not inconsiderable, was nevertheless insufficient. In spite of all these defects, Bunge's efforts did improve the lot of the popular masses, particularly the peasants. By smoothing out the difficulties that had been created by the reform of 1861—and that were already glaring at the end of the reign of Alexander II—Bunge furthered the task that Loris-Melikov had set himself.

Count Ignatyev, Loris-Melikov's direct successor in the Ministry of the Interior, aligned himself with Bunge. Although he did not disown his predecessor's concept of associating the population with the work of its government, he resorted to more cautious means for its accomplishment. Instead of calling together elected zemstvo and urban representatives, as Loris-Melikov had intended, he himself selected, among those men in the provinces who had gained distinction by their public activities, certain "competences" with whom he conferred on the government's proposed measures. He employed this method on two occasions in 1881, presenting a number of questions that were of concern to the government for consideration by the "competences." He went further. In agreement with the Slavophile circles, by which he was influenced, he sought to reestablish the ancient *Zemsky Sobor*, "in order to enable the tsar to consult the country." In this assembly, which was to be purely consultative, he wished to gather the high dignitaries of the Orthodox church, the members of the Imperial

Council and the Senate, the ministers, the marshals of the nobility of all the governments, the mayors of provincial capitals and of some district capitals, and the delegates of all the social classes and all the territories of Russia. He hoped to make its first session coincide with the day of the new tsar's coronation, and in May 1882, with this end in view, he drafted the proposed manifesto that he intended to submit for the tsar's signature.

It was this project that caused his downfall. The conservatives had not got rid of Loris-Melikov in order to keep his policies alive, even in the attenuated form given to them by Ignatyev. Besides, the archaic character of his ideas cost the new minister of the interior the sympathies of the liberals as well. Thus, with the vigorous support of Katkov, Pobyedonostsev had no difficulty in obtaining the rejection of these proposals and completely discrediting their author in the eyes of the tsar. Ignatyev was removed from office.

The Triumph of Reaction and the Appointment of Tolstoi as Minister of the Interior

On the advice of Pobyedonostsev, Alexander III replaced Ignatyev with Count D. A. Tolstoi, formerly minister of public education under Alexander II until that tsar had dismissed him at the instigation of Loris-Melikov. Tolstoi's appointment signaled the final victory of the reactionary group under Pobyedonostsev's leadership. Thereafter power was in the hands of a spokesman of the provincial nobility, an adherent of reaction, who was determined to achieve, with persistence and methodical procedure, that basic idea of the nobility that a contemporary memorandum phrased in these words: "Each canton must be ruled by a mayor of noble stock." In his very first conversation with Alexander III, who had sent for him in order to apprise him of his appointment, Tolstoi told the tsar that he "absolutely knew nothing of any peasant Russia." If there was a peasant Russia, for him it was merely an amorphous mass intended to be molded by the Russia of the nobility. "Your ancestors," he told the tsar, "created Russia, but they created it with our hands." It was his intention that the function that he attributed to the nobility in the past be preserved to it in the present and the future. Thus he was the resolute adversary of all the reforms of Alexander II that had in any way impaired the privileges of the nobles, and he conceived it to be his task to work for the restoration of those privileges, fully prepared to change any institutions and methods of the previous reign that were out of harmony with his conception. To restore the nobility's political preponderance, to protect its economic interests by every possible means, to guarantee it as privileged a place as possible in the social hierarchy: this was Tolstoi's program, and it became the government's as well. During the celebrations of his coronation in 1882, Alexander addressed the cantonal leaders, who had been invited to the ceremony in the character of peasant delegates, and he called on them to place no credence in tendentious rumors of a new redistribution of the land; he urged them emphatically to obey always and unquestioningly "their" marshals of the nobility. What this meant was that he regarded the marshals of the nobility as the natural and legitimate, if not the direct, leaders of the peasant class. Three years later, in the manifesto that he issued in 1885 on the occasion of the centennial of the charter granted by Catherine II to the nobility in 1785, he expressed the hope that he would see, in the future as in the past, "the Russian nobles preserve their preponderance in the command of the army, in local government, in the courts, and in the propagation, by their example, of the precepts of faith and fidelity, as well as of sound principles of popular education."

II / SOCIAL, ADMINISTRATIVE, AND RELIGIOUS REACTIONISM

The Creation of the Bank of the Nobility

The manifesto of 1885 also announced the creation of a special Bank of the Nobility, the purpose of which was to safeguard and advance the material position of the landed nobility. The brainchild of Tolstoi, the new bank offered mortgage loans to noble landowners in search of credit, and on terms much more favorable than those set for the clients of the Peasant Bank. Through these privileged loans Tolstoi hoped to halt the rapid decline in the nobility's landed wealth and to make it possible for the nobles to rebuild their fortunes. The average nobleman immediately gave all his confidence to the bank, and the mere possibility of obtaining state loans at reduced rates assuaged the anguish of an army of bankrupt aristocrats. But the many loans granted by the bank were only rarely employed for the improvement of the land. In fact, as it was soon to become apparent, the operations of the Bank of the Nobility led to results quite different from what had been anticipated. The loans were used not so much for the reinforcement of the nobility's landed property as for the increase of its burden of debts.

The creation of the Bank of the Nobility was followed by a series of measures, this time juridical in nature, all of which tended toward the reconstruction of a system based on distinctions among social classes.

The Inauguration of "Rural Chiefs" and Judicial Reactionism

Convinced that what was in fact essential was to organize "a firm governmental power close to the people" and founded on the principle of division into castes, Tolstoi proposed to inaugurate a new judicial and administrative arm, the *zemsky nachalnik*, or "rural chief." This proposal was so contrary to all existing judicial and administrative customs and so thoroughly confounded them that the Imperial Council, for all its conservatism, opposed it by an effective majority. But Alexander III endorsed it, and in 1889 he gave it the force of law.

Everywhere, except in a small number of major cities, the new law abolished the elective justice of the peace created by Alexander II. In the cities it replaced him with municipal judges appointed by the minister of justice, on whom they were in part dependent; in the districts the Minister of the Interior appointed the "rural chiefs," recommended by the marshals of the nobility from the noblemen of the region. The rural chiefs had complex functions. Besides serving as judges for the entire population in their districts and supervisors of the peasant tribunals in their cantons,* they were administrators exercising broad powers over the peasant population and its elected representatives; these powers included the right to impose disciplinary punishments. No great schooling was needed to become a rural chief: any noble who owned a stipulated number of *desyatini* in the district could get the job, not only without having studied law but even without having completed his secondary education. Thus the peasant class was turned back to all-powerful noble guardians, for whom birth alone was adequate compensation for ignorance, and who were recruited with the cooperation of the nobility but who were entirely dependent on the governors. It was obvious that, in the performance of their duties, these guardians, in whom Tolstoi incarnated his "firm power close to the people," would be largely guided by caste prejudices and would ignore legality in favor of whim and despotism. But there was nothing in such a prospect to perturb the minister: fundamentally, he had forseen it when he created the rural chiefs, and it was what he wanted.

Reaction in the judiciary was not restricted to the virtually complete elimination of the justice of the peace. In 1885 the principle of judicial independence and permanency of tenure was abolished in fact: the minister of justice was empowered to call on any judge at any time to defend his work; in certain cases the minister could resort to such

*See p. 16.

disciplinary measures as transfer or dismissal. In 1887 limitations were placed on public court proceedings. In 1889 the normal court of first instance was stripped of its jurisdiction over cases in which the government was particularly interested.

The Rule of Authoritarianism

Under Tolstoi the field was opened wide to authoritarianism, especially in the administration, where it was in full accord with the old traditions of Russian bureaucracy and where higher officials were amply equipped with means of exerting pressure on their subordinates. Immediately on taking office, the minister of the interior appointed and encouraged, by preference, those governors who were determined to support the nobility and in no way allow themselves to be hampered by law in the application of the concept of a "firm power," especially when it was a question of the peasants. The governors speedily adopted the minister's point of view and saw to it that it was diffused among their subordinates. Administrative tyranny, which it had been sought to limit during the previous reign, sprang up again everywhere. Its major representatives crowned their careers with membership in the Imperial Council and the Senate, the highest bodies in the country. Those who were thus rewarded were sometimes so compromised that in 1890 Manassein, minister of justice, as accommodating a servitor as he was, nevertheless petitioned Alexander III "to take pity on the Senate and not humiliate it by appointing dubious members to it" and not to include in its membership certain honorary governors whose nomination might "represent an affront to the other senators." Such requests, of course, made no change in the established order.

The Limitation of Provincial and Municipal Autonomy

The system of authoritarianism could not be adapted to local self-government even when this was merely relative. Therefore Tolstoi proposed drastic changes in the zemstvo and the municipal institutions and the application of the principles of bureaucratic administration to them as to the rest of the governmental machinery. He died before he could achieve his plans. But his successor, I. N. Durnovo, who pursued the same policy, radically altered the status of zemstvo and city through the laws of 1890 and 1892.

The 1890 law on the zemstvo introduced the principle of the hierarchy of social classes into the election of delegates to the provincial assemblies, increasing the percentage of noble delegates at the expense of all the rest. In thirty governments before 1890, the nobles and the officials held 42 per cent or 43 per cent and the peasants 38 per cent or 39 per cent of the total delegations in the district zemstvo. After 1890 the share of the nobles in these governments was 57.1 per cent, the urban and rural middle class had 13.3 per cent, and the peasants had 29.6 per cent. Furthermore, the peasants could no longer elect their delegates directly: they voted for candidates, among whom the governor chose delegates. But in practice these candidates were pre-selected by the rural chiefs. Thus constituted, the zemstvo was wholly dominated by the nobility and the agents of government. In addition it was subjected to governmental supervision. Now it was only the legality but the wisdom of the decisions of the zemstvo on which the governor could rule; he had the right to veto whatever he regarded as contrary to the general needs of the state or clearly prejudicial to local interests. Finally, in certain instances, the government reserved for itself even the right to appoint the members of the permanent delegation of the zemstvo.

The law of 1892, which modified the "statute of the cities," was conceived in the same spirit. The former electoral system of "three classes" was replaced by the system of election districts, but the property qualification for the suffrage was increased and thus the number of voters was substantially lowered: in Petersburg it fell from twenty-one to eight thousand, in Moscow from twenty to seven thousand, and in all the other cities in virtually the same proportion. The law also reduced the number of municipal councilors provided by the "Statute" of 1870. Thus the management of municipal affairs became the monopoly of a very tight circle of men who represented the richest part of the population and also that least concerned with good city government. At the same time the cities were made more closely dependent on the central administration. All decisions of municipal councils had to be approved by the administration, which, here again, concerned itself not only with their legality but also with their wisdom. The mayors and the members of the executive bureaus elected by the councils had to be confirmed by the authorities. Moreover, all their work was closely supervised by the central government on which, at bottom, they were more dependent than on the municipal councils that had elected them. In spite of their elective character, they had become no more, so to speak, than functionaries of the central administration. The municipal institutions, in sum—perhaps even more than the zemstvo—were thrust under strict bureaucratic tutelage with a view to preserving the political order and defending the interest of the privileged classes.

The Russification of the Border Provinces

After the Polish insurrection of 1863, ultra-conservatism and Russian nationalism tended to merge into each other. Every assault against the political system was viewed as an attack committed or inspired by local "natives" against the old Russian traditions. Therefore the nationalists insisted on the necessity of making certain that everywhere and in everything there was an absolute preponderance of the Russian element over the "natives." When it opted for the road of reaction the government embraced the program of nationalism as its own and adopted a policy that was sharply hostile to regions of non-Russian population as it was to local tribes in general. The policy of Russification was especially vigorous in the grand duchy of Finland and in Poland.

Alexander II had treated Finland as a state united with Russia and provided with an individual organization guaranteed by its own constitution. He had officially granted Finland a special military status. Alexander III began by following his father's policy. In 1881 he started to establish Finnish military units. In 1886 he granted the Finnish Diet the right to initiate legislation. But, as his reactionary policy grew sharper, he began more and more to look on Finland as a mere province incorporated into Russia, whose individual system and institutions could be altered by the unilateral will of the Russian absolute sovereign, and in various ways he endeavored to bind Finland more tightly to Russia. In 1890 he placed the Finnish postal and telegraphic services under the Russian Ministry of the Interior. In the same year, on the pretext that it was out of harmony with Russian laws, he suspended the application of the Finnish Penal Code, which had been voted by the Diet and which he himself had ratified only a year before. Modified and thus submitted to the Diet, which adopted it, this code was confirmed in 1892 and its effective date was fixed for 1894. These steps, and especially the comments to which they gave rise in government circles, whose desire to disregard the Finnish constitution was apparent, made a profound impression in Finland. Public opinion in the grand duchy, which had always been virtually unanimous in its manifestations of complete loyalty, began to change, and the idea of struggle against the imperial power for the defense of the country's freedoms became more and more popular.

In Poland Alexander III continued the rigorous application of the harsh system established after the 1863 insurrection. He hoped in this way to rob the Poles of their last illusions on the independence of their country and thus to bind the Polish provinces more closely to Russia. In official documents the very name of the *Kingdom of Poland,* which evoked the idea of a distinct and separate country, was replaced by a new term, the *Region of the Vistula.* In order to Russianize the entire administration of the country as much as possible, Poles were barred from public employment in their own country and in the governments bordering on western Russia; public officials of Polish origin and Catholic allegiance were permitted only in the provinces at the center of the empire. In 1885 the use of Russian except for teaching the catechism and the native speech of the pupils was made mandatory in elementary and secondary schools.* In 1892 it was extended to the teaching even of the Catholic religion. At the same time, "as a result of the current absolute impossibility of establishing general supervision in the combat against certain secret procedures of Polish Catholic propaganda, and especially against clandestine education," the government issued a "provisional regulation relative to the measures to be taken against clandestine education in the governments of the northwest and the southwest." This was an extremely harsh order: to teach children in their native language became a crime subject to severe punishment by the authorities. Far, of course, from attaining the desired result, this policy only augmented the Polish population's hostility to the autocracy and its repulsion to the Russian language and civilization that it sought to force on the Poles.

In 1887 consideration had been given to compulsory teaching of the Russian language in the Moslem higher institutions; but in 1890, because of the fear of Moslem opposition, the government confined itself to ordering all members of the Islamic clergy to know Russian. In the Caucasus too, although it was more moderate there, Russification led to the resistance of the local population against Russian domination and prepared fertile soil for separatist movements.

The Policy of Anti-Semitism

The government's hostility and suspicion toward non-Russian peoples was particularly evident against the Jews, whose rights, even

*In 1887 the same step was taken in the Baltic provinces and in 1889 it was broadened to include all private schools. Three gymnasia that refused to conform were closed by order of the tsar.

though they had already been rigidly restricted, were constantly being further reduced throughout the reign.

First of all, the extent of the territory on which their presence was tolerated, the famous "residence zone," was markedly diminished. In 1882 they were forbidden to live in the rural areas of the "zone" itself, and—on the pretext of protecting the peasants against possible exploitation by them—to acquire buildings there. In 1887 access to the cities of Rostov on the Don and Taganrog was prohibited to them, except for a few categories among them that were anything but numerous. In 1891 a new restriction gravely damaged a large number of them. Jewish artisans, who although they could not obtain the necessary licenses, had previously been permitted to establish themselves outside the "residence zone," were now forbidden to enter the city and the government of Moscow. The consequences of this ban were all the more serious because it was made retroactive: seventeen thousand persons were turned out of their homes; a very large number suffered very heavy economic losses, some of them being utterly ruined.

Every effort was made, moreover, to keep the Jews out of the liberal professions. In 1887 the inception of the *numerus clausus* restricted the number of those who might be admitted to institutions of secondary and higher education. In order to "establish a more normal proportion between the numbers of Jewish and Christian students," a ministerial bulletin established a Jewish quota of 10 per cent in the "residence zone," 5 per cent outside that zone, and 3 per cent in Petersburg and Moscow. While the wealthier Jews, if they had to do so, could get round the restrictions by having their children tutored at home or by sending them to schools abroad, the less fortunate, who were also the more numerous, were thus effectively prevented from giving their children an education of any extent. In 1889 Jewish aspirants to the bar lost some of the rights that were normally conferred by the diploma: they could not practice law professionally and, even when they had completed their clerkships, they remained clerks. This injustice condemned brilliant lawyers, some of whom were the glory of the Russian bar, to a humiliating position.

Finally, still persisting in viewing the Jews as only a kind of second-class citizens, the government totally erased them from the municipal voting lists through the Statute of the Cities of 1892. In cities in the "residence zone" the administration had the right of choosing a certain number of city councilors among those Jews who, if they had not been Jews, would have met the qualifications for suffrage, but the number of such councilors could not exceed 10 per cent of all the councilors.

Religious Reactionism

The anti-Semitic policy, which was aimed not only at the Jewish religion but also at the Jewish "race," was accompanied by a purely religious reaction. The government, which advocated a return to the "age-old Russian traditions," in particular the close union of the throne and the altar, wanted to support the state religion. It devoted every means, including persecution, to this end.

At the same time, it not only forbade the Kalmuki and the Buriates, who belonged to the Lamaïc faith, to build shrines and practice their rituals, but also strove with vigorous propaganda to win them over to Orthodoxy; the authorities laid a heavy hand on those who, having become converts if only *pro forma*, sought afterward to return to their former faith.

Catholics and Lutherans were likewise the targets of harassment. But the most harshly dealt with of all were those who had left the Orthodox church, especially the rationalist sects of the *Pneunamotomachi (Dukhobori)* and the *Stunde,** which were at that time very widespread among the peasants. Led and egged on by Pobyedonostsev, the Orthodox clergy sent special missionaries to battle these sects, and forceful backing was supplied by the authorities. Again at the instigation of Pobyedonostsev, outright persecutions were launched against them. Their religious gatherings were prohibited and broken up by the police, and their propagandists and their most zealous and stubborn disciples were deported. At times their children were taken from them by force, to be brought up under "better" influences.

In this official alliance of throne and altar, whose methods of action recalled those of the Middle Ages, there was more fanaticism than genuine faith. What the government was protecting in the dominant church, which it had subjugated and made the instrument of a predetermined political doctrine, was solely the defender of that doctrine. That was why some of the Orthodox clerics—the more conscientious and the more sincere—seemed to have so much difficulty in accommodating themselves to the situation that had been created for them, but they lacked the courage to stand out openly in opposition to it and were satisfied to nurse an unspoken resentment.

---

*The *Pneumatomachi* (also known as the Macedonian heretics, who followed Macedonius, a fourth-century bishop of Constantinople) denied the uncreated nature of the Holy Spirit.—Translator. The *Stunde* was a sect of German origin whose members assembled to perform all their religious practices in common.— Author.

III / REACTION IN EDUCATION AND CULTURE

Public education could not be immune to the universal reaction. Not only did the conservatives want to delay the evolution of the country; they sought in fact to lead it backward. For this they could see only one means: to arrest the intellectual advance of the people. This was the direction toward which, beginning early in 1882, all governmental measures were oriented. At that time, on the recommendation of Pobyedonostsev, Delyanov became minister of public education. Like Count Tolstoi in the Interior, he became the docile, obsequious executant of the attorney general's program.

The Attacks on the Primary Schools

In 1884, with Delyanov's backing, Pobyedonostsev succeeded in obtaining the promulgation of a law that brought under the control of the Holy Synod all village primary schools of the most elementary kind, known as "ABC" schools. This step did not content him. He wanted to set the clergy's hands on all popular schools intended for the peasants in order to correct their errors and lead them along a "truly Russian" path. Under Alexander II, he said, "the ecclesiastical ideal of universal education was denatured by the mistaken and fantastic notion of the popular school, conceived as a means of spreading positive knowledge among the people with the help of artificial methods of teaching borrowed from foreign experience"; the real object of the popular school was to cultivate piety in the people and therefore only the church school could suitably perform the task. But this great project encountered obstacles that were not easy to overcome. First of all, the government could not ask the Treasury to meet all the expenses of primary education. Furthermore, the zemstvo, which had no confidence in the church school, stubbornly refused to hand over to the clergy either its schools or the funds that were allocated to them. Even after the law of 1890 had increased the nobility's representation in the provincial assemblies and reduced that of the peasant class to virtual nullity, the zemstvo clung faithfully to its educational policy. Compelled to give up the complete fulfillment of his plan, Pobyedonostsev restricted himself to setting up, side by side with the zemstvo schools, similar institutions administered by the local clergy and called parish schools. Each year, in the section of its budget devoted to the Holy Synod, the government allocated substantial sums for their establishment and maintenance. Furthermore it protected them against the competition of the zemstvo by forbidding the establishment of a zemstvo school not only in any village where a parish school already existed but also in any where such a school was merely planned. Under such conditions the parish schools multiplied rapidly: from forty-five hundred in 1882 to almost thirty-two thousand in 1894. But the level of their education was always very low. The great majority of them, and, with even more reason, the old "ABC" schools, could not survive any comparison with the zemstvo schools. The Orthodox parish clerics, who, in general, remained totally aloof from the policy of militancy and who were mainly concerned with problems of a material nature, very simply took no interest in the pedagogical mission that was entrusted to them. In actuality the increase in the number of parish schools indicated a regression rather than an advance. By vigorously supporting these schools, the majority of which had only a precarious existence and often none, except on paper, and by exerting every effort, on the other hand, to hobble the activity of the zemstvo schools, which it deliberately hampered in their recruitment of teaching staffs and which it prevented from broadening their teaching programs, the government arrested the development of public education. It reduced schooling systematically to the most rudimentary needs of the villagers: reading and writing were the sole goals set for elementary schooling in rural areas.

This conception of the school led the government logically to restrict postschool education through books by allowing the people access to only a small part of the publications approved by the censor. In 1882 a very severe statute regulated the foundation and operation of free libraries and reading rooms. In 1889, on the pretext that "works that hardly match the intellectual level of the major users of free libraries and are not within their grasp" had made their way into these institutions, the scientific committee of the Ministry of Public Education was instructed to review their general catalogue. In 1890 a special rule established extremely severe control of libraries and authorized them to have only those books that were expressly approved by the scientific committee. Of the 12,000 titles available in Russian bookshops in 1890, only 1150, plus 450 textbooks, were permitted in the libraries. Even this number seemed too high for the authorities, and the Ministry began to give thought to cutting it down.

Reaction in Secondary Education

In principle Delyanov held that the secondary school, and in particular the classical Gymnasium, which was the gateway to the university, should be exclusively reserved to an elite composed of the upper layers of society. This was the conception to whose realization he dedicated himself.

In 1887 he proclaimed the necessity of "barring from the secondary schools those pupils whose parents' position is such that they ought not to aim for the Gymnasia or, later, the universities." Consequently, in order to close the doors of the Gymnasia to poor pupils whose parents could not afford to have them tutored at home for the admission examination for the secondary schools, he ordered the abolition of all the preparatory classes that already existed in the Gymnasia. In the same year, since this step seemed inadequate to them, certain ministers, including Pobyedonostsev, Tolstoi, and Delyanov, proposed specific legislation to prohibit access to the Gymnasium to every youth whose parents were of a social status inferior to that of merchants of the second guild. This proposal having been shunted aside because its realization seemed "premature and full of problems," they sought to reach the same end by way of ministerial orders. In 1887 Delyanov decreed that the trustees of school districts should thereafter admit to the secondary schools only those children "entrusted to persons" who had previously been found on investigation to be capable of exercising proper supervision over them at home and assuring them of the "conditions of comfort necessary to their scholastic pursuits"; all other applicants were to be "resolutely turned away" and directed to those "scholastic establishments whose programs require less time and are more suited to their environments." At the same time Delyanov raised the fees for the Gymnasium. Thus it would be possible "to eliminate from the Gymnasium the sons of coachmen, lackeys, cooks, laundresses, small shopkeepers, and other persons of that kind," and "not snatch these children, with perhaps the exception of a few who might be gifted with unusual capacities, out of the environment in which they belong and thus, as long experience has proved, lead them to hold their parents in contempt, to be resentful of their own situations, and to revolt against the social inequalities that exist and that by the very nature of things are inevitable." This was an unmistakably clear reversion to the principles of the days of Nicholas I; the secondary school tended to become once more, if not the school of the nobility exclusively, at least that of the upper levels of society.

The organization of the secondary schools did not undergo any notable change. True, the program of the classical Gymnasium was revised in 1890, but this revision, which did not bear on fundamentals, was limited to some diminution of the ratio of classical instruction, which was chiefly grammatical, in favor of more concentration on religious education and more attention to the Russian language at the expense of Russian literature. As far as moral instruction was concerned, the school administration devoted itself almost exclusively to maintaining strict outer discipline among the pupils and guarding them from all "free thought." It was in fact a requirement that the pupils be kept completely ignorant of any idea or any conception that the government regarded as subversive. Calling on his teachers to maintain ceaseless watch over their pupils not only in the classroom but also outside the school and in their homes, the minister of public education continually reiterated in his bulletins that "teachers, headmasters, and inspectors will be liable to punishment if, in the classes entrusted to them, there is discovered any baneful influence of seditious ideas inspired by evil-minded individuals." Most of the time, consequently, teachers and pupils were divided by reciprocal distrust, and the physical life of the schools was weighed down under a gloomy, depressing formalism.

Naturally the government applied the same policy in the education of women. Delyanov criticized the secondary Gymnasia for girls for trying to attract those for whom elementary education would be more appropriate. "Moreover," he remarked in one of his reports to the tsar, "when the girls have completed their secondary studies they apply for admission to various higher institutions both in Russia and abroad; but what motivates the majority of them toward this is not so much a passion for study as the fallacious dream and wish to live apart from their families and their environments, to put aside their daily tasks in order to obtain rights that seem most inappropriate to their condition as women." Therefore he wanted to establish Gymnasia for girls where the course of study would be sensibly narrower than that for boys. His dream was not fulfilled; no schools of this kind were set up except in a few border regions of the empire and on the Don; but the Ministry of Public Education and the department of Tsarina Marya, which supported a certain number of full-fledged Gymnasia for girls, made no effort until the end of the reign to establish more of them.

The Enslavement of the Universities

In spite of a number of restrictions, the university statute of 1863 was still in force when Alexander III began his reign. Delyanov supplanted it with the statute of 1884, which in large part fulfilled for higher education the desires expressed by the reactionary press under Katkov's leadership.

The new statute abolished the autonomy of the university councils and completely subordinated the teaching corps to the Ministry. Henceforth rectors, deans, and professors would no longer be chosen by the university council but would be appointed by the minister. Moreover, the statute cut off the professors from the students. The inspectors charged with supervision of the students within the university precincts were independent of the council of professors and directly answerable to the trustees of the school districts. "State examinations" were no longer the province of the university schools; they were put into the hands of special juries appointed by the government. During their tenure in the university the students were regarded as "isolated visitors," who could not belong to any corporative organization. On admission they had to sign an oath not to join any secret group, even if it were devoid of all "criminal intent"; since there were no legally constituted student societies or clubs, because, however unexceptionable their purposes, virtually none was ever authorized, it was impossible for the students to sustain any consistent commerce with one another. Finally, in order to keep the poor out of the universities without fail, the statute almost trebled the existing fees and added a special tax for the benefit of the professors.* Three years later, in 1887, university fees alone were increased to 50 rubles— in other words, quintupled.

The enactment of the statute of 1884 made it possible for the government to be assured of the docility of administrative and teaching personnel. Professors with outstanding reputations but an excess of independence were made to resign. Young scholars who did not give evidence of sufficient tractability to the Ministry's views or whose political opinions did not seem "safe" enough were frequently denied access to professorships. A sickly climate little calculated to foster the growth of true learning invaded the universities.

The students, who were under the constant threat of stern administrative penalties for the most trivial offenses, were totally passive at first, and the government could hope that the statute of 1884 would be enough to restore calm among them and guide them back to the right road. But in 1887 serious disorders broke out in the Universities of Moscow, Kazan, and Petersburg. The students, who took part in large numbers, vigorously demanded the end of the degrading internal supervision, the reestablishment of the jurisdiction of the professorial council in all matters affecting students, the restoration of the council's autonomy, and the right of free association among students. The

*This was the German *Kollegiengeld* (lecture-fee) system.

government responded with harsh penalties: hundreds of young men were expelled from the universities and a large number of them, without trial, were exiled for long terms to distant provinces. Nevertheless, trouble broke out again three years later at the University of Petersburg, where the students made the same demands. However sternly the administration retaliated, it could not wholly stifle this movement of protest, which sprang up again on a number of occasions at various universities.

The Impotence of the Press

At the start of the reign the press endeavored to maintain a free and forceful utterance. The day after the assassination of 1/13 March 1881, *Strana (The Country)*, a liberal Petersburg newspaper, asserted that the existing system must be drastically altered, that the person of the tsar ought to be no more than the symbol "of national unity," and that it was the function of "the representatives of the country to set the course of internal policy and therefore to be responsible for it." Another liberal paper, *Golos (The Voice)*, endorsed this viewpoint. Both journals were at once given warnings by the minister of the interior, Loris-Melikov, who felt that "such remarkably out-of-place arguments" could have a disastrous influence.

His successor, Count Ignatyev, evidenced much more severity toward the press. He was not satisfied to send warnings to the newspapers; he suspended them for many months when they were not lucky enough to print what he liked. His excesses led *Poryhadok (Order)*, the most serious and the most intelligent of the liberal press, to suspend publication voluntarily at the beginning of 1882.

Count Tolstoi outstripped Ignatyev. As soon as he took over the Ministry of the Interior, he strengthened the rules that were already curbing the periodical press. Under the "provisional regulations" of August 1882 he decided that publications that were temporarily suspended after three warnings would have to submit to prior censorship as a condition of resuming publication. This censorship was so ordered that it made it impossible for newspapers to give their readers news that was not stale; by depriving them of the means of arousing their readers' interest, it in effect prevented them from staying alive. The "provisional regulations," moreover, endowed a special committee, composed of the ministers of the interior, justice, and public education and the attorney general of the Holy Synod, with the power to put permanently out of business any publication in which it found "pernicious tendencies" and to prohibit its editor from undertaking any new publishing venture whatever. Making extensive use of these new penalties, Tolstoi lost no time in making the existence of a liberal press virtually impossible. Almost all the liberal newspapers in Petersburg and Moscow had to stop publishing, and in the provinces, where the despotism of the local administration put teeth into the censor's yoke, there was no chance of publication for a liberal publication of any importance. The magazines shared the fate of the newspapers. Early in 1884 a review called *Otechestvennya Zapiski (The Fatherland Annals)*, edited by the famous satirist Saltykov and the eminent publicist, critic, and sociologist Mikhailovsky, whose contributors included many great writers and whose circulation was high in cultivated circles, was suspended. Its social-affairs section propagated the views of radicals and Socialists, who thus lost their most influential forum. Various other radical publications soon suffered the same fate. Finally the liberal press of the two capitals included only three publications: *Vyestnik Evropy (The European Messenger)*, a Petersburg magazine, and, in Moscow, *Russkya Vyedomosti (The Russian News)* and a magazine, *Russkaya Mysl (Russian Thought)*; even they lived under the constant menace of interdiction. On the other hand, the government strongly supported the reactionary press, which, under the leadership of Katkov and Suvorin, made fanatical war on all the institutions created under Alexander II and unwearyingly reiterated all the jargon of the most unbridled nationalism.

Coincidentally with the decline in the number of publications, the matter offered by the survivors was being visibly impoverished, under the double influence of governmental rigors and the general discouragement that had taken hold of the public. Such liberal journals as were left devoted themselves almost exclusively to the defense of what remained of local autonomy. They set themselves a special doctrine, that of "modest endeavors," the followers of which, who were numerous among those men whom politics had left disabused, aspired now to nothing more than the slow, gradual improvement of society. This state of mind was favorable to the diffusion of the ideas of Lev Tolstoi, who called on the intellectuals to "become simple," emphasized the necessity of moral reorientation, the sole inspiration for progress, and proclaimed the principle—the basic dogma of his theory —of "not resisting evil by violence." It was futile for the Orthodox clergy, led by Pobyedonostsev, and the civil authorities to wage their vigorous campaign against a doctrine that, in spite of its religious foundations, was flagrantly contradictory of the official religion. Just as in the previous decade clandestine revolutionary literature had been widely diffused among the educated youth, so Lev Tolstoi's writings, even though for the most part prohibited by the censor, continued to be printed and distributed in secret. A large sector of the youth was brought under the influence of "Tolstoism," which, while it drew them out of their revolutionary fantasies, also made them forget their dreary realities.

Socialism too continued to grow, but with modifications. The Socialists, who had refused to join The Will of the People and who had condemned terrorist activity, had founded the association called *Cherny Peredyel* ("The Black [i.e., General] Portion") in 1880, but its adherents, who, with Plekhanov and Akselrod, had completely embraced the sociological theory of Karl Marx, far from enlisting in The Will of the People, had drawn even farther away from it and were conducting a fierce campaign against it. Living abroad, where they published their propaganda texts, they were endeavoring to create a Social Democratic Party in Russia. About 1890 Social Democratic clubs began to take shape in Russian intellectual circles, and especially among the young in the schools; these groups categorically repudiated political terrorism and set as their purpose the organization of economic struggle by the factory workers against their employers. Social Democracy spread all the more easily because, in its original form of a relatively pacific economic doctrine, it was more suited than the revolutionary theory and practice of The Will of the People to the prevailing mood of discouragement.

This discouragement began to dwindle toward the end of the reign. Little by little a new generation was growing up that had known nothing of the zeal of the revolutionary or his frustrations, and it was beginning to inject itself into public life. Governmental policy, furthermore, which was directed only toward the consolidation of caste privileges, the oppression of the popular masses, and the persecution of every public activity and any independent thought, was creating grave repercussions on the economic life of the population, whose discontent was increasing. Its consequences were becoming evident by 1890, and the famine of 1891, which tore the last scales off the eyes of educated men, clearly revealed all its dangers. From that time forward, a new movement of social opposition emerged unmistakably. The tone of the Russian press grew sharper. New liberal magazines were founded. The number of scientific and sociological works devoted to current problems rose, and literary output became more varied. But the reign of Alexander III was to end before the press could substantially broaden its field of action.

IV / ECONOMIC POLICY

The government's economic policy, like its domestic policy, was aimed exclusively at the protection of the interests of the higher social classes, mainly those of the landed nobility. When the interests of the rest of the population were not specifically sacrificed to these goals, they were left in pure and simple oblivion.

Agrarian Policy

In order to foster the exploitation of the nobles' estates by assuring them of the labor force that they needed, a special law of 1886 set the conditions for the employment of farm workers: any such laborer hired for a specific term would be subject to penal action and could be compelled to return to his employer if he left his job before the expiration of his contract. In practice, the landowners preferred to resort to methods less obviously brutal in order to be certain of a cheap labor force: by granting loans to the peasants in their districts, or leasing lands to them, the nobles imposed on them the obligation of performing certain work for the lenders or landlords. But, though the law on the employment of farm workers remained a dead letter, it no less clearly demonstrated that the government would not boggle at any means, however harsh, to protect the landed property of its nobles.

In contrast it endeavored to limit the right of land ownership by peasants. In 1886, in order to create obstacles to the division of peasant holdings, a new law made it subject to the approval of the appropriate administrative authorities. After 1889 this approval was in practice almost the exclusive monopoly of the "rural chiefs"; since the majority of them, subservient to the instructions of the central authorities, disapproved of such distributions, they devoted their efforts to compelling the peasants not to convey. In 1893 a further law—the promulgation of which was of particular importance because the period of redemption was approaching its end—prohibited the peasants from selling the parcels that they had received under the 1861 reform to persons who were not members of the peasant community. Some theoreticians approved of this because they believed that it was essential, in the interests of the rural class itself, to protect and preserve the peasant community. But its purpose was not to prevent the peasants from becoming proletarians by alienating their land. Its intent was solely to deny them the right of full ownership of their parcels and to keep them on the land in order to assure the great landed proprietors of a continuing cutprice labor force.

Financial and Industrial Policy

In the first half of the reign, as long as Bunge was finance minister, the government was still interested in easing the harsh living conditions of the masses, revising the taxation system, and to some degree curbing the excessive exploitation of the factory workers. But this policy angered industrial and commercial circles, which criticized the government for neglecting the interests of Russian industry and were not backward in their assaults. Under their pressure Bunge was compelled to abandon his Ministry in 1887. He was succeeded by Vyshnegradsky, who to a large extent was the representative of industry and finance. During his term of office and that of Count Witte, who succeeded him in 1892 and who, in sum, was led by the same influences, financial and industrial policy was profoundly altered.

In the area of finance Vyshnegradsky dedicated his efforts to raising the foreign-exchange value of the Russian currency by making the Treasury take part in stock-market operations abroad. In order to carry out such operations on a large scale, he concentrated all his activity on accumulating large reserves of currency and placing them at the disposal of the Finance Ministry. In addition he endeavored to relieve the Treasury by reducing the burden of foreign debt: he paid off some of the older loans and negotiated new ones at lower interest rates and more distant maturity dates. The closer ties with France made it possible for him to offer a substantial part of the state bonds on the French market. All these activities, so different from Bunge's more cautious methods, failed, however, to bring any true assistance to Russian finances, and their success was more apparent than real.

Vyshnegradsky also instituted a new industrial policy. As soon as he was appointed, Russian industrialists plied him with evidence that Russian industry had received insufficient backing from his predecessor. He was receptive to this campaign and he endorsed the aspirations of the industrialists. Above all he endeavored, much more through ministerial orders rather than legislative means, to weaken the functioning and the importance of industrial regulations. Furthermore, by restoring industry's right to employ women and children more or less under its own terms, he nullified virtually all the steps that Bunge had taken to protect them against exploitation. And with the tariff of 1891 he reinforced customer protectionism. Of the 372 items included in this document, only 15 benefited from a reduction in import duties; 178 were left unchanged; 15 previously undutiable items were now subject to customs, and duties were increased on 164 others. Inasmuch as the increases, which were ordered mainly for items in general use, reached and even exceeded 20 per cent of the former duties, the tariff was clearly protectionist and was intended to bar many products of foreign origin from entry into Russia. Its enforcement compelled Witte, Vyshnegradsky's successor, to wage a customs war, with reasonable success, against Germany, which retaliated by making access to her markets difficult for Russian farm products.

Already benefiting from protectionism, industry also profited heavily from the rapid increase in the construction of railway lines. The total trackage of the rail network under Alexander III rose from 22,500 to 36,500 versts. Here the state was the dominant factor. It was chiefly the state that built the new lines. It made every effort, in addition, to buy out the old lines belonging to private companies. Between 1881 and 1894 it purchased twenty-four of them owned by fifteen companies and comprising 12,500 versts. In sum the state railway network was increased by 22,000 versts, while the private companies' trackage dropped to about 7500. Through the good offices of protectionism this huge network provided new markets for the mineralogical and metallurgical industries, which, under such powerful stimulation, were beginning to develop rapidly in southern Russia with the financial assistance of heavy foreign investment, chiefly French and Belgian. There was also another national industry that the state sought to encourage by building railways: the textile industry, whose home market was too poor to absorb its entire output. In order to provide it with outlets in central Asia, where Russia had just acquired immense territories, and in the Far East, the government began work in 1891 on the Trans-Siberian Railway, a giant ribbon of iron that was to cross all Siberia and join Moscow to Vladivostok.

The Industrialization of the Country and the Impoverishment of the Worker and Peasant Classes

The Finance Ministry's policy made notable contributions to the industrialization of the country. Many of the older industrial and commercial enterprises expanded, new ones arose in large numbers, and many towns that until now had been no more than insignificant settlements were transformed into great industrial centers. At the same time when it was constantly attracting more workers, industry was also becoming concentrated. Between 1881 and 1893 the number of factories and workshops dropped from something more than 31,000 to 22,650, but the number of their workers rose from 770,000 to 1.4 million. Thus in a dozen years industry virtually doubled the size of its payroll and almost trebled the average size of its component enter-prises. It was above all in the southern provinces, bordering on the Black Sea, that the surge was most striking; the development there was almost as rapid as that in America.

The economic prosperity brought about by this industrialization was more appearance than reality. From the outset there was some-thing artificial in this expansion of industry, for it was the result not so much of the needs of a free market as of the orders and premiums of every kind that came from the state. Then too it was based exclu-sively on the exploitation of the working class and the impoverish-ment of the peasant masses.

In spite of the rapid growth of the working class, the government took not the slightest notice of its needs. On the contrary, the state sought only to assure industry of all the profit that it could wrest out of the industrial expansion. Far from wishing to oppose exploitation of the workers' labor, the government invariably sided with the em-ployers in every dispute between management and labor. Hence the situation of the majority of industrial workers was extremely cruel and their anger was equally acute. In direct proportion to the growth of awareness of its strength and its importance, visible evidences of the discontent of the working class became more frequent and more violent.

What was still more serious was the fact that the industrial advance had been accomplished only at the price of the impoverishment of the agricultural population, which represented by far the majority of the nation. The threatening symptoms of this drain became clearly evident in 1891, when, as a consequence of the poor harvests in Russia's twenty most productive agricultural governments, a horrible famine struck the country. In spite of this terrible omen, the government of Alexander III did not waver in its class policy; without regard for the danger, it continued in its ruthless sacrifice of the interests of the popular masses to those of the great landowners and the industrialists.

V / FOREIGN POLICY

German-Russian Relations at the Beginning of the Reign

Determinedly conservative at home, in the international arena Alexander III moved perceptibly away from the policy followed by the Russian autocracy since the beginning of the nineteenth century.

At the time of his accession Russia was virtually isolated. Since the

Congress of Berlin the close friendship that had bound German and Russian court circles had suffered severe shocks. Alexander III, who as tsarevitch had shared the sharp resentment of the Russian nationalists against Bismarck, remained profoundly suspicious of German policy and its major instigator. But N. K. Giers, to whom he had entrusted foreign affairs after Prince Gorchakov's retirement in 1882, endeavored to preserve the old ties of friendship and alliance with Germany. Although Alexander was given to reiterating that he was his "own foreign minister" and, according to Witte, he "regarded Giers as his secretary for foreign affairs," the tsar occasionally listened to this minister, who, though he had no great talents, was at least a conscientious and hard-working official. While the counsels of Giers and the efforts of the Foreign Ministry succeeded for a while in averting a break with Germany, German-Russian relations were nonetheless visibly strained. As long as old Kaiser Wilhelm I lived and no further divergencies between Russian and German policies supervened, this strain was not heightened.

Expansion in Asia and Anglo-Russian Relations

Under Alexander II Russia had begun to seek compensation in central Asia for the diminution in her influence in the Balkans. These conquests were pursued under Alexander III. In the early years of his reign he succeeded in finally subduing the Tekes. Transcaspian Turkmenia and its capital, Merv, also recognized his authority. By now Russia's borders reached to Afghanistan's. The Afghans were uneasy. Relying on English help, which the British authorities in India indicated that they would have, in 1885 they attacked General Komarov's forces encamped near the Kushk River. Not only did they suffer a great defeat, but they were disillusioned by the stand of Prime Minister Gladstone, who had no desire to enter into open conflict with Russia and professed satisfaction with the explanations that he received from the Russian government. Hence the new Russian border now ran between the Murghab and Amu-Daria rivers, in the immediate vicinity of Afghanistan, which recognized the frontier in 1887. Five years later, during a new clash on the Pamir, Russian troops defeated an Afghan detachment. The incident did not lead to serious complications, and Russia, England, Afghanistan, and China entered into an agreement for the partition of the Pamir region.

While the possession of part of this region, which was only desert, was of hardly any advantage to Russia, this was not the case with Turkestan, which was fertile and rich. Russian industrialists looked on that area as their road to emancipation from their dependence on

English cotton. That was why they soon began the large-scale cultivation of cotton there. Their activity and their progress were all the greater because of the assistance provided, at the expense of the state, by the construction of a railway linking Samarkand and the Amu-Daria to the eastern shore of the Caspian.

This expansion of central Asia, which was highly profitable to Russian industry and therefore most warmly endorsed by it, was not, however, devoid of problems. Aside from the fact that it subjected the Treasury to large expenditures, it made England apprehensive and more and more suspicious of Russia. Germany, on the other hand, as Russia's immediate neighbor in Europe, was not at all displeased to see her turn eastward into Asia.

Balkan Policy and Relations with the Central Powers

Far from giving up hope of Russian dominance in the Balkans, Alexander III intended to solidify it. Since the treaty of San Stefano had taken Serbia and Rumania out of Russia's sphere and moved them closer to Austria-Hungary, it was Bulgaria, which owed the restoration of her independence only to the Russians, to which he directed all his attention. He expected to make her a willing instrument of his policies. But his intention ran into unanticipated obstacles. First of all, in spite of all the importance of Russian support, Alexander v. Battenberg, the reigning prince of Bulgaria, had no wish to become a kind of Russian governor general, and both his own personal ambitions and respect for the interests of the country that had elected him made him firmly opposed to this threat. In addition, the Bulgarian political parties, which embraced the best educated elements in the country, were hardly inclined to bow to the tutelage of Petersburg and blindly serve the aspirations of Russia. Therefore the policy of Alexander III brought on a series of grave conflicts in Bulgaria, and these ended in a major blow to Russia.

In April 1881, very soon after the death of Alexander II, to whom he was indebted for his throne, Prince Alexander v. Battenberg executed a *coup d'état* with the active assistance of his Russian advisers. He abrogated the democratic constitution of Trnovo, conferred on Bulgaria at the time of her creation as an independent principality, and procured a seven-year grant of very broad powers to himself that in effect assured him of virtually absolute dictatorship. Far from protesting this *coup*, the Petersburg government, which wanted to maintain its guardianship over Bulgaria, lost no time in dispatching two of its generals, Sobolev and Kaulbars, to Sofia. Sobolev was made premier and Kaulbars was made minister of war in the new Cabinet formed by Prince Alexander; their assignment was the preservation and the expansion of Russian influence in Bulgaria. They did not carry it out successfully. The Bulgarian liberals turned their backs on Russia because she had accepted the *coup d'état*. While the conservatives joined the new government, they vigorously defended their independence against Petersburg's representatives, and a bitter conflict soon erupted between the two Russians and their Bulgarian colleagues. Prince Alexander himself had no intention of meekly following the counsels of the Russian generals who expected to be his mentors or his preceptors; at times he requested their backing and cloaked himself in their authority, but at other times he skillfully played off his Bulgarian ministers against them. The stronger the tone taken by the Russian generals and the greater and more specific their demands, the more clearly defined the attitude of Alexander and his Bulgarian ministers became. Against Russia's exorbitant demands they sought to assure themselves of the support of Austria-Hungary, which was rejoicing in the frustrations of Russian policy and seeking to profit thereby.

When he saw that he could not influence Prince Alexander and his conservative government, Sobolev gave thought to restoring the constitutional system in Bulgaria. But the prince anticipated him and reinstated the Trnovo Constitution. Two years later, in order to strengthen his popularity, he took a further step. Serious disorders having broken out in eastern Rumelia, which the Congress of Berlin had detached from Bulgaria and left under the administration of a governor appointed by Turkey, Alexander seized on this development to enter the region at the head of his troops and proclaim its union with his principality. This union, which Russia had earlier sought to realize in the treaty of San Stefano, was officially refused the approval of Alexander III, who was angered by the spirit of independence that the prince had manifested. Thus Russia made herself the ardent defender of the treaty of Berlin that had once been forced on her by the powers—an attitude that was all the more surprising in that no other signatory of the treaty joined in her protest and Turkey herself, in the end, accepted the accomplished fact and, purely to save face, was content with the fiction of appointing Prince Alexander governor of eastern Rumelia. Only Serbia attacked Bulgaria, but, after one major defeat, she too had to recognize Bulgarian unification.

Nevertheless Russia continued to enjoy so great a prestige in Bulgaria that the position taken by Alexander III, who had broken all relations with Prince Alexander, brought about the prince's downfall. In the autumn of 1886, as the result of a conspiracy organized by a few Bulgarian officers with the backing of Russia's official representatives, he was arrested in his palace, forced to abidcate, and removed across the border. Power was transferred to a Regency Council. In order to help the Bulgarians to make their way out of the chaos that had followed the *coup d'état*, Alexander III once more dispatched General Kaulbars. This officer was so devoid of tact, so contemptuous of the constitution, so arrogant in his behavior toward the Bulgarian authorities and people, that his mission was a total failure. He very soon aroused so much indignation against himself and his government that he was compelled to leave in haste. Official relations between Bulgaria and Russia were severed again, and for a long time to come.

The Petersburg government could not resign itself to accepting this defeat. Alexander III in particular was long reluctant to recognize it. In his view, every reverse was the product of fortuitous circumstances and individual scheming, and he would not give up his insistence on intervening in Bulgarian affairs. He wanted to give the Bulgarian throne to a candidate who would be completely devoted to him, and he indulged himself in proposing one name after another. He did not hesitate to engage in a purely personal policy for the fulfillment of this dream. Without the knowledge of his foreign minister and in total disregard of his counsels, the tsar employed Katkov's intercession to enter into relations with Bulgarian exiles who were conspiring against the Regency Council; he gave his approval to their plans and added financial help. When Giers called his attention to the danger of a Bulgarian revolution prepared in this fashion, Alexander replied with equal parts of simple-mindedness and assurance: "There is no question of a revolution, but of restoring order; it is your business to know that." His passion and his blindness were such that not only did he envisage the occupation of Bulgaria but he considered such an occupation to be without danger, "because no one would dare to do anything." It was only with difficulty that his foreign minister convinced him that in such a venture Russia would run the risk of colliding with a vast coalition of European powers, that in any event "rebellious" Bulgaria could be sure of having Austria-Hungary's support, and that Vienna in turn would be backed up by her ally, Berlin. In fact, despite the treaty of friendship that also bound her to Russia and that was due to expire in 1887, Germany decisively supported Austria-Hungary's Balkan policy. At the end of 1886, then, Russia could not rely on a single ally; she was indeed wholly isolated in Europe.

The French-Russian Alliance

The Austrian-German alliance was even more menacing for France than for Russia. Ever since the scare of 1875, when a German attack on France had been prevented by the intervention of Alexander II, Paris had lived in dread of German aggression. Only Russia could guarantee her the defensive alliance that she wanted. That was why, in spite of the differences in political systems that divided the two countries, France was giving more and more consideration to an understanding with Russia.

When the Russian government recognized its isolation in consequence of its Balkan policy, it hastened to offer evidence of its friendship to France. While French Foreign Minister Flourens did receive a delegation from the Bulgarian National Assembly that was seeking to enlist the aid of the European powers against Russia's claims to dispose of Bulgaria's destinies, he did so only in order to remind the Bulgarians of the gratitude that they owed to Russia and to urge them to give obedience to Petersburg. This stand was all the more acceptable to the Russians because the other powers did not give the same advice to Bulgarian delegations. It was particularly welcomed by Alexander III, who almost immediately had an opportunity to make the French government aware of his satisfaction. When Bismarck, who accused General Boulanger, the French war minister, of wanting and preparing a war of revenge, inquired of Petersburg whether, in the event of war between France and Germany, Russia would observe a benevolent neutrality on behalf of Germany, Russia could not accept a new destruction of France by Germany; not only had she no desire to help as against France an ally of Austria-Hungary, which was pursuing an anti-Russian policy in the Balkans, but she would find it impossible to pledge herself to neutrality if there should be war between Germany and France. When Bismarck, who was still relying on the solidity of the old Russian-Prussian friendship, attempted nevertheless to provoke France into action, Alexander very forcefully repeated his warning. The German chancellor had no choice but to abandon his warlike plans, and the danger that threatened France was dissipated.

This laid the groundwork for French-Russian reconciliation. As yet it amounted to no more than "association," a friendly understanding born of a certain community of interests, but not yet solemnized by any treaty. Alexander III had not yet made up his mind to an actual alliance with a country whose republican system, in spite of its government's good intentions toward Russia, was basically against his grain. He was equally hesitant, even though his alliance with Germany offered him no more than a modicum of sympathy and confidence, to break with Berlin. He was simultaneously under the influence of the urgings of his foreign minister, who regarded the German alliance as indispensable to Russia, of an already venerable tradition, and of the personal friendship that he felt for old Kaiser Wilhelm I. As for Bismarck, haunted by the dread of an anti-German coalition, he was in no hurry to break with Russia in spite of the disappointment that she had just inflicted on him. Although Germany was already closely bound to Austria-Hungary, Russia's adversary, in his confidence in his own expertness in the game of diplomacy he did not hesitate to renew for three years the German-Russian treaty of mutual reassurance that was about to expire in that same year of 1887.

Nevertheless, relations between Germany and Russia grew steadily more strained. There political disagreements were aggravated by an economic conflict. The more and more aggressive protectionism in which the Russian government was engaged during the second half of the reign of Alexander III was a grievous blow to the interests of German industry. Bismarck replied to the 1887 tariff with a considerable rise in German duties on Russian raw materials. At the same time, he endeavored to close the German financial market to the loans that Russia had hitherto been able to obtain there with such facility. This was made all the easier for him by the fact that the demands of German industry, whose growth at this time was extremely rapid, were enough to absorb all the nation's capital. But, in spite of the customs war, Russia maintained her tariff, and she found the capital that she needed in France; beginning in 1888, Finance Minister Vyshnegradsky succeeded without too much difficulty in transferring Russian state borrowings to the French market, which in fact was looking for investments abroad. Thus a new bond was forged between Russia and France. The nascent friendship between the two countries was strengthened by this, while a reciprocal hostility was driving Russia and Germany farther and farther apart.

The death of Wilhelm I, which loosened the personal ties between the tsar and the Hohenzollerns, precipitated the German-Russian rupture. Toward Wilhelm II, who succeeded his father, Friedrich III, after three months, Alexander III did not have the same feelings that the first Wilhelm had aroused in him. The new Kaiser himself, a man of impulse, was less inclined than his grandfather to respect the traditional Russian-Prussian friendship. His first visit, however, was paid to Alexander III. At that time and again in March 1890, when Bismarck was dismissed, the Kaiser, in conformity with his grandfather's desires, proclaimed his ardent devotion to and his unshakable friendship for the tsar, but for all that he categorically refused, to the great disappointment of the Russian foreign minister, to renew the German-Russian treaty of mutual assurance that was expiring in this same year of 1890. With his new Chancellor Caprivi he followed a policy of reconciliation with England. Hence they regarded the Russian alliance as superfluous now, and even embarrassing. Furthermore, after the formation of the Triple Alliance with Austria-Hungary and Italy in 1882, Germany felt that she was strong enough not to have to be afraid of Russia.

The respective isolations of France and Russia compelled them to an understanding. Therefore the French-Russian reconciliation made swift progress; witness the French squadron's visit to Kronstadt in 1891 and the Russian squadron's visit to Toulon in 1893. In August 1891, in an exchange of notes, France and Russia pledged themselves to assist each other in the event of attack by a third power. Then, on the instance of the French government, a military convention, signed on 5/17 August 1892 by the French and Russian chiefs of staff, Generals de Boisdeffre and Obrutchev, stipulated that each country would back the other with all its available forces in the event of war with one or two members of the Triple Alliance. Finally, on 18/30 December 1893 the Russian government, and on 23 December 1893/4 January 1894 the French government, approved the military agreement officially. This was the official seal on the purely defensive French-Russian alliance that restored the European equilibrium broken by the Triple Alliance.

Russian Aims in the Far East and the Construction of the Trans-Siberian Railway

Although the French-Russian alliance protected both parties against a possible attack by Germany, it was not enough to make it possible for Russia immediately to recapture her former preponderance in the Balkans. The Russian government was aware of this. Hence, in the last years of the reign of Alexander III, it directed all the efforts of its policy toward the Far East.

In 1887 the governor general of Irkutsk had pointed out the value of building a railway in eastern Siberia. The commission appointed by the government especially for the study of this question had approved the proposal; it had arrived unanimously at the conclusion "that, from the national point of view, and especially from the strategic point of view, the acceleration of exchanges between European Russia and the Far East was becoming more urgent year by year, even though the construction of a railway across Siberia, given the primitive level of Siberian commerce, could hardly offer any tangible advantages in the immediate future and could pay for itself only over a long period."

With some delay, work actually began on the project in 1891. In May, shortly after the appointment of Witte as minister of communications, Tsarevitch Nicholas went to Vladivostok for the solemn ceremony of laying the first railway tie for the Trans-Siberian. When he became finance minister, Witte retained his interest in this railway, on which he too based great expectations: "The Trans-Siberian Railway," he wrote in 1892, "opens a new avenue and new horizons to world commerce; in this regard its construction takes its place in the rank of events of universal import that mark the beginnings of new eras in the histories of peoples and that often lead to radical changes in the economic relationships established among states."

The Trans-Siberian, which was to be completed during the reign of Nicholas II, was not to bring about any "radical changes" in the economic sphere, but it was to play a most important part in the history of Russia.

Nicholas II (1894–1917)

—————————————— ·+◄⋅❖⋅►+· ——————————————

I / THE CONTINUATION OF REACTION [P A U L   M I L I U K O V]

When Nicholas II succeeded his father, who died of nephritis at Livadia in the Crimea on 28 October/1 November 1894, he was twenty-six years old. Alexander III had made every effort to prepare him for his task; but the weakness of Nicholas' character and the instability of his emotions, on the one hand, and the influence of the environment in which he had grown up and lived before his accession, on the other, made him absolutely incapable of governing his huge empire.

The Education of Nicholas II

In his youth Nicholas II had been subject above all to the domination of his father, for whom he felt an emotion of commingled respect and fear and whom he obeyed blindly. Lord and master in his own family, where his will, his merest wish were law and where everyone trembled when he grew angry, Alexander III had entrusted the education of the tsarevich, in conformity to his own ideas, to Pobyedonostsev, the attorney general of the Holy Synod, and to General Danilovitch. Himself lacking in education and not intelligent enough to be aware of his own lacks, Alexander had thought, as did the court, which attached considerably more importance to manners and protocol than to breadth of culture, that his son would be learned enough when his store of knowledge matched his father's. An English tutor, Heath, taught the boy English, which Nicholas knew thoroughly —he was also fluent in French and German—horseback riding, and other sports, as well as all the rules of polite behavior. Nicholas owed it to Heath that he was, as Count Witte often called him in his *Memoirs*, "a well bred man." Pobyedonostsev had taught the tsarevich that autocracy was the finest government that the Russian Empire could have. But the boy's lack of aptitude and of eagerness to acquire the scanty intellectual equipment that was considered indispensable for him often discouraged both his teachers and his father. When he came to power, Nicholas knew just about as much as the average officer of the guard, in which, for the furtherance of his theoretical studies in the art of war, he had himself served as an infantry, cavalry, and artillery officer. Moreover, he had given evidence of a greater liking for regimental life than for the study of the historical, juridical, or social sciences. With his fellows in the Preobrazhensky Regiment, the hussars, or the guard artillery, he was a typical gay young officer. They were his companions not only in military maneuvers but also in late suppers, parties, theater attendance, and the courting of amenable young women like the dancer Kshesinskaya, with whom he became infatuated and who was briefly his mistress; and these pleasures were far more attractive to him than intellectual endeavor.

In 1891, with his brother Georgi* and a rather large entourage, which included his cousin, Prince George of Greece, Nicholas made a long study tour through Greece, Egypt, India, China, and Japan, returning by way of Siberia. When he was visiting a shrine in Japan, a local policeman, Sanzo Tsuda, struck him violently on the head with a saber; if Prince George of Greece had not been able to prevent the assailant from striking again, Nicholas would certainly have been killed. The wound left him with a sclerosis of the bone tissue that pressed on his brain and caused him frequent and violent migraines.

His Character

Nicholas II did not possess the natural endowments that might have been able to compensate for the gaps in his education. Weak and docile, he was easily influenced by those around him: his father first of all—and Alexander's advisers, notably Pobyedonostsev, knew how to make the best use of the father's influence in shaping the son's decisions—then, at the very start of his reign, there were the rival influences of his mother, Tsarina Marya Fyodorovna, and the grand dukes, particularly Alexander Mikhailovitch, his sister's husband, and Sergey Aleksandrovitch, governor general of Moscow and the husband of the tsar's sister-in-law. Subsequently Nicholas fell under the influence of the two "Montenegrins," the daughters of Prince Nicholas of Montenegro. These two princesses, brought up in Petersburg and married to two brothers, Grand Dukes Peter and Nikolai Nikolayevitch, won the confidence of the young tsarina—who was later to conceive a

*The second son of Alexander III and heir to the throne after Nicholas first became tsar. He died of tuberculosis at Abbas-Tuman on 28 June/10 July 1899.

violent hatred of them and never speak of them except as the "black women"—by doing little personal favors for her. It was they who made spiritualism fashionable, as well as traffic with various "saints," such as "Dr." Philippe, whom they had imported from France and who played on the imperial couple's credulity by promising a son, supplying amulets, and fortifying the tsar's conviction of the divine origin of his power.

But all these influences were little by little wiped out by the growing ascendancy of the tsarina. Alix von Hesse, daughter of Archduke Ludwig IV von Hesse, was born in 1872; through her mother she was a granddaughter of Queen Victoria of England. Reared in the English manner, she knew the language fluently and used it for her correspondence with her husband. She had met Nicholas at the court of Alexander III during her visits to her sister Elisabeth, the wife of Grand Duke Sergey Aleksandrovitch. Engaged to Nicholas in the spring of 1894, she became his wife, under the name of Alexandra Fyodorovna, less than a month after his accession, on 14–26 November of the same year. Physically she was more like an Englishwoman than a German. Tall, beautiful, with regular features, she gave the impression of a cold, reserved, extremely willful nature. In her resoluteness and her capacity to make decisions she was intellectually far superior to her husband. It was easy for her to win his love and devotion. Initially she stayed clear of politics, but during the second part of the reign she played a larger and larger part in the government of the Empire, and she was tireless in encouraging the tsar's reactionary tendencies.

While he was easily influenced, Nicholas II, as is so often the case with the weak, was also capable of extreme obstinacy when it was a matter of questions to which his own preferences or some third person's opinion caused him to attach special importance. He was notably intransigent in everything that had to do with the absolute and exclusive power that was his by the right of inheritance. He evidenced an extreme distrust toward those whom, occasionally not without reason, he suspected of wanting to place curbs on the scope of his autocratic rights. Whether a minister or a friend, any man who seemed to him to be attacking his prerogatives was certain to be thrown into disgrace. This was to be the fate of Witte, for whom he had no great fondness and whom he never forgave for his participation in the constitutional reform of 1905–1906; the same thing was to happen to some ministers who, during the First World War, sought to dissuade him from assuming the supreme command of the army.

His feeling that he derived his power from Providence and the stubbornness to which he resorted in order to exact respect for all his rights as a sovereign did not prevent him from always behaving with cordiality toward recalcitrant ministers, even when he had decided to dismiss them and even occasionally when he had already signed the orders for their dismissal. The nearer their day of doom came, the more affable and affectionate his behavior toward them appeared. More than one minister, leaving an audience at which Nicholas had received him with much graciousness, returned to his office to find the letter notifying him that he had been removed. The signs of special good will that were displayed toward any given individual enabled experienced courtiers of the tsar to gauge the imminence of the man's disgrace.

Very reserved and timid, Nicholas felt quite handicapped by his lack of experience in public affairs. Though he was conscientious in his attentiom to them, this attention was the fruit of duty and went against his wishes. He much preferred not only court life but also family life. He was really happy only in the company of his wife and their children. The tsarina, who was very arrogant, was offended that she had not been received by the court with sufficient cordiality—but the fault lay rather in her own withdrawn character. Therefore, court receptions were abolished, and the imperial couple, taking up residence at Tsarskoye Selo, very definitely lived only within the restricted circle of a simple family life. At the first opportunity, after he had replaced Cherevin, the chief of the palace guard and an alcoholic brute, with General Gesse, a nothing who was available for every base action, Nicholas removed the minister of the court, Count Vorontsov, a favorite of the dowager tsarina who attempted to exercise too much pressure on him, and replaced him with Baron Fredericksz, an easygoing old man who did not get in the way of his family life and who was deeply devoted to him. Thus the court isolated itself not only from the country but even from the highest Russian society.

The Preservation of Autocracy and Reaction

Among the public, which knew little of the new tsar's personality, the mere fact of having a young sovereign, married to a German princess who was steeped in English ideas, as the successor to a retrogressive old man gave rise to the hope that the order instituted by Alexander III would be modified. People wanted to think that the new tsar would back more liberal ideas and show his support of the constitutional system that was so ardently desired. The anticipation that revived all classes of the population was evident in the many resolutions, adopted by government zemstvo or city council, in which the accession of the new monarch was hailed. Very moderate in both manner and matter, they declared that it was essential to go back to the liberal reforms of 1860–1870 and they expressed the hope that the new reign would inaugurate an era of economic and political well being for Russia. Some of them, especially the resolution adopted by the zemstvo of the Tver government, spoke of the necessity of creating legislative institutions for the whole empire. The word *constitution* had not yet been uttered, but constitutional ideas were coming back to life in Russian society.

Delegates elected by every zemstvo, assembly of the nobility, and city council to go in person to acclaim the young tsar and present the good wishes of their constituents were supposed to be received on 17/29 January 1895. One day earlier it was learned that, under the influence of Pobyedonostsev and some of his father's other advisers, Nicholas II had expressed angry resentment at the resolution of the Tver zemstvo. During the reception, from which one of the Tver delegates, F. I. Roditchev, was barred, the tsar said bluntly:

I am happy to see the delegates of all social classes united here to convey their sentiments of loyalty to me. I believe in the sincerity of these sentiments, which from the beginning of time have been characteristic of Russians, but I have learned that voices have recently been raised in certain zemstvo assemblies that have allowed themselves to be seduced by the insensate fantasy of participation by zemstvo delegates in the internal administration. Let all men understand that, pledging all my energies to the well being of my people, I will defend the principles of autocracy as immovably as my father. I state this frankly.

It would have been impossible to find a clearer declaration that nothing had changed, that nothing would change, and that the thought of a constitution was an "insensate fantasy." This speech, the text of which had been written in advance and read by the emperor, assumed the appearance of a program of government. It was a mortal disappointment to the assembled delegates and to public opinion. Sanctions were subsequently imposed on the entire Tver zemstvo and two of its delegates, Roditchev and Golovachev: they were stripped of the right to take part in zemstvo, nobility assembly, and city-council elections; restrictions were imposed on zemstvo activities in general. This convinced public opinion of the futility of its anticipations. The new tsar had rudely rejected the first opportunity presented to him for bringing the society and the government closer and inspiring confidence in himself.

Far from abandoning his father's reactionary policy, Nicholas was determined to intensify it. His first step was to confirm in their posts all the ministers who had served Alexander III—Pobyedonostsev, Witte, Delyanov. When it came to choosing new ministers, he followed the advice of his intimates at first but soon took as almost his sole guide his own personal preference, and he could not tolerate any man of independent character or liberal tendency. When he dismissed Ivan Durnovo, minister of the interior, whom the tsar's mother disliked, he was urged to appoint Pleve or Sipyagin. On the advice of Pobyedonostsev, who told him that "Pleve is a swine and Sipyagin is an imbecile," he chose Goremykin on 3/15 April 1895. This man, who had once enjoyed the reputation of a liberal, had found it easy to go over to the government's side. But Nicholas could not forgive his liberal past, and, on 21 October/2 November 1899, Goremykin, while on a journey, received the surprise of learning that he had been replaced by his former competitor, Sipyagin. It mattered little to the tsar that Sipyagin might be the "imbecile" that Pobyedonostsev had called him, or the man of mediocre intelligence and limited knowledge that Witte considered him to be in 1895. He was satisfactory to the tsar because, to quote Witte again, he was "firmly devoted to the nobility," profoundly dedicated to the principle of autocracy, and a convinced believer in the patriarchal system of local government. Krivosheyin, minister of communications, was removed on suspicion of embezzlement and, for lack of any other candidate, replaced by a friend of the dowager tsarina; on the other hand, General Vannovsky, minister of war, was ousted because of his relative independence; and his successor, General Kuropatkin, who was to learn the road to the emperor's heart by following the signposts of servility, writing amusing reports, and being a charming guest at those luncheons of the imperial couple to which he had the remarkable honor of always being invited, was the personal choice of Nicholas II.

II / WITTE'S ECONOMIC AND FINANCIAL ACCOMPLISHMENTS
[PAUL MILIUKOV]

Among the advisers who furthered reaction during the first part of the reign of Nicholas I, Finance Minister Sergey Witte* held a special place. He remained loyal to the liberal traditions of Bunge, who under Alexander III had endeavored to follow a modern scientific economic policy.

Witte was not a member of the upper bureaucracy and high no-

*His achievements during the peace negotiations with Japan at Portsmouth, New Hampshire, in 1905 gained him the title of count.

bility that made up the tsar's entourage. He came from the railways, in which he had begun his working life as an ordinary office employee in the southeastern system and successively risen through the ranks from station-master to director. During the Russian-Turkish War of 1877–1878 he had already earned the reputation of an exceptionally able administrator, but it was above all as director of the system that he had been able to demonstrate the full extent of his capacities, until in the end Alexander III made him minister of communications and then finance minister. Throughout his ministerial career he remained a "new man." He could never accustom himself either to the climate of bureaucracy or to the caste spirit that prevailed at court. In his own mind, as his posthumous *Memoirs* showed, he despised the majority of the ministers of Nicholas II and had no great opinion of the tsar himself. Furthermore, neither his colleagues nor the tsar had much love for him, for all their recognition of his capacities for his work, his ability, and his spirit of initiative; if they tolerated him, it was only because they could not find a replacement adequate to the task to be performed.

Witte entered the Finance Ministry in 1892 and governed it until 1903. During these eleven years his achievements were of major importance. For one thing, he fostered the economic transformation of Russia with all his energies, accelerating her industrial growth, especially in metallurgy and textiles. For another, he made every effort to stablize the financial system, create a stable currency, and balance the state's budget.

Railway Development

Between 1894 and 1905 the railway network doubled its length, from 29,394 to 59,718 versts. Some of the new lines were built by the state, others by private companies. But the state bought up many of the private lines that were of fundamental importance: in 1894, Petersburg-Moscow, Petersburg-Warsaw, and Moscow–Nizhni-Novgorod, all owned by the Russian General Railway Company; in 1895, all the lines in the southeastern network, amounting to 3296 versts; in 1896, Moscow-Brest-Litovsky; in other words, in the six years between 1891 and 1897, a total of 14,201 versts of trackage. Thus the state took over not only the management of railway policy but also the operation of the major lines and ownership of three-quarters of the national network.

The growth of the railway network and the policy followed in customs duties were powerful factors in the stimulation of Russia's productive energies. Above all they hastened the country's industrial expansion. Indeed, they put an end to the economic isolation of many areas and made it possible for capital to be invested in the exploitation of the country's natural wealth and in the establishment of new factories and mills. In addition, the construction of railways required the collaboration of many ancillary industries, principally metallurgical, such as the manufacture of rails, locomotives, rolling stock, etc., which the government encouraged with every means at its command. On the other hand, the operation of this network imposed quite heavy sacrifices on the state. Gross revenues were not enough to meet either the costs of operation or the amortization of the capital investment in the construction of the roads. In 1900 the state had to put up large sums in order to guarantee this amortization. The causes of the deficit, investigation into which was made the task of a commission created in 1903 under the chairmanship of Ivashchenkov, a member of the Imperial Council, lay chiefly in the establishment of relatively low freight and passenger rates and in the construction of lines like Bologoye-Polotsk that were notoriously unprofitable but of the highest strategic importance.

The largest of the railway lines built during this period was unquestionably the Trans-Siberian, which, extended by the Chinese State Railway,* linked Petersburg with Vladivostok and ran through the whole of Siberia and northern Manchuria. The construction of its 8731 versts had been marked by extreme difficulties in very many areas, notably in the *taiga*, the immense, swampy Siberian forest, and in the deserts and mountains on the southern shores of Lake Baikal.† It had devoured enormous sums—375 million rubles; the cost per verst to the Treasury was 70,000 rubles. The Chinese State line, built by a private company, had cost even more; its shorter length had absorbed 375 million rubles too, but in this instance the cost per verst was 150,000 rubles. But, apart from their political and military value, which will become apparent presently, these railways opened the Russian market and even the world market to Siberian products.

Industrial Growth

Russia possessed enormous natural resources, most of them still intact: oil in the northern Caucasus and the Transcaucasian regions, manganese in the Caucasus, coal in the Donets Basin, iron in the

*See p. 187 ff.
†The sector that went round the lake, almost 170 versts long, was begun in 1899. Until it was completed, trains were carried across the lake on an ice-breaking ship.

Urals and the region of Ekaterinoslav, gold and platinum in Siberia. All that was lacking was capital for the Russian mineralogical industry to assume a major rank in European and even world industrial life. Witte found this capital in other countries, sometimes through the issuance of state bonds, sometimes by encouraging the incorporation of companies in which foreign shareholders predominated. It was her ally, France, above all, to which Russia turned for financial help: between 1888 and 1896 Russia borrowed 5.519 million gold francs there in thirteen separate loans, and, between 1901 and 1906, 2.424 million. Whereas investments of foreign capital between 1831 and 1888 had never been more than 1.5 million rubles, they averaged 5 million between 1889 and 1894 and rose to 21 million in 1895 and 52 million in 1896; they declined to 38 million in 1897, then rose to 98 million in 1898, only to fall back to 93 million in 1899.

Thanks to these foreign investments, Witte provided a solid foundation in the country for struggling young industries and brought new ones into being. Between 1894 and 1899 the business corporations already existing substantially enlarged their activities, increasing their capital through new issues of both shares and bonds; at the same time 927 new companies were created with a nominal capital of 1.42 billion rubles. The annual rise in industrial capital went from 26 million rubles between 1878 and 1887 to 42 million between 1888 and 1892 and 161 million between 1894 and 1897. Many firms were set up by French and Belgian companies that infused them with exceptional vigor. The Donets Basin in particular was profoundly changed: the steppe was quickly covered with mines and factories; small towns like Bakhmut and Lugansk became cities; cities of no importance, like Ekaterinoslav, Rostov, and Taganrog, were transformed into major centers of industry. Everywhere the population of the industrial regions rose, and in the cities new neighborhoods came into being that were inhabited almost exclusively by the working class.

Labor Legislation

The upsurge of industry compelled the creation of an ever larger working class, and the signs of an organized working-class movement were not slow in appearing.

In Russia at the end of the nineteenth century the strike, the workers major weapon for the defense of their interests, was not only prohibited but punishable as common-law crime; the mere act of participation in a strike was subject to penalty. Nevertheless, strikes multiplied during the last ten years of the nineteenth century. Their frequency was such as to disquiet the government, which decided to give some of its attention to the lot of the workers and sought to develop labor legislation. Under the previous reign the factory inspectors had been created to supervise workers' output and conditions of labor. The number of these inspectors was increased, and, toward the end of the century, all industrial enterprises, regardless of size, were placed under their supervision. After a few timid efforts to protect women, children and adolescents employed in industry, the government promulgated the law of 2/14 June 1897. It had been driven to speed up this action, in spite of the anguished outcries of refractory industrialists against even the concept of regulation of labor, by violent strikes that had erupted at many places in the Empire.

This law marked the first attempt to limit the length of the working day in Russia: eleven and a half hours for adults. The appropriate ministries, however, had the right to extend it when this was required by the special conditions of a given enterprise; they were empowered also to shorten it in cases of employment especially dangerous to health. Night workers, even if only part of their employment was nocturnal, were limited to ten hours. The law also sought to assure the worker of free Sundays and holidays. It left to worker and employer the problem of reaching agreement on overtime, but no worker could be compelled to work overtime except in those industries where it was absolutely essential, such as chemicals or those seasonal industries that had to operate at full speed for a fixed and usually short period.

Although the labor inspectors were under orders to see to it that the law was strictly observed, there were no enforcement provisions in it; hence, in practice, violations by management were seldom punished by administrative action. Moreover, resort to the inspector, who had the power to arbitrate in disputes between employers and workers, was still the sole means of dealing with labor conflicts; there were neither mediation facilities nor boards of arbitration. Thus it was still only timidly that Witte inaugurated state intervention in the relations between workers and management.

Monetary Reform

By means of a series of measures adopted between 1895 and 1897 Witte stabilized the value of the ruble, established a gold reserve, and introduced the gold standard.

Disrupted by the issuance of paper money not mandatorily redeemable in specie during the Russian-Turkish War of 1877–1878, the monetary system had been unable to recover its stability throughout the reign of Alexander III. Bank notes could not be converted into gold without a loss of 30 per cent. Consequently the ruble had become a speculative item in foreign markets, especially on the Berlin *Börse*. In order to stabilize its value and protect it against the fluctuations that were making it an object of speculation in European markets, Witte decided to undertake a devaluation. Having accepted the simultaneous circulation of paper money acceptable for payment at the current rate and of gold coins, he sought, by taking as a basis the approximate value of the paper ruble, to establish a fixed rate for the conversion of paper to gold. The imperial ukase of 29 August/10 September 1897 stabilized the paper ruble at two-thirds the value of the gold ruble, and it provided that further bank-note issues, which would be authorized only "within the limits strictly imposed by the pressing needs of money in circulation," would have to be guaranteed by a gold reserve. This was established at half the value of the notes to be issued provided that the issue did not exceed 600 million rubles; beyond that figure the bank notes would have to be totally backed by gold at the stabilization rate; in other words, each 15-ruble note would be guaranteed by 1 gold imperial, which would no longer be worth 10 gold rubles, as in the past, but 15 paper rubles. The new bank notes issued under the date of 14/26 November 1897 bore this legend: "The State Bank will exchange bank notes against gold without limitation as to amount, at the rate of one ruble for one-fifteenth of one imperial." Like the paper money, the gold currency was devalued in its turn. New 5- and 10-ruble coins were minted, containing, respectively, only one-third and two-thirds of the gold weight of the old imperial. They were put on a par with bank notes, and the new gold ruble was worth only two-thirds of its predecessor's value.

In order to carry out this currency reform Witte had been compelled to set up a major metal reserve sufficient to guarantee both the old bank notes still in circulation and the new issues. He did this step by step, partly by means of borrowing, partly with the help of budget surpluses. The Treasury, furthermore, had embarked on the redemption of the old coins and was buying gold in ingots. At the time of the reform, when the face value of the bank notes in circulation was 1.121 billion rubles, the gold reserve represented 900 million, a more than adequate guaranty.

The creation of a stable monetary standard, the new gold ruble, which was the culmination of Witte's reform, made it possible to survive without disaster the financial difficulties created by the Russian-Japanese War.

The Monopoly in Spirituous Liquors

In addition to indirect taxes and customs receipts, the major source of budgetary revenues at the end of the nineteenth century was the monopoly in spirituous liquors established by Witte.

Distillers and wholesalers in the eastern provinces were trying to get the monopoly of vodka sales for themselves. Since each commune had the right to authorize or prohibit the sale of liquor in its own jurisdiction, they bought up all the licenses and in the cities they competed for the benevolence of the municipal governments by laying out large sums for "works of charity." Having made themselves the masters of the trade, they held regular meetings in which they fixed the prices of their wares, which they could increase at will while at the same time lowering the quality of the product.

Their abuses impelled Witte to supplant their monopoly with a state monopoly. He viewed this as a means of protecting the population against fraud, by controlling the quality of vodka, and of assuring the Treasury of a major source of revenue. Under the law of 6/18 June 1894 the monopoly in the sale of liquor was instituted in four eastern governments: those of Perm, Ufa, Orenburg, and Samara. Subsequently and gradually it was extended to the governments of southern, western, and then central Russia. Henceforth the state controlled the distillation of liquor, which it alone had the right to sell to the public; it became the sole customer of the distilleries; it set prices and regulated production. A whole sector of the national output, all the more important because the country was primarily an agricultural one, fell under the close domination of the state, which, by assuring it of a permanent market and relatively high prices, also established it in a privileged position.

As Witte had anticipated, the new monopoly, in contrast to the operation of the railways by the state, became a source of great profit to the Treasury. In 1894 its gross receipts rose to 543 million rubles and the net to 376 million. But public opinion and the press, except a few newspapers wholly loyal to the government, greeted it with hostility, and, because it represented the chief source of state revenues, they called the state budget "the drunkenness budget."

Budget Balance

When he succeeded Vsyhnegradsky, Witte found a rather shaky financial situation. By persistent effort he managed to restore balance to the budget and to keep the budget balanced as long as he remained in office.

As a first step, he set up two budgets, the ordinary and the extra-ordinary: the law of 4/16 June 1894 classified as extraordinary expenditures the construction of the new railways, the Treasury's purchase of the privately owned lines, the anticipated amortization of state debts, disbursements occasioned by war or public disasters such as bad crops, epidemics, etc. Next he increased revenues by raising the rates of existing taxes, especially the indirect levies, and mainly, as we have seen, by instituting the liquor monopoly. He soon had in hand a surplus of income over outgo, which he allocated in part to accelerated repayment of debts and in part to the Treasury's reserve fund. Through the conversion of a number of bond issues he succeeded also in alleviating the interest burden on the public debt.

The Aggravation of the Farm Crisis

In spite of its scope Witte's economic and fiscal policy contained one serious defect. By putting the country's industrial development above everything else, the government was neglecting or indeed damaging the interests of the agricultural masses, and this was the more grievous by reason of the fact that agriculture, since it was the chief source of public prosperity in Russia, was the foundation of the entire national economy.

Now the agricultural crisis had grown steadily worse since the emancipation of the peasants. It was especially acute in the south, the largest producer of wheat for the market. By 1900 peasant holdings there had fallen to 51 per cent and even 36 per cent of what they had been in 1861, crops had declined to 88 per cent and 62 per cent, livestock was down to 83 per cent and 51 per cent, and liquor consumption had dropped to 63 per cent and 37 per cent, while tax arrearages had risen by 782 per cent to 2015 per cent and peasant migrations within the country had increased by 708 per cent to 2023 per cent. The peasants' hardships were made worse by the increases in taxes, which were becoming heavier and heavier: the total tax burden rose 29 per cent between 1883 and 1892 and 49 per cent between 1893 and 1902, whereas the population increases for these two periods were 16 per cent and 13 per cent respectively. While Witte succeeded in creating a gold reserve of a billion rubles in the eight years 1893–1900, tax arrearages rose by 314 million rubles, which the peasants could never liquidate, and the Treasury had to spend 275 million for the relief of those who were suffering from famine. An official report submitted to the Imperial Council in December 1902 had to acknowledge that "there are limits to the taxpaying capacities of the population" and that "any increase in taxes would be unproductive and in fact intolerable in the existing economic situation." The rural population's buying power, which was the essence of the home market, was so low, and industrial output, to the development of which Witte had dedicated himself, had risen so quickly, that part of the industrial production had to be sold abroad at prices below the actual cost of production—sugar and iron were examples—while the Russian peasant was paying twice or three times as much as the foreign buyer for them.

Hence Witte's industrial policy contributed to the heightening of the farm crisis. Therefore it made enemies among the landed nobility, who called for assistance to agriculture and were far less interested in having a gold standard for their currency than in getting "cheap" money, regardless whether coin or paper. Witte himself, moreover, in the end became aware of the problems that were crippling agriculture. At the end of his term in office he recognized that in Russia rural interests were entitled to at least as much attention as those of industry. On 4/16 April 1902, with the tsar's approval, he appointed a committee, headed by himself, to investigate the needs of agriculture. In order to assemble the data required for its work, the commission set up provincial government and district committees, composed of zemstvo members and experts in farm problems—the total number was eleven thousand. But in 1903 Witte fell into disgrace and left the Finance Ministry, and in 1904 the commission's work was halted by the war against Japan.

III / THE GROWTH OF THE OPPOSITION AND THE PREPARATIONS FOR REVOLUTION (1894–1904) [PAUL MILIUKOV]

The opposition aroused by the government's reactionary policy assumed a wholly new dimension. It was no longer confined to enlightened circles alone. Unquestionably it was still the extreme radicals and Socialists and the young students who constituted the skeleton of militant revolutionary organization, but they changed their tactics, they organized, and they gained the support of the people, especially the workers in the cities. Discontent, aggravated by Pleve's brutal policy, spread not only among all classes of Russian society but also among all the outlying local populations. In vain Pleve counted on the war against Japan to shatter opposition at home; the defeats abroad merely hastened the revolution.

The Organization and Work of the Socialist Parties

Economic conditions fostered the propagation of Socialist ideas among peasants and workers. In rural areas the peasants were still too uneducated and too poor to try through intensified exploitation of the land to compensate for a relative overpopulation. Therefore they denounced the short supply of land as the source of all their troubles. The best means of influencing them was to insist on the necessity of enlarging the extent of their holdings, and it was this increase that was to be the aim of all the radical programs for agrarian reform. In the cities, where the swift development of industry had multiplied their numbers, the factory workers were suffering as much as the peasants; poorly paid, poorly protected, in spite of the law of 1897 against exploitation by their employers, they were to provide the revolutionaries with the troops that hitherto had always been lacking to them. After a decade of passivity the revolutionary movement was coming back to life. But the new revolutionary generation, which had grown to maturity under the reign of Alexander III, was different from its predecessors. It did not have their idealism. On the other hand, it was far more skilled in "scientific analysis." Steeped in the thinking of Karl Marx, it predicted that the growth of industrial capitalism would culminate automatically and spontaneously in Socialism, and it found in "economic materialism" the philosophical and historical foundation for its "scientific" Socialism.

The young Russian "economic" Marxists were sharply critical of their predecessors, the Populists, who continued to contend that in Russia, even in the absence of all capitalism, the system of peasant agrarian communities must lead to economic collectivism. The weapon on which the Marxists relied was completely professional: it was workers' strikes for purely economic objectives. They triumphed when in 1896, without any visible help from the intellectuals, the workers in twenty-two Petersburg cotton mills organized a major strike, such as had never been seen in Russia, during which more than thirty thousand workers relied on peaceful means alone to win the ten-and-a-half-hour working day. Their propaganda was so peaceful that, in spite of the rigors of the censorship, they were able to diffuse their ideas in writing and to criticize the Populists within the procedures permitted by law.

But soon the old Social Democratic leaders who had emigrated, Plekhanov and Akselrod, rose against their opportunist interpretation and defended "orthodox" Marxism against "economism" and "revisionism." In 1894–1895 a clandestine organization, the Union for the Victory of the Emancipation of the Working Class, was formed in Petersburg. Its members included Lenin and Martov and it broke away from the "legal Marxists." * Establishing revolutionary action as a primary step, this Union set a political objective as its immediate goal: the overthrow of the autocracy and the conquest of political freedom by associating itself with "every social movement that may rise up against the vestiges of serfdom and the survival of castes." In Minsk on 1/13 March 1898 the Russian Social Democratic Party was founded during an initial congress that was attended by only ten delegates from various groups. At the end of 1900, its publication, *Iskra (The Spark)*, began to appear abroad under Lenin's direction and turned it resolutely toward revolutionary action. The second Social Democratic Congress, held in Brussels and London in July and August of 1903, confirmed the growth of this tendency. It restored the unity of the party, decimated by police persecutions, and, on the urgings of Lenin, at that time supported by Plekhanov, it introduced the strictest centralization into the party's organization. But this centralization, imposed by the majority of the party, was contested by national groups, mainly by the Jewish *Bund*. It was to bring on a long and bitter struggle between the "majority," or *bolshinstvo*, which followed Lenin—and whose members later adopted the name of *Bolsheviki*—and the "minority," or *menshinstvo*—the future *Mensheviki*—led by Martov and Akselrod. In five years, between 1895 and 1900, the Social Democratic Party had organized 220 workers' strikes, in which altogether 200,000 men had taken part, published 30 issues of an underground publication printed in six different localities, and lost 5942 of its members through arrests.

At the end of 1900 the old revolutionary Populist party, the "Revolutionary Socialists," was reorganized and began to issue a publication, *Revolutsionnaya Rossya (Revolutionary Russia)*. In 1901–1902 it unified all its local groups in Russia, which soon numbered forty-nine. It directed its activity toward two matters in which the Social Democrats were particularly weak. In the first instance, the Social Democrats, whose agrarian program was barely outlined and inadequate, were interested almost exclusively in the working class and called for organized demonstrations by the workers; the Revolutionary Socialists declared themselves without reservation for the nationalization of the

*That is, those who held legal passports and who lived under police control rather than in hiding.

land and its distribution to its workers, and they formed an "agrarian league" to propagandize their ideas in rural areas. In the second instance, in order to carry on individual resistance to the government and resume the old terrorist methods, they organized a "combat battalion" composed of the most enthusiastic representatives of the young. The excitement that virtually never subsided among the students of all the universities and against which the government fought back without quarter—as when the Cossacks savagely broke up a demonstration taking place near the Cathedral of Our Lady of Kazan in Petersburg—encouraged the return to terrorism. The "provisional regulations" that made it possible to force students into the army as a disciplinary measure impelled Karpovitch, a former student, to kill the reactionary minister of public education, Bogolyepov, with a revolver shot on 14/27 February 1901. General Vannovsky, the new minister, who had ordered a reasonably impartial investigation into the student disorders under Goremykin, replaced the "provisional regulations" with "friendly guardianship," but in vain; it was equally futile for him to try to appease the poorer students by providing scholarships for them, or to sway public opinion by cutting back the Latin and Greek studies that had been the symbol of educational reaction ever since D. Tolstoi's reform. The disorders went on, and on 1/14 April Vannovsky had to yield his post to Senger, an advocate of the domination of classical studies, who attempted, though with no greater success, to restore order by establishing disciplinary councils made up of professors. Not only did the students persist in their demands with respect to the universities; their agitation assumed a more and more pronounced political character. "We need not reforms but Reform"— the singular noun meant a constitution: this was the slogan that spread among the public. A second terrorist attack bore witness to this state of mind: on 1/15 April 1902 Balmashev brought down Minister of the Interior Sipyagin.

Peasant, Zemstvo, and National-Minority Opposition during the Repressive Pleve Ministry (1902–1904)

After the assassination of Sipyagin, Nicholas II did not hesitate in the selection of his successor. On the advice of a reactionary journalist, Prince Meshchersky, who enjoyed a considerable influence over him, the tsar appointed Pleve, "the swine," as Pobyedonostsev called him. An intelligent official but an opportunist bare of the slightest principle, an agile turncoat who had twice changed his religion, Pleve initiated his career as a minister by making a pilgrimage to the monastery of Troika-Sergyevo; in the hope of winning the good will of the believers at court, he went to kneel before the relics of Saint Sergey. His ministry was fatal for Russia and for autocracy. His ultra-reactionary policy drove into the arms of revolution that part of the population that had thus far held itself aloof from all agitation: the peasants, the zemstvo, and the national minorities.

He set himself at once to combatting the agrarian movement that had begun in March 1902 among the peasants in the governments of Poltava and Kharkov. He ousted Governor Belgard of Poltava, who had not been sufficiently vigorous in putting down the disorders by force, and he lavished honors on Prince Obolensky, governor of Kharkov, who had outraged all Russia by the beatings that he had inflicted on the peasants. Then Pleve imposed a heavy money penalty on all the peasants without any effort to distinguish between the innocent and the guilty. His severities angered the opposition, and, when Obolensky fell victim to an assassin, the minister's associates became convinced that he too would certainly be killed in spite of all the precautions in which he armored himself.

Witte had hoped that the creation of his commission to explore agricultural needs and the organization of its district fact-finding committees would influence the moderate zemstvo elements and palliate the effects of Pleve's policy. But, as was to have been expected, the district committees did not confine themselves to the limited task that had been assigned to them. They associated the farm problem with the more general problem of the establishment of a constitutional rule of law in Russia: their liberal members adhered to the epigram of Montesquieu that one of them quoted: "the cultivation of a country is to be judged not by its fertility but by its freedom." Pleve manipulated this attitude against Witte. Once he had succeeded in bringing the local committees under his own authority, he persecuted their liberal members and forbade them to examine "general problems" such as public education, zemstvo autonomy, the legal status of the peasants, etc. He succeeded only in intensifying the spirit of opposition in the zemstvo; more especially, the harassments with which he pursued the zemstvo statisticians, in whom he smelled revolutionaries, simply drove the moderate elements closer to the most advanced.

Because public meetings were forbidden, the zemstvo representatives of the various governments had since 1900 acquired the habit of gathering from time to time for private "conversations," usually in Moscow. There they drew up a program of joint action: thus in 1901 they had demanded compulsory public education, the extension of the elementary-school program, and the abolition of corporal punishment.

In June 1902, pursuant to the desires of the meeting held in Petersburg in March, they set up a clandestine publication abroad, *Osvobozhdenye (Liberation)*, which appeared first in Stuttgart and then in Paris and of which P. Struve, who had turned from Socialism to liberal ideas, was the editor in chief. In the summer of 1903, with the collaboration of intellectuals and university professors, they founded a secret association in Russia, *Soyuz Osvobozhdenya* ("Union for Liberation"), which, rejecting "the class struggle and revolutionary combat," intended to achieve the unification of public opinion on the foundation of a democratic constitution—it was this Union that in 1905 would spawn the party known as *Konstitutsionno-Demokraticheskaya*, the Constitutional Democrats or "Cadets." *

It did not take Pleve long, of course, to learn of the secret gatherings of the zemstvo delegates. Nineteen marshals of the nobility who took part in them were censured by the tsar, a rebuke that they merely shrugged off. More rigorous punishments—for instance, the removal of Prince Peter Dolgorukov from his post as chairman of the permanent delegation of a district zemstvo—accomplished no more. The liberal sector among the titled nobles, the princes and courts, went over openly to the opposition. Pleve came to the point of relying on a foreign war to put an end to domestic opposition: "In order to stop the revolution," he told General Kuropatkin, "we need a small victorious war." Confident of easy victory over little Japan—"those monkeys," as he was pleased to call them—the tsar did not hesitate to declare the war the Pleve wanted. In the end it was to compel him to capitulate before the popular demands that he wanted to stamp out.

Finally, Pleve provoked and exacerbated the national minorities—the Finns, the Poles, the Armenians, the Jews.

As minister-secretary of state for Finland after August 1899, Pleve supported the policy of General Bobrikov, who had made a name for himself through his campaign of Russianization of the Baltic provinces. To the Finns the Grand Duchy of Finland was a state in its own right, in which the tsar was merely the grand duke, limited in his power by the basic laws, which had been recognized by all the Russian emperors, and by the national representative body, the Diet. Bobrikov, however, in conformity with the thinking of the Russian nationalists who had succeeded in 1898 in having him made governor general, regarded Finland as an ordinary province of the Russian Empire, discrete only in its special local institutions. His point of view, which was also that of War Minister Kuropatkin, was formalized by the manifesto of 3/15

---

*This nickname came from the initials, K. D., by which the party was designated.

February 1899, which ordered the Finnish army merged into the Russian, and by a number of decrees that, between 1901 and 1904, extended the rights of Russian subjects and the Russian language in Finland, strengthened the prerogatives of the governor general, restricted freedom of the press and of assembly, etc. Immediately on the publication of the manifesto, the opposition of the Finns was unanimous: at once a petition bearing more than five hundred thousand signatures protested the violation of their Constitution. It was not even officially recognized. The tsar refused to receive the delegation of five hundred persons sent to Petersburg to present the petition to him; in order to put his decisions into action, he changed the composition of the Finnish administration and Senate. But, far from laying down its arms, the national opposition redoubled after the promulgation of a new army law in July 1901. The clergy refused to read the text of the law aloud in the churches. A more vehement petition than that of 1899 was signed by 473,000 persons, many of them officials who rose above the fear of laying themselves open to reprisals. The population invented numberless obstacles to the mobilization of the class of 1902, organizing a "conscription strike": 59 per cent of the conscripts refused to appear. The universal resentment finally drove a young functionary of the Senate, Eugen Schauman, to kill Bobrikov on 5/18 June 1904, and his act was approved by public opinion. After the Russian revolution of 1905 the tsar was compelled to condemn everything that Bobrikov had done and, in the manifesto of 23 October/5 November 1905, to abrogate all the measures that contravened the Finnish Constitution.

In Poland, where, during his youth, Pleve had perpetrated one of his most loathsome actions by betraying his benefactor, a wealthy Pole, the effects of the Russification policy were manifest. Prince Imeretinsky, the governor general and a moderate, pointed out that "discontent is general" and that "the revolutionary movement is spreading among those classes of society that it had not yet reached," that the Russian officials were "ignorant and gross," and that it was necessary to put a stop to persecutions against the Polish language and the Catholic religion "if it is desired to pacify the country." But his counsels of moderation were not observed.

The national opposition in the Caucasus, which had begun under Alexander III, had increased, especially after the appointment of Prince Golitsyn as governor general in 1897. He was not satisfied with closing the Armenian schools, as he had already begun to do under the previous reign. In 1902 he proposed the confiscation of the property of the Armenian church, the income from which was used to support the national schools. This suggestion was so preposterous that the majority of the ministers opposed it. But Pleve seconded it, and the tsar pronounced himself in favor of it. Deeply wounded in its religious feelings, the Armenian people defended the possessions of its church by force of arms, and in many towns it fought bloody battles against Russian troops. Later the Russian government was to go to the extreme of inciting the Tartars against the Armenians and creating what amounted to a climate of pogrom.

It was above all the Jews who were the objects of Pleve's fury, with the backing of part of the court, notably Grand Duke Sergey Aleksandrovitch, who, as soon as he had been made governor general of Moscow, had undertaken the infamous expulsion of twenty thousand Muscovite Jews in 1891–1892. Pleve resolved to "drown the revolution in Jewish blood," and at the same time he hoped, by inflaming national hatreds, to distract the people from revolutionary notions. Under the immediate management of an agent of the police and with the participation of reactionary monarchist groups, he made the plans for a pogrom in Kishinev that broke out on Easter, 8/21 April 1903, lasted two days, and abruptly ended when Petersburg ordered it to end. Encouraged by the connivance of the authorities and heartened by drink, the mob tore down Jews' residences, threw itself on the Jews themselves, butchered them without regard to age, and stole their belongings: 500 houses and apartments were sacked and destroyed, 131 persons were killed or seriously injured, and 500 were less gravely hurt. The press was forbidden to say anything about this pogrom, but *The Times* of London published the letter in which Pleve enjoined the governor of Bessarabia not to resort to armed force in the event of a pogrom lest this "arouse the animosity of the Russian population against the government." On 29 August/12 September of the same year another pogrom, directly supported by the army, was staged in Gomel. The Governor of Mogilev told the Jews: "It is your own fault: you bring up your children badly." Pleve told them frankly: "Stop the revolution and I will stop the pogroms." * Far from intimidating them, he succeeded only in encouraging them in revolutionary tendencies and nationalist sentiments.

His labor policy was no more fruitful. Before he took office, the police had accepted the offer of a Moscow student, Zubatov, to organize workers' meetings with government help as a means of holding the labor movement in check. Thus, about 1900, Zubatov had set up "labor unions" in Moscow, Petersburg, Odessa, and a few other cities,

---

*The remark was recorded by Count Witte.

and the government had carried its tolerance of them to such a point that, when they went on strike, its representatives forced the employers to meet the workers' demands. Pleve regarded Zubatov's work as dangerous and dismissed him but not his methods, which acquired the name of *zubatovshchina* (Zubatovism). For all his certainty that he was controlling the labor movement, Pleve was merely reinforcing it.

His brutal policy came to the end that might have been predicted for it. On 15/28 July 1904, as he was riding in his carriage to the railway station from which he would take the train to Peterhof to present his report to the tsar, he was torn to shreds by a bomb thrown by a Revolutionary Socialist, Sazonov.

Opposition at the Beginning of the Conciliatory Svyatopolk-Mirsky Ministry (1904)

The assassination of Pleve, which coincided with the Russian defeats in Manchuria, impressed the tsar far more profoundly than the earlier assassinations. This time, instead of selecting a man of the right as minister of the interior, he turned to Prince Svyatopolk-Mirsky. Upright and honest, but weak in character and wholly without experience in high politics, the new minister was hardly equal to his task. But he was able to assuage the opposition by responding to the aspirations of the country as a whole. Before his appointment he had laid his program before the tsar: to reconcile Russian society with the government by satisfying those of its legitimate demands that it was timely to grant and to win over the national minorities by recognizing the validity of their just claims. Relying on the tsar's response—Nicholas told him that he shared his view—the prince promised the representatives of the press that he would move in this direction.

His appointment immediately incited the opposition of the moderates, the zemstvo, and the intellectuals, whose representatives banished by Pleve were recalled from exile. In August 1904 it was agreed that there would be a zemstvo congress to address a petition to the tsar and present the demands for a constitution. At the same time the Union for Liberation, which represented a more advanced sector of opinion, decided to organize a series of dinners in the autumn in various Russian cities in order to procure the adoption of resolutions of a constitutional and democratic character in order to back up the demands of the zemstvo congress. Informed of the convocation of this congress, Svyatopolk-Mirsky suggested that the zemstvo delegates gather in Petersburg rather than in Moscow, as they had intended.

They agreed, but on 1/14 November, when they had already arrived in Petersburg, their congress was prohibited. They could hold only private meetings. Between 6/19 and 8/21 November they debated and adopted the eleven articles of the memorable document that may be called the "Bill of Rights" of Russian liberalism. During the debates basic differences had emerged between the majority (108), which favored a constitution, and the minority (27), which, under the leadership of Shipov, opposed any limitation on the tsar's absolute power. While all the delegates had agreed in demanding the inviolability of the home, individual liberty, freedom of conscience, religion, speech, the press, assembly, and association, civil and political equality for all, the peasants as well as the other social classes, the democratization of the zemstvo, and the enlargement of its powers, only the majority, however, had declared in favor of authority for the national representative organ to make laws, vote the budget, and supervise the executive arm. The demands of the Petersburg congress, which also governed the composition of future zemstvo congresses, were approved in a whole series of local meetings held at the end of 1904 and the beginning of 1905. Public dinners staged by the Union for Liberation extended them in a still more radical direction. In December 1904, in a conference in Paris, the representatives of the Union for Liberation reached agreement with various groups of Revolutionary Socialists and national-minority patriots for a struggle against the autocracy. While each ally reserved the right to select its own tactics, all set themselves a common end: the establishment of a democratic system founded on universal suffrage and the right of each nationality to determine its own course.

The Ukase of 12/25 December 1904 and the Promise of Reforms

The zemstvo congress had not been able, as it had hoped, to present its demands to the tsar in person. Nevertheless Svyatopolk-Mirsky deemed it essential to take cognizance of demands that had been formulated in what was undoubtedly a private meeting but one held with his tacit consent. He submitted to the tsar a proposal for a ukase that would grant certain freedoms to Russian subjects and announce the introduction of elective members into the Imperial Council.

The tsar summoned his ministers and put this question to them: should Pleve's policy be continued, or, in the light of the growth of the revolutionary movement, must satisfaction be granted to the desires of the moderate elements in society? Pobyedonostsev argued that religion forbade the tsar to alter the political system. Witte, on the contrary, insisted that the prosecution of reaction would lead to disaster and that the existing system was condemned by all social classes, but that it could not be modified without "taking the road that would certainly lead to what is called a constitution." On the tsar's order he drafted a proposed ukase that was signed by all the ministers present. But, the day before it was to be promulgated, Nicholas II sent for Witte and, in the presence of Grand Duke Sergey Aleksandrovitch, he expressed his doubts on the wisdom of admitting elected members to the Imperial Council. Witte replied that "in his heart and his conscience" such an admission would in effect be the first step toward the limitation of the absolute power and that, in consequence, "if His Majesty had reached the sincere and irrevocable conviction that it was impossible to resist the universal tide of history, this paragraph must be retained in the ukase, but that, if His Majesty found that such a form of government was inacceptable, it would be wiser to eliminate it." In agreement with Grand Duke Sergey Aleksandrovitch, the tsar replied that never in any case would he accept a representative system, for he regarded it as "noxious to the people that God had entrusted to his care," and the paragraph dealing with national representation was eliminated. At the same time, even though the tsar declared in the ukase of 12/25 December 1904 that it was his duty to "provide for the welfare of the state that God had put into his hands" and that he intended to maintain "intact the basic laws of the empire," he added, in contradiction to these statements: "But, if the necessity for some changes becomes clearly evident, we believe that it is essential to undertake them, even if such a reform must introduce a substantial innovation into our legislation." The ukase, which was completely silent on political rights and liberties—as if the "necessity" had not become "clearly evident"—called on the Imperial Council in cautious terms to examine the following matters: the transformation of the peasants into free rural citizens enjoying the fullness of their rights, the provision of the benefits of social insurance for the workers, an increase in zemstvo and municipal independence, the revision of the "vexatious laws" on national minorities, the abolition of "excessive restrictions" on the freedom of the press, the inauguration of the "necessary independence" of the courts, "the maintenance of all the force of law," and limitations on the "discretionary power of the administrative authorities" in the punishment of crime. At the same time the government issued a communiqué that forbade all institutions and associations of whatever nature, under penalty of prosecution, to concern themselves with questions the study of which was not permitted to them by law; it also called on the press to "do whatever is necessary to tranquilize public opinion."

Naturally the ukase of 12/25 December 1904 satisfied no one. The gulf between the demands of public opinion and the intentions of the government was too deep.

IV / FOREIGN POLICY FROM 1894 TO 1905* [B. MIRKIN-GUETZEVITCH, P. GRONSKY, and G. DANILOV]

The foreign policy of the first part of the reign of Nicholas II was peaceful in Europe and aggressive in the Far East. On the one side, Russia endeavored to consolidate the French-Russian alliance, to make certain of Austrian-Russian understanding in the Balkans, and to convene the first Conference of The Hague. On the other, Russia's occupation of Manchuria and her aims in Korea set her in opposition to Japan and led to the Russian-Japanese War.

The Consolidation of the French-Russian Alliance

Nicholas II remained loyal to the alliance concluded by his father. In October 1896 he went to France, where he was given an enthusiastic welcome. In August of the following year President Félix Faure returned his visit and was a guest at lavish celebrations in Petersburg and Peterhof. In August 1899 Delcassé, the French foreign minister, negotiated a new arrangement in Petersburg: an exchange of secret letters with his Russian counterpart, Muravyev (August 9), synchronized the duration of the 1893 military convention (previously based on that of the Triple Alliance) with that of the diplomatic agreement of 1891. Thus the French-Russian alliance was reinforced.

The Austrian-Russian Accord of 1897 and the Mürzsteg Program of 1903

Austrian-Russian rivalry in the Balkans was growing weaker. Russia was looking more and more toward the Far East, a direction in which Wilhelm II was making every effort to push her. In addition, Foreign

*Professor Mirkin-Guetzevitch was responsible for all except the sections on the construction of the Chinese-Eastern Railway and the leasing of the Liao-Tung Peninsula, written by Professor Gronsky, and the Russian-Japanese War, written by General Danilov.

Minister Goluchovski of Austria-Hungary was taking a conciliatory attitude.

In April 1897 Russia and Austria-Hungary concluded the Petersburg accord. They announced publicly that they "were resolved to preserve the general peace, the principle of order, and the *status quo*," and they agreed secretly that, if the *status quo* could not be preserved, they would put aside "in advance all spirit of conquest" in the Balkans and enforce respect for this principle by any other power that might give evidence of contrary intentions. In addition they evolved a program of reforms in Macedonia. The Porte, pursuant to its custom, forestalled any foreign intervention by publishing its own reform project (November 1902), and appointed Hilmi Pasha as inspector general. But Russia and Austria-Hungary were insistent, and on February 21, 1903, in a joint memorandum, they demanded that the Porte embark on a more thorough reform of the administration, the police, and finances, and permit the participation of foreigners in the reorganization of the police.

Russia clung loyally to the policy of the *status quo*. In 1903, when the Macedonian insurrection spread, Foreign Minister Lamsdorf declared that the tsar would never support "the revolutionary activities in Macedonia." In February of that year the Russian *Official Messenger* asserted that, while Russia intended to protect "the vital necessities and the normal interests of the Christian populations in Turkey," she would sacrifice "neither a single drop of the blood of her sons nor the smallest tittle of the Russian people's wealth if the Slav states, in spite of the counsels of wisdom that had been given to them, sought by violent and revolutionary methods to alter the established order of things in the Balkan Peninsula." On October 9, 1903, at Mürzsteg in Steyr, the emperors and foreign ministers of Russia and Austria-Hungary drew up the new program of reforms intended to guarantee the protection of the Christian populations of Macedonia, and two "civil agents," one Austrian and one Russian, were attached to the inspector general to see to the execution of the program. In 1905 representatives of England, France, Germany, and Italy were appointed to assist the "civil agents"; the Porte did not submit to this supervision until it saw the powers' warships approaching the Dardanelles.

The Mürzsteg program seemed to be the confirmation of the final reconciliation between the two major rivals in the Balkans. Certain journalists and politicians looked on it as the inauguration of a new era. But first of all Austria-Hungary was not sincerely abandoning her predominance in the Balkans, where v. Aehrenthal, who succeeded Goluchovski in October 1906, was to renew the old policy of the Habsburgs. Furthermore, the reform programs were incapable of restoring peace to Macedonia, where the secret nationalist organization persevered in its struggle against Turkish domination.

The First Conference of The Hague (1899)

On 12/24 August 1898 Foreign Minister Muravyev let it be known that Nicholas II wanted the convocation of an international conference to explore the reduction of armaments, the humanization of methods of warfare, and the peaceful solution of international disputes.

The preservation of the general peace and a possible reduction in the burden of armaments that weighs heavily on all nations [he wrote] appear in the present state of the entire world as the ideal toward which the efforts of all governments ought to be directed.

In its conviction that this lofty aim fulfills the most essential interests and the legitimate desires of all the powers, the imperial government believes that the present moment would be most favorable to the quest, by way of international discussion, for the most effective means of assuring to all peoples the benefits of a real and lasting peace and, above all, putting an end to the increasing expansion of current armaments . . .

Imbued with this belief, His Majesty has deigned to command me to propose to all governments whose representatives are accredited to the Imperial Court that they meet in a conference whose task it would be to concern itself with this grave problem.

With the help of God, this conference would be a happy omen for the century that is about to begin; it would bring together in a forceful whole the efforts of all states that are sincerely striving for the triumph of the great concept of universal peace over the causes of disorder and discord. At the same time it would cement their agreements with a joint consecration of the principles of equity and law on which are based the security of states and the well being of peoples.

In a circular bulletin of 18/30 December 1898 Muravyev outlined a concrete program for the conference:

1. An accord stipulating that there would be no increase, for a period of time to be determined, in the current land and sea forces and the war budgets thereunto appertaining; a preliminary study of means by which in the future it would be possible even to achieve reductions in the forces and budgets above referred to;

2. The prohibition of the use of any new firearms and new explosives by armies and navies, including any more powerful than those currently employed both for rifles and for artillery;

3. Restrictions on the use of already existing highly powerful explosives

in land warfare and the prohibition of the launching of projectiles or explosives of any kind by air from balloons or by similar means;

4. A ban on the use of submarine or diving torpedo boats or other destructive equipment of the same nature in naval warfare; and a pledge not to build ram-equipped warships in future;

5. The adaptation of the terms of the Geneva Convention of 1864 to naval warfare, on the basis of the supplementary articles of 1868;

6. On the same basis, the neutralization of all rescue craft charged with the retrieval of crews during or after naval battles;

7. The revision of the declaration of the laws and customs of war prepared in 1874 by the Conference of Brussels and not yet ratified;

8. Agreement in principle on the use of good offices, mediation, and optional arbitration in all circumstances that lend themselves thereto in order to prevent armed conflicts between nations; agreement on the method of their application and the establishment of a uniform practice for their employment.

On May 18, 1899 the representatives of twenty-six powers gathered in The Hague to open the first peace conference. Certainly it did not succeed in lightening the burden of the armed truce that hung over Europe. Nonetheless it represented a major advance in the development of international law. Russia's initiative, supported by France, led to a series of conventions of the utmost importance.

The Construction of the Chinese-Eastern Railway and the Leasing of the Liao-Tung Peninsula

In January 1895, after the death of Giers, who had directed Russian foreign policy throughout the reign of Alexander III, the Foreign Ministry was put into the hands of Prince Lobanov-Rostovsky, who had been Russia's ambassador in Vienna. In full agreement with Nicholas II* and his advisers, the new minister turned his whole attention to the Far East.

The Chinese-Japanese War ended with victory for Japan in the spring of 1895. The peace treaty of Shimonosaki gave the victor the island of Formosa, the peninsula of Liao-Tung with the fortress of Port Arthur, and the port of Niu-Tchuang in southern Manchuria. Russia, Germany, and France protested against these Japanese acquisitions on the Asian mainland, and, while at the same time demanding the restitution of all except Formosa to China, they concentrated large naval forces in the Gulf of Tchili. Japan was compelled to give in; though she obtained, by way of compensation, an increase in

---

*In 1896 the tsar told Wilhelm II: "I have no interest whatever in Constantinople; all my interest and attention are directed toward China."

the amount of war reparations that China had to pay her, she was nonetheless cheated of the major fruits of her victory.

Russia hastened to make the most of her intervention on behalf of China. She saw a possibility of changing the route of the Trans-Siberian. If the line could be run through northern Manchuria, it would not only eliminate 514 versts from the Irkutsk-Vladivostok leg but also save huge sums in construction costs because of the working difficulties that would be obviated. For this she needed China's consent. In order to win Peking's friendship, Witte helped China to borrow in France the money that was required for the payment of the reparations due to Japan. Then he created the Russian-Chinese Bank and won larger shares for France and Russia in the administration of the Chinese customs services. In 1896 the emperor of China sent Li Hung-tchang, who was viceroy of Pe-Tchili and who shaped Chinese policy, to represent him at the coronation of Nicholas II. The Russian government seized the opportunity to negotiate a treaty of defensive alliance with China against Japan and to obtain for the Russian-Chinese Bank the concession to build the Trans-Manchurian or Chinese-Eastern Railway. The convention of September 1896, signed by the Chinese minister in Petersburg and the board of directors of the Russian-Chinese Bank, authorized the bank to build and operate this railway, whose Tchita-Kharbin-Vladivostok branch had been envisaged by Witte. A private Chinese-Eastern Company was at once organized: its headquarters was in Petersburg; the chairman of its board of directors was appointed by the Chinese government and the directors were chosen by the stockholders. In actuality it was the Russian Finance Ministry that held the whip hand over both the Chinese-Eastern Company and the Russian-Chinese Bank. Behind these two private companies the moving force was the Russian state, which, with the full knowledge of everyone, was prosecuting a political undertaking of major scope, the progressive penetration of northern Manchuria.

In December of the next year, after the occupation of Kiao-Tcheyu by Germany, the Russian fleet took possession of Port Arthur at the instigation of the new foreign minister, Muravyev. Under the Chinese-Russian convention of March 27, 1898 Russia gained a lease, for a renewable term of twenty-five years, on the southern part of the peninsula of Liao-Tung, with Port Arthur and Ta-Lien-Wan, as well as the right to establish a military port and a commercial harbor in Port Arthur and on the peninsula and to connect Port Arthur with the Manchurian section of the Chinese-Eastern Railway. Thereupon the Chinese-Eastern Company acquired the concession for a new line, from Kharbin to Port Arthur by way of Mukden and Liao-Yang, with a branch to the Chinese port of Inku on the northern shore of the Gulf of Liao-Tung; this opened the whole of southern Manchuria and the Liao-Tung Peninsula to Russian political influence. Russia was also commissioned to organize shipping in the Pacific waters and, in the Bay of Ta-Lien-Wan, to build a Russian commercial port, to which the name of *Dalny* ("The Faraway") was given. The construction of Dalny cost the Treasury a great sum, but it spent the money without hesitation, in spite of criticisms in the press, notably in Siberian newspapers, which declared—and the Russian-Japanese War was to vindicate these predictions—that, in the event of a landing by an enemy force on the Liao-Tung Peninsula, the new town would most certainly become a major base for military operations against Port Arthur.

Russian-Japanese Rivalry in Korea

While she was penetrating into southern Manchuria and establishing herself in the peninsula of Liao-Tung, Russia was also hoping to extend her influence over Korea, which had been made independent in principle by the treaty of Shimonosaki. Here she came into conflict with Japan, which had insisted on the independence of the Korean kingdom only in order to be able in fact to bring it under her own protectorate.

King Li-Khui of Korea seemed at first amenable enough to the influence of the Japanese minister, who spurred him to a series of reforms and gave him the technical advisers who could carry them out. On the other hand, the queen's sympathies—like those of her party, the Min, which was hostile to the reforms—were with Russia; it was she who was responsible for a reversal at court in favor of Russia and for the dismissals of the pro-Japanese ministers. But a popular revolt broke out in October 1895; the rebels forced their way into the palace and assassinated the queen and her partisans. The king fell back under Japanese influence until February 1896. At that time naval forces, landing at Shemulpo from the Russian warship *Admiral Mornilov,* dispersed the leaders of the Japanese party and took custody of the king, who, having fled his palace, had taken refuge in the Russian mission, where he lived until February 1897, under guard by Russian naval riflemen. When Li-Khui returned to his court, it was to Russian officers that he turned over the command of his personal guard and the palace guard. Thereupon Russia and Japan pledged themselves, under the treaty of Seoul (May 14–July 29) , to respect Korea's independence; the king assumed the title of emperor. But Russian-Japanese rivalry persisted nevertheless.

Russian competition in Korea irritated Japan the more sharply because the Russians were established in Manchuria, which the European powers had forced Japan to give back to China. Through the intermediary of Baron Rosen, the Russian ambassador in Tokyo, Japan suggested to the Russian government that the zones of Russian and Japanese influence in the Far East be officially defined. Japan was prepared to abandon Manchuria and the peninsula of Liao-Tung to the Russians, provided that she gained recognition of her predominance in Korea, and she wanted to establish the Yalu River as the line of demarcation between the two spheres of influence. In 1898, after the occupation of Port Arthur, Russia agreed to make concessions. A Russian-Japanese convention of April 25, 1898 once more guaranteed the independence of Korea, in which the two contracting parties would share commerical concessions and advantages. In fear of intervention by England, which had sent a naval detachment to Shemulpo, Russia left Japan a free hand by recalling her financial adviser and her military instructors from Seoul.

In order to allay the anxieties of Japan, which had begun in 1897 to enlarge her army and her fleet and had fortified the Tsushima Strait in order to cut the Russian line of communications between Port Arthur and Vladivostok—thus leading the Russians to attempt to fortify their own positions on the Korean coast, in the vicintiy of the port of Ma-San-Po—it would have been necessary at the very least that Russia respect the 1898 convention. On the contrary, in spite of Witte and Kuropatkin, the tsar allowed himself to be drawn into a policy of conquest and material gain in the Far East that was steadily to augment the antagonism between Russia and Japan. Two influences in particular had a profound effect on Nicholas II.

The first was that of Wilhelm II, who was striving to upset the European equilibrium restored by the French-Russian alliance. In order to divert Russia from Europe and to supplant her in the Balkans to the advantage of Germany and Austria-Hungary, the Kaiser consistently urged her eastward. In his correspondence with Nicholas II he liked to address him as "the emperor of the Pacific" and to call himself "the emperor of the Atlantic." He hoped that Russian expansion would culminate in a clash with England and that, by putting France in a delicate position since she was trying to establish closer ties with the British Empire, this would weaken the alliance between France and Russia.

The second influence was that of a "military party," which was

really only a businessmen's party and which had its center at court.
In 1898 an extremely enterprising business magnate named Vonlyal-
yarsky suggested the creation of a company to exploit the natural
resources of Korea, which was rich in iron, coal, forests, gold. . . . It
was his intention to obtain a concession from the Korean government
and, by laying his hands on the whole kingdom step by step to prepare
it for annexation to Russia. Submitted by Grand Duke Alexander
Mikhailovitch, his project was approved by the tsar and the company's
charter was published in the *Bulletin of Laws.* In 1899, through the
backing of Russian diplomacy, the company obtained some forest
concessions in Korea. The Boxer Rebellion forced the postponement
of further operations, the leadership of which had been given to a
former officer, Bezobrazov, who had just bought the concessions for
some 80,000 rubles and built a lumber mill on the left bank of the
Yalu, in the Japanese sphere of influence. But these concessions,
which violated the commitments made by Russia to Japan, aroused
the protests of the Tokyo government.

The Military Occupation of Manchuria by Russia

The Boxer Rebellion of 1900 was directed not only against the
propaganda of foreign missionaries but also against the concession of
territories under lease and the construction of railways. This gave
Russia the opportunity for the military occupation of Manchuria.
While some of her troops marched on Peking, where they joined the
detachments of the other powers, the rest took over the protection
of the Trans-Manchurian. Once the Boxer Rebellion had been put
down, Russia kept her troops in Manchuria, in spite of the protests
by China, which demanded the evacuation of her territory; the pretext
was the necessity of the troops presence as protection for the continuing work of building the railway.

This stand brought Russia's two rivals, Japan and England, together. The Anglo-Japanese accord of January 20, 1902 guaranteed
Chinese and Korean independence while at the same time recognizing
Japan's special interests in Korea. It assured Japan of England's
neutrality in the event of war against Russia and England's help if
some other power—it was France that was meant—should align itself
with Russia. The accord was given a term of five years, renewable
automatically unless either party gave a year's advance notice to the
contrary.

Russia sought to counter this with an agreement with the French.
But France was hesitant to make the specific commitment of support-

ing an active Russian policy in the Far East. In the declaration of March 20, 1902 these two allies also reaffirmed the principle of Chinese and Korean inviolability, but they confined themselves to reciprocal promises to "consult on possible means" of safeguarding their special interests in the Far East against "agressive action by third powers." On the suggestion of France, to which she had given the pledge of evacuation of Manchuria, Russia promised under the Russian-Chinese convention of April 9 to carry out the evacuation in three stages, at six-month intervals, before October 8, 1903, contingent on observance of the convention concluded in 1896 between China and the Russian-Chinese Bank for the protection of the Manchurian railway.

The Russian-Japanese Rupture

The execution of the Russian-Chinese convention had been barely begun when Bezobrazov and his associates came back into the picture. Bezobrazov, who had become secretary of state attached to the person of the tsar, went to the Far East, where he not only negotiated new concessions on both banks of the Yalu but also arrived at an understanding with Admiral Aleksyeyev, the commander in chief at Port Arthur, to halt the evacuation. When the second stage fell due, on April 8, the Russian troops did not move; only Mukden was evacuated. Witte and Kuropatkin vainly contested this policy, which had to lead to war. The group surrounding Bezobrazov was a powerful one. The company that had been established for the exploitation of the Talu River concessions included men like Admiral Abaza, the tsar's secretary for Far Eastern affairs; Count Ignatyev, a member of the Imperial Council; Count Hendrikov, master of the horse to the tsarina, and Prince Yusupov; some of the concessionnaires had sufficient influence to infiltrate Russian soldiers, in the guise of workers, into the areas under exploitation. This gang of "adventurers of the lowest sort," as Kuropatkin called them, of "thieves," in Witte's expression, found the highest backing in the court itself—the minister of the interior, the all-powerful Pleve, who was persuaded that the Russian revolutionaries were behind the Japanese and that a speedy and victorious war would make it possible for the government to make an end of the revolutionary movement forever; and the tsar, who was going to play Pleve's game.

Far from criticizing the halt in the evacuation procedure, Nicholas II ordered Aleksyeyev to present to China on April 18 a list of conditions to which the application of the 1902 convention would be made subject. In particular it required that China grant Russia alone special rights in Manchuria and that she admit no foreigners other than Russians to that territory. This demand evoked sharp protests not only from Japan and England but also from the United States, which offered its financial help to the Japanese. Even while she was feverishly preparing for war, Japan still tried to negotiate. On August 12, 1903 she submitted to the Russian government, which had agreed to parley, a draft convention embracing a mutual commitment to respect the independence and integrity of China and Korea and reciprocal recognition of Japan's interests in Korea and Russia's special interests in the railway ventures in Manchuria, as well as mutual assurance that the contracting parties would interpose no obstacles to each other's industrial and commercial activities, and Russian recognition of Japan's exclusive right to intervene in Korea in the interests of the reforms and of good government. It was on the very next day after the presentation of this proposal that Nicholas II, by decree, appointed Admiral Aleksyeyev lieutenant general for the Far East and decided that the diplomatic negotiations between Tokyo and Petersburg would be carried on by the lieutenant general, who would submit them to the "special committee on the Far East" of which the tsar was the chairman. The "new viceroy" was working hand in glove with Bezobrazov, who joined him in order to serve as what might be called his foreign minister. Witte, who recommended moderation and peace and who was in conflict with Grand Duke Alexander, chairman of the finance committee, was called on to tender his resignation and relegated to the honorary post of chairman of the ministerial committee. This was a triumph for the Yalu company. As the viceroy's *Official Journal* stupidly put it in print, the purpose of the appointment of Aleksyeyev was to assure Russian predominance in the Pacific.

In vain Baron Rosen, the Russian ambassador in Tokyo, warned Petersburg that, if Russia did not give up Korea, war was inevitable. Bezobrazov and his gang, who looked on the conquest of Korea as their own get-rich-quick scheme, specifically wanted war. It was Bezobrazov who first drafted or revised several Russian notes sent from Petersburg to the Japanese; it was in fact he who subsequently directed the negotiations when they were removed from the foreign minister's hands and put into those of the viceroy and shifted to Tokyo. He was not interested in any compromise. When Japan proposed that a thirty-mile-wide neutral zone be established on either side of the Yalu, he refused. He was seeking merely to gain time for the reinforcement of the Russian troops in Manchuria, and the transfer of the actual forum of negotiations to the Far East facilitated this dilatory tactic. It was not until a month later, on October 3, that

Japan received an initial reply, in which Russia put forward her claim to keep Manchuria for herself without granting Japan reciprocity in Korea. Japan responded on October 30, but she had to wait until December 21 for the next word from Russia, which rejected her counter-offers. This calculated delay continued to the very end. If Tokyo insisted on an answer with respect to the evacuation of the Russian troops, back came the information that the tsar had gone to Darmstadt, where the tsarina was ill. . . . On January 13, 1904 Japan made new proposals to Petersburg, which did not reply. Two weeks later she asked for a formal response by the end of January or the beginning of February. When she did not get it but did see the Russian troops concentrating on the whole length of the Yalu, she broke off diplomatic negotiations on February 5 and, during the night of February 8-9, without any prior declaration of war, Japanese torpedo boats attacked the Russian fleet in the roadstead of Port Arthur and knocked seven heavy warships out of action.

The Russian-Japanese War (1904-1905)

Thoroughly persuaded of her own prestige, Russia had never envisaged the possibility of a Japanese attack. Furthermore, she was barely emerging from a period of great financial difficulties. Therefore she was not prepared when the war started. In Asia she had only 120 battalions, which, moreover, were scattered over the immense area of Siberia, the Amur region, and Manchuria, and which required 40 to 50 days to be put on a war footing. The mobilization program called for the initial transfer of 2 army corps and 4 reserve divisions—in other words, 128 battalions—from Europe. But, given the vastness of the distance to be traveled—up to more than 7500 versts—the very limited capacity of the single-track lines of the Trans-Siberian and the Chinese-Eastern, the extremely burdensome necessity of shipping troops and supplies at the same time, and the uncompleted state of the Trans-Siberian—which compelled the soldiers to march 60 versts over ice in order to cross Lake Baikal—the concentration of these reinforcements required several months. Furthermore, the defenses of Port Arthur, the home base of the Russian Pacific fleet, had been only poorly ordered; the day before the rupture, Kuropatkin, who had been there, declared that the city could not withstand a Japanese attack.

Thanks, in contrast, to a powerful naval fleet and a large merchant marine, the Japanese army, which was organized on the European model and consisted at the very start of 13 divisions, or 156 battalions, all on a war footing—as the war went on, these were to be supplemented by 20 reserve brigades, or 160 battalions—could very speedily be moved to the mainland and consequently seize the initiative in operations there.

Japan also had the moral advantage. For a long time and with great perseverance she had been preparing herself for the struggle against her powerful neighbor, and she was fully aware that her entire future depended on it. To Russia the war was a mere colonial conflict. While great interests were at stake, they were in no way vital to the country. The people did not feel directly threatened; the masses could not even understand what reason there could be for taking them off their land and sending them to far-off Manchuria to fight the Japanese, of whom they had never even heard.

Condemned for a long period to wage a war of defense, Russia concentrated her main forces between Liao-Yang and King-Tcheyu. The Japanese, who had gained naval supremacy through their sudden attack on the Russian fleet, decided to land their advance guard in Korea, move it swiftly to the Yalu, and, threatening to cut the railway between Mukden and Liao-Yang, immobilize the Russians and thus protect the landing of the rest of their own army on the Liao-Tung Peninsula. In spite of the serious losses inflicted on the Russian fleet by the Japanese torpedo boats on the night of February 8–9, Admiralissimo Togo, who had been given the difficult mission of covering the landing of all the Japanese forces, was in dread of intervention by the Russian Pacific fleet throughout February and March; it was under the command of that remarkable warrior, Admiral Makarov. It was only after he had gone down with the battleship *Petropavlovsk*, sunk by a Japanese mine on 31 March/13 April, that Togo felt no further immediate menace.

The first major land battle was fought on 18 April/1 May on the Yalu between the Japanese First Army under General Kuroki and the Russian eastern forces established at the Manchurian border. It was a most humiliating defeat for Russian national pride. The Japanese turned the Russians' right flank and forced them to fall back into the Fei Chung Lin mountain range, while themselves occupying Fin Kwan Tchen.

A few days later the Japanese transports anchored off the Elliot Islands, near the Liao Tung Peninsula, and landed their soldiers at Pi Tse Wu. These troops took the offensive toward the south and on 13/26 May they captured the position of H'sinung Yo, regarded as the key to Port Arthur and Dalny. Thereafter Port Arthur and its garrison, consisting of two infantry divisions, were cut off from the rest of the Russian forces, known as the Manchurian Army, which, under Kuropatkin's command, was still proceeding with its concentration in the region of Liao Yang, some 148 to 198 versts from the battlefield. After the battle of H'sinung Yo, the Japanese, who had continued to land fresh forces, first at Pi Tse Wu and then at Ta Ku Shan, assigned the mission of capturing Port Arthur to four divisions of General Nogi's army and turned Generals Oku's and Nodzu's armies against Kuropatkin's Russian army.

Kuropatkin could attempt to prevent the junction of the enemy forces marching against him—the armies of Generals Kuroki, Oku, and Nodzu—and try to defeat them separately. His alternative was either first to attack Kuroki's army, which was threatening Mukden, the nearest Russian base, or else to move against the Japanese forces in the south under Oku and Nodzu in order to restore communication with Port Arthur. In either case, obviously, he must put aside speculation and launch a decisive action. But he could not make up his mind to do so. In spite of the urgings of Viceroy Aleksyeyev, who insisted on the necessity of swiftly freeing Port Arthur, in which the Russian Pacific fleet was bottled up, Kuropatkin preferred to cling to his initial plan and proceed with the concentration of the reinforcements that were being sent to him. This tactic led to a succession of indecisive battles, all broken off before their issue could become clear, at Wa Fang Tcbo, Da Shi Tchao, Kai Tchen, and the heights of the Fei Chung Lin; little by little they undermined the Russian army's confidence in victory and made it possible for the three Japanese armies to effect their junction in the area of Liao Yang.

Kuropatkin, who had now got his reinforcements,* was compelled to accept the major battle that the Japanese were seeking under the command of Marshal Oyama. The Russians, with two hundred battalions, enjoyed superiority of numbers; but the much finer organization of the reserve officers and noncommissioned officers in the Japanese army made the two contesting forces virtually equal in terms of reality. After a series of clashes that engaged the opposing outposts between 11/24 and 16/29 August, the real battle began on 17/30 August at the outskirts of Liao Yang, where the Russians had set up fortified positions. They fought with amazing tenacity, and the Japanese, in spite of fanatical efforts, could not take their positions frontally. That evening, recognizing the failure of his frontal attacks, Oyama ordered Kuroki's army to begin crossing the Tapusi He River in order to turn Kuropatkin's left flank. This maneuver decided

---

*The Siberian Fifth Army Corps, the Tenth and Seventeenth Corps, and the first battalions of the First Line Army Corps.

the fate of the whole battle of Liao Yang. Kuropatkin of course ordered part of his force to go to the aid of the threatened flank, but his counter-maneuver did not succeed, and on the evening of 20 August/2 September he was obliged to fall back on Mukden; moreover, he did so in very good order. Once again he had not fought the battle to the end. Caution, temporization, and lack of confidence in its own troops were to be the characteristics of the Russian command throughout the war.

During September the Manchurian Army* received some of the reinforcements that it needed. In addition Admiral Aleksyeyev augmented it with the Siberian Sixth Army Corps, which was put under his orders. Kuropatkin, who now had 260 battalions available, finally considered his forces adequate to go over to the offensive, which had been made more urgent than ever by the situation of Port Arthur, tightly ringed by the Japanese. His plan was to maneuver in such a way as to turn the Japanese right flank, established in the mountains in the east, while the enemy's main force was north of Liao Yang, also in the mountains. But the lack of mountain artillery and pack animals made it difficult to carry out this maneuver, and the requisitions sent to Chinese suppliers merely unmasked the Russians' plans to the Japanese. They prepared a countermaneuver: they would remain on the defensive in the mountains in order to maintain their positions there, and they would attack in the plain in order to try to outflank the Russians on the west. The Russians took the offensive on 21 September/4 October, but a few days later they had to halt because the mountains were inaccessible and the Japanese were retaliating by counterattacking the Russian center and right flank. Kuropatkin very soon abandoned his plans of attack and took up defensive positions all along the Sha Ho River. There was ferocious fighting along the entire front, lasting until the morning of 4/17 October. During the previous night the Japanese won control of the "Tree Height," which overlooked the Russian positions, and set up artillery and machine guns there. But during the next night, in a daring stroke that wound up in hand-to-hand fighting, the Russians recaptured the height and renamed it *Putilovskaya,* in honor of General Putilov, who had won it back. It was this brilliant feat of arms that was the real conclusion of the so-called battle of the Sha Ho, which lasted for several days without producing a decisive result. During their offensive the Russians had been able to gain only about nineteen versts to the south

---

*At that time it consisted of the Siberian First, Second, Third, Fourth, and Fifth Corps and the First, Tenth, and Seventeenth Line Army Corps.

of Mukden. Exhausted, both sides rested on their positions, and for four and a half months there was no fighting on the whole length of the Sha Ho. Both armies dug in, protected their fronts with wildernesses of barbed wire, and concentrated as many artillery pieces as they could. It was the inception of trench warfare, which was to develop so much farther during the First World War.

While Kuropatkin's and Oyama's armies stood face to face in Manchuria, Nogi's had pursued the siege of Port Arthur. In July the garrison had had to abandon its perimeter defenses and fall back on the line of forts. This retreat had exposed the city and the inner port, in which the Russian fleet was anchored, to the shells of the Japanese siege guns. Rather than risk being destroyed at its moorings, the fleet had made a desperate gamble and tried on 28 July/10 August to get to Vladivostok. In the open sea it had made contact with the stronger Japanese fleet and lost its commander, Admiral Witheft, in the battle. Some of its units had been able to find shelter in neutral ports; such others as had not been put out of action had had to return to Port Arthur, where their crews and their weapons, as at Sebastopol, had been used to reinforce the army on land. From 4/17 to 10/23 August General Nogi strove to take Port Arthur by storm. After his failure, which cost him heavy losses and convinced him of the impossibility of capturing the fortress by a general attack, he had decided to proceed by a series of localized and progressive attacks.

The suspension of operations in Manchuria allowed the Japanese to concentrate their entire attention on the siege of Port Arthur. Kuropatkin was fully aware that the city's surrender would mean the loss of the whole Russian Pacific fleet—with the exception of a few cruisers at anchor at Vladivostok—and would cause a new and grievous disillusionment in Russia. But, while he was willing to return to the offensive, he did not believe it possible to do so before the following year, when he would have received the reinforcements that he was expecting from Europe and that were arriving only irregularly. The Japanese, however, had decided to end the war sooner. At the end of October they began a series of violent assaults against a few positions that seemed especially important to them—the High Mountain, which dominated the city and the port; Forts II and III, and Redoubt 3. The Russians fought back savagely, and this whole unequal struggle was nothing but a long succession of dazzling exploits of arms. It was not until 22 November/5 December that the Japanese gained a foothold on the High Mountain, and it was only two weeks after that that they captured Fort II, where the heroic leader of the defense, General Kondratenko, was killed, and Fort III. After this the defenders' days were numbered. On 20 December 1904/2 January 1905, General Stoessel, in command of Port Arthur, capitulated. Port Arthur had held out for more than seven months. Not only did its surrender satisfy the national pride of the Japanese, who, having already conquered it in 1894, had been compelled by Germany, France, and Russia to return it to the Chinese; the victory freed Nogi's army to throw itself against the Manchurian Army. In contrast, it completed the discouragement of the Russians, already sorely tried by the loss of their fleet; they were so thoroughly demoralized by it that the continuation of the war seemed to them to have no further sense.

In order to restore the morale of his men and also to prevent Nogi's army from moving northward, Kuropatkin launched a cavalry raid on Hin Koi and the Port Arthur–Liao Yang railway at the beginning of January. This sortie, led by General Mishchenko, did not succeed in stopping Nogi. Marshal Oyama, who had received reinforcements consisting of newly activated brigades, was to have Nogi's entire army at his disposal by the middle of February. The Russian forces, which had also been substantially increased,* were divided into three armies: the Second, on the right flank, under General Grippenberg; the Third, in the center, under General Kaulbars, and the First, on the left flank, under General Linevitch; the supreme command was held by Kuropatkin, who became generalissimo in place of Admiral Alekseyev, who was recalled to Petersburg. The opposing forces, each of which consisted of 250,000 to 300,000 bayonets, were approximately equal. Kuropatkin launched his January offensive some time before the final concentration of the Japanese troops. The Second Army, which was supposed to envelop the Japanese left flank, scored some successes at first: by 15/28 January it had conquered almost the whole region of Sandepu. But Kuropatkin halted his attack and pulled back his troops when he learned that the Japanese were concentrating their strength against his center, the Third Army. When he decided, a month later, to resume the interrupted offensive, it was too late; the Japanese had anticipated him, for Nogi's army, arriving from Port Arthur, had undertaken a flanking movement on both shores of the Liao Hô River. Kuropatkin made a number of attempts to counter the Japanese maneuver, but, in spite of the heroic comportment of some of his units, he could not prevent Nogi from forwarding his attack. Kuropatkin was forced to pull back his right flank not only toward the west but also toward the north, in order to defend Mukden, which

---

*They had been augmented by the Eighth and Sixteenth Line Army Corps and five brigades of riflemen.

was the starting point for the only northbound rail line and the best road, known as the Mandarins' Road. The battle round Mukden swung in favor of the Japanese. Afraid lest communications with some of his army corps be severed, Kuropatkin began to withdraw toward the north during the night of 25 February/10 March. He had to fight as he retreated, and he could not regroup his troops before they had moved north of Tye Ling, on the Si Pin Hai heights. He yielded the supreme command to General Linevitch, whom he replaced at the head of the First Army.

After the Mukden defeat a new and bitter ordeal was awaiting Russia: the destruction of her Second Pacific Squadron. At the start of the war Petersburg had decided to send the Baltic and Black Sea fleets to the Far East. Only the Baltic fleet, under the command of Admiral Rozhdestvensky, had set out in October 1904. Composed of ships of extremely various types and speeds, compelled to drag cargo vessels filled with food and coal behind it, this fleet, some units of which had to cover 16,400 miles, had made its way through three oceans with extreme slowness. It was only at the end of April/beginning of May 1905, when Port Arthur had surrendered and the First Pacific Squadron had ceased to exist, that Rozhdestvensky concentrated all his vessels near the coast of Annam. There was only one possibility for him: to try to reach Vladivostok. He decided to force his passage through the Tsushima Strait. Excessively slow, overloaded with coal, inadequately armored, armed with guns too short in range, his ships were far inferior to the enemy's. In an unequal battle on 14/27–15/28 May they were shot to pieces by the Japanese guns; except for two armored cruisers and two destroyers that managed to escape and reach Vladivostok, the greater part of the fleet was sunk; what was left, the older ships, was surrounded and captured.

The Tsushima disaster meant the end of the war. The Russian government, disturbed by the revolutionary movement that was being abetted by the military defeats, was ready to make peace. As for Japan, she was eager to end a costly war, and she secretly requested the mediation of the President of the United States. Summoned by President Theodore Roosevelt to initiate preliminary peace talks, both sides agreed.

The Treaty of Portsmouth (1905)

In August the plenipotentiaries gathered in Portsmouth, New Hampshire: for Russia, Witte, Baron Rosen, the former ambassador in Tokyo, and Professor Martens; for Japan, Baron Komura and the ambassador to Washington, Takahira.

The extremely extensive Japanese conditions were most humiliating for Russia: the cession of the island of Sakhalin and the Liao Tung Peninsula, the evacuation of all Manchuria, the surrender of all warships interned in neutral harbors, restrictions on Russian armament in the Far East, and war reparations totaling 600 million dollars. The Russian emissaries protested vigorously against the last three conditions. Japan, which had just renewed her alliance with England, was immovable at first, but, under pressure from Roosevelt and England, she finally moderated her position and dropped the terms that Russia had rejected.

Under the Treaty of Portsmouth, signed on 23 August/5 September 1905, Russia recognized Japan's protectorate over Korea, gave up the peninsula of Liao Tung, ceded Port Arthur and Dalny to Japan together with the various installations and the railway that were connected with them, as well as the southern part of the island of Sakhalin, granted the Japanese privileges in the fishery areas north of Vladivostok, accorded Japan most-favored-nation privileges on the basis of reciprocity and before the conclusion of a new trade treaty, and, finally, pledged herself to evacuate Manchuria.

As painful as these terms were for Russian national pride, the Russian government could no longer put off the conclusion of peace, for revolution was about to explode.

Nicholas II (1894–1917): The Reign Continued

[P A U L M I L I U K O V]

I / THE FIRST REVOLUTION: FROM RED SUNDAY TO THE MANIFESTO OF 17/30 OCTOBER 1905

At the end of 1904, when the ultra-cautious Svyatopolk-Mirsky was as incapable of persuading Nicholas II to embark on real reforms as he was of renewing the repressive policy of his predecessor, Pleve, the battle against absolutism was being carried on almost exclusively by the Socialist parties, the intellectuals, and the zemstvo. These three opposition groups had taken advantage of the period of relative freedom that followed Pleve's death, first to organize and attempt unification and then to clarify and publicly state their demands, which at that time were relatively moderate. In 1905, as the war against Japan turned more and more into a disaster, their organization made rapid gains; they were no longer alone in their assault on autocracy. The new phenomenon that dominated the entire year of 1905 was the emergence of the popular masses into the political arena. On "Red Sunday," 9/22 January 1905, for the first time in the history of Russia and without either the anticipation or the intention of the leaders of the movement, the people took the stage in the shape of the workers. This action infused the whole opposition movement with a special energy that made it a menace. Although absolutism strove to persevere in its intransigence, it was beaten back into a series of increasingly important concessions. The manifesto of 17/30 October, without either the anticipation or the intention of the government, was the first constitutional concession to be made by the autocracy, and this concession was to lead to the convocation of the first Imperial Duma.

Red Sunday: 9/22 January 1905

The date of 9/22 January, which inaugurated the revolutionary year of 1905, had been planned not in intellectual and zemstvo circles but among the factory workers of Petersburg. Nor was it the Socialist parties that were its instigators: its inspiration came from a priest, Gapon, who at the same time enjoyed a remarkable prestige in workers' circles and maintained relations with the police and the Ministry of the Interior—so that it may be said that the government itself expedited the beginnings of the revolution. In February 1904 Gapon had become chairman of the five "labor unions" established, in pursuance of Zubatov's method, at the expense and under the auspices of the police. Gapon was a man of dubious background, devoured by inordinate ambition, and endowed with a remarkable talent for oratory. In the "unions," the number of which he increased to twelve, he had brought together some thirty thousand well-disciplined workers over whom he exercised an unhampered ascendancy, thanks to his own demagogic eloquence and also, to a certain extent, to the money with which the police supplied him in order to meet his organizations' needs. Eleven days before "Red Sunday," the workers' representatives had called a strike at the Putilov factory and submitted a list of purely economic demands. In the ensuing days the strike had spread to other factories: on 7/20 January 93,000 workers employed by 74 companies were on strike; a day later 1614 firms and 250,000 workers were involved. Gapon, who had spent months in its preparation, decided to employ this strike for purposes that had in no way been foreseen by the police.

Through the intermediary of his sections, he suggested that the workers go to the palace to present the tsar with a petition setting forth their grievances. This idea of an appeal to the tsar, which could come from neither the Socialist groups nor the intellectuals, was bound to be understood by the popular masses. It brough back the seventeenth century and the times of Alexis Mikhailovitch. But the text of the appeal included wholly modern political demands: the convocation of delegates of all social classes, the introduction of all liberties, equality for all citizens before the law, amnesty for political offenders, the cession of land to the peasants, the eight-hour day, recognition of the right to strike, etc. It concluded with a remarkable threat: "Tsar, if you are deaf to our entreaties, there is no choice for us but to die here where we stand." In a series of public meetings

Gapon collected one hundred and thirty-five thousand signatures. In order to present the petition to the tsar, it was decided that on 9/22 January tens of thousands of workers coming from every working-class quarter in the city would converge in a solemn procession on the Winter Palace. The tsar was advised by letter that, if he did not appear before his people at two o'clock in the afternoon, he would cut the moral bonds that linked him with his people by destroying its confidence and blood would flow.

Nicholas II withdrew to Tsarskoye Selo. On the appointed Sunday troops were posted at every point that the procession might be expected to pass. The intellectuals, who foresaw a massacre, tried to prevent it; their emissaries, eminent men of letters such as Arsenyev, Annensky, and Gorky, intervened in vain with Svyatopolk-Mirsky and Witte, who were unable to take any action; the next day they were arrested on charges of having tried to form a "provisional government." At noon the workers formed ranks in their quarters and set out for the center of the city. They carried ikons and portraits of the tsar in order to leave no doubt as to their loyalty to their sovereign. They were confident of a fatherly reception and hearing from the tsar. But they did not move far. Everywhere, as soon as they came within range of the barricades erected by the troops, they were met with rifle fire. This unexpected attack paralyzed them at first; then they gave way to panic as they saw the dead and the wounded fall; they fled in disorder, pursued by the soldiery, and the most atrocious excesses of extermination followed, in which innocent spectators shared the fate of the demonstrators. The chase and the gunfire went on until late in the night. Gapon, who had led one column in person almost to the steps of the Winter Palace, fell at the first shots; rescued by friends, he was able to flee abroad a few days later. In a very few areas the workers, recovering from their panic, attempted to put up real resistance; they tried to set up barricades on Vassilyevsky Island. But on the whole the demonstration preserved its peaceful character to the very end, and the outrages perpetrated by the troops were therefore all the more flagrant; the balance sheet for this bloody day that became known as Red Sunday was a thousand dead and another thousand wounded.

The Resurgence of Opposition and the Unification of the Revolutionaries

Red Sunday launched a new period in the conflict between the opposition and the government. The authorities decided to make a display of "firmness." They reinstituted the post of governor general of Petersburg and gave it to D. G. Trepov, son of the prefect of police assassinated by Vera Zassulitcha. An extremely close collaborator of Grand Duke Sergey Aleksandrovitch, governor general of Moscow, Trepov had already proceeded most energetically against the revolution from this post. In Petersburg he ordered the dissolution of all labor unions and the arrests of a number of intellectuals. But, as Gapon had admitted was his aim after 9/22 January, in the eyes of the people the tsar's reputation was irreparably destroyed. The most peaceful citizens who had gone to the square in front of the Winter Palace to be heard by the tsar or "die" had gone home converts to revolution. A few days later, when the tsar had come to grips with the position in which he now found himself, Trepov ordered thirty-four reliable workers to be selected in the factories, told them how they must behave in the tsar's presence, and took them to Tsarskoye Selo. Nicholas II received them and informed them that he "forgave" them; he implored them "to be patient" and he "would take steps." After the audience he ordered lunch served to them; but, when they returned to Petersburg, a number of them was roughly handled by the workers there. This comedy did not succeed in restoring the tsar's prestige. Henceforth it was impossible to believe in the legend of the people's loyalty and obedience. Not only did the mass of the urban population go over at once to the revolution, but, since the government frequently resorted to the forcible return of workers to their villages by way of reprisal, revolutionary tendencies soon penetrated into peasant circles. The industrial strikes that mushroomed after Red Sunday and spread to almost all the country's industrial centers, especially those in the border regions, Poland, the Caucasus, and the western governments were complicated by agrarian disorders that erupted in March in all the governments. The intellectuals themselves cast off their pacifist approach and uttered no moral strictures against the armed attacks on the police and the terrorist activities that were becoming more and more frequent. In one such assault Grand Duke Sergey Aleksandrovitch was killed near his palace in the Kremlin by a bomb thrown by a Revolutionary Socialist, I. Kalyayev, and this made a profound impression on the tsar. When he learned of it, Nicholas II buried his head in his hands and cried amid his tears: "My God, why such a frightful crime?" Nothing could better have revealed his lack of understanding of his country's aspirations than this *why*. It was not until twelve years later, when he was abdicating, that he would weep again as he asked himself: "Have I been wrong for twenty-two years?"

The most serious consequence of Red Sunday was not that it had driven the terrorists back into action; it was that it had unified all the opponents of the government, from the extremists to the most moderate. A number of organizations were formed; in order to avoid reprisals by the authorities, they called themselves professional or technical "unions." Unquestionably this method of organization was less flexible than that of political parties; but, if the Russian intellectuals allowed themselves to be persuaded by their instincts not to go beyond this transitional form, it was because it was still too soon to think of establishing genuine parties. The first groups were the creations of university men and lawyers.

In Petersburg the funeral of Savinkin, a student who had been among the victims of Red Sunday, was the first pretext for an impressive demonstration organized by his comrades and their professors. Then, when the university reopened—it had closed the day after Red Sunday—its council decided not to resume classes. At the end of January, 16 members of the Academy of Sciences, 124 university professors, and 201 *Privatdozenten*, in the name of all Russian scholars, signed a declaration that concluded with the assertion that "freedom of knowledge is incompatible with the existing Russian social system." On 7/20 February, during a meeting at the university, students and professors castigated the "criminal adventure" of the war against Japan and the "bloody events" of 9/22 January, proclaimed the solidarity of workers and intellectuals, and called for the convocation of a Constituent Assembly elected by universal suffrage, a general amnesty, and the right of autonomy for national minorities. In April three separate organizations were formed for teachers in higher, secondary, and elementary schools.

On the day after Red Sunday, 325 lawyers met for a week of discussions, after which they expressed their sympathy with the workers, appointed a commission to investigate the recent events, and staged a week-long protest strike. On 16/29 the board of directors of the Bar Association itself adopted a motion declaring that a change in the political system was an inescapable condition to the proper rendition of justice. On 25 February/10 March representatives of the lawyers of both capitals and several provincial cities agreed to summon a general assembly of all the lawyers in Russia. It convened on 28 March/10 April; in vain Trepov's men demanded that it adjourn: it did not miss a single session. The 180 delegates who attended decided to organize a professional and political union, to propagandize on behalf of a constitution, and to proclaim their solidarity with all parties and associations of revolutionaries or other oppositionists.

The legal and university unions were augmented by many others, such as those of the railway workers, the engineers, the writers, etc. Recognizing that they shared a common constitutional program—it was that set forth in the declaration of the zemstvo delegates of 8/21 November 1904, though considerably amplified and expressed in more vigorous language—they all joined in a "Union of Unions."

The press shared the general mood, and, in spite of the harshness of the censorship and the capricious tyranny of the authorities, it joined the opposition movement. This trend was so strong and so unanimous that in practice the press no longer paid any attention to the restrictions that had been imposed on it; in "declarative sentences," as they were jokingly called at the time, it assumed a freedom of expression such as it had never known. Not only the liberal press but even the conservative press fell under the common influence. Thus *Rus*, which belonged to Alexis Suvorin, Jr. and than which nothing could have been less liberal, published an article that created a forceful impression. Under the title "A Grave Moment" and the subtitle "There Is Still Time," it pointed out, quoting Bismarck, that "the interest of the state requires a change in its institutions," it added that the hour for this change had struck in Russia, and it chastised the government for its inaction. The reactionary Prince Meshchersky too acknowledged in his turn the need for a "union with the people," and he stated openly: "Let us thank God that we were beaten by the Japanese, for the laurels of victory would have hidden our gaping wounds."

Governmental Temporization and the Rescript of 18 February/ 3 March 1905

The government's attitude was not calculated to allay the general excitement. Witte, who in his capacity as chairman of the committee of ministers* was charged with executing the promises of the imperial manifesto of 29 November/12 December 1904, had indeed set to work with his habitual dedication. But the numerous commissions appointed to prepare the necessary draft laws, which the liberals refused to join because they expected no good from them, were most often rather less eager to come to conclusions; it soon became apparent that the government had no intention of really making the concessions that it had promised but rather that it was preparing a purely verbal camouflage.

---

*A purely honorary title not to be confused with that of president of the Council of Ministers, or premier.

In his report to the committee of ministers on 11/24 January, Witte painted an appalling picture of the abuses by local administrations and concluded with a demand for the revision of all laws bearing on the maintenance of public order; the tsar gave his approval. But not a single step was taken toward the elimination of the specified abuses. A commission that liberal writers refused to join was formed on 23 January/5 February for the reform of the press laws. Its chairman, Kobeko, was a champion of press freedom. But, while the commission called for the abolition of administrative censorship, the newspapers went on being harassed by the government's vexations and the Imperial Council increased the authority over the press that the Minister of the Interior already possessed. The ukase of 12/25 January pledged the execution of a rigorous separation of the legislative and administrative powers and ordered that every proposed law would unconditionally have to be ratified by the Imperial Council and promulgated by the Senate. But, even in the case of provisional and extraordinary measures, the ministers continued to obtain the tsar's signature for decrees that were given the force of law. A commission was set up to study the problem of freedom of thought, but for all practical purposes it had no effect. A broad program of labor legislation was outlined by Witte, but the commission appointed to analyze it, under the chairmanship of Kokovtsev, had not yet produced a single draft bill after six months. On 29 January/11 February, as a result of Red Sunday, a special commission was created, supposedly including elected representatives of the workers, under the chairmanship of Shidlovsky. But, when the 420 workers' delegates met on 17 February/2 March and demanded personal immunity and freedom of speech for all commission members, the complete and undistorted verbatim publication of its proceedings, and the restitution of the labor unions abolished by the government, the tsar ordered the commission dissolved, and this provoked a new strike in Petersburg.

The government's hesitations were visible even in the selection of the new minister of the interior. Svyatopolk-Mirsky, shorn of his illusions, weak, incapable of action, had served his time. It was almost as a spectator that he had been involved with the events of Red Sunday and the ensuing period. He had long wished to resign, but to find a successor for him was not easy. When at last he did give up his post on 2/15 February, he vanished from the political scene and no one even noticed his disappearance. On Trepov's advice the tsar replaced him with Bulygin, who had been an associate of Grand Duke Sergey Aleksandrovitch in the government general of Moscow. This former governor of Kaluga and Moscow was no mere functionary

amenable to the orders of his betters. He had some of the characteristics of the *grand seigneur*. But, though he scorned to further the
base intentions of the ultra-reactionaries, no more did he carry out
any reforms. His appointment was not a solution but a postponement.
He had no more of a program or a plan of action than the government. The real master of the situation was not he but the new
governor general of Petersburg, Trepov, who enjoyed the personal
trust of the tsar.

Nevertheless the resurgence of revolutionary passions made it incumbent on the government to do something. Even the conservatives
insisted on this necessity. They wanted neither the constitutional
system favored by the liberals nor the Constituent Assembly advocated
by the radicals, but they enlisted increasingly in the ranks of those
supporting the idea of reviving the ancient institution of seventeenth-
century Muscovite Russia, the *Zemsky Sobor*. They believed that, if
the tsar had to enter into relations with the representatives of the
country, these ought to be not delegates of the intellectuals or even
of those noblemen tainted with liberalism, but those of the mass of
the people, the peasant class, which contituted 85 per cent of the
Russian population. The peasants, they thought, were conservative;
they longed for property; they clung firmly to the old traditions and
would not betray their tsar. Why not address them directly and ignore
the upper classes? It was among the peasants that the government
would find the support that it so desperately needed. This conception
of national representation was perfectly compatible with absolutism:
as in the seventeenth century, it was possible for the people to state
its views and for the tsar to make the decisions. With that minority
of zemstvo delegates who in 1904 had followed Shipov, then, the
moderate conservatives pronounced themselves in favor of a Consultative Assembly; and it was their thinking behind which the tsar,
who did not want to give up his autocracy, was to entrench himself
in order to combat the rising exactions of the majority of the country.

Certain ministers also recognized that the situation required more
precise positions and statements by the tsar. On 17/30 January 1905,
at the end of his weekly report, Agriculture Minister Ermolov described to Nicholas II the frightening position of the country, the
unprecedented agitation that had seized on the nation; he enumerated
the demands of the various groups, he emphasized the necessity of
making voluntary concessions if fatal consequences were to be averted,
and he showed the tsar what a brilliant opportunity was offered to him
to become Russia's second "Liberator Tsar." After some resistance,
Nicholas agreed to call a representative national assembly and sent

Ermolov to Witte; but two weeks later he had still done nothing. On 31 January/13 February Ermolov returned to the assault with a new memorandum. A private conference, convened and presided over by the tsar, produced a majority for Ermolov. On 3/16 February Nicholas told the ministers that he had decided to convoke the deputies but that he reserved the right to choose the appropriate time for announcing his decision through a rescript. Knowing the tsar's character, Witte offered some objections, but in the end he fell silent. Three draft rescripts were submitted to the tsar, and again a barren fortnight passed.

On the morning of 18 February/3 March, the day before the anniversary of the emancipation of the serfs, which seemed to be a propitious date for the publication of the "liberating" rescript, the ministers were amazed to read in the *Government Courier* not the rescript that they expected but a manifesto of a wholly opposite character. It denounced the creators of disorder who were attacking the foundations of the state, hallowed by the church and confirmed by the law, rending the ties that bound the present to the past, and hoping to create a new power on bases alien to Russia. Having recalled how the assassination of Grand Duke Sergey Aleksandrovitch "had profoundly wounded the national feelings," the manifesto voiced the sovereign's confidence in the devotion of his loyal people and in the support of "right thinking" citizens. He had as his immediate aims only the destruction of the foreign enemy's obstinate resistance and "the extirpation of the roots of sedition" within the country; it was only when these aims had been achieved and men's minds had been restored to serenity that efforts could be devoted to "the renewal of the moral factors in the national life." By way of conclusion he invoked the blessing of God on "the consolidation of the foundations of true autocracy." In this document, which, without consulting anyone, the tsar had transmitted directly to the minister of justice, everyone at a glance recognized the hand, the thinking, and the rhetoric of Pobyedonostsev.

On the same day, under the tsar's presidency, the ministers attended the weekly Cabinet meeting in Tsarskoye Selo. After some minutes of strained silence, Kokovtsev mentioned the need to allay the fears of foreign creditors. Ermolov and Bulygin raised the question of the rescript, which, they insisted, must be published without delay. The tsar replied irritably that the rescript was not yet in final form, since none of the drafts that had been submitted to him had satisfied him. After lunch the ministers resumed their attack, declaring that they would not be responsible for the maintenance of order or the safety of "threatened" persons—those, that is, in danger of being the targets of bombs. The tsar did not mask his impatience. "One would think you were in fear of a revolution," he told Bulygin, who replied: "Sire, it has already begun." Then Nicholas took from his pocket the text of a rescript that he himself had written, basing it on the three drafts that had been given to him. He read it aloud and, the ministers having approved it, he signed it and dated it, like the manifesto published that morning, as of 18 February/3 March.*

Thus on the one day two mutually contradictory documents would have appeared if the tsar had not inserted into the second certain reservations that annihilated its "emancipatory" effect. Indeed the rescript did proclaim that "the most deserving citizens, clothed in the confidence of the nation," would be summoned to take part in "the preliminary preparation of legislative proposals." But, when it added that reforms would be introduced only "in proportion to the acuteness of their need," and on condition that they make no break in "the bonds with the historic past" and preserve "the unshakable character of the basic laws," it placed remarkable restraints on the function, already so far from "constitutional," assigned to the deputies. While the rescript offered a compliment or two to the assemblies of the nobility, the zemstvo, and the various organizations that had presented their felicitations to the tsar when the tsarevitch was born, it said not a word of their demands or of the hopes of public opinion.

Nothing could demonstrate better than these two documents of 18 February/3 March the intensity with which the last of the Russian autocrats clung to the past. Is it to be believed, as Dowager Tsarina Marya Fyodorovna supposedly said to one of her ladies in waiting, who repeated it to a French journalist, Bourdon, that by signing the manifesto first the tsar had meant to "show that in issuing the rescript he was doing so under no constraint"? It is more accurate to say that he had endeavored, as he was to go on doing until his abdication, to use the manifesto to nullify the effect of the rescript that had in fact been forced on him. He was simply making game of his ministers and his subjects; for lack of decisiveness he resorted to trickery.

Nonetheless the rescript led public opinion completely to overlook the manifesto. Undoubtedly in their own minds the liberals were convinced of the tsar's duplicity and the radicals did not believe for even a moment that he was capable of making concessions spontaneously. But the press rejoiced, because it was to its interest to interpret the tsar's involuntary half-concessions in the sense of the national

*Witte described this incident in a rather different fashion in his *Memoirs*.

aspirations. The director of *Novoye Vremya*, Suvorin, "wept with joy and felt rejuvenated," and he declared that, with this "historic day, Russia was growing wings"; and it was true, in spite of the manifesto. The rescript was the most important step along the road to constitutional government since the declaration of the zemstvo delegates in November 1904.

The rescript did not lay down the procedures for convening those "most deserving" citizens who were to represent the nation. It turned over this task to a commission that was to be headed by Bulygin. But the government, which was accused of wanting to await the outcome of the battle of Mukden, was by no means eager to set up this commission. Flooding Bulygin with proposals, various administrative and social bodies insisted on being represented in it. On 12/25 March Bulygin told a delegation of the Moscow City Council that urban and zemstvo representatives would be among its members. On 18/31 March an official announcement stated that, in addition to the representatives of the government, "persons known for their activities would take part in it." Two weeks later a further announcement specified that the commission's members would be "named" by the tsar. On 6/19 May it was made known that the "preliminary steps" were "almost" completed and that there was reason to "hope" that the commission would meet on 15/28 June. So at the end of three months the commission had not yet been called to its first meeting; even its membership was still unknown. Having waited for Mukden, the government was waiting now for the disaster of Tsushima. In the face of a new explosion of public anger, the government hastened to give assurance that the Bulygin "commission" would not be constituted and that, in order to save time, the Minister's proposal would be submitted directly for study to the committee of ministers and the Imperial Council, then to the tsar for ratification. On 26 May/8 June the committee of ministers, in the utmost haste, examined the first twenty-five chapters of the proposal, the tenor of which was beginning to become generally known. It fully justified the skepticism of the liberals toward the ambiguous rescript of 18 February/3 March. While it provided for a Duma, this was only a modest consultative assembly, which could not make it possible for the nation to exercise its sovereignty. Its legislative function would be restricted to the preparation of draft laws that could not become final unless they were adopted by the Imperial Council and approved by the tsar. In budgetary affairs the Duma would have only a consultative voice, and matters concerning national defense would be outside its jurisdiction. The method of its election would be based on the principle of separation of classes, and it was reminiscent of the zemstvo electoral law of 1864.

The Zemstvo Petition of 26 May/8 June 1905

The government's shifts and dodges were hardly calculated to endear it to the country, of whose unanimous sentiment it could entertain no further doubt after the congress of zemstvo delegates in Moscow from 24 May/6 June to 26 May/8 June 1905.

Since November 1904 delegates to zemstvo congresses were elected no longer in their individual capacities but rather as representatives of their respective assemblies, the majority of which invested them with official mandates; moreover they were the delegates not of a party but of a "coalition" of oppositionists, and this gave their deliberations even more weight. In the congress of 22–26 April/5–9 May, the left wing of the November 1904 congress, composed of constitutionalists, had officially formalized the position of the liberals on the subject of the electoral system and the agrarian problem, calling for universal direct suffrage and the compulsory sale of part of their lands by private owners. It had also demanded that the "first representative assembly" be empowered to "establish the legal political system" on its own initiative: in other words, that it be endowed with the prerogatives of a Constituent Assembly. On all these points, in flagrant contradiction to the principles of the "Bulygin Duma," it had not been followed by Shipov's group: this faction was content with a "Zemstvo State Council" chosen by cantonal, district, and government zemstvo electoral colleges and charged with the "preliminary preparation" of draft laws, which were then to be put into "final form" by a "special governmental institution" and resubmitted to it for study; but the left wing had mustered an overwhelming majority: 127 votes for universal suffrage and 8 against; 87 for direct suffrage and 49 against; 123 for the principle of a legislative, not merely consultative, national assembly and 13 against.

The Moscow congress, the last "coalition" congress, was called by Shipov and began on 24 May/6 June, after the disaster of Tsushima, when the basic features of Bulygin's proposals had been made known. Since this was a grave and solemn moment, the congress resolved to address itself directly to the tsar and to appoint a delegation to present a petition to him. As delegates it chose Princes Sergey Trubetskoy and G. E. Lvov—the future premier of the Provisional Government in 1917—Count Heyden, Golovin—who was to be the president of the second Duma—Petrunkevitch, Roditchev, Princes Shakhovskoy and

Dolgorukov, and two representatives of municipalities, Fedorov and Nikitin. The petition, framed on 26 May/8 June, was most specific. It stressed the danger that threatened "the throne," it qualified the war as the result of "criminal abuses and negligence on the part of the counselors" of the tsar, and it emphasized the state of "civil war" and the guilt of "the ignorant and evil bureaucracy" that had "distorted" the tsar's orders or omitted to carry them out. It complained that, in spite of the serious events that had occurred, "the tsar's promise to call together the representatives of the nation" had not been fulfilled, and it protested against the intention, generally ascribed by rumor to the government, of substituting class representation for national representation. It prayed the tsar, "while there is still time," to order "without delay" the convocation of the representatives of the nation, "elected by all his subjects without distinctions of any kind." It declared that these representatives must "decide," in agreement with the tsar, "the vital question of war and peace" and "define or reject the terms of peace," a step that would convert the war into a "national" war and unite everyone "round a single national flag," and that, again in agreement with the tsar, the representatives "must establish the organization of the reshaped state." It concluded in two sentences freighted with warning: "Do not temporize, Sire. In this terrible hour of national ordeals, your responsibility before God and before Russia is great."

This was a way of speaking that was unaccustomed in Russia, and Trepov told the delegates that they would not be received. Thereupon they addressed themselves to Nicholas II directly. The tsar agreed to receive only some of them—he particularly abhorred Petrunkevitch —and only on condition that they refrain from presenting their petition and that they make the texts of their speeches available to Trepov. In the end, when they refused all his terms, the tsar received the entire delegation in Peterhof on 7/20 June. Prince Trubetskoy delivered a speech in a tone more moderate than that of the petition, and his deeply felt remarks seemed to touch the tsar. Nicholas replied with a prepared speech. While he called on the delegates to banish their "doubts," while he asserted that his "determination as tsar"—and he stressed this phrase—"was unshakable" and that "those who are elected will certainly be admitted to take part in political activity," he also did not fail to point out that he hoped that, "as in the past," the union between the tsar and the people of the soil of Russia would be reestablished "in order to serve as the foundation for an order of things in harmony with the traditional principles of Russia." Obviously the tsar was still thinking in terms of absolutism; even at the most critical moments he remained true to himself. But, even though he had made no new promise, the mere fact that he had received the delegation and listened to Trubetskoy's speech was a gain, the importance of which was immediately emphasized by the press.

The petition of 26 May/8 June was the last step taken in common by the constitutionalist and monarchist zemstvo members, because the publication of Bulygin's Duma proposal succeeded in splitting the coalition. In the congress of municipal and zemstvo delegates that met in Moscow from 19 July/1 August to 21 July/3 August, the constitutionalists voted a draft constitution prepared by S. A. Muromtsev. While, nevertheless, they decided to take part in the elections for Bulygin's Duma, they did so only with a view to continuing the struggle, to demanding for the Duma the right to make laws and vote on the budget, and to fighting for civil liberties and universal suffrage. Inasmuch as they considered it necessary to establish contact with the popular masses and to present candidates for election with a single, complete program, they resolved to form a political party of constitutional and democratic inspiration. It did no good for Trepov to declare this congress illegal and to order the police to break it up; its members refused to obey. It was in the next congress—the last to be officially authorized in view of the Duma elections—which was held openly from 25 September/8 October to 28 September/11 October, that the basic points of the program of the future Constitutional Democratic party (the "Cadets") were formally adopted.

Revolutionary Disorders and Strikes

What was more disquieting was the revolutionary demonstrations that increased throughout the country and at the most unexpected social levels from the beginning of 1905. In the cities, for the most part, they took the form of strikes with a more and more emphatically political character. Everywhere the strikers called for the convocation of a Constituent Assembly elected by universal suffrage; and two slogans were heard more and more often: *Down with autocracy!* and *Long live armed revolt!* In the wake of Red Sunday strikes broke out in the border provinces: Poland, and the Baltic countries, the Caucasus, and especially in Warsaw, Riga, Reval, Vilna, and Tiflis. The more backward labor groups—bakers, cobblers, coachmen, small artisans—followed the example of the factory workers. In February a wave of peasant risings surged out of the government of Kursk and swept over the whole of Russia. The rioters' tactics varied with the local demands of the peasants. In some places they seized the landowners' wheat and livestock, cut down their trees, worked their fields, and occasionally even drove them out and burned their houses. Elsewhere, for example in the Caucasus, they went to the extreme of refusing to pay taxes and literally chasing out the local authorities. The government sent soldiers and Cossacks to the aid of the landed proprietors; the unmerciful repression of the risings intensified the peasants' hatred of the nobility and the autocracy. With the help of the workers, the peasants met in congresses and, at the end of June, they founded the All-Russian Peasants' Union, whose second congress, in November, was to bring together 187 peasant delegates, irregularly elected without question—sometimes even as the result of a fictitious vote—but coming from 20 governments.

Although political propaganda had not infected the army, since 1903 it had been gaining among the sailors, who were more aware than the soldiers. In the summer of 1905 the crews of a number of ships of the Black Sea Fleet joined the revolutionary movement, and, with the help of the Social Democrats, went as far as to prepare a plan for a squadron revolt at Sebastopol. Pure chance—the foulness of the food—brought about a rising by the sailors of the battleship *Potemkin Tavrichesky* on 27 June/10 July. The rebels sailed the ship to Odessa, where bloody clashes between the army and striking workers were then under way. Feldman, a Social Democrat, called on the sailors to go ashore, take over the city, and, under the protection of their ships' powerful guns, make it the center of the struggle against the autocracy. But the crew was not yet ready for this step; it could not make up its mind to land and it waited for the whole of the Sebastopol squadron to join the *Potemkin Tavrichesky*. The squadron did appear off Odessa on 30 June/13 July, but only the battleship *Georgi Pobyedonostsev* joined the insurgents. But then, a day later, the sailors of this ship reconsidered and decided to go to Sebastopol and surrender themselves. The men of the *Potemkin Tavrichesky* could not even entertain such a notion, because they had killed a number of their officers at the start of their revolt, and they had fired the ship's guns on Odessa. Their leader, a sailor named Matyushenko, was advised to head for Rumania. At Constanza the Rumanian authorities suggested that they surrender and promised them their freedom. The sailors refused, going on to Theodosia to take on food and coal. But in Theodosia soldiers fired on the ship's delegates and captured Feldman and some of the other leaders of the revolt. On 6/19 July the *Potemkin Tavrichesky* returned to Rumania, and two days later she surrendered to the Rumanian authorities.

In order to root out revolutionary agitation the government would have to make major concessions. But it was still unprepared to do so. After it had been studied by the Cabinet, Bulygin's proposal for an Imperial Duma was discussed in a Peterhof conference under the presidency of the tsar and in the presence of the grand dukes. During the discussion the tsar and his entourage made it quite clear that they had greater faith in the peasants, whom they considered more loyal, than in the nobility, which they suspected of having been seduced by the political ideas of the intellectuals. Finally the conference approved indirect suffrage and the division of voters into three colleges: peasants, landed proprietors, and city dwellers, representing respectively 43 per cent, 34 per cent, and 23 per cent of the total electorate. The manifesto of 6/19 August, which announced the creation of the Duma, was the greater a disappointment to public opinion because it forbade, under penalty of prosecution, any public discussion of political problems. By robbing the opposition of its last hope of an understanding with the government, the manifesto definitively thrust it on to the path of revolution.

In the renewed conflict, the extremist or Bolshevik wing of the Social Democrats played a major part. During its third congress, held in London from 12/25 April to 27 April/10 May, it had at first decided to take part in the elections for the Duma in order to organize an armed revolt and contribute to the victory of a bourgeois republic in the hope of achieving entry for its representatives in the provisional government that would follow the proclamation of the republic. But, even while agreeing to support the middle class "as long as it backed the revolution or even only the opposition," it had also decided to enlighten the workers as to the "anti-revolutionary and anti-proletarian nature of the *bourgeois* democratic movement." But after the manifesto of 6/19 August, unlike the democratic middle class, the congress did not confine itself to disapproval of the Duma; it decided to boycott the elections. In September it began to make a reality of the watchword, *Let us organize the revolution!*, that Parvus, a Social Democrat, had first voiced shortly after Red Sunday in January. The Bolsheviki sought to consolidate the fragmented labor strikes and to instigate a general strike. In the autumn propaganda among the workers was considerably expedited when the students, taking advantage of the autonomy granted to the universities, opened their lecture halls to public meetings. Trepov, who had agreed to autonomy for the universities, could not prohibit these meetings, and he tolerated them as long as they did not overflow into the streets. Such meetings became more and more numerous, the speeches grew more and more fiery, and the resolutions adopted turned more and more revolutionary.

An attempt at a general strike by the Moscow typographical workers was a resounding success; no newspapers appeared between 2/15 and 18/31 October, and the Petersburg printers went out in a three-day sympathy strike. With the help of the Social Democrats, Moscow became the birthplace of the first unified workers' organization, the "soviet* of deputies of the typographical and lithographic workers."

The printers' strike was not enough to launch a general strike by workers in all trades. On the other hand, a railway strike, by halting traffic and communications and thus immediately paralyzing the country's economic life and hobbling governmental action, might be capable of accomplishing the general stoppage. In order to prevent this, the government called a congress of railway workers in Petersburg on 3/16 October on the pretext of improving their economic conditions. But six days later this congress voiced the political demands that were those of the entire country: the abolition of the state of siege and capital punishment, individual freedom and full civil liberties, the right of self-determination for national minorities, the convocation of a Constituent Assembly, and immunity for strikers. A rumor having spread that the delegates to the congress had been arrested, the workers of the Moscow-Kazan rail line went out on strike. During the next three days the strike spread throughout the entire Moscow rail network, and communications with Petersburg were cut off on 11/24 and 12/25 October.

At the same time, executive organizations, strike committees, federal councils, and soviets of workers' deputies sprang up in various centers of the empire. The most important of all these groups was the Petersburg soviet of workers' deputies, which met for the first time on 13/26 October. As Lenin said of it in November, it was "neither a workers' parliament nor an agency of proletarian autonomy, but a battle organization pursuing certain definite ends." Its purpose was the realization of the Bolshevik agenda: armed revolt, provisional government, democratic republic, and Constituent Assembly. It regarded the general strike as merely the first of its means of combat against the autocracy; it began at once to arm the workers and organize "combat battalions." The demands that it laid before the government were identical with those of the printers' union.

At the same time, a congress of zemstvo members and the Union for Liberation met in Moscow with a view to organizing the People's Freedom party—the Constitutional Democratic (Cadet) party. The Cadets acknowledged the identity between their own goals and those

*Sovyet, meaning "council."

of the strikers—the immediate establishment of civil liberties, free elections for a Constituent Assembly, the selection of deputies by equal, direct, and secret universal suffrage, and a general political amnesty—but they rejected armed revolt.

The Manifesto of 17/30 October 1905

It was now beyond the government's capacities to put down the revolution by force, for it had broken the structure of the autocratic system; the garrisons were weak and anything but reliable, and the regular army had not yet returned from Manchuria. Neither the *de facto* dictator, Trepov, nor the nullities who were his ministers were capable of quieting the country. In the universal opinion of official circles, there was only one man who could do so. He was Witte, who, for his accomplishments in the treaty of Portsmouth, had been rewarded with the title of count and was returning from America in triumph. Therefore Nicholas II consented to ask his views.

On 9/22 October Witte gave the tsar a memorandum in which he asserted that there were only two choices: either to institute a rigid dictatorship in order to stamp out sedition, or to "grant the institutions and adopt the legislative organization that would meet the political demands clearly expressed by the majority of Russian society and that would actually assure the solidity of the civil liberties accorded to the nation." He made no secret of his own opinion that the first solution seemed to have no slightest chance of success, and he insisted on the second, on what he called "the rule of law," lest he utter the word *constitution,* which revolted the tsar. In order to establish such rule, he believed, governmental activity must be unified and must produce proof of absolute sincerity in the accomplishment of the promised reforms by guaranteeing freedom in the election of the Imperial Duma, showing confidence in the national representation, and respecting its dignity. At once the sycophants of the court went into battle to make certain that the document certifying to these freedoms should not be signed by Witte; the beneficences bestowed on the people by the tsar, Trepov argued, ought to be announced in a manifesto by the tsar himself in order to enhance his prestige. Such reasoning convinced the tsar, and he asked Witte to draft the manifesto. He received this draft in Peterhof on 15/28 but, since he did not like it, he asked Goremykin and Baron Budberg to prepare two others, in which there was no longer any mention of giving the Duma the initiative in legislation and which, instead of charging the government with vigilance over the introduction of the promised freedoms, merely announced that they had been bestowed on the people—as Trepov had insisted, it was intended that the glory of this gift illuminate the tsar and not, as court circles were already calling Witte, "the president of the future republic." The tsar sent these two drafts to Witte, who replied that whoever wrote the one that was finally approved would have to be made premier. Since a general strike was raging, the government needed Witte, and on 17/30 October he was summoned to Peterhof again. The tsar was still hesitant; but Grand Duke Nikolai Nikolayevitch, who had just arrived in a panic over the railway strike and was frightened at the prospect of being appointed dictator, threatened to shoot himself if the tsar did not sign the manifesto drafted by Witte. At this Nicholas made up his mind at last and signed the manifesto of 17/30 October.

This document, which, for all its reservations, opened the first breach in the absolute power of the tsars and which, for that reason, Nicholas would never pardon Witte for making him sign, "imposed on the government the duty of carrying out the resolute will of the tsar":

1. to grant to the people "solid civil liberties founded on actual individual freedom, freedom of thought, freedom of speech, freedom of assembly, and freedom of association";

2. to "accept the immutable principle that no law can become effective without the approval of the Imperial Duma, and to guarantee to the elected representatives of the nation the means of effective cooperation in the supervision of the legality of the acts" of the government;

3. to "effect participation in the election of the Duma—without delaying the elections already scheduled and to the extent to which this is possible in the light of the imminence of the sessions of the Duma—by those classes of the population that have hitherto been completely deprived of the right to vote, by entrusting to the new legislative system the task of executing the principle of universal suffrage."

In his report, published simultaneously with the imperial manifesto, Witte emphasized the terms for the reconciliation of government and country. In his opinion the disorders were neither the product of extremist propaganda nor the consequence of minor imperfections in the system, but the result "of the desire of the whole of Russian society for a rule of law founded on civil liberties." Without waiting for the Duma to approve the new order, it was essential to put into practice at once its major elements: "freedom of thought, of the press, of assembly, and of association, and individual liberty," as well as the equality of all citizens before the law, "whatever be their religion or their nationality." "It will then be the duty of the government to establish a rule of law in conformity with the political wishes clearly voiced by the majority of the country." Since it was impossible that "a country of 125 million inhabitants belonging to various nationalities accept and at one step adapt to the principles" of the new system, it was "essential to form a homogeneous government tending toward this same end." "The government ought not to set up obstacles to the decisions of the Duma." "The status of the Duma may be modified and enlarged in proportion to recognition of its imperfections and in response to current needs." It was also essential to enlarge the Imperial Council with elected members in order to establish "normal relations between this body and the Duma." Finally, in order to accomplish these measures, it was essential, even while combatting "acts that openly threaten the society and the state, to act on the foundation of law and on the basis of close alliance with the moderate majority in society" and to demonstrate "good faith and sincerity" in the execution of the new principles. Obviously Witte was deliberately emphasizing all the flaws in the system. Since none of the conditions that he set forth was to be carried out, his report explained in advance why the manifesto of 17/30 October did not bring about social peace.

II / FROM THE OCTOBER MANIFESTO TO THE MEETING OF THE DUMA

While the general public greeted the manifesto of 17/30 October with enthusiasm, and the politicians, more concerned with its realities, received it with circumspection, both the ultra-reactionaries and the revolutionary parties, if for different reasons, resisted it with equal vigor. The interval between its publication and the first meeting of the Imperial Duma was abundantly marked by their savage struggles.

The opposition parties, which had thus far been united in the pursuit of a common end, the overthrow of autocracy, broke apart once they had wrested the first major concession from the tsar. Henceforth each sought to attain its own ends: the most moderate were satisfied with a consultative Chamber of Deputies; others insisted on a genuine constitutional system; the Socialists aspired to a democratic republic and, in order to achieve it, called for armed insurrection by the workers; the peasants, little influenced by propaganda, remained aloof from political agitation and were satisfied to take over the lands of the nobles; and the government continued to view the peasants as loyal champions of autocracy. On the other side, the opponents of reform took heart again and closed their ranks. Those industrialists who had backed the purely political demands of the liberals abandoned them when the workers joined against the employers as the representatives of the capitalist system. The nobility, which at first was in large part terrorized by the peasants who were seizing its lands, attacking its houses, and beating their residents, and which was therefore ready to reach an understanding with them even at the cost of major sacrifices, also regained courage once the "government had come back." It swiftly organized the defense of its caste privileges by creating a Union of the Nobility, which embraced the most reactionary of its members. It exploited what loyalty to the tsar still survived among the most backward groups of the urban population—for example, small artisans —and recruited members among them for an avowedly monarchist organization, the Union of the Russian People. With the complicity of the police and the financial help of the government, it launched an open battle against the revolutionary movement, during which it unleashed nationalist and anti-Semitic passions and itself resorted to the use of terrorist tactics. In direct proportion to the growth of the counterrevolutionary organizations, the tsar's confidence returned and the government recovered its composure. Nicholas regretted having given ground, and he found Count Witte less and less necessary. On the eve of the opening of the first Duma, when Witte had supplied him with the money and the troops that he had lacked for effective reaction, he felt strong enough to embark openly on a campaign against the national representative body that he himself had convoked.

The Creation of Witte's "Caretaker" Government

After the publication of the manifesto of 17/30 October the tsar bowed to necessity and appointed Witte premier. This act entailed the dismissal of his former advisers. Bulygin departed freely and with pleasure. Nicholas, whose ingratitude toward his most dedicated servitors was the dominant trait of his character, had a very cold parting with his former tutor, Pobyedonostsev, the chief ideologist of autocracy; but he was unwilling to deprive himself of the services of his dictator of the moment, General Trepov, who was nevertheless the major factor in the government's impotence against the popular insurrection. While he relieved him of his posts as governor general of Petersburg and deputy minister of the interior, his purpose was to bring Trepov into his immediate entourage as commander of the Peterhof palace, without a word to Witte. The exchange of Petersburg, noisy with the anger of revolution, for the quiet of the imperial residence further enhanced Trepov's influence over the tsar, whom one could keep under one's own ascendancy only by never allowing him out of sight. Hereafter Nicholas saw everything only through Trepov's eyes, and the tsarina, in gratitude for the services that he had performed as the collaborator of Grand Duke Sergey in Moscow, showed the same confidence in him. Witte was able to write in his *Memoirs*: "In sum, Trepov became the irresponsible chief of the government and I became the responsible Premier, but devoid of influence."

Detested by the imperial couple, Witte was likewise unable to count on support from the advocates of the reforms. They knew how fragile and equivocal were the freedoms bestowed by the tsar. They knew also that the presence of Witte in power was not an adequate guaranty that the government would pursue, with "good faith and sincerity," the expansion of political liberties, the extension of the right to vote, and the enlargement of the powers of the Duma. A loyal servitor of Alexander III and a convinced monarchist, Witte was obviously not the man to head a constitutional cabinet. Hence his invitations to liberal leaders to join his government in November were fruitless. First he summoned to Petersburg two zemstvo congress delegates, Prince G. E. Lvov and young F. Kokoshkin, who insisted that the Constitution be drafted by a Constituent Assembly elected through universal suffrage. In the face of this pertinacity, Witte turned to the right wing of the zemstvo congress—to A. Y. Gutchkov. D. N. Shipov, Stakhovitch, and Prince E. Trubetskoy, to whom the step demanded by Lvov and Kokoshkin seemed too abrupt and even revolutionary. But at the same time Witte wanted to include in his Cabinet not only them but an old reactionary bureaucrat, P. N. Durnovo. No liberal leader could tolerate collaboration with Durnovo, whom Alexander III had once thrown out of the post as head of the police* with one sentence: "Get rid of this swine for me within twenty-four hours." First Stakhovitch and Trubetskoy and then Gutchkov and Shipov took evasive action, alleging, moreover, that they did not represent the opinion of the majority of zemstvo members. Finally Witte decided to create a temporary "caretaker" government with those of his ministerial associates who had not previously compromised themselves during their careers.

The Black Hundreds and the Pogroms

It took no one very long to recognize that real power eluded Count Witte. In the first days of elation that followed the October manifesto, many parades and meetings were held in all the cities of Russia; there

---

*For having abused his authority in a love affair in which he was involved.

were great displays of red flags and the *Marseillaise* was much sung; young orators delivered inflammatory speeches. But these peaceful manifestations of the universal rejoicing were soon drowned in blood.

When the manifesto was published, the Union of the Russian People rallied the representatives of the extreme right. Its director, Dr. Dubrovin, under Durnovo's patronage and with the backing of Grand Duke Nikolai Nikolayevitch himself, with whom he had private meetings, organized secret meetings of members of the titled aristocracy. When there were liberal demonstrations, the Union of the Russian People staged counter-demonstrations that ran through the streets singing the national anthem, *God Save the Tsar*, and carrying patriotic emblems, ikons, and portraits of Nicholas II. In the street fighting between the two sides, the police threw their strength behind the Black Hundreds—this was the popular name for the monarchist and nationalist counter-demonstrators. These gentlemen were always careful to orient the hatred of the mob against the Jews, whom they accused of being the instigators of the revolution, and the street fights degenerated into pogroms. In the single week that followed 17/30 October there were one hundred pogroms in which three thousand persons were killed and almost ten thousand were injured. The most terrible of these occurred in Odessa immediately after the publication of the manifesto: it raged for four days and almost five hundred persons— men, women, and children—were killed; more than fifteen hundred homes were looted. The complicity of the police in the pogroms was blatant, and the subsequent investigations proved as much. In the police department itself, with the full knowledge and consent of the director, a squad leader, Komisarov, was printing propaganda for pogroms on presses seized from the revolutionaries, and these leaflets were strewn throughout the provinces. When Witte learned of this and went to inform the tsar, he saw that Nicholas II was anything but uninformed. After the Gomel pogrom the tsar received a report that singled out the guilt of a constabulary officer, Podgorichany; Nicholas II wrote testily in the margin: "Is this any business of mine?" The Black Hundreds enjoyed the tacit approbation of the tsar.

The Mutinies of Kronstadt and Sebastopol and the Rout of the Petersburg Soviet

Convinced that there was no chance of success for its strike, the Petersburg Soviet of Workers' Deputies resolved on 18/31 October and 19 October/1 November to end it at noon of 21 October/3 November. But it also decided at the same time to continue its struggle for the creation of a Constituent Assembly. As its method of action it chose to arm the proletariat and create a national militia, in order to get rid of the police and force the garrisons out of the cities. It also insisted on the general political amnesty that the manifesto had not even mentioned, but the decree of 22 October/4 November granted only a limited amnesty. The preparations for armed revolution were carried out by the left wing of the Social Democrats, and barricades had been erected in a number of southern cities as early as 17/30 October. But the workers were still poorly armed, and the Soviet had to restrain their ardor for combat. On 29–30 October/11–12 November it attempted through their direct action to win freedom of speech and the press and the eight-hour day. But the employers, who thus far had observed a strict neutrality as far as political action by the workers was concerned, responded to the demand for an eight-hour day with the threat of a lockout, and, when they began to carry out this threat, the Soviet had to give ground and defer the realization of its demands. Work was resumed under the same conditions as before.

Consequently the Bolsheviki were all the more insistent in their pressure on the Soviet to prepare for armed revolt. From 26 October/ 8 November to 28 October/10 November, under the influence of Socialist propaganda, the soldiers and sailors of Kronstadt mutinied. Poorly organized, the mutiny was quickly suppressed by Guard regiments summoned from Petersburg; twelve hundred sailors were arrested and there was a rumor that they would be tried by courts-martial. At the same time, as a result of the labor strikes, a state of siege was proclaimed in Poland. In support of the Kronstadt sailors and the Polish workers, the Petersburg Soviet called a new political strike for 2/15 November. This act merely emphasized the finality of the divorce between the moderate opposition and the revolutionaries, as well as the weariness of the working class. The purely proletarian strike was a complete failure. The Soviet at once tried to make it appear to have been a mere gesture and ended it at noon of 7/20 November in view of the "decisive conflict" that was in preparation. Furthermore, the government officially announced that the Kronstadt sailors would not be court-martialed and that the state of siege in Poland had been lifted. The Cadet party, which had supported the October strike, denounced the November action as a major political and tactical error. The leaders of the Soviet contended that, on the contrary, it had "aroused the masses of the soldiers from their torpor for the first time" and assured the success of an armed rising.

They were apparently vindicated by the rebellion that broke out among the crews of the warships at Sebastopol on 11/24 November.

The men elected a "Soviet of Sailors' Deputies," disarmed their officers, and physically removed them from the ships and the barracks.
As in Kronstadt and, earlier, aboard the *Potemkin Tavritchesky*, the
action lacked all political character; it was merely the manifestation
of resentment against the rigorous living conditions imposed on the
sailors. Generally the mutineers were without organization and held
no clearly defined political views, and the soldiers of the regiments
based in the city did not follow them. The sailors entrusted the leadership of their operation to a Lieutenant Schmidt, "a great enthusiast
of moderate tendencies," a supporter of the Cadets, and a very well-
liked officer. Schmidt accepted on condition that there be no blood-
shed and that the men add the demand for a Constituent Assembly
to their purely technical grievances. Meanwhile, the authorities disarmed ships that were under suspicion, and Admiral Chukhnin
himself visited the squadron and exhorted the sailors to keep faith
with the oath that they had sworn. On the evening of 14/27 November Schmidt went on board the *Ochakov* with the intention of subsequently assuming command of the entire squadron. But only seven
or eight other ships besides the *Ochakov* were flying the red flag.
Nevertheless, in the name of the Black Sea Fleet, Schmidt sent a telegram to the tsar demanding the convocation of a Constituent Assembly. At three o'clock on the afternoon of 15/28 November the shore
batteries and the guns of the ships that had remained loyal to the
government opened fire on the *Ochakov*, which was totally disabled by
a hail of shells. Schmidt attempted to swim to safety; he was picked out
of the water and removed to the citadel of Ochakov, for which the
ship had been named. It was not until February 1906 that he was
brought to trial before an extremely biased tribunal, which condemned this courageous man to death. His execution on 18 Feb-
ruary/3 March on the island of Berezan plunged Russian public
opinion into deep mourning.

The Sebastopol mutiny finally drew the government's attention to
the Soviet of Workers' Deputies—that "second government," as it was
ironically denominated by Suvorin's reactionary newspaper, *Novoye
Vremya*. The various defeats had undermined the Soviet's moral authority. Witte resolved to put an end to it. On 26 November/9 December he ordered the arrest of its chairman, Nosar-Khrustalev. Unable to
organize a new strike or an armed revolt, the Soviet turned over its
work to an expanded executive committee. On 2/15 December this
committee published its reply, a "financial manifesto" that called on
the public to hasten the bankruptcy of the government by refusing to
pay taxes and withdrawing its deposits in the savings banks and the

State Bank and insisting on payment in gold. This cut Witte where he was most vulnerable, for at that very moment he was busy negotiating a loan abroad. His reaction was immediate: he suspended the publication of the newspapers that had been forced to print the manifesto and he ordered their directors held for trial; on 5/18 December he had all 230 members of the Soviet arrested in the premises of the Free Economic Society.

The Moscow Risings

Far from crushing the revolutionary movement, the arrest of the Petersburg Workers' Soviet drove it to further extremes, to armed revolution. After the mutiny at Sebastopol, agitation had spread throughout the country. In the army, soldiers led by reservists—that is, peasants—had mutinied in Kiev, Ekaterinodar, Elizavetpol, Kursk, Lomzha, and Moscow; in the rural areas, peasant disorders had multiplied; in provincial labor centers there had been a burgeoning of workers' soviets. On 29 November/5 December a soviet was convened in Moscow by the "federative committee" of all the revolutionary parties. After the arrest of the members of the Petersburg Soviet, Moscow assumed the leadership of the revolutionary movement.

On 6/19 December the Moscow Soviet decided to take reprisal for the Petersburg arrests with a political general strike that would begin on the following day and be converted into armed revolt. Delegates from twenty-nine railways, meeting in Moscow, endorsed this decision. "Combat battalions" composed of Bolsheviki were supposed to try to bring in the soldiers. But this time the government was on the alert. Long since informed about the plans for an armed revolt in Moscow, Witte had insisted on the timely dispatch of troops from Petersburg and had appointed Admiral Dubasov, known for his forcefulness, as governor general of the city. Two days—7/20 and 8/21 December— went by without incident. But on 9/22 December the troops surrounded the Fidler School, where the combat battalions had gathered, and, when the revolutionaries refused to surrender, the soldiers shelled them. On the same day strikers began to erect impromptu barricades in the streets and to block them with coils of barbed wire. But they refused to give battle on their fragile barricades and fled when the troops approached. During the night the conflict became sharper. The combat battalions fired from the windows and roofs of houses when the police and the Cossacks tried to tear down the barricades. Dubasov, who had no faith in the Moscow soldiery, was waiting for the arrival of the guard regiments, and he ordered special precautions at the

Petersburg station. On 11/24 December he began occupying the various quarters of the city, one by one, with the rest of his men. Finally, on 15/28 December, the Semenovsky Regiment arrived under the command of Colonel Min and Lieutenant Colonel Riman. The regiment concentrated its "punitive expedition" chiefly on the railway network of the Moscow region; it butchered railway workers and office staff without mercy. One section of Moscow, Pryesnya, defended by two to three hundred armed workers alone, put up a savage resistance against the government's forces. During the night of 17/30 December the area was surrounded and shelled. The workers carried on with their defense. It was not until 20 December 1905/2 January 1906 that the revolt was finally put down. Their forces drained by their earlier struggles, the Petersburg revolutionaries had not gone to the assistance of those of Moscow.

The Election Law of 11/24 December 1905

Although the smashing of the Moscow rising did not put an end to the agitation in the provinces, at least the general staff of the revolution had been overpowered. What was important now was to prepare for the convocation of the Duma. The manifesto of 17/30 October had promised a limited revision of the election law in order to enlarge the number of voters. Universal suffrage had won many supporters. Even moderate politicians were most emphatic in their advocacy of it. Moreover, the ruling circles, which were confident of the peasants' allegiance, and the conservatives were prepared to accept it in the hope that the votes of the intellectuals, whom they hated, would be drowned by the ocean of peasant votes. Shipov and Gutchkov themselves offered to draft a law establishing universal suffrage.

But Witte had a plan of his own, which retained the system of voting by electoral colleges while at the same time increasing the participation of the workers and the small holders of land. He submitted this to the committee of ministers. A new debate began in a special meeting at which the tsar was in the chair: the issue was limited against universal suffrage. Count Bobrinsky, a conservative who had always opposed universal suffrage before, now declared in favor of it, arguing that "no other proposal would satisfy Russia." Witte vigorously defended his own plan, which was adopted. The new election law was promulgated on 11/24 December 1905, and on 12/25 February 1906 it was decided that the Duma would hold its first session on 27 April/10 May 1906.

The new law made no alteration in the method of voting provided by the statute of 6/19 August for the "Bulygin Duma." The electors were divided into three groups or *curiae*: landed proprietors—the majority of these being nobles—urban voters, and cantonal peasants. Elections were conducted in two stages, and even, for the peasants, in four: the electors of the first *curia*, numbering 1918 for the 51 provinces of European Russia, were elected by district electoral assemblies; those of the second *curia*, totaling 1344, were elected by municipal electoral assemblies; those of the third *curia*, the *upolnomochennye* or "delegates" of the peasants, who numbered 2476, were elected by district electoral assemblies, which in turn were elected by the cantonal electors. All these electors gathered in provincial (government) assemblies. In each such assembly the peasant "delegates" first elected, by themselves, their deputy to the Duma—there were in all 54 peasant deputies*—and then all the electors chose the rest of the province's deputies, the number of whom, in proportion to the population, ranged from 1 to 15 (there were in all 330 seats to be filled) ; the 26 large cities, separately, chose 28 deputies. Thus European Russia sent 412 deputies to the Duma, which also included representatives of Poland, Siberia, the Caucasus, and a few other outlying areas.

On the other hand the new law changed the rules of electoral eligibility. Under the August law, the ordinary voter had not only to be at least twenty-five years old but also to meet other conditions: in the districts, ownership of land varying in area from one hundred to six hundred *desyatini*, according to the district; in the cities, payment of a minimum of 50 rubles in taxes or ownership of a building or tenancy of a residence valued at 1500 rubles. Under the new statute, the ownership of any area of land, the payment of any tax, or the rental of any apartment for a year was sufficient. In addition, the workers were given the right to vote in a special *curia*, and in the provincial assemblies their representatives took part in the election of deputies to the Duma. In spite of this extension of the suffrage, the law of 11/24 November still seemed anything but liberal, especially to the Socialist parties, which reaffirmed their decision to boycott the elections.

Conflicts Between the Tsar and Witte

Since the promulgation of the manifesto of 17/30 October and the appointment of Witte as premier, the tsar's state of mind had undergone considerable modification. In January 1906 he received the delegates of the Union of the Russian People whom Dr. Dubrovin

---

*One for each of the fifty-one governments and one for each administrative district, known as the *oblast* ("region").

presented to him, and he graciously accepted the badges of membership in the Black Hundreds that were offered to him and the tsarevitch. When the delegates begged him to preserve autocracy inviolate, he promised them that soon "the sun of truth will shine over the soil of Russia." This reversal threw him into conflict with his premier on a number of occasions early in 1906.

Appeasement of the rural populations was of the essence. The most extreme conservatives, such as Trepov, were in agreement in their acceptance of the fact that some of the landowners' properties must be expropriated—besides, the peasants had already seized some of these lands—if they wanted to preserve the rest of their holdings or be assured of compensation for what they lost. This belief had led Witte to instruct Kutler, a minister deeply versed in the agrarian problem, to prepare a draft expropriation law. While Kutler was working on this draft, the panic that had swept through the nobility dissolved. Therefore the landed proprietors looked on Witte and Kutler as nothing but revolutionaries who wanted to dispossess them. Witte had interrupted the preparation of the expropriation project, but he had been unable completely to prevent its disclosure. Influential noblemen complained to the tsar, Nicholas insisted that Witte get rid of Kutler at once, and the minister was removed in February without even the customary severance indemnity, which consisted of appointment to the Imperial Council or the Senate.*

The tsar's dislike of Witte, fueled by the noblemen's complaints, grew more and more acute. On advice from the right, Nicholas contemplated appointing Krivosheyin and Rukhlov to the government. On 12/25 February Witte wrote to the tsar that it would be impossible for him, in the Duma and the revised Imperial Council, to champion measures that had been taken without his knowledge and approval, and he urged the tsar not to disorganize the Cabinet by new appointments before the Duma had met. If, as he reported in his *Memoirs,* he remained in power against his own wishes for two months after this letter, it was only because he was still needed. Because of the lack of money and troops, the "situation was still uncertain." Once he had "negotiated a substantial loan abroad and assured the prompt return of the army beyond Lake Baikal," and once the Duma had met, the tsar would be able to get along without him, because "any imbecile would have been able to put down the revolution."

Convinced that on its return to Russia the Manchurian Army would be a "force for order," he strove to accelerate its repatriation.

---

*It was this same Kutler who would later work with the Cadet party in the preparation of an agrarian law calling for compulsory expropriation, against just compensation, of part of the estates of the great landowners.

That was why, because he knew that since 17/30 October the area had been "contaminated by the revolutionary spirit," he took it on himself to order Generals Rennenkampf and Meller-Zakomelsky to lead a punitive expedition in Siberia. In February this expedition extinguished the mutinies by methods devoid of mercy; it then restored the Trans-Siberian traffic that had been interrupted by the disorders, and thus the speedy repatriation of the Manchurian Army was made possible. On the other hand, it was against Witte's will that General Orlov, a favorite of the tsarina, was dispatched against the Latvian peasants in revolt against their German lords and that at the tsar's personal insistence the repression there was characterized by a special cruelty. The executions, the deportations of peasants, the searches, the arrests, the reprisals of every kind that proliferated through the whole of Russia in the beginning of 1906 attested to the gains of reaction. They were hardly suited to bring about appeasement. In fact, the Revolutionary Socialists, who had held a congress from 11/24 to 17/30 January, retaliated with a series of successful assassination attempts against governors and police officials.

The Negotiation of a Loan from France

From the moment of his appointment as premier, Witte had begun to consider the negotiation of a loan to reinforce the money in circulation, threatened by the low estate of the public finances. By his own admission he was in a hurry to accomplish this before the meeting of the Duma; he did not wish it debated on the floor, lest the deputies advert to the catastrophes of the war and thus "the bankers set less advantageous terms, and the government, because it is short of money, lose all freedom of action." He initiated talks with French bankers and their government for the negotiation of a loan of 2.25 billion francs at interest of 6 per cent. France at this time stood in need of Russia's backing in the Conference of Algeciras. Even though French opinion was cognizant of the peril that menaced the Duma if the loan was granted before it met, Finance Minister Maurice Rouvier acquiesced in Witte's request provided that Russia support France on the Moroccan question; he promised to float the loan as soon as France had obtained a favorable solution at Algeciras. But the Moroccan conference dragged out, and Rouvier's successor, Raymond Poincaré, was anxious to know whether the Russian government had the right to borrow without action by the Duma. Wilhelm II, furious at Witte for his contribution to the destruction of the Russian-German alliance of Björkö,* forbade German bankers to subscribe to the loan. In the

*See pp. 269 ff.

United States the Morgan bank followed his example. Nevertheless, on 5/18 April 1906, three weeks before the first session of the Duma, the contract for the loan was signed. Now the Russian government had complete freedom of action for the execution of its campaign against the Duma.

The Preparation of the "Basic Laws"

The manifesto of 17/30 October had merely promised, without actually creating it, the establishment of a new political system. The promises had still to be transmuted into action. According to the traditional idea of the Russian intellectuals, adopted by the new political parties of the left, it was a new Constituent Assembly elected by universal suffrage that was the proper source for the promulgation of constitutional laws. The conservatives and the reactionaries, on the other hand, argued that nothing should be altered in the old organization. Witte felt that both points of view were equally menacing to the autocracy. While he believed that the old order was obviously bankrupt after the October manifesto, he felt that the new one should be handed down from above by the absolute power itself and that precautions should be taken to safeguard the sovereign's prerogatives against the demands of the national representative body that was about to convene.

This was the aim of his revision of the draft of the "basic laws,"* though it was fashioned on the most conservative of models—the Constitutions of Prussia, Austria, and Japan—that had been prepared by Baron Uxkull, secretary of state, and a commission headed by Count Solsky and the initiative for which he ascribed to General Trepov. Witte found it too liberal and suggested a variety of amendments designed to preserve all the tsar's prerogatives in matters of war and foreign policy, to extend substantially his regulatory power and his discretionary power in administrative questions, to limit the functions of the Duma in the domain of the budget, and to remove the principle of ministerial responsibility to the people's representatives, which had been accepted by Solsky's commission. Having obtained Cabinet approval for all these changes, Witte submitted his final draft to the tsar on 20 March/2 April 1906. Ten days later it was discussed in a meeting of imperial dignitaries and grand dukes over which Nicholas II pre-

---

*This is the literal translation of the Russian term *osnovnye zakony*. The French and English equivalent would be "Constitution," but, since in actuality there was no real constitution, we shall use the Russian term, which more truly represents the ambiguity created by the tsar.

sided. During the discussion Goremykin argued that the Duma must be forbidden to express itself on the expropriation of noblemen's land for the benefit of the peasants and, if it disobeyed, it must be dissolved. Witte vehemently opposed any such treatment of the Duma.

Simultaneously with the preparation of the basic laws, two very important ukases, both issued on 20 February/5 March, altered the composition and procedure of the Imperial Council and the Duma. The first augmented the membership of the Imperial Council appointed by the tsar with a larger membership elected by the clergy, the nobility, the zemstvo, the universities, business, and industry, and the Council became an Upper House, endowed with legislative capacity equal to that of the Duma, whose excesses it could prevent and whose reformist ardors it could quench. The second ukase, even though granting the Duma more rights than the August 1905 statute, limited its jurisdiction, restricted the rights of its members, and regulated its methods of work.

The Duma Elections and Witte's Resignation

The instruction of 17 February/2 March had established the procedure for the elections; the ukases of 4/17 March had prescribed, without a shadow of liberalism, the rules for associations and the organization of public meetings; that of 8/21 March had assured the freedom of the elections, which were to be held on three dates: 26 March/8 April in one group of governments, 14/27 April in the second, and 20 April/3 May in the third.

Contrary to the government's predictions, it became evident as soon as the first election returns were available that the peasants would not send a docile majority to the Duma. The Socialists boycotted the elections, and it was the new radical organization, the People's Freedom or Cadet party, that won the largest number of seats. All the court's anger thereupon descended on Witte, who had insisted on the overly liberal election law of 11/24 December and freedom of election. By his own admission his position became untenable. "The tsar avoided me," he wrote in his *Memoirs*, "he had recourse to subterfuges, he embarked on all kinds of measures without my participation and even without my knowledge." Considering his mission concluded, since he had put down the revolution and contracted a loan, he tendered his resignation, with his reasons for it, on 14/27 April.

He did not approve of the activities of Durnovo, minister of the interior, who, having repressed the revolution, continued to oppress the country, "thus angering the majority of the population and contributing to the election of extremist elements to the Duma";* it was impossible for him to go before the Duma and defend actions that Durnovo had carried out "without my knowledge or against my advice," nor could he "share the opinions of the conservatives of the extreme right, whose profession of faith has recently been adopted by Durnovo as his own with respect to the agrarian, Jewish, religious, and other problems"; in the agrarian domain he disapproved of the tactics of Goremykin, which "determined the character of the work of the Duma in advance"; attacked from the left by the revolutionaries and the liberals, he was "not supported from the right by the ultra-conservative nobles and high dignitaries, who had the tsar's ear and aroused his suspicions toward the actions and even the intentions of men whom they disliked"; whatever policy was resorted to, whether conciliation or "extreme measures," he could no longer usefully function as the intermediary between the government and the Duma; finally, he pointed out that by negotiating the loan he had released the tsar from the necessity of making concessions to the parties. These explanations, so rare in the mouth of a Russian minister and so remarkable in their political precision and the feeling of dignity that inspired them, were not calculated to change the prejudices of the tsar. Nicholas II lost no time in accepting Witte's resignation on 16/29 April, and the premier's departure entailed those of all his associates—even Durnovo was removed.

Goremykin became premier; P. A. Stolypin, who for the first time was to move at the top level of politics, became minister of the interior in place of Durnovo; Izvolsky replaced Lamsdorf as foreign minister; V. Kokovtsev became finance minister; Stishinsky, a conservative and a spokesman of the nobility, assumed the head of the Agriculture Ministry, and Shcheglovitov, who had gone over to the conservative side, became minister of justice, while Count Shirinsky-Shikhmatov, whom even Pobyedonostsev called a reactionary, replaced the liberal Count Obolensky as attorney general of the Holy Synod.

The Promulgation of the "Basic Laws" (27 April/10 May 1906)

The basic laws that Witte had drafted had not yet been promulgated when he left his post. Their publication had been delayed because at the last moment Trepov feared that they would not satisfy the coun-

---

*To this the tsar retorted that "the Duma is extremist through the fault of the excessively liberal electoral law of 11/24 December, the inertia of the conservative elements of the population, and the authorities' remissiveness in having abstained from intervening in the elections, something that never occurs in other countries."

try's desires. He submitted the text to a few liberal politicians, who, on 18 April/1 May, suggested certain indispensable changes. But the date for the meeting of the Duma was coming closer and there was some apprehensive question whether it would not want to discuss the "Constitution" on its own. Hence, even though he was no longer in power, Witte pressed the tsar to publish the basic laws. Nicholas yielded to his insistence. At the very last moment—27 April/10 May, the same day when the Duma first met—he issued the laws with some slight changes of his own.

Like the new institutions created by the ukase of 20 February/5 March on the organization and procedure of the Upper House, the basic laws of 27 April/10 May were intended to restrict the rights of the national representative entity. Although the Imperial Duma became a true legislative chamber, since no law could be either promulgated or abrogated without its concurrence, its competence was singularly limited by the prerogatives of the tsar and the Upper House.

The tsar, whose title of *autocrat* was preserved in the basic laws, retained very broad prerogatives. First of all, the army and navy and all matters connected with them,* diplomacy, the conclusion of treaties, the right of declaring war and making peace, everything that concerned the succession to the throne, the imperial court, the crown's estates, and the "appanages" fell within his sole authority. He also retained all his powers over the Orthodox church. At his pleasure he set the dates for the opening and closing of the annual session of the Duma; he could indeed dissolve it, provided that the ukase of dissolution established dates for the election and convocation of the New Duma. In the event of "emergency"—and the concept of "emergency," as we shall see, could be most elastic—he had the right to make laws on his own initiative in the intervals between the annual sessions of the Duma, but, within two months of the opening of the new parliamentary session, he had to submit these "emergency laws" to the approval of the Duma, which could veto them. He held the initiative in legislation. Legally both Houses did have means of indirectly taking such an initiative; each, indeed, had the power of presenting proposals for the amendment of laws and even debating them on its own instance, if after a month the Cabinet refused to convert them into draft laws. But in practice this power was too indirect to be effective. In any event, the Duma could not on its own initiative change either the fundamental laws or the electoral law, which, however, the tsar could

*Nevertheless, when new expenditures were required in these areas, they had to be voted by both Houses.

not modify without the participation of the Lower House. Further-more the Duma had only very limited financial powers. As a budget basis it had to accept, unmodified, the budget of 1906; it could make no changes in it without voting a separate law for each item that it sought to modify. Nor was it privy to all ordinary expenditures. What were called "protected" expenditures,* such as those for the court, service on state loans, etc., were outside its jurisdiction. As for the others, which in the majority were only credits that could not be pre-cisely established in advance but had to be estimated approximately at the start of each year, such as those of the state departments, it could disapprove them; but in that event the relevant credits of the previous budget were automatically granted to the government. Nor was the Duma to be concerned with the costs of war or preparation for war, emergency disbursements, trade treaties, railway concessions, rates of import duties, or foreign loans. Finally, the administration and application of laws were the monopoly of the tsar alone, and simi-larly all officials and ministers were answerable only to him. The Duma did receive the right† to challenge the illegal and arbitrary actions of ministers and their subordinates, but the ministers did not have to answer to it: the minister involved could refuse to reply, or postpone his reply for a month; if, at the end of that time, the Duma was still interested in the question and, by a two-thirds vote, decided that the minister's response was insufficient, the president of the Up-per House referred it to the tsar.

The Imperial Council, which had been hastily made over into an Upper Chamber and, like the Duma, been given the power to legislate, was so constituted as to act as a barrier to the desires of the Lower House. Half the Council's members were appointed by the tsar; the rest were elected for nine-year terms, one-third of them being chosen every three years: fifty government zemstvo representatives who could meet especially high property qualifications, eighteen councilors from the nobility, six from the Orthodox clergy, six from the Academy of Sciences and the universities, twelve from the chambers of commerce and industrial associations. Of all the elective members, only the rep-resentatives of the intellectual and business communities were likely to be liberals, but together they numbered only eighteen in a body of ninety-two men. As for the councilors appointed by the tsar, the list

*In the 1908 budget these represented 1.164 billion rubles, or 47 per cent of the total disbursements.

†Deputies did not have the right personally to raise questions. Each such request had to be signed by thirty deputies and presented to the Duma as a whole for its approval or refusal. The questioner therefore spoke in the name of the assembly.

of whom was prepared each year, they could not risk showing any trace of liberalism without exposing themselves to immediate removal. That was why the Imperial Council approved only those laws initiated by the government; in the ten years between 1907 and 1917 only one of the laws originated by the Duma, that dealing with freedom of thought, was to succeed in gaining the Council's approval—and even so it became a nullity by reason of the tsar's veto; all the rest found the peace of the graveyard there.

The terms of the basic laws, like their promulgation, clearly showed the Duma how limited its rights were. Thus the first Russian national assembly came together under the most unfavorable auspices. Not only had the revolution been vanquished on the barricades of Moscow; the liberal impetus that had been provided by the manifesto of 17/30 October had already diminished considerably. Against the aspirations of the country were arrayed the apprehensions of the nobility and the monarchy, the one fearful for its property, the other for the inviolability of its absolute power. An uneven struggle began.

III / THE FIRST DUMA, OR "DUMA OF POPULAR ANGER" (27 APRIL/10 MAY–7/20 JULY 1906)

The Meeting of the Duma

The first Imperial Duma became known as the "Duma of popular anger." Nevertheless, when it opened its sessions on 27 April/10 May, "anger" had not yet invested the spirits of the deputies. On that day their hearts were as glad as the sky was clear. It was as if they had forgot all the inauspicious circumstances that had surrounded the convocation of the Duma: the imperfections of the electoral law, the promulgation of the basic laws that restricted their assembly's rights, the manifest illwill of men in high office, the hostility of the privileged classes, the tsar's distrust. They had only one thought: that they were taking part in the meeting of the first Russian national assembly, called into being in order to make laws, to change the old order, to satisfy the people's aspirations—in other words, to launch the new era of Russian history that had so long been only a dream and for which so much energy had already been sacrificed and so much blood had been shed. In the face of the dream turned reality, everything else seemed secondary, insignificant, and easy of correction.

The opening session of the Duma was held in the Winter Palace. In the sumptuous setting of the imperial palace, the deputies, some in business suits, some in peasant dress, some in the costumes of the various national minorities, some in the black cassocks of the clergy, were surrounded by the blazing uniforms of the court dignitaries. In the coldly observing eyes of the courtiers the newcomers could see around them the reflection of a world as old as it was hostile. But that world was the past, and now everything was going to change. In his speech of welcome, the tsar seemed not at all to belie this hope: "May this day," he perorated, "be a milestone henceforth for the moral regeneration of Russia and the rebirth of her forces! I myself will guarantee the impregnable survival of the institutions that I have bestowed upon her."

When they left the Winter Palace, the deputies were transported by boat on the Neva to the old palace of Potemkin, the "prince of Tauride," which had been remodeled to house the first Russian Parliament. The journey took them past the Kresty (Crosses) Prison, whose windows were crowded with prisoners waving their handkerchiefs and shouting: "Amnesty!"—a cry that was taken up by the spectators. A general amnesty and the effacement of everything that had hitherto been regarded as a political crime seemed the logical and natural consummation of the end of the battle, the pledge and the symbol of reconciliation. To make it a reality was for the deputies the first of their obligations, a sacred duty to the country and the voters. Since they did not have the power to effect it by decree, they desired that the first words to be heard from the floor of the Duma be consecrated to it, and they called on I. Petrunkevitch, former member of the Tver zemstvo and the patriarch of Russian neo-liberalism, who enjoyed the respect of all his colleagues, to demand it. After the unanimous election of S. A. Muromtsev as president of the Duma and the delivery of his speech, which was devoted to defining the rights of the Duma in relation to the prerogatives of the sovereign, the deputies settled down to their labors.

The Composition and Conflicts of the Parties in the Duma

The composition of the Duma was quite complex. Initially rather confused, little by little it was clarified, and the deputies fell into nine discrete groups: 178 (37.4 per cent) belonged to the radical People's Freedom or Cadet party, 94 (19.6 per cent) to the Workers' party, 32 (6.7 per cent) to the Polish Kolo,* 26 (5.4 per cent) to the moderate Peaceful Renewal party, 17 (3.5 per cent) to the Social Democratic

*Kolo, meaning "Circle."

party,† 12 (2.5 percent) to the group of independent autonomists, 12 (2.5 per cent) to the Progressive party, 6 (1.25 per cent) to the Democratic Reform party, and 100 (20.9 per cent) to no group.

Classified in terms of nationality, 59 per cent of the deputies were Great Russians, 17 per cent were Ukrainians and White Russians, 22 per cent came from the national minorities (Poles, Balts, Moslems, Jews); thus the great majority (75 per cent) consisted of Orthodox believers. In terms of social origin, the most numerous were the peasants (45 per cent), followed by the nobles (37 per cent); 14 per cent were genuine landed proprietors; 25 per cent were farmers; 25 per cent were members of the liberal professions (lawyers, physicians, teachers, university professors); only 6 per cent were industrialists and merchants. It was the People's Freedom party in which the level of culture was the highest, but it was in the Workers' party, which represented a great variety of views, that there were the most peasants. In actuality these two parties represented the majority of the Duma; they had a common aim: the fight against the old order in the social and political spheres. At the same time, their outlooks on the tactics to be adopted in this struggle were quite divergent and indeed opposed. The Workers' party combined two different elements: pure peasants and pro-Socialist intellectuals. The peasants entered the Duma with the ingenuous conviction that it could do anything and that it was the Duma that held the responsibility for the redistribution of land and the preparation of the laws that they deemed necessary. The Socialists encouraged them in this belief, even though they did not share the peasants' illusions. Precisely because they knew that political conditions made it in effect impotent, they were prepared to sacrifice the Duma. They looked on it only as a means of organizing the popular masses and transplanting the political struggle from constitutional to revolutionary soil: "We want to lead the Russian people into a movement that it will be impossible to stop," one of their leaders, Aladyin, said. Another, Zhilkin, added: "It is time to recognize that we are the observers of a titanic struggle and that we have been placed here as an advance-guard detachment of that popular army that has sent us out to occupy forward positions." That was why they argued that the Duma ought to dare anything. "We are all-powerful legislators," Aladyin said, "and we have only to will." Their concept of omnipotence was most simplistic: "The Duma will make a law and the people will assume the task of executing it"; invested with full powers,

---

†In spite of the party's boycott of the elections, these seventeen, in the majority, were deputies elected in the Caucasus. In the final stages of the legislature the Social Democrats numbered twenty-six.

the Duma should combine the legislative with the executive and judicial powers; in order to organize the people, the deputies would establish direct contacts with their constituents and form local committees that, in conjunction with the Duma, would resolve the agrarian question and such problems as food supplies in times of famine; in their eyes the basic laws, the ministers, the existing legislation, and the regulations of the Duma were mere details, superfluous formalities, that need not be reckoned with; the ministers could be got rid of, and besides they were not members of the Duma. When one minister told a correspondent of *The Times* of London that the Duma was "only a revolutionary assembly on the order of the Soviet of Workers' Deputies," Aladyin retorted that no better compliment could have been paid to the assembly: "The Soviet has so brilliant a past that there is nothing offensive in the minister's statement." In fact the Workers' party's concept of the Duma, which was shared also by the Social Democrats, was precisely that of the revolutionary authority that the Soviet of Workers' Deputies of 1905 had sought to establish and that, with greater success, would be executed by the Soviets of Workers and Soldiers in the second revolution.

If this conception had been entertained by the Duma as a whole, the assembly's existence would probably have been extremely brief. Fortunately, the group whose members' number and political experience made it the most important, the People's Freedom or Cadet party, followed a less dangerous and more useful policy, which it had long since determined in its congresses. It recognized the absolute necessity of remaining within the strictest limits of legality, even though it hardly regarded that legality as perfect. By acting within the Duma itself and keeping it alive as long as possible, the party hoped gradually to broaden the Parliament's rights. To this end it believed that conflict with the government must be avoided whenever a legal foundation for the issue was lacking but that the rights granted to the Duma must be used. It had decided, for instance, to raise those problems most important for the people, such as the agrarian question, and to pursue their solution through strictly constitutional means without allowing itself to be halted by possible government opposition. In contrast to the left wing of the opposition, it did not count on any immediate action by the popular masses to support the Duma, because it was aware that such action could succeed only if it had had the benefit of prior organization and that revolutionary methods were those least likely to achieve that organization.

The conflict that was created in the Duma by these tactical divergencies among its parties made the task of the constitutional nucleus extremely delicate. At every step it encountered obstacles that it surmounted only at the cost of constant vigilance and the utmost diplomacy. Unquestionably, when the government attacked the Duma as a whole, the assembly reforged the union of all its parties against the assault. But, once the crisis was over, the internal battles began again. Above all they were supported from without by the leaders of the left-wing parties, who had not been elected to the Duma but who were striving to make it serve their purposes. Their major target was the Cadet party, which opposed their tactics and their objectives. They accused it of betrayal of the people's cause, they depicted all its parliamentary activity in a hostile light; and alliances between the left group and the right wing in the Duma, for all the latter's lack of numbers and influence, became more and more frequent as a means of placing the Cadets in the minority.

The Struggle Between the Government and the Duma

The dissensions of the left accorded perfectly with the aims of the government, which had no intention of giving any heed to the Duma.

Goremykin's initial tactic was simply to ignore the assembly. The ministers did not appear at the Tauride Palace or submit proposed legislation to it. It was not until 15/28 May that they first presented legislation to the Duma—a proposal, which has since become famous, for the erection of a greenhouse and a laundry at the University of Dorpat. It was apparently their intention to condemn the Duma to inactivity—and Goremykin thought that the deputies' own attitudes would greatly further him in this endeavor—so that as a consequence it could be branded "unfit for its labors," as in fact the government was later to accuse it of being. But the Cadets were resolutely determined to act. If they could not convert the Duma into a Constituent Assembly, they decided, they would at least embark at once on the realization of the reforms without which the manifesto of 17/30 October would remain illusory. They were prepared to present bills on their own initiative, even though this procedure, by the terms of the basic laws, must postpone any debate on them for a month—and in these circumstances a month was an eternity, as witness the impatience of that journalist who, in the early days of the assembly's existence, burst out during a meeting: "Three days have gone by and the Duma has done nothing!" With the Cadets the majority of the Duma resolved to initiate real work without delay. Aware of their obligation to the people, the deputies were willing to work day and night.

In consonance with proper constitutional procedure, the Duma began by preparing a response to the address delivered by the tsar in the Winter Palace; this address was treated as a speech from the throne. It was the version prepared by the Cadets, with some insignificant amendments contributed by the Workers' party, that was adopted in the fifth session of the Duma by a vote only six short of unanimity. The six were the men of the moderate right, who, with Count Heyden, had sought, however, to avoid weakening the effect of a unanimous vote by simply withdrawing when the question was put. In this memorable document, the Duma, putting its faith in the promise that the institutions created by the tsar would remain "unshakable," set forth the program that must be carried out in order to assure the normal and progressive evolution of the country: a bill for the establishment of universal suffrage; the abrogation of the emergency laws in which administrative despotism was cloaked; the extension, in concert with the tsar, whose legal prerogative it was to initiate it, of the legislative and budgetary powers of the Duma; the promulgation of specific laws on individual liberties and the freedoms of religion, speech, the press, assembly, association, and the strike; complete equality for all citizens before the law and the abolition of all special rights and privileges of any class, nationality, religion, or sex; the abolition of the death penalty; the solution of the agrarian problem on the principle of compulsory conveyance of land; recognition of the just claims of the various national minorities, and the creation of a cabinet answerable to the Duma in order to set limits on the omnipotence of government officials who stood as a barrier between the tsar and his people and in order, too, to assure the harmonious collaboration of the legislative and executive arms. The Duma appointed a delegation to go to the tsar with this document, which it was impossible to regard as "revolutionary" because it had rejected all the subversive proposals offered by the extreme left.

The constitutional parties hoped that the meeting with the tsar would strengthen their position with respect to the Cabinet. But, after three days of fevered waiting, the Duma was told by Goremykin that the tsar refused to receive the delegation. The Cadets succeeded, though not without difficulty, in persuading the Workers' party not to raise an issue on this account. On 13/26 May, in the presence of the entire Cabinet, for which this was its first appearance before the Duma, Goremykin read to the Duma the government's reply to its address. While he made some concessions on matters of subsidiary importance, he adamantly rejected the basic demands of the Duma: it was his view that experience had not yet demonstrated the necessity for any change in the electoral law and that it was his duty to state that "compulsory conveyance of land is absolutely unacceptable"; he believed that he did not have the right even to discuss the demand for changes in the basic laws and that "there could be no question of revision on the initiative of the Duma"; he favored the adoption of laws on the "freedoms bestowed," but only in order to "give the administrative arm effective means of preventing abuses of them"; he emphasized the firm determination of the Cabinet to retain the emergency laws because of the "assassinations, looting, and revolting violence that were taking place on the entire territory of the country"; in sum, he reminded the Duma that its only right against the government's decisions was that of raising questions.

This reply, which in addition wore the guise of a rebuke, was a declaration of war. It offended the most moderate of the deputies, such as Count Heyden, who contended that the government's reply was destroying any hope of peaceful collaboration. The Cadets, after having answered Goremykin in the person of their most forceful speakers, Nabokov and Roditchev, joined the Workers in preparing a resolution in which the Duma would declare that, "in the light of the government's refusal to meet the demands of the nation, without the satisfaction of which neither the pacification of the country nor fruitful labor by the national representative assembly is possible," it withheld its confidence from an irresponsible government. This denunciatory resolution was adopted almost unanimously, except for seven votes.

Nevertheless, neither the Cabinet nor the tsar was ready to draw from this constitutional cleavage the conclusions that it made necessary. Although the majority of the Duma had adopted a constitutional procedure, the government was determined to demonstrate that there was no constitution in Russia. The ministers seized on every opportunity to show their enmity to the Duma.* The deputies, who for the first time had the opportunity to put themselves openly on record against the abuses and the illegal acts of the government, naturally wanted to make the most of it; they submitted innumerable petitions for question and challenge—a total of 373. But the law gave the government the right to enforce an interval of a month between the question and its reply. This right it exercised to the full, even when the issue was one of capital punishments, which the Duma wanted to prevent, or of pogroms, which were sometimes staged even

---

*Thus the *Government Monitor* published the telegrams in which the extreme right petitioned the tsar to dissolve the Duma. When on 16/29 May a question was formally raised to determine who was responsible for this publication, Goremykin refused a week later to answer.

while the assembly was in session. In the face of this behavior, inevitably, the Duma could not maintain its composure, and there were
violent outbreaks and interruptions that prevented governmental
delegates from presenting the Cabinet's negative responses to legislative questions. Symbolically the Duma enacted a law abolishing the
death penalty, and, when the government asked for appropriations for
the relief of areas stricken by famine, the Duma reduced them to the
absolute minimum required and then granted them only under the
express proviso that it be empowered to control their disbursement.*
It also sent an investigating commission to Byelostok in order to
establish on the spot the origins of the pogrom that had just been
staged there, and Prince Urusov, a deputy who had once been governor
of Bessarabia, accused the police itself of having organized the pogrom.

It was principally, as Goremykin had anticipated, the agrarian
problem that intensified the antagonism between the government and
the Duma. Because the peasants wanted the question to be resolved as
quickly as possible, and even though the Cadet party intended to concern itself solely with "constitutional" legislative proposals, its
deputies had decided even before the Duma first met to insert this
issue into the assembly's agenda. Consequently they drafted a very
radical program that drew its inspiration from the thinking of the
party's left wing, and they managed to obtain the chairmanship of the
agrarian commission for one of the best qualified experts on the subject, Hertsenstein. In order to put off the decisive conflict and, by
playing for time, to familiarize the people with the need for proceeding by parliamentary methods, they refused to follow the Workers' party in its demand that any decision reached by the assembly be
made public in the form of a pure and simple decree by the Duma.
Similarly they offered absolutely no support to the suggestion for the
establishment of local committees by means of which the revolutionary members of the Duma intended—as was to be the case in 1917—
not so much to settle the agrarian question on the spot through the
seizure of land as to develop the revolutionary organization of the
population with a view to the decisive battle, the prospect of which
governed all their tactics. What also contributed to the delay in the
study of the agrarian problem was the large number of speakers—
almost two hundred—who had demanded time to state their views;
all the peasants and all the Workers' deputies wanted to have the floor,
and the talking went on until 18 June/1 July. The agrarian commis-

---

*This lack of confidence was subsequently fully vindicated by the scandal over
their expenditure that involved the deputy minister of the interior, Gurko.

sion had a complicated task; hence it was only on the eve of the dissolution of the Duma that Hertsenstein, having reconciled the views of the various parties, was to succeed in persuading the Duma to adopt the Cadets' proposals as the basic principles for the reform.

Uneasy at the activities of the agrarian commission, Goremykin decided to move first. On 20 June/3 July an official statement was published in the *Government Monitor.* Distributed in thousands of copies, it declared that the government had submitted its own proposal for an agrarian law that would distribute state lands among the peasants on terms that were to their advantage and, in addition, would enable them, through the help of the Peasant Bank, to purchase more land whose present owners were willing to sell; but the statement added that the rumors of compulsory conveyances of privately owned land were absolutely false and that, far from counting on a revolution, the peasants should put their hopes solely in the tsar's peaceful efforts and his loving care. This statement did not succeed in impairing the peasants' confidence in the Duma, of which so many of their representatives were members, but it was a challenge to the assembly, which in so vital a matter could not brook such a derogation of its legislative function.

Inasmuch as the country was, so to speak, officially apprised of the conflict between the government and the Duma, all the deputies were in agreement on a declaration to the people that the land problem could not be resolved without the participation of the Duma and that the assembly was at work on the development of a program of its own that envisaged a solution different from that offered in the government's communiqué. A proposal for an "appeal" to the people "from the Imperial Duma" was submitted by the agrarian commission on 27 June/10 July. It expressed the hope that "the population will wait patiently and calmly for the Duma to complete its labors," in other words "the draft of a law based on careful deliberation and drawn in legal form." This proposal was opposed by the Workers' party, which suggested a declaration that the Duma had no doubt of the support extended to it by the nation in the accomplishment of its purposes. One member of this party, Zhilkin, argued that the Duma could provide no guaranty that the land law would be the version that it had prepared and that therefore it was in no position to exhort the people to wait calmly. "What should prevail," he said, "is not peace and calm but anxiety. . . . We ought to be talking about an organized struggle. . . . What should be mounting is indignation in order to destroy the old order and establish a new one." The Cadets, far from following the Workers, offered some emendations to the "appeal"; they added, for example, a note to explain that compulsory conveyance, as the agrarian commission had agreed, must be understood to mean "the conveyance to the land workers, in conformity with legal provisions and against just compensation, of lands sold by the government." The Workers' party seized on these modifications as the pretext for voting against the "appeal," which, because of the Poles' abstention, was voted by only 124 members of the Cadet party.

There was nothing unconstitutional in the "appeal," or else the "constitutional" party would not have voted for it and the left wing of the Duma would not have found it insufficiently revolutionary. Nonetheless it served as the basis on which Goremykin's government ordered the dissolution of the Duma.

The Dissolution of the Duma

The government had not come to this decision without a certain hesitancy. Most of the deputies were convinced of the inviolability of the Duma; those of the left in particular asserted that only its existence prevented the outbreak of revolution, and the government was not too far from the Workers' party in its belief that the population would not placidly accept the announcement of the dissolution. That was why, at the same time, in government and especially in court circles there was much talk of the timeliness of finding a basis for agreement with the moderate sectors of society. D. N. Shipov, who was approached, declined, observing with his usual frankness that he was not representative of the majority. During an audience with the tsar, he advised the initiation of talks with the Cadets, who were the ruling party in the Duma, and he suggested calling on the combination of P. N. Miliukov and S. A. Muromtsev. In complete conformance with his custom when confronted with ideas contrary to his own—that is, by putting questions to the other man and pretending to share his views—the tsar gave every appearance of recognizing the utility of such a combination. On his order, talks were held between Miliukov and Stolypin. They proved that the government had in mind neither a purely Cadet Cabinet nor concessions that could satisfy the majority in the Duma. Carried on on a purely private basis because of the mood of the Duma, they were broken off when it became clear that an agreement was impossible between the government, which challenged the very existence of a constitution, and the constitutional party in the Duma.

The Cabinet thereupon opted for dissolution. Since Goremykin could not nerve himself to this perilous step, its execution was finally turned over to P. A. Stolypin, who was made premier. He first took military precautions not only in the capital but throughout the Empire. It would appear that the date for the dissolution was not settled until the last minute. During the Duma session of 7/20 July, Stolypin asked its president to schedule for the following Monday, 10/23 July, his reply to the question on the Byelostok pogrom. But the deputies who arrived at the Tauride Palace on the Sunday morning found the doors closed and under guard by sentries, and a large military force backed up by artillery was occupying all the neighboring streets in anticipation of an insurrection.

The Duma was not "dissolved" but, rather, "dispersed," like a band of criminals, without even the courtesy of prior notice to its presiding officer. The communiqué announcing its dissolution, in violation of Article CV of the basic laws, did not set a date for new elections; in contravention of Article LXXXVI of the same laws as well, it scheduled the convocation of the new Duma after 1/14 December— that is, after the expiration of the period provided for parliamentary study of the new budget; and finally, since the ukase of dissolution bore the counter-signature of no minister, no one was officially responsible for it. In the light of these violations of the basic laws the future seemed ominous, and there was reason even to fear that there would never be another Duma.

The first Duma, as one of its most respected members, I. Petrunkevitch, observed,

. . . had serious defects. It lacked experience in many areas, but could it have had any when it was the first [national assembly]? Its leadership structure might have been more perfect; but it was already amazing that the people's common sense, in spite of all the obstacles and the absurdities of the electoral law, had been capable of filling it with representatives who no doubt were not perfect but who were qualified. The deputies' temper was inclined to be quick, the ardor of certain of them disturbed the calm of debate and their anger sometimes took coarse forms; but the atmosphere in which they were living and working was not conducive to intellectual balance or serenity or parliamentary courtesies. All these faults were counterbalanced by the deputies' total dedication to the national purpose, by their keen awareness of their obligations toward the country, and by a profound confidence in the people, on whom the great future of Russia rests. The life of the first Duma was short, but the mark that it left in the country's social and political life was deep; the furrow that it cut brought virgin soil to life, and no reactionary force would be able to reduce the soil to its original state. In spite of its apparent impotence, it demonstrated to the nation all the vigor and the importance of national representation, the sole means by which the people can attain its rights, its freedom, and its prosperity. The Duma thrust out deep roots that its dissolution could not tear out of the popular consciousness: the idea of national representation remained a living force, and, in spite of all the efforts of the government and its reactionary supporters, the population invested all its hopes in the second Duma.

IV / FROM THE FIRST TO THE SECOND DUMA (9/22 JULY 1906– 20 FEBRUARY/5 MARCH 1907)

The Viborg Appeal

On 9/22 July, the same day when the government ordered the gates of the Tauride Palace closed, P. N. Miliukov—who already knew that the dissolution of the Duma had been decided on—presided, at four o'clock in the morning, in Petrunkevitch's home, over a meeting of deputies belonging to the Cadet party's central committee. They were unanimous in their view that they could not adjourn without protesting. Loyal to their strictly constitutional principles, they rejected the idea of the revolt nurtured by the Workers' party and the Social Democrats; they agreed to go to the extreme limit of their parliamentary rights. Consequently they decided to issue a call to the people to refuse to pay taxes or submit to induction into the army until a date for elections for a new Duma had been announced. They knew very well that this appeal could produce no immediate result, because neither the new conscript levy nor the collection of taxes would take place until autumn, but they wanted to have time to learn the mood of the people and, on the basis of that attitude, to organize passive resistance; furthermore this, in their view, afforded a means of making it possible for public anger to manifest itself. They knew too that they were laying themselves open to prosecution and to the loss of their civil rights in the next legislative elections, but they assumed this risk without hesitation. The text of the proposed appeal was drafted at once and communicated to the Workers' party, which approved it both in substance and in form. Since it was absolutely impossible to hold a meeting in Petersburg even to discuss the matter and vote on it, it was agreed that such a meeting would be held in Finland, where on several previous occasions parties forbidden in Russia proper had held their congresses. That Sunday evening 180 deputies—Cadets, Workers, and Social Democrats—gathered in the Hotel Belvedere in Viborg after a four-hour train journey from Petersburg. By common accord the chair was given to S. A. Muromtsev. The representatives of the "left" agreed to abide by the Cadets' proposals as the minimum of demands supported by all, but they reserved the right to go beyond this minimum in their individual capacities. At noon the next day, when the discussion of the text of the appeal was still under way, the governor of Viborg sent for Muromtsev. The governor informed him that he had received orders from Petersburg to prevent the meeting, and he pointed out reprovingly the delicate situation in which it had placed the Finnish authorities; then he requested that the deputies adjourn voluntarily. Thereupon the appeal was hastily adopted, signed by all present, and taken to Petersburg. The Social Democrats and the Workers' party subsequently undertook to organize risings in Sveaborg and Kronstadt, but the Cadets refused to be associated with these activities.

Stolypin's First Measures

The population was deaf to the Viborg appeal. On the other hand the extreme right, in agreement with the Union of the Nobility, demanded that the government, if it could not wholly reestablish autocracy, radically revise the electoral law in order to assure a majority in the Duma for the supporters of a return to the old order. But, fearing a popular protest, Stolypin's Cabinet dared not go so far, and the law of 11/24 December 1905 remained in force for the new elections.

During the early period that followed the dissolution of the first Duma, while there were serious agrarian disorders at Voronezh, Odessa, and Shusha in the Caucasus, military risings at Poltava, Brest-Litovsk, and Sveaborg, and a mutiny aboard the cruiser *Pamyat Azova* in the Baltic, Stolypin even tried to make some overtures to the moderate liberals. He held talks with D. N. Shipov, Count Heyden, Prince G. E. Lvov, and A. I. Gutchkov in the hope of persuading them to join his government. Shipov and Lvov set conditions: half the portfolios for themselves and their political friends and the promise that bills would be submitted to the Duma for the implementation of the essential points of the manifesto of 17/30 October and for the achievement of major land reforms. Stolypin refused: "Only a government that capitulates accepts programs," he wrote in reply. Under these conditions the moderates backed off; Count Heyden made a joke of the matter, saying it had been an attempt to "pass off the moderates as the putative children of ladies of flexible morals." Only Gutchkov agreed to work with the government, and even so he refused to join the Cabinet, pledging only his support as a deputy and as the head of the governmental or "Octobrist" party.*

*So called because its political program was based on the principles of the manifesto of 17/30 October 1905.

On 12/25 August an attempt was made to assassinate Stolypin, but he was unharmed by the bomb that wrecked part of his villa and killed almost thirty persons. Thereafter he concentrated on a course of repression. He invoked Article LXXXVII of the basic laws, which authorized the use of "provisional" laws in the event of emergency when the Duma was not in session, with the condition that they must be submitted to the new assembly within two months of its first session, and he issued such emergency laws. On 19 August/1 September courts-martial were set up and military expeditions were dispatched to the trouble spots. Other emergency measures were taken in order to prevent the new Duma from adopting any radical solution to the land problem. Stolypin adopted the doctrine of certain noble public men who professed to believe that all the evils sprang from the fact that, after the emancipation of the serfs in 1861, the peasants had not been assimilated to the other classes but had preserved a special system of land ownership (the mir) and that, instead of being brought under the common law (Volume X of the Code), they were governed by local customs. The ukase of 4/18 October 1906 abolished all the last vestiges of the special system that had applied to the peasants. The ukase of 9/22 November was intended to convert collective peasant property into individual holdings: every peasant received the right to demand that the commune separate his parcel from the common property. This right was to redound principally to the benefit of the richer peasants, who, with the government's help, received the best plots. By "banking on the strong," the government succeeded, as it had reckoned on doing, in dividing the peasants. Thus it hoped, by diverting their attention from the nobility's lands, to create a new class, a kind of class of aspiring landowners who could be called on to reinforce the former ruling class, which was growing poorer and was increasingly disposing of its land.

The Elections to the Second Duma

Stolypin was also quite particularly concerned with the preparations for the elections to the second Duma. Although he had retained the old electoral law, he was firmly determined to employ every means to make its application innocuous; in this effort his deputy in the Ministry of the Interior, Kryzhanovsky, an adept in the art of exerting pressure on the voter without overstepping the letter of the law, seconded him most ably, and the Senate, with its "interpretations" that changed the law, equally furthered his aims.

It was of the utmost importance to strike at those political figures who in the first Duma had proved themselves to be the irreconcilable antagonists of the government. Immediately after the dissolution of the assembly, reprisals were taken against its members. The peasant deputies, returning to their homes, were particularly persecuted: they were even officially forbidden to give any accounting of their labors to those who elected them; efforts, not always successful, were made to arrest them and banish them, but the peasants, who were convinced that their best defenders were the men whom the government persecuted, occasionally resisted these attempts by force. Prosecutions were initiated against 180 deputies, including 120 members of the Cadet party, for having issued the Viborg appeal. Since mere accusation was legally sufficient to deprive a man of political rights, the elite of the intellectuals and politicians was thus removed from the electoral campaign. "The Duma will have no head," the minister of the interior announced complacently. Having brought down their chiefs, the government soon attacked the political parties themselves. Any campaign activity was forbidden to parties that were not "authorized"; the only "authorized" parties were the extreme right Union of the Russian People, Gutchkov's Octobrists, and the Peaceful Renewal party; even this group, which included the moderates whom Stolypin had sought to bring into his Cabinet, was approved only after much hesitation; authorization for the Cadet party, of course, was refused.

At the same time, everyone whose electoral backing was anticipated, especially clerics and functionaries, was mobilized: they, like their subordinates and even the employees of private enterprises, were forbidden to belong to unauthorized political parties, and the clergy was ordered by its hierarchic superiors to take part in the elections. As a result of the Senate's "interpretations," the most democratic elements were stricken from the electoral rolls. At the end of 1906, 260 daily newspapers had been suspended and 207 editors in chief were being prosecuted; in January 1907, at the height of the election campaign, 77 more publications were suppressed and 60 more editors in chief were indicted. Every possible step was adopted to paralyze the propaganda of the prohibited parties and to abet that of the right-thinking parties, which had at their disposal Stolypin's official publication, *Rossya (Russia)*; at political meetings there was no pressure tactic that was not brought into play: elections of undesirable delegates were invalidated and opposition candidates were persecuted.

What was the outcome of these manipulations? The extreme right won 63 seats; the moderate right, the Octobrists, took 34; the Cadets obtained 123; the Polish party got 39; the left, or Workers' party, won 97; the various Socialist parties—Revolutionary Socialists, Social Democrats, and "Populist" Socialists—captured 83; there were 22 deputies without party affiliation. In spite of all its efforts, then, the government had been unable to force the election of a docile majority. Its candidates represented only about one-fifth of the Duma, while the opposition as a whole remained virtually as strong as in the first Duma—it had dropped only by one percentage point, from 69 per cent to 68 per cent.

The striking aspect of the second Duma was the progress made by the extreme parties that had no intention of restricting themselves to constitutional action. The extreme right entered the Duma with the clear purpose of destroying it completely and restoring the autocracy. It enjoyed the sympathies of the nobility and the powerful court party; it controlled a network of "sections," which, by concerted declarations, attempted to create a false picture of public opinion; it possessed a secret organization, the Union of the Russian People, which was supplied with arms by the government and which resorted to terrorism against its political opponents.* Similarly, on the extreme left, the Socialists, who for the first time had openly taken part in elections and the number of whom had tripled, pursued only destructive ends; they had preserved all their illusions and they believed that forceful action by the Duma would help them to organize the popular masses and arouse a powerful revolutionary force. Only the center party, the Cadets, was definitely determined to employ all the rights conferred on it by the basic laws in order to consolidate the national representative assembly and accustom the government, like the nation, to the methods of parliamentary action. But its number was smaller than in the first Duma: instead of its 37.4 per cent in that assembly, it now had only 24 per cent of the deputies.

V / THE SECOND DUMA (20 FEBRUARY/5 MARCH–3/16 JUNE 1907)

Although in part the second Duma was more radical than the first, the state of mind of all the opposition parties had undergone notable change since the dissolution of July 1906. The glorious expectations that had been awakened by the opening of the first Duma had vanished. It was now a known fact that the national representative assembly was not inviolable and that the government could easily shatter this fragile instrument without any reaction by the country. Hence the pri-

---

*It was this organization that was responsible for the assassination of Hertsenstein a short time after the dissolution of the first Duma and for the murder of one of his friends, Iollos, a deputy, during the session of the second Duma.

mary concern was not so much for the defense of its power as for the preservation of its very life; it was universally recognized that it could survive only as long as it avoided mortal conflicts. "Save the Duma!" was the watchword tacitly adopted even by the Socialist parties at a time when they were reproaching the Cadets for following it. The government, on the other side, wished no immediate conflict with the Duma: on the contrary, by submitting proposed legislation and a budget to the assembly, the government made clear its desire for collaboration with it.

The first obstacle to be overcome was the governmental declaration that Stolypin read to the Duma on 6/19 March. In order to avoid a vote of censure that might afford the pretext for its immediate dissolution, the Duma resorted to the tactic of silence, which was infringed only by the Social Democrats. Moreover, Stolypin's declaration, which discussed the proposed legislation, was quite moderate in its tone; it even conceded that the government's proposals might be subject to revision by the assembly. It was only in the speech that he delivered later, as a reply to the Social Democrats, whom he clearly divorced from the other opposition parties, that Stolypin showed more intransigence: he asserted that "the sovereign's will has not authorized the Duma to express its lack of confidence in the government," and he concluded with a shout: "You will not frighten us!"

But its abstention from the adoption of a motion of lack of confidence did not disarm the enemies of the Duma. On 16/29 March, the same day when Deputy Iollos was murdered by the extreme right's secret organization, a black cross appeared in the newspaper *Russkoye Znamya (The Russian Flag)*. At this signal, as they had been ordered by Deputy Purishkevitch on 28 February/13 March, the sections of the Union of the Russian People launched a campaign to demand the dissolution of the Duma and the amendment of the electoral law. The government itself, basically, clung to its old position and had no intention of giving up the benefits of the "provisional" laws that it still had the right to enforce for two months after the meeting of the Duma. When the left called for the immediate abolition of the courts-martial instituted by these laws,* Stolypin retorted summarily on 13/26 March: "If you want an end to the courts-martial, put an end to the red madness and be the first to disarm." The effect of this was to range the entire Duma solidly behind the terrorist parties; it amounted in essence to demanding that the Duma "denounce the terror" as a condition of its own survival, and, since it did not want to pick up the

*The laws remained in force until 20 April/3 May.

challenge and give the government the backing of its moral authority, it was to live from then until the end of its session under the unremitting threat of dissolution.

Nevertheless the Duma set itself to serious work. It began to study the land problem, as well as the budget, which it turned over, in spite of opposition from the left, to the appropriate committee. But the discussion of both questions was never more than purely academic. The Cadets had taken full cognizance of the tangible realities and, even while retaining its essential features, they had substantially revised their agrarian program with the collaboration of Kutler, who was now a deputy, and the government did not pronounce it unacceptable. In addition, they were devoting every effort to organizing the operations of the Duma and making it more effective. They obtained approval of a new rule that set restrictions on the deputies' eloquence; fixed one day each week for questions, the flood of which had submerged the first Duma; and established two night sessions for the discussion of matters of secondary importance so that all the remainder of the time could be given to debate on legislation that was purely organic, such as proposals for the reform of the judiciary and of local self-government, which—like those on the abolition of capital punishment, amnesties, etc.—could not be construed as political manifestations. Because of the difficulties and the delays that were encountered by those proposals presented directly by the Duma, they believed that a start must be made by debating the government's proposals, with the understanding that any necessary amendments in them would be made. For lack of a stable majority, they had to maintain a permanent communication among the various parties and unite them in working out a general plan for the parliament's work.* Fifteen committees of the Duma worked untiringly on legislation and the budget. In spite of the government, which utilized every means at its disposal to impede their endeavors, opposed their resorting to experts who were not members of the Duma, and refused to provide them with the documentation that they required, by the end of May these committees completed their discussions of proposals for local courts, on individual freedoms, and on the laws issued under Article LXXXVII of the basic laws on freedom of belief and the establishment of compulsory schooling. The agrarian committee reached agreement on the adoption of the basic principles of the Cadets' proposals. The committee on local autonomy made useful progress. Other committees studied proposals for labor

---

*This method did not begin to show real results until almost the end of the third month.

legislation, states of siege, the expansion of the budgetary powers of the Duma, etc.

These visible results of the work of the Duma served only to heighten the apprehensions of its enemies. Specifically they feared, as the congress of the Union of the Nobility had shown on 14/27 November 1906, the eve of the elections, that, "strengthened by its past experience, it would adopt a proper and irreproachable attitude so that there would be no ground for criticism of it, and then, under the cover of the authority conferred on it by the seeming legality of its activities, it would promulgate fatal laws"—fatal for the nobility. In order to prevent parliamentarianism from "taking solid root in Russia," the Duma from "becoming a permanent institution," and Russia from "ceasing to be a great power," they had hoped for the success of the extreme-left parties at the expense of the Cadets and for elections that would be "as bad" as possible. That was why the deputies of the right made every effort to compromise the Duma by inciting their left-wing colleagues to rash actions and even by occasionally voting with them in order to turn the constitutional center into a minority. In mid-April, meeting in Petersburg, the Union of the Nobility addressed a petition directly to the tsar to dissolve the Duma and change the electoral law. Above all else the nobles feared that, if the Duma survived until the summer vacation, the left-wing deputies would go into the provinces to stir up new agrarian disorders with their propaganda. These fears, moreover, were not altogether devoid of foundation, because the Socialists were still in favor of organizing revolution by means of local committees, as they publicly stated from the floor of the Duma on more than one occasion.

The center, which was beginning to attract the allegiance of the left-wing peasant deputies, who understood the important part that would devolve on the Duma in the accomplishment of land reform, tried in vain to avoid any conflict with the government by rebuffing the Socialists' arguments; the cautious conduct of the center was canceled by the behavior of the left. Aside from the terrorist attacks that were carried out not only by the Revolutionary Socialists' "combat legions" but also by the new organization of the "Maximalists," * the left was carrying on a revolutionary propaganda campaign in the army that frightened the government and that had already brought about the arrests of a number of Social Democrats. The inevitability of the conflict became apparent on 7/20 May, when the agenda of the Duma

---

*A group with anarchist tendencies; it regarded the Socialists' tactics as ineffectual and preferred to resort to violent methods such as assassination and expropriation.

showed a question by the Social Democrats on the invasion of Deputy Ozol's residence by the police.* The next day, under question from the right, Stolypin confirmed that on 13/26 April twenty-eight persons had in fact been arrested on charges of planning the assassination of the tsar and Grand Duke Nikolai Nikolayevitch. On 1/14 June, Stolypin went to the Duma, demanded a closed-door session, and then called for the arrests of fifty-five Social Democratic deputies—in other words, the party's total parliamentary representation—whom he accused of criminal conversation and a nationwide conspiracy to provoke an armed revolt and proclaim a democratic republic; he asserted that sixteen deputies must be arrested at once and that written evidence of their incrimination had been discovered during the search of Ozol's home. The Duma was thus forced into an extremely delicate position. It must take a stand on a question that bore profoundly on the principle of parliamentary immunity. The charges made against the Social Democratic deputies, for all their *a priori* plausibility, seemed too summary and were not equally serious with respect to all those accused. Furthermore, this was not a question of seeking individual exemptions from parliamentary immunity, such as the requests that had previously been made, and referred to a special committee of the Duma, against deputies accused of political crimes; this was a collective demand against an entire party. What the Social Democrats were doing had long been common knowledge: why was it not until now that charges were being made? Obviously reasons of a political nature were entwined with the common criminal charges. After some discussion, the Duma referred Stolypin's demand to its committee, which was to make a report within twenty-four hours.

It had been known for some days that the dissolution of the Duma had been decided on; the fact that Stolypin did not want to wait for the outcome of the committee's discussions clearly showed that his demand for the abrogation of immunity was a mere pretext. The next day, which was 2/15 June, the Duma convened with the conviction that it was meeting for the last time. Among the items on the agenda was legislation dealing with local courts. Ninety minutes before the sitting was scheduled to conclude, the left deputies requested that the bill be tabled and that the Duma vote to reject the budget and abrogate the agrarian laws promulgated under the authority of Article LXXXVII of the basic laws. They hoped that this move, which could produce no practical result, would redound to the benefit of their propaganda, because they expected to be able to profit by a dissolution to provoke a

*The police had broken into Ozol's home during a meeting and had searched not only the premises but the persons of all present, including four deputies.

popular rising. But it was clear that such a tactic could only discredit the very principle of national representative government at a time when it was already under the gravest of menaces. The center refused to be drawn into this course, and the debate on the judiciary measure continued calmly until the sitting ended. The special committee not having completed its report, that matter was postponed for the next day's session. But there was to be no such session. During the evening Deputies Maklakov and Struve labored in vain to convince Stolypin that the committee's hesitations were well founded; the government had made up its mind.

The Duma was dissolved on 3/16 June, new elections were set for 1/14 September, and the opening of the third Duma was scheduled for 1/14 November. At the same time the government issued a new election order, which could not be described as a law because it was a direct contravention of the basic laws, which made any change in the election law subject to the approval of the Duma. Triumphant, the right-wing parties hardly tried to conceal the fact that from a constitutional point of view they had achieved what amounted to a *coup d'état*. To them this was one more proof that there was no constitution in Russia: "The tsar gave it and the tsar will take it away" was the phrase that summarized their view. The accusations made against the Duma in the manifesto of 3/16 June were without foundation. In actuality its great crime was its dual refusal to disavow the terror and at the same time to give the government its moral support. The publication of a new electoral decree left no further question as to the basic, even if unadmitted, reasons for the dissolution. This decree was not drawn and published between one dusk and one dawn; it was the product of an accord between the nobility and the government, and it was not by mere coincidence that the Duma was dissolved at the precise moment when this masterpiece of the art of politics, the handiwork of Kryzhanovsky, was coming off the government's presses. The country was not deceived; it grasped at once that the second Duma was a pure and simple sacrifice to the interests of the nobility.

VI / THE THIRD DUMA, OR "DUMA OF THE LORDS" (1907–1912)

The "Government Bloc" and the Opposition

The electoral decree of 3/16 June 1907 drew its inspiration from the methods of Napoleon III. It allowed the minister of the interior and his agents to alter the boundaries of election districts and to divide voters into groups (producers, landowners, etc.), each of which would have the right to choose its own delegates. Ecclesiastics, for instance, could be grouped into special colleges, and small landowners could be divided among various colleges in accord with the size of their holdings; under the decree's own terms, city residents were divided into two *curiae* each of which elected the same number of deputies: the first *curia* consisted of the rich and the second consisted of everyone else. The number of electors to be chosen by the peasants in each district and each government was substantially reduced, while the large land-owners' representation was enlarged. Furthermore, in each district, the number of urban voters in the first *curia* was so calculated that, added to those of the landowners, they would have a majority over the combination of peasant electors and those of city dwellers in the second *curia*. In short, in the electoral assembly of a province (government), which elected the deputies, the number of electors was in inverse proportion to the size of the population group that it represented: in fact, it was one for every 230 landowners, one for every 1000 rich urban residents, one for every 15,000 middle-class city dwellers, one for every 60,000 peasants, and one for every 125,000 workers. Thus the government possessed the means of wielding effective influence over elections, and therefore it was the government, much more than the political parties, that determined the outcome. Its watchword was "Combat the revolution," and all its efforts were directed toward assuring the success of those parties "obedient to the law." An agreement reached between Stolypin and the leader of the Octobrist party, A. I. Gutchkov, guaranteed this party the support of the right and the nationalists, themselves backed—one might say created—by the government.

The "incomparable Chamber" thus brought into being was profoundly different from the first Duma: it was composed in large measure of supporters of the government. The government's majority included the three groups of the right, the nationalists, and the Octobrists—in other words, more than 300 of the 442 deputies. The opposition, which was led by the Cadets, was reduced to somewhat more than a hundred members, and it included: on the right, the Progressives, with twenty-three deputies, and the Moslems, with eight; in the center, the fifty-four Cadets; on the left, thirteen Workers' party deputies and twenty Social Democrats. Between the majority and the opposition, the Polish fraction, composed of the Polish *Kolo* and the Polish-Lithuanian-White Russian group, with eighteen deputies, remained independent, voting sometimes with one side, sometimes with the other.

The majority called itself the "government bloc." The Octobrists, who had pledged themselves to follow a program "of pacification and reforms," assumed its leadership. Captives of the parties that sat to the right of them and eager to serve the purposes of the government that had assured them of victory, they proved to be extremely bad "constitutionalists." The majority denounced the members of the opposition as enemies of the nation and accused them of plotting the destruction of the state and of yielding to the pernicious influence of the Jews; it also cast suspicion on the national-minority groups—the Poles, the Moslems, and the representatives of the other minorities.* Not only the speakers of the right but also those of the Octobrist center engaged in unrestrained attacks against the opposition as a whole and against the Cadets in particular. A Bessarabian landowner, Purishkevitch, and an engineer from Kursk, Markov II, both of whom sat at the extreme right, gained opprobrious notoriety by dishonoring the dignity of the assembly and lashing out savagely at the leaders of the left; but, every time they denounced the opposition, the principle of a constitution and popular representation, and the prestige of the Duma itself, they did so with the backing of the majority and almost always with the approval of government circles and the reactionary faction at court. The opposition deputies were barred from the committees dealing with military matters on the ground that they were lacking in patriotism. In the beginning the atmosphere was so charged with hate, the torrent of insults to some of them was so fierce, the efforts to discredit them were so shameless that the position of their spokesmen was extremely painful. Interrupted by offensive shouts and organized noise-making from the right-wing benches, they encountered the utmost difficulty in defending their views. Nevertheless, relations between the opposition and the Octobrists improved notably after the third session. The Octobrists began to evidence a greater tolerance for their opponents, who included many experts and eminent parliamentarians. When the Octobrists wanted to put through their technical program—the balancing of the budget, the development of the army, the introduction of certain liberal reforms whose usefulness was beyond question, for example in local courts and public education, or the creation of the cantonal zemstvo—they found themselves compelled to rely on the various groups in the opposition.

The Policy of Russification

With the support of the majority in the Duma the government pursued a policy of oppression of national minorities.

*The electoral decree of 3/16 June had reduced Polish representation from thirty-seven to fourteen deputies; the forty-four representatives of the Asian possessions were cut back to fifteen, and the twenty-nine Caucasus deputies were reduced to ten.

While it viewed virtually all the minority groups in the empire with the same suspicion, it was above all the Finns against whom the nationalist policy was most forcefully applied. The accord concluded in 1809 between the Diet of Borgå and Alexander I had united the Grand Duchy of Finland to the Russian Empire while at the same time preserving its autonomy and its Constitution. The existence of an autonomous province enjoying a European-style Constitution within a few versts of Petersburg was intolerable to the nationalists and the government. Therefore Stolypin turned back to the policy of Governor General Bobrikov, who, at the outset of the reign of Nicholas II, had suspended the activities of the Finnish constitutional system. Early in 1908, when he had prevailed on the tsar to decree that henceforth the governor general and his deputy would be appointed on the recommendation of the Russian government and no longer on that of the Finnish, he incited the deputies of the "government bloc" to raise a series of extremely antagonistic questions on Finland and in particular to demand that the Russian government refer Finnish matters to his control. Under the decree of 20 May/2 June 1908 "concerning the procedure to be followed for dealing with Finnish matters affecting the interests of the Empire," he ruled that the grand duchy's authorities could no longer present any proposals to the tsar without the prior knowledge and consent of the Cabinet. Then he took up the so-called Empire legislation question that had been posed by the manifesto of February 1899. A mixed commission composed of six Russians and five Finns was assigned to define those Finnish matters that would be governed by imperial legislation. The Russian members' proposals were approved by the Cabinet and made into a draft law. In contravention of the Finnish Constitution, this draft established the hegemony of imperial legislation over a large number of questions that were vital to the grand duchy—for example, its obligation to share in costs designated as imperial expenditures, military service, the position of Russians and the rights of Russian citizens in Finland, the adaptation of local public education and the local penal code to the interests of the Empire, legislation on public meetings, association, the press, and the import of foreign books, the currency, postal and telegraphic services, customs, etc. Submitted to the Duma at the end of March 1910, and discussed in plenary session on 23 May/5 June, the draft aroused fierce protests not only from the opposition but even from some members of the "government bloc." The cause of Finland and justice was pleaded by Miliukov for the Cadets; Roditchev, Luchitsky, General Babyansky, and Bulat, for the opposition, and Baron Meyendorff of the government bloc, who was Stolypin's cousin; they contended that the proposal violated both the Finnish and the Russian Constitutions at the same time. It was useless. Eager to please the government at any price, accepting the government's assertion, which it could not prove, that its proposal was vital and legal, the majority decided to curb the debate and accelerate the vote. The discussion was carried on in an atmosphere of such chauvinism and the rights of the minority were so flagrantly violated that about 120 members of the opposition and some members of the majority refused to remain in the Chamber and withdrew. Voted within an hour,* the law was finally adopted on 31 May/ 13 June by the Duma and then by the Imperial Council. After its promulgation on 17/30 June, the Russian government had the two Russian Chambers† enact two new laws, of which one gave all Russian subjects in Finland the same rights as Finns and the other provided that, until further notice, personal military service by Finns would be supplanted by a money payment to be made by the Finnish Treasury to the Russian Treasury.

The government and its bloc practiced a similar nationalist policy toward the other minorities in the Empire, especially the Poles and the Jews. Draft laws were proposed for establishing municipal governments in the cities of the Caucasus, the northwest and southwest provinces, and Poland, that provided for the creation of special electoral colleges for Russian municipal electors, even though they represented an infinitesimal minority in many cities; for Polish municipal elections three colleges were provided: Polish, Russian, and Jewish, the Jews being represented by the smallest number of city councilors in spite of the fact that they constituted the majority of the population in the Polish cities. Another proposal, for the disannexation of Khelm— known as "the fourth partition of Poland"—knifed deeply into Polish national feeling; its intent was to combine the non-Polish (i.e., Orthodox) populations established in the two governments of Lublin and Syedltse and create a single new government, that of Khelm, which would be detached from Poland.

The Jewish question was put on the agenda by the congress of the Union of the Nobility, which took over the political leadership of the country during the third Duma. A savage campaign of anti-Semitism was unleashed in the Duma with the obvious approval of the center and the leadership; the mouthpieces of the extreme right—Markov II, Purishkevitch, Zamyslovsky—delivered a number of orations against the Jews, seizing every opportunity of a new draft law to demand their

*Of the 307 deputies present when the session began, only 187 remained in their seats; and 23 of them voted negatively.

†The Duma in November 1911, and the Imperial Council in January 1912.

exclusion from the army, the zemstvo, and the municipality, as well as still further limitations on their already extremely restricted access to the schools.

The Policy of Caste and the Agrarian Laws

While it was parading its militant nationalism, the majority, which was meekly following the social and political program of the Union of the Nobility, was dedicating great effort to the protection of the nobles, whose landed estates were breaking up. It was not for nothing that the mass of the people called this third Duma "the Duma of the lords." Its majority, like the Cabinet, was wholly won over to the theories of A. D. Pazukhin, marshal of the nobility of the Simbirsk government and a notorious collaborator of Pobyedonostsev and Katkov during the reign of Alexander III; he contended that as servitors of the state the nobles must "become once more the dominant caste in the Empire." In order to implement the law of 1890 that had assured the nobility of a majority in the zemstvo and placed the administration of every district in the hands of marshals of the nobility chosen by its own assemblies, further legislative and administrative steps were taken that consolidated the nobles' predominance in local government and afforded them privileged credit terms with the land banks.

It was this policy of caste that explained the haste with which the Duma adopted measures dealing with the peasant problem, especially those laws establishing the character of property in peasant lands and fostering individual peasant ownership. The Stolypin Cabinet's agrarian program, carried out by Krivosheyin as minister of agriculture, was intended to divert the people's thoughts from the dream that had obsessed them for centuries: the redistribution of the hereditary seignorial fiefs among the peasants. The law of 14/27 June 1910, which ratified and strengthened the ukase of 9/22 November 1906* and which itself was supplemented by the law of 29 May/11 June 1911, was intended to replace collective ownership by the peasant commune with small individual holdings. In Stolypin's view it should have served to prevent that "lack of land" from which the peasants were so acutely suffering. The political reasons behind it can be truly understood only

---

*The new law differed from the ukase only in that it established as private property those parcels held by peasants in villages in which there had been no redistribution of land during the preceding twenty-four years, and, further, in order to prevent the kulaki (the "rich men") from dispossessing the poor, it set limitations on the right of free conveyance of these parcels to other peasants.

if it is viewed in terms of the nobility's attempts to protect what was left of its estates against falling into the hands of the peasant masses. Undoubtedly its basic principle was equitable, because private ownership by peasants represented a more advanced form of exploitation of the land than the old system of the agrarian community that prevented the peasants from applying the necessary technical developments for optimal use of their land, but the manner in which Stolypin put it into practice made brutal inroads on the rights that the rural communities had acquired over their holdings through the 1861 law; in reality, even though the communities were owners both *de facto* and *de jure*, under the 1910 and 1911 laws they could be compelled to give up communal property and to allow it to be converted into new individual holdings. That was why the peasants were split into two opposing factions in the governments in which the law was enforced by the land commissions set up by the Ministry of Agriculture: on the one hand there were the individual peasant owners who were the gainers by the right conferred on them by the law to withdraw from the community and establish independent farming operations on the best lands, taken away from their neighbors, while on the other hand there were the peasants who remained members of the community and fought vigorously to defend its property against the greed of their rivals encouraged by the government.

Thus the consequence of Stolypin's legislation was a further complication of the land problem. Side by side with the old conflict between landlords and peasants there was now the new struggle between peasants who became private owners and those who clung to the community. This conflict created by the third Duma was to be a potent factor for social agitation in rural areas during the 1917 revolution.

Although this social policy protected the "dominant order" of the nobility, it ran counter to the basic needs of the country, which had just adopted the course of broad industrial development. Such a policy neglected the interests of the cities, which, since the time of Alexander III, had grown much larger, had become major industrial and intellectual centers, and were guiding public opinion, but which had been unable to obtain in the "Duma of the lords" the representation to which their importance entitled them. Stolypin's policy tended solely to sacrifice the interests of the vast Russian Empire to those of a single class, a self-centered caste that was degenerating and diminishing; and, of course, as this policy impeded the normal growth of trade, it sapped the economic vitality that marked the beginning of the twentieth century.

The Reconciliation Between the Octobrists and the Opposition

In the country at large the general interests as well as those of the peasants were defended by the intellectuals of democratic persuasions who had always been the champions of the people and many of whom were connected with the press, the universities, the city governments, and the zemstvo—which in practice, despite the election system instituted by the 1890 law, had been able to preserve its tradition of 1864: that is, concern for the welfare of the peasants. In the Duma these same interests were supported first of all by the opposition—many outstanding members of which had been elected by the cities—which had revived the program of social and democratic reforms presented by the first Duma in its response to the speech from the throne. But soon even the center began to be made uneasy by the reactionary policy that the government, the prisoner of the nobility, was seeking to put into practice.

In 1908 the rift between this policy and the beliefs of the center became clearly evident. Gutchkov, the leader of the Octobrists, went into battle against the Navy minister, who, like the War minister, was immune to control by the Duma. Given the restrictions of the national assembly's powers, this conflict assumed the character of the attack on the sovereign's prerogatives. With the backing of the opposition, the center undertook to defend the rights of the Duma in matters of military and naval legislation. Article XCVI of the basic laws gave the tsar the right to make laws without Parliament in questions that concerned the army and navy but only those that did not require new appropriations. But the very fact that it included new expenditures for the Treasury made the naval budget subject to discussion and vote by the two Houses. The Duma took advantage of the opportunity to reduce the budget. The tsar refused to approve it with these changes, and, in a rescript, he assigned to Stolypin the task of defining the respective powers of the Chambers and the government in the domain of naval and military legislation. The regulations governing procedures for establishing new credits for military and naval needs, issued on 24 August/6 September 1909, were already severely restrictive of the budgetary powers of the Duma, but the War and Navy ministers interpreted them in the most arbitrary fashion and utilized them to insert new cost items without submitting these to prior study by the Chambers. During a request for a question in the Duma on the illegality of these new regulations, the opposition spokesmen—Miliukov, Maklakov, and others—proved that their publication without the consent of the Duma was a perversion of the spirit of the basic laws. But the majority, including the Octobrists, could not bring itself to vote against the government, and the question petition was defeated by 161 votes to a hundred.

The center also collaborated with the left in order to defend the budgetary jurisdiction of the Duma. This jurisdiction was extremely narrow: a large sector of the budget, as we have seen, was "protected" and thus exempt from any attack or change on the part of Duma. During a debate on the railway system's budget in the spring of 1908, the assembly's budget committee presented a resolution for the creation of a commission to investigate the railways. Miliukov having pointed out that the Parliament enjoyed the right of engaging in such investigations, Finance Minister Kokovtsev took the opposite view, which he expressed in a sentence that became famous: "We have no Parliament, thank God!" The reaction was violent, and not only from the opposition spokesman, Miliukov, but also from the Octobrists' representative, Count Uvarov. The presiding officer of the Duma, Khomyakov, an Octobrist, declared that Kokovtsev's remark was "out of order," but a few days later, before the whole Chamber, he was made to offer his apologies to the minister. During the same year an imperial ukase, without the approval of the Duma, extended the provisional appropriations for the Ministery of Communications, whereupon Count V. Bobrinsky, a nationalist right-wing deputy, proposed that as an act of protest these appropriations be reduced by one ruble. The majority of the Duma, which on more than one occasion involving matters of far greater importance and expenditures of many millions had meekly yielded to the government, supported Bobrinsky's motion, which, of course, was of only symbolic significance. It was principally during the two final sessions of this third legislature that the Octobrists and the opposition joined forces fairly frequently on budgetary matters. But, when the Cadets offered a bill to amend the rules that set such extreme limits on the budgetary powers of the Duma and to grant it the rights customarily enjoyed by the Lower Chambers of all other countries, the Octobrists did not support them, but united with the nationalists and the right in defeating the proposal.

The government was apprehensive over the behavior of the Octobrists. In the spring of 1909, when the premier was recuperating in the Crimea after an illness, government circles had suggested that Stolypin's Cabinet be removed in favor of one more strongly right-wing, and, in order to lay the groundwork for the creation of a frankly reactionary government and create a counterweight to the "constitutionalist" policy of the Octobrist majority under the leadership of Gutchkov, one faction of the party, led by Deputy Golobolov, had broken away from the center and gone over to the right. After the session of 22 February/7 March 1910, during which Gutchkov delivered a speech attacking the government and directing its attention to the fact that "the unhappy necessity for emergency rule no longer exists and that, under such conditions, he and his friends could see no further grounds that would justify the delays imposed on the inauguration of civil liberties," Stolypin could no longer rely on the docility of the center. Fearful of the creation of a left majority, the omens of which had been visible on a number of occasions in connection with matters of the budget, the restoration of the justices of the peace, and the organization of the cantonal zemstvo, he turned to the right in search of backing against the center. With the help of P. N. Krupensky, a Bessarabian deputy, he formed a solid nucleus of all the representatives of the right, the ultra-monarchists, the nationalists, and the dissident Octobrists of Golobolov's faction—altogether more than 150 deputies. At the same time, Stolypin and the other ministers repeatedly went before the Duma to attack the Octobrists, whom he accused of being in opposition not only to the government but to the throne itself, and to whom the right gave the label of "the young Turks." Gutchkov, who had nevertheless only recently proffered his hearty support to the Cabinet, lost his popularity in rightist and especially in court circles. The government's attitude and the pressing problem of the next general election—for their policy had antagonized their electors, who threatened to repudiate them—impelled the Octobrists to increase their opposition. During the debate on the introduction of the zemstvo into the western governments, they attacked the government's proposal, particularly those stipulations in it that assured the Russian element of overwhelming predominance in the zemstvo. One Octobrist deputy submitted an amendment that would have restored a Polish representation of 30 per cent in the zemstvo, and, in spite of Stolypin's personal intervention against it, this amendment was defeated by only seven votes. The final passage of the bill by the Duma in June 1910 did not bring the conflict to an end. Indeed, in the following March, when the Imperial Council had defeated the bill, Stolypin procured an imperial ukase that ordered the work of both Chambers suspended for three days, and, under the authority of Article LXXXVII of the basic laws, he at once promulgated the law in the form in which it had been approved by the Duma. This arbitrary action united the Duma and the Imperial Council in shared indignation against what they regarded as an offense to the legislative institutions, and Gutchkov, recognizing that his alliance with Stolypin had been broken, resigned the presidency of the Duma, which he had accepted after Khomyakov's withdrawal.

The Government's Alliance with the Extreme Right and the Reprisals Against the Universities

In its systematic amputation of the prerogatives of a Parliament already severely hamstrung by the basic laws, the government made itself increasingly unpopular; anger spread even into the more moderate sectors of the population that had supported the Octobrists. The differences that widened the gulf between himself and the center compelled Stolypin to turn toward the right and to place preparations for the next general election high on his agenda. His aim was to achieve a distribution of political forces that would make it possible for him to exploit a totally docile majority with the right and the nationalists and without the Octobrists. But on 5/18 September he was fatally wounded in a Kiev theater by one Bogrov, a revolutionary and a member of the *Okhrana*.* Stolypin's successor, Kokovtsev, made no major change in the government's policy. He pushed on with preparations for the elections to the fourth Duma, relying for support only on the nationalists and the right.

The reprisals undertaken against the University of Moscow and in part against the University of Petersburg by Kasso, the new minister of public education appointed in 1910, were among the most brutal manifestations of governmental reaction. Kasso, a Bessarabian landowner and former professor of civil law at the University of Moscow, forced Manuilov, the rector of that university, and Menzbir, the vice rector, to retire at the beginning of 1911. Outraged by this violation of the autonomy of the higher institutions, the majority of the university's professors declared its solidarity with the rector and vice rector, and the professors announced that they would be unable to continue in their duties unless the government agreed to restore to their posts the two officials elected by the University Council. Basically quite delighted that these "left-wing" professors were retiring on their own accord, the minister refused to rescind his order. The University of Moscow was thus deprived of many scholars and outstanding teachers. Kasso replaced them with men from the provincial universities, who once they had accepted their appointments at the hands of the ultra-reactionary

---

*The *Okhrana* (the word means "security") was a secret service of the political police whose origin went back to the period of the terrorist conspiracies against Alexander II.

minister, became the faithful supporters of his policy toward the higher learning. At the University of Petersburg, in defiance of the wishes of the professors, the majority of whom was opposed to his policy, Kasso also appointed right-wing candidates to various empty chairs. At the same time, in order to fill the posts of the professors who had resigned, Kasso sent several dozen young men who had barely graduated to prepare themselves abroad, at public expense, for professorships; in many instances the recipients of these fellowships were selected by the minister in spite of the universities' opposition.

CHAPTER 6

Nicholas II (1894–1917): Foreign Relations

·◀◼▶·

I / FOREIGN POLICY FROM 1905 TO 1914 [B. MIRKIN-GUETZEVITCH]

The war against Japan had laid bare the vital flaws in the structure of the army and navy. The accomplishment of the drastic reforms that were essential required huge sums that could be provided neither by taxation nor by internal borrowing. It was once more to France that the government turned for financial help. Nevertheless, it did not devote all the money thus obtained to its professed purpose—that is, to the acceleration of military and naval reforms; it used some of the money to furnish itself with means of combatting revolution after the dissolution of the first Duma. In spite of the fact of a national representative assembly, in spite of the majority that the government obtained in the third Duma through the new election law and its own pressures in the elections, it was still as free as before to conceive and execute foreign policy untrammeled by any control.

After 1905, and particularly after the unexecuted treaty of Björkö, this foreign policy was determined by the new situation that the Anglo-French alliance created in Europe. French diplomacy made special efforts to bring London and Petersburg together; as a result of its success, Russia was able to conclude an agreement with Japan, and, relieved of her anxieties in the Far East, to turn her attention once more toward Europe.

The Russian-German Treaty of Björkö (July 24, 1905)

Germany, which had taken advantage of the Russian-Japanese War to wage a diplomatic offensive against France in Morocco, cherished the dream of forming a continental coalition against England or else breaking the French-Russian alliance. Earlier, on October 30, 1904, after the Hull incident,* Wilhelm II had endeavored to prove to Nicholas II that the real threat to him came from England; therefore the Kaiser had suggested the following treaty:

Their Majesties, the Emperors of All the Russias and Germany, in order to localize the Russian-Japanese War as much as possible, have agreed on the following articles for a treaty of defensive alliance:

ARTICLE I: In the event that either of the two empires shall be attacked by any European power, its ally will assist it with all its land and sea forces. In case of necessity, the two allies will act in concert in order to remind France of the commitments made by her under the terms of the French-Russian treaty of alliance.

ARTICLE II: The high contracting parties pledge themselves not to conclude a separate peace with any common enemy.

ARTICLE III: The pledge of mutual aid shall remain in force in the event that the actions of either of the high contracting parties during the war, such for example as the delivery of coal to one of the belligerents, should result after the end of the war in a protest on the part of a third power with respect to any alleged infringement of the rights of neutrals.

While this proposed treaty was aimed against England, obviously it concerned France as well. Nicholas II had recognized this, and he had requested that the draft be altered and submitted to France; in particular he had insisted that it be made known to her before it was signed. Even though Wilhelm II proposed a new version on November 17, he was opposed to any such prior disclosure; he had contended that the French government would in its turn inform the British and thus conflict would be unavoidable; hence France must be confronted with a signed treaty in order to compel her to adhere to it. Under these conditions Nicholas II had refused his signature, and Wilhelm II had been left hanging.

In July 1905, after the Russian defeats in the Far East and the Kaiser's own services rendered to Russia during the negotiations that followed President Roosevelt's offer of mediation, Wilhelm II considered the moment propitious for the renewal of the interrupted treaty talks. While Witte was in the United States for the peace negotiations with the Japanese, the Kaiser requested a meeting with the

*Steaming through Dogger Bank during the night of October 21, Admiral Rozhdestvensky's fleet thought it had spotted Japanese torpedo boats and therefore opened fire, hitting a number of British fishing vessels and killing and wounding some of their crews. British public opinion had been angered, and, if it had not been for the intervention of France, which gained acceptance for the appointment of a board of inquiry in accordance with the procedure established at The Hague, the incident might have led to serious Anglo-Russian complications.

tsar. The two sovereigns met aboard the tsar's yacht at Björkö on July 23–24, and Wilhelm offered a third version:

Their Majesties, the Emperors of All the Russias and of Germany, in order to guarantee the preservation of peace in Europe, have agreed on the following articles of a treaty of defensive alliance:

ARTICLE I: In the event that one of the two empires shall be attacked by a European power, its ally will assist it in Europe with all its land and sea forces.

ARTICLE II: The high contracting parties pledge themselves not to conclude a separate peace with any common enemy.

ARTICLE III: The present treaty shall become effective immediately on the conclusion of peace between Russia and Japan and shall remain in force until either party shall have given one year's notice of its abrogation.

ARTICLE IV: The Emperor of All the Russias, after the effective date of this treaty, will take the necessary steps to inform France of this agreement and to commit her to associate herself with it as an ally.

Nicholas II found this draft "absolutely excellent," and Wilhelm II bestirred himself to persuade him to have it signed at once on July 24. It was countersigned by Secretary of State Tschirschky for Germany and Admiral Birilev, minister of the navy, for Russia.

What Birilev, without asking or receiving any explanations, had signed in the belief that it was a treaty of defensive alliance in Europe would be a new continental Triple Alliance if France accepted it. But the treaty was never to become effective. When Foreign Minister Count Lamsdorf learned on September 12 what the tsar had done, he explained to his "poor dear August Sovereign" the real significance of the treaty and its international dangers.

Nicholas II at once wrote to Wilhelm II that he would not allow the treaty to become effective until France had signed it. Russian diplomats in Paris were convinced that there could be no reliance on such action. As a result, on November 23 Nicholas II suggested to Wilhelm II that an annex be appended to the treaty:

In the light of the difficulties that impede the immediate adherence of the French government to the treaty of defensive alliance signed at Björkö on July 24, 1905, such adherence having been provided in Article IV of the said treaty, it is understood that the first article of this document cannot apply in the event of war with France and that the mutual pledges that bind her to Russia shall remain in force until the establishment of the triple alliance.

In vain Wilhelm II replied to the tsar: "We have given each other our hands and we have affixed our signatures in the sight of

God. . . . Therefore it seems to me that this treaty could very well be made effective. . . . What is signed is signed! And God was our witness." But the tsar stood firm on his position, which was an "indirect invalidation" of the treaty of Björkö, and the pact remained a dead letter.

The Russian-Japanese Agreement (July 30, 1907)

Thanks to the efforts of French diplomacy, Russia became reconciled with Japan in order to assure peace in the Far East. After the French-Japanese convention of July 10, 1907, Russia and Japan signed the accord of July 30, which ratified the terms of the Treaty of Portsmouth and guaranteed the "territorial integrity" of both powers in Asia.

The Anglo-Russian Agreements (August 31, 1907)

It was again through the good offices of France that an end was made to the traditional hostility between England and Russia. By abandoning any policy of expansion in central Asia, Russia gave England reassurance; and England, herself apprehensive of Germany's intentions and especially of her activity in the near East, was desirous of closer relations with Russia. On August 31, 1907 Russian Foreign Minister Izvolsky and the British Ambassador, Sir Arthur Nicholson, signed three agreements.

The first dealt with Persia, which was divided into three zones of political and economic influence: the northeast was reserved to Russian influence, the southeast was assigned to British influence, and the area between, in which both states could compete for influence, was designated as "neutral."

The second accord covered Afghanistan. Giving ground on a number of issues, Russia acknowledged that this state fell within the British sphere of influence; in addition, she pledged herself to maintain relations with the emir only through the intermediary of the British government.

The third pact concerned Tibet. Britain promised to evacuate that area; the two contracting powers guaranteed its independence and agreed that neither of them should maintain a representative there.

A year later the reconciliation of England and Russia was solemnized by the visit of King Edward VII to Reval, in June 1908. A new entity, the Triple Entente of France, England, and Russia, was taking shape against the Triple Alliance.

The Second Conference of The Hague (1907)

On the initiative of the United States and with the concurrence of Russia the Second Conference of The Hague was convened on June 15, 1907. Its chairman was Nelidov, the Russian ambassador in Paris; forty-four states took part. During its long session, which lasted into October, it was no more successful than its predecessor in bringing to reality the aspirations of the most enlightened sectors of European public opinion. Germany forced the rejection of the principle of compulsory arbitration; it was Germany again, this time with Russia's backing, that opposed any limitation on armaments. The Conference was not wholly fruitless, however; it adopted a number of resolutions that represented undeniable advances in international law.

The Balkan Crisis of 1908–1909

In 1908 the entire attention of Russian diplomacy was focused on the Balkan crisis.

Baron von Aehrenthal, who was in charge of Austro-Hungarian policy, was a member of the group of "young men" who were attempting to stave off the collapse of the Dual Monarchy through an audacious foreign policy. In his view it was essential to battle Slavic influence within the country by adopting a threatening attitude toward Serbia and by resolutely advancing in the Balkans. What he sought was the annexation of Bosnia and Herzegovina, of which the treaty of Berlin had made Austria-Hungary merely the administrator, with the right of maintaining garrisons in the *sandjak* of Novi-Bazar. He decided to proceed once he had made certain of the approval and backing of Germany. This violation of the treaty of Berlin entailed the risk of arousing the protests of the powers that had signed it, and especially of Russia, but this did not frighten Aehrenthal. Before becoming foreign minister, he had been ambassador in Petersburg from 1899 to 1906, and there he had been able to cultivate friendly contacts in Russian conservative circles. He had been especially close to Shvanebakh,* who had introduced him into the most influential quarters of the capital. The impressions that he had gathered during his diplomatic mission had convinced him that Russia was too weak to offer any opposition to an Austro-Hungarian offensive in the Balkans.

His plan for linking the Turkish railways with the Austro-Hungar-

---

*At that time secretary of state to the Ministry of Agriculture, and an expert in financial matters.

ian system through Bosnia and Macedonia, in order to open the Dual
Monarchy's path to Salonika and Constantinople, resulted early in
1908 in the rupture of the Austrian-Russian alliance of 1897. Russia
drew closer to England. During their meeting in Reval in June of
that year, Nicholas II and Edward VII prepared a new plan for increasing the effectiveness of European supervision over the reforms in
European Turkey. But this plan had barely become known when the
Young Turks' revolution compelled the sultan to grant a Constitution; the powers postponed the "Reval program" and recalled their
civil and military representatives from Macedonia.

The Young Turks' revolution persuaded Aehrenthal to accelerate
the annexation of Bosnia and Herzegovina. On September 15, 1908
he and Russian Foreign Minister Izvolsky conferred in the castle of
Buchlau in Moravia. What actually occurred in this meeting? Aehrenthal alleged—he wrote as much to Chancellor Bülow of Germany—
that Izvolsky had agreed to the annexation of Bosnia and Herzegovina
by Austria-Hungary on condition that the Straits be opened to Russia.
In contrast, during the endless controversy that followed, Izvolsky consistently maintained that he had never given his acceptance but that,
while putting forward his demands with respect to the Straits, he had
insisted in the most emphatic fashion possible on the immediate convocation of a conference of all the powers that had signed the treaty
of Berlin. Wherever the truth lay, Izvolsky felt reassured when he left
Buchlau for Paris. Three weeks later, on October 5, Franz Josef signed
the decree of annexation. On the same day Prince Ferdinand of
Bulgaria assumed the title of tsar and proclaimed his country's independence.

These two actions brought on a series of important conflicts. The
Young Turks' government reacted with a boycott of Austro-Hungarian
products. Russia's position was extremely delicate; Izvolsky demanded
the convocation of a conference, and Aehrenthal, opposed to any international discussion, categorically refused. Furthermore, even
though he told the Duma that he had "not concealed from the
Bulgarian government the painful impression produced in Russia by
its method of procedure," Izvolsky was compelled by Russia's traditional sympathy with Bulgaria to recognize Bulgarian independence—
in other words, to approve the success of Austro-Hungarian diplomacy, whose connivance with the new Bulgarian tsar was patent. In
Serbia and Russia the annexation aroused great indignation: the
Serbs regarded it as a deliberate intimidation and demanded indemni-
ties and guaranties; Russian public opinion—in the Duma as in the

independent press—insisted openly and forcefully that the Serbs be protected against the Austro-Hungarian menace.

Meanwhile, two of these conflicts were resolved. In the one instance, Aehrenthal, with Germany's help, negotiated directly with Turkey, to which he restored the *sandjak* of Novi-Bazar; he took advantage of the financial crisis that had struck the Young Turks' new government to buy its recognition of the annexation for 54 million crowns on February 26, 1909. In the other instance, through Russia's intercession, the question of Bulgarian independence was settled. The Turks agreed to recognize it in exchange for the payment of the tribute due them from eastern Rumelia. Russia suggested that this be offset against the indemnity that the Turks still owed her after the Russian-Turkish War of 1877–1878. On March 19, having received an advance of 25 million rubles, the Turks formally accepted the independence of Bulgaria.

On the other hand, the Austrian-Serbian conflict still raged, and it was threatening to become a Russian-German conflict. At first Russia had deserted the Serbs: "I cannot at all understand your excitement," Izvolsky told them in effect. "You cannot drive Austria out of Bosnia by force. And we Russians cannot go to war against Austria for Serbia." But Austria-Hungary sought to press her gains. On March 19 she presented Serbia with an ultimatum: it required not only that Serbia recognize the annexation but also that she demobilize her army within three days and that she pledge herself "to change the course of her present policy toward Austria-Hungary in order henceforth to live on a good-neighbor footing with her."

Izvolsky then sought to intervene on behalf of the Serbs. On March 20 he asserted that he was still prepared to counsel peace to Belgrade, but he called on Germany to follow a similar course with Vienna, while at the same time repeating his request for a conference. Germany replied with an ultimatum to Russia. On March 22 the German ambassador in Petersburg, Graf de Pourtalès, called on Izvolsky to state, "yes or no," whether he accepted the Austro-Hungarian note "and gave formal consent without reservation to the abrogation of Article XXV" of the treaty of Berlin—in other words, to the annexation of Bosnia and Herzegovina and the threat of German intervention in the event of conflict with Austria-Hungary. Russia was in no position to face a war. The Cabinet urged Izvolsky to yield. He resigned himself to this course, and Serbia, abandoned by Russia and under pressure by the powers, affixed her signature on March 31 to all the humiliating provisions of the Austro-Hungarian ultimatum.

Russian-Italian Friendship (1909) and the Question of the Straits

Frightened by Austria-Hungary's triumph in the Balkans, Italy was ready to arrive at an understanding with Russia. On October 22, 1909 Nicholas II and King Victor Emmanuel met in Racconigi. Two days later a secret agreement was concluded: its intent was the preservation of the *status quo* in the Balkans, or, if this were impossible, "the application of the principle of nationalities by the development of the Balkan states to the exclusion of all foreign domination"; it stipulated further that "Italy and Russia pledge themselves to look with goodwill the one on Russian interests in the question of the Straits, the other on Italian interests in Tripolitania and Cyrenaica."

In 1911, during the Italian-Turkish War and after Italy's proclamation of her annexation of Tripolitania and Cyrenaica, the Russian ambassador in Constantinople, Charykov, raised the question of the Straits. On November 27 he submitted a "draft convention" to the Porte; its key article provided that Russia would furnish "effective support" to Turkey in the maintenance of the existing situation in the Straits, "extending the said support also to adjacent territories in the event that these should be threatened by foreign armed forces," and that the Porte, "in time of peace as in time of war," would open the Straits to Russian warships. Backed by Germany, Turkey rejected this draft; England evinced no partisanship for it; France was not inclined to support her ally's action. In these circumstances Russia abandoned all thought of pursuing her negotiations with the Porte.

The Potsdam Talks (1910) and the Russian-German Agreement on Persia (1911)

Sazonov, the new Russian foreign minister, who, as German Chancellor Bethmann-von Hollweg observed, was primarily concerned with "the internal consolidation of Russia," favored a "thaw" in Russian-German relations. On November 4–5, 1910 Nicholas II and Wilhelm II met in Potsdam, where the major subject was that of Persia. The German chancellor took the opportunity to attempt to cause a rift between Russia and England by distorting the meaning and the scope of the statements exchanged by the two emperors. Although he did not succeed in this, there can be no doubt that the Potsdam meeting, by raising his hopes for the impairment of Russian-French friendship, contributed to his adoption of a provocative stand in the Moroccan question and his execution of the "Agadir incident." Finally, after long negotations, Germany and Russia concluded their agreement of August 19, 1911, which was confined to Persia. Germany recognized Russia's "special interests" in Persia and stated that she herself was pursuing only "commercial aims" there; she promised to request no public-works concessions in northern Persia; in exchange, Russia promised to build the Teheran-Khanikin railway within two years of the completion of the Baghdad-Khanikin line; in the event of default, Germany would be free to seek this concession; Russia, in addition, would not interfere in any way in the construction of the Berlin-Baghdad railway.

The Balkan League (1912)

Russian diplomats in the Balkans had embarked on vigorous negotiations that resulted in the creation of the Balkan League. Its first achievement was the reconciliation of Serbia and Bulgaria, which were divided by a number of issues; the Bulgarian-Serbian agreement was signed on March 13, 1912. Each state was pledged to provide the other with complete military support if either was attacked or if a great power attempted to annex or occupy militarily, even on a temporary basis, any part of the Balkan territories still held by Turkey; the two countries agreed on a future partition of Macedonia, although without definitively establishing their respective borders, and they agreed that, in the event of their inability to reach agreement on the matter, it should be arbitrated by the Russian tsar. On May 29 a treaty of "defensive" alliance was concluded between Bulgaria and Greece. Early in the year Montenegro had arrived at an understanding with Serbia.

The Balkan League thus created was the fruit not only of the efforts of Russian diplomacy, which was attempting to carry out its plan for the political organization of the Balkans. The League also owed its existence to the Balkan peoples' desire to liberate their compatriots and co-religionists who were still under the yoke of the Turks. But the fact that other populations racially related to the Balkan peoples were also under the domination of Austria-Hungary infused this highly ambitious project with many dangers. France, which Sazonov had not kept informed of the details of his Balkan negotiations, was keenly aware of these dangers. Premier Poincaré told the Russian government in unminced words that he wanted to know these details, though at the same time asserting that he intended to make no commitment on the subject of the Balkan League; he emphasized that he did not wish to allow himself to be drawn by Russia into some adventure that might compromise the peace of Europe. In August 1912 he went to Petersburg and demanded complete information on all the Balkan treaties; once he had studied them, he made no secret of the fears that they aroused in him.

The Balkan Wars and the Conflict Between Russia and the Central Powers (1912–1914)

The first Balkan war ended with complete victory over Turkey for the allies; but the peace treaty evolved during the London conferences in May 1913 was not executed. The Macedonian question set the Serbs and the Bulgarians against each other. In June, Nicholas II sent telegrams to the rulers of both countries to remind them of the clause in the Serbian-Bulgarian treaty dealing with arbitration by himself: "I learn with sorrow," he said, "that the Balkan states are preparing themselves, as it appears to me, for a fratricidal war that would tarnish the glory that they have earned together. . . . The power that first launches hostilities will have to answer for its act before the whole Slavic cause . . ." In principle both sides of course accepted arbitration by the tsar, but this acceptance was left without practical implementation. The Bulgarians launched the second Balkan war by attacking the Serbs. Surrounded completely, since the Rumanians had aligned themselves with the Greeks and the Serbs, Bulgaria was soon defeated; not only did she lose Macedonia but also, under the Treaty of Bucharest, she had to give up some of the territories that she had gained under the treaty of London.

It was natural that Austria-Hungary should be made apprehensive by the victories of the Balkan states over Turkey, the expulsion of the Turks from the peninsula after the first war, and, especially, the aggrandizement of Serbia. Austrian-Russian rivalry came back to life. In February 1913 Franz Josef sent Prince von Hohenlohe-Schillingsfürst to Petersburg in order to seek to avert "new misfortunes," which meant a collision between the two empires. An agreement was reached: Austria promised to demobilize and Russia pledged the discharge of three hundred and fifty thousand reservists. The communiqués issued on this agreement did not coincide; the Russian text contained a sentence that did not appear in the Austrian and that angered the Vienna government: "The Austro-Hungarian monarchy has no aggressive intentions with regard to its neighbors to the south." The antagonism between the two powers persisted, and it was clearly demonstrated in the discussions that arose over the question of the Serbian, Rumanian, and Albanian frontiers. On March 15, 1913 the

German Chancellor Bethmann-Hollweg made a speech in reaction to the refusal by the king of Montenegro to give up the town of Scutari, which the powers wished to incorporate into Albania. Speaking first of "the rebirth and the reinvigoration of racial instincts" and "the struggle of Germanism against Slavism," the chancellor pointed out that the equilibrium of the Balkans had been altered to the advantage of the Slavs; he stated frankly that the help that, as an ally, Germany was obligated to provide to Austria-Hungary "is not limited to diplomatic mediation." In April Austria-Hungary made her final decision to attack Serbia. In conformity with the Triple Alliance, she called on Italy to take part in joint action. The positions taken by Italy and Russia caused the threat of general war to be postponed. Italy did not wish to "shed her blood in a war that, in the event of victory, would end by giving Austria a situation in the Balkans that would be incompatible with Italian interests." As for Russia, she refused to stand with Nicholas of Montenegro, who, in spite of the decision by the powers, was still laying siege to Scutari, and a Russian communiqué bluntly accused him of having sought to drag Russia and all Europe into war.

The second Balkan war, which made enemies of its predecessor's allies, gravely impaired Russia's prestige in the Balkans, particularly in Bulgaria, where the pro-Russian parties were defeated in the elections and removed from power, and the new government called for a pro-Austrian policy against Serbia's demands. In similar fashion Russian influence in Constantinople was also much damaged. Russia's hesitancy in numerous quarrels and her lack of vigor in the defense of the Balkan peoples' interests against Germany and Austria-Hungary led Turkey to the view that Russia need no longer be reckoned with. In this respect the case of the assassin of Mahmud Shevket Pasha was already significant: arrested aboard a Russian vessel while it was in transit through the Straits, in spite of the fact that he held a Russian passport he was turned over to the Turkish authorities by the Russian consul at the request of the Porte. There were further, more significant indications. At the end of 1913 a German military mission was sent to Constantinople and its head, General Liman von Sanders, was appointed to the command of the Turkish First Army Corps, garrisoned in the capital. When Russia protested to Germany, Germany offered the vague reply that she would bear Russian interests in mind and would change the nature of the general's mission; but she actually did nothing. The grand vizier declared that there was no political aspect to the German mission and that the general's command did not extend to the Straits, but in spite of this,

Russian Ambassador Giers demanded that "the existing situation in the Dardanelles be guaranteed," that the projected restoration of the former fortifications and construction of new ones be dropped, and that Russian commercial interests be reimbursed for whatever losses they might suffer; the Porte arrogantly refused to reply. True, on January 8, 1914 General von Sanders gave up the command of the Turkish First Army Corps, but three days later he was made a marshal in the Turkish army and inspector general of all the armed forces. Russia's anxiety mounted when at the end of January the Porte bought two battle cruisers, the *Moltke* and the *Goeben*, from Germany and tried to purchase other warships in South America. The growing influence of Germany in Turkey and the activities of the Austro-Hungarian war party, which feared the unification of the two Serbian kingdoms of Serbia proper and Montenegro, were forcing Russia to make ready for war. In March a German newspaper denounced her rearmament; an angry press controversy between the two countries ensued. A Petersburg newspaper printed an unsigned article under the headline: RUSSIA WANTS PEACE BUT SHE IS PREPARED TO MAKE WAR; ascribed to War Minister Sukhomlinov, the article declared that the Russian army was not only prepared to sustain a defensive war but capable of mounting an offensive. It was the subject of much excited discussion in Europe, and it was exploited in Germany by military and conservative quarters.

The Austrian-Serbian Conflict and the Declaration of War
(July–August 1914)

In June 1914 Archduke Franz Ferdinand, heir to the throne of Austria-Hungary, went to observe military exercises in Bosnia, whose population was rubbed raw by Austrian rule. On June 28 he was assassinated in a street in Sarajevo by Gavril Prinzip, a Bosnian student.

Two weeks earlier Wilhelm II and the archduke had met in Konopishte to discuss, among other matters, Balkan problems. As a result of this conference the Austro-Hungarian government had drawn up a detailed memorandum in which it set out a plan for an alliance with Bulgaria and Turkey intended to combat Russia's Balkan policy, which, the memorandum said, was aimed at Germany by way of Austria-Hungary. This memorandum had not yet been sent when the archduke was assassinated at Sarajevo, whereupon the Austro-Hungarian government seized on the opportunity "to settle accounts with Serbia." On July 5 Count Hoyos took the memorandum to Berlin with a hand-written letter from Franz Josef, who stated that hence-forth his government "must strive to isolate and reduce Serbia" and that it would not be possible to form a new alliance with Turkey, Bulgaria, Rumania, and Greece until Serbia had been "eliminated as a political factor in the Balkans." Angered by the assassination of the archduke, Wilhelm II not only approved of Austria-Hungary's desire to launch "a warlike action" against Serbia but also reckoned that, if this was her decision, it would be best to execute it at once, "as long as Russia, which is still far from being prepared for war, hesitates to take up arms." Chancellor Bethmann-Hollweg too declared that "immediate action would be the best solution." Under orders from Wilhelm II the German ambassador in Vienna laid special stress on the fact that in Berlin "it is expected that Austria-Hungary will act against Serbia and it would be impossible to understand if the Austrians did not take this opportunity to strike at her." Count Hoyos, summarizing the impressions he had gathered in Berlin, asserted: "German ruling circles and the Kaiser himself are virtually forcing us to undertake action against Serbia."

Under the influence of Count Berchtold, the foreign minister, and in spite of the objections of the Hungarian premier, Count Tisza, the Austro-Hungarian Crown Council decided on July 7 and 19 to prepare and justify the initiation of hostilities by presenting Serbia with an unacceptable ultimatum. While it professed the desire to respect Serbia's territorial integrity, the Vienna government intended ultimately to distribute some of Serbia's soil among Bulgaria, Rumania, Greece, and Albania, to impose revisions of the Serbian border to the advantage of Austria-Hungary, to put the remainder of Serbia under military occupation, to install a new dynasty, to enforce acceptance of a military convention, and to place Serbia "under the dependency" of Austria-Hungary. Since the president of France and Premier Viviani were at the moment the guests of Nicholas II, Austria-Hungary waited —on the pretext that the "bellicose" Poincaré might be able to influence the "peaceful" Sazonov—for their departure, the date of which was communicated to her in advance by the German embassy, before sending her ultimatum to Serbia. The ultimatum was formally submitted to the Serbian government at six o'clock on the evening of July 23, immediately after the battleship *France*, with Poincaré and Viviani aboard, had cast off. Although an investigation made by an Austrian official had conclusively shown that the Serbian government was totally guiltless in the Sarajevo assassination, this "unacceptable" ultimatum demanded that Serbia violate all her own laws and sacrifice her sovereignty in order to guarantee the "suppression of the subversive movement" on her own soil and search for Prinzip's accomplices with the help of Austro-Hungarian officials, and an answer was required within forty-eight hours.

In the face of such extortionate terms there was little that could be done by European diplomacy. Nevertheless for six awful days diplomats exhausted all their efforts to avert the consequences of the Austro-Hungarian design, which was backed *in toto* by Germany even though she did not know its details in full. Russia was indeed unready for war, and, in the words of Wilhelm II, could only "hesitate to take up arms." Foreign Minister Sazonov first urged Vienna to extend the time limit of the ultimatum; then, by way of the Serbian minister in Petersburg, he advised the Serbian government to bow to all Austria-Hungary's terms except the condition that infringed Serbian sovereignty. In conformance to this counsel, the Serbian government submitted a reply steeped in humility to Baron Giesl, the Austro-Hungarian minister in Belgrade, at six o'clock in the evening of July 25. The reply rejected only one demand: participation by Austro-Hungarian officials in the investigation on Serbian soil; but, if Austria-Hungary still felt that further satisfaction was required, Serbia was prepared to refer the matter to the International Court in The Hague. Baron Giesl, obedient to his government's instructions, barely glanced at the Serbian reply before he denounced it as unsatisfactory; a half-hour later, with the entire staff of his legation, he left Belgrade. The next day both Serbia and Austria-Hungary began mobilization and Crown Prince Alexander of Serbia sent a telegram imploring help to Nicholas II. Determined to bring matters to a head, Berchtold rebuffed an overture by Russia, which was seeking to initiate direct negotiations, while at the same time the German chancellor rejected an offer from England, which at first proposed to call a conference of the four great powers "foreign to the Serbian matter," Germany, England, France, and Italy, and then sought to set up a mere meeting of the four ambassadors of these states. On July 28 Austria-Hungary declared war on Serbia. Such precipitate action was all the more remarkable because General Conrad von Hoetzendorf had told his government that the Austro-Hungarian army was not yet ready and that he would be unable to mount a serious offensive before August 12. Austria-Hungary's behavior altered Europe's sentiments to her own disadvantage, and, above all, it made Russian intervention inevitable. At the time of the presentation of the Austro-Hungarian ultimatum Sazonov had told the British ambassador, Sir George Buchanan, that, if Germany did not restrain Austria-Hungary, Russia "would not shrink back from the risk of a general war." Confident of support from France, Russia had requested England to clarify her position at once in order to avert a world war. On July 27 England evaded the issue, but she decided not to demobilize her fleet, which had just completed maneuvers. On the same day France had suspended the major maneuvers on which she had just started. Also on July 27 Nicholas II told the Serbian crown prince that, if his personal efforts to prevent catastrophe failed, Russia "would not remain indifferent to the fate of Serbia." On the same day when Austria-Hungary declared war on Serbia, Bethmann-Hollweg urged the Vienna government to proclaim that it had no ambitions toward territorial acquisitions and would occupy Serbian soil only temporarily. The inadequacy of such a pronouncement, which was obviously intended simply to dilute the impression created by the aggressive nature of Austro-Hungarian actions, could not be reassuring to Russia. She felt that war with Austria-Hungary was inevitable, and, on this same day, the Cabinet met under the chairmanship of the tsar and decided to order mobilization in four military districts of southern Russia: this meant thirteen of the thirty-seven army corps available to the country. The mobilization order was made public the next morning, July 29.

In the twenty-four hours that followed the declaration of war there were exchanges of fire between Austro-Hungarian and Serbian troops. These further aggravated the situation. Wilhelm II, who was aboard a cruiser in the North Sea, returned to Berlin on July 28 to find a telegram from the tsar that requested his friendly help after the "cowardly" declaration of war by Austria-Hungary against her weaker neighbor. On July 29, at Russia's request, Sir Edward Grey reiterated the British proposal for a conference of the four "disinterested" powers. He did not confine himself, as Russia wished, to suggesting the suspension of military operations; he even agreed to Austro-Hungarian occupation of a part of Serbian territory until the conference had arrived at a decision and the Vienna government had received full satisfaction. Not only were all these proposals rejected; on Austria-Hungary's demand the German ambassador in Petersburg, Graf de Pourtalès, called on Sazonov on this same day and told him flatly that, if Russia did not halt her mobilization, Germany would mobilize too. This statement finally convinced Petersburg that war with Germany was unavoidable; in a communiqué addressed to the powers, Sazonov concluded: "Given the fact that it is impossible for us to bow to Germany's wishes, there remains no other course for us but to accelerate our own preparations with full recognition of the fact that war appears inevitable." Nevertheless Nicholas II still strove on July 29 to avoid the unavoidable: he sent another telegram to Wilhelm II: "It would be proper to refer the Austrian-Serbian conflict to the Court of The Hague. I rely on your wisdom and your friendship." He sent this telegram without the knowledge of his Cabinet—Sazonov himself did not learn of its existence until six months later—and the German government at first kept it secret.

For Berlin there was now only one concern: to prevent, as it had pointed out in its dispatch of July 28 to its ambassador in Vienna, the unshakable obstinacy of the Austro-Hungarian government from "arousing against it the whole of European public opinion," and, on the other hand, to maneuver in such fashion that "the responsibility for the extension of the conflict to parties not directly concerned shall fall on Russia at all costs," because "under such conditions a successful war cannot be undertaken on three fronts." As a result, Pourtalès asked Sazonov on July 30 whether he would not be satisfied with Austria-Hungary's promise not to infringe Serbia's territorial integrity. Sazonov replied that the matter had assumed a European aspect and that it was also essential to preserve Serbian sovereignty; if Austria-Hungary would strike out of her ultimatum the clause that violated that sovereignty, Russia would be prepared to break off her preparations for war. Germany rejected this proposal as "unacceptable" to her ally.

Moreover, the activities of the diplomats on this same July 30 were supplemented and countered by those of the general staffs. All the armies, convinced that war was inevitable, were dedicating all their attention to taking the necessary steps as quickly as possible: on each side they insisted that it was the adversary who had first resorted to preliminary mobilization measures before the issuance of any official order. The diplomats did not give up at once. Bethmann-Hollweg asked Wilhelm II to suspend his mobilization order, which had already been made public in an official communiqué appearing that day in the *Lokalanzieger;* but he was able to obtain nothing more than an official denial of the communiqué, because both the minister of war and the chief of the General Staff refused all responsibility in the event of any postponement. The same was the case in Russia. Since July 25 all Russia's attention had been concentrated on the military measures to be taken against Austria-Hungary, whose forces had already been placed on a war footing. On July 26 a conference presided over by the tsar had decided to proclaim a state of "pre-mobilization." But limited mobilization presented serious technical problems; it could not be carried out as an operation planned and detailed in advance but only as a kind of improvisation that might gravely hamper a subsequent general mobilization. Hence the military authorities considered it impossible to separate limited from general mobilization. On July 29 Nicholas II agreed to proceed with general mobilization, but, when he had sent Wilhelm II the telegram in which he suggested the submission of the matter to The Hague Tribunal, he revoked his decision and ordered that mobilization be carried out only in the four military districts. This seemed inadequate for waging war in the eyes of the General Staff, even if the sole antagonist were to be Austria-Hungary, which in recent years had become a formidable military power. In two further dispatches the tsar gave Wilhelm II his word of honor that the Russian armies would not initiate hostilities as long as talks went on with Austria-Hungary, and he asked the Kaiser, on the other side, to pledge that German mobilization did not mean war and that negotiations could continue. Sazonov made new concessions: he agreed that Austria-Hungary should occupy Belgrade and he assented to the submission of the amended text of the Austro-Hungarian ultimatum to the judgment of Europe. But at one o'clock in the morning of July 30 the tsar received the Kaiser's reply: Wilhelm II threw the full responsibility for war on Nicholas if Russia mobilized against Austria-Hungary. As the day went on, the Russian government was informed that Germany was arming and that the mobilization decree had been published in the *Lokalanzeiger*. At two o'clock in the afternoon, during a conference among War Minister Sukhomlinov, Sazonov, and General Yanushkevitch, chief of the General Staff, the generals demanded urgently that the limited mobilization be enlarged to general mobilization, and they implored Sazonov to convince Nicholas II of the necessity for this. Yanushkevitch added that it would be impossible for him to take the responsibility for the consequences that would arise out of any further delay. Sazonov at once was received in audience at Peterhof, and, during a report that consumed the hour from three to four o'clock, he apprised the tsar of the reality of the German menace and the necessity of general mobilization. Fully aware of the responsibility that he was about to assume, the tsar hesitated, but he yielded when Sazonov protested to him that Russia would lose "the influence that she has gained in the Balkans throughout her history" and that she would be "condemned to a miserable existence at the whim of the central powers." After a long silence the tsar said to Sazonov: "You are right: give the General Staff my order to mobilize." As soon as he received this order by telephone, Yanushkevitch, afraid lest the tsar change his mind, gave orders that all callers be told that his telephone was out of order. At 10:40 A.M. on July 31 the decree of general mobilization was made public; two hours later Germany proclaimed a state of *Kriegsgefahrzustand*,* which was equivalent to general mobilization; then, a few hours later, she issued a double ultimatum to Russia and France.

The German ultimatum was handed to Sazonov at midnight. Without making any commitments in the name of Germany, it demanded that, "within the term of twelve hours, Russia halt all measures of war," not only against Germany but also against Austria-Hungary, or else "German mobilization will be proclaimed." Russia made no reply. Curiously, at the very moment when Germany was issuing her dual ultimatum, Austria-Hungary suddenly agreed to resume the interrupted negotiations. It was obviously her intention to place all responsibility for war on Russia. But this design was thwarted: it was Germany that declared war. At seven o'clock in the evening of August 1 Graf de Pourtalès called on Sazonov in a state of extreme agitation and handed him the German declaration of war. Austria-Hungary, well aware that she was not yet ready to take the offensive, made no haste to emulate her ally's example. It was only six days later that, on the insistence of Germany, which had been left standing alone, Austria-Hungary also declared war on Russia. The First World War had begun.

II / FOREIGN POLICY FROM 1914 TO 1917 [B. MIRKIN-GUETZEVITCH]

During the war Russia took part in a series of collective diplomatic steps taken in the name of all the Allies. In addition she engaged by herself in diplomatic negotiations with various countries, sometimes with a view to common ends, sometimes for ends of her own. In this history we shall restrict ourselves, in discussing the collective actions, to a general outline that will bear on the major stages of Allied policy; more attention will be given to the more or less isolated political activity of the Russian government: relations with those countries— Turkey, Bulgaria, Rumania, Italy, Greece—that, having begun by preserving their neutrality, finally took part in the war on either the Allies' or the Germans' side; the question of Constantinople and the

*That is, an imminent danger of war.—Translator.

Straits; the relations between the Allies and Russia; the question of a separate peace; and the Polish problem.

Russia's Refusal of a Turkish Alliance

From the start of the war the influence that Germany enjoyed in Turkey, chiefly as the result of von Sanders' mission, acquired the character of definite control of Turkish foreign policy by Berlin. It was perhaps only because of Russia that this was the case.

In August 1914 in fact, Giers, the Russian ambassador in Constantinople, transmitted to Foreign Minister Sazonov a proposal from Enver Pasha for an alliance: Turkey was prepared to commit herself to the dispatch of a strong army to Thrace against Austria-Hungary or any Balkan country that aligned itself with her, on condition that Turkey receive the western part of Thrace and the Aegean Islands, as well as a five-to-ten-year alliance with Russia. This proposal, the acceptance of which might have altered the course of the war and opened fruitful avenues to the Allies, gave rise to the exchange of a number of dispatches between Giers and Sazonov. The ambassador implored his minister in the most pathetic terms to accept Enver Pasha's offer, sending a more pressing message every day; Sazonov gave evasive answers and counseled the prolongation of the negotiations in order to gain time while he waited for a clarification of Bulgaria's stand. The Russian General Staff was contemptuous of Enver Pasha's offer to withdraw his Ninth and Eleventh Army Corps from the Caucasian border. In vain Giers telegraphed that Enver Pasha's proposals must be taken advantage of without a moment's loss; Petrograd* refused. Izvolsky, now the Russian ambassador in Paris, instead of informing the French government of the Turkish offer, which had been communicated to him by Sazonov, confined himself to mentioning it in a private conversation to Delcassé, who had not yet become foreign minister,† and then sent Sazonov a telegram saying that Delcassé disapproved of it and urged that every effort be exerted toward the reconstitution of the Balkan alliance.

In spite of Giers' insistence, Turkey's offer of an alliance was not accepted. The political situation in Constantinople soon became

*The city's German name, St. Petersburg, was replaced with the Slavic form when the war began.

†This conversation between Izvolsky and Delcassé was held on August 17; Delcassé became foreign minister nine days later.

clearly hostile to Russia and the Allies, and on October 29 the Turks shelled the Russian coast.

The Failure of Russian-Bulgarian Negotiations

If the Russian government refused an alliance with Turkey, it was partly because it hoped for one with Bulgaria.

The initial talks with Sofia were limited at the start to efforts to reconcile the respective claims of Bulgaria and Serbia on the territories that had been in dispute between them since the first Balkan war. But the Serbian government showed no desire to compromise, and Pashitch emphatically demanded certain disputed areas for his country even when Austrian troops were already occupying a substantial part of Serbia.

The Russian diplomatic effort in Sofia conflicted not only with the Serbs' territorial claims but also with the personal attitude of Tsar Ferdinand of Bulgaria, who had long been under the influence of the central powers and who was hardly likely to be driven into the arms of the Allies by the military successes of his Austrian and German protectors. When Mackensen was already on the Danube and Pashitch was clinging to his intractability, Premier Radoslavov of Bulgaria, as intercepted dispatches clearly showed, was maintaining close relations with Germany under the blessing of his tsar. Finally, on September 6, 1915, Bulgaria concluded a secret alliance with the central powers. At the end of that month she ordered general mobilization and proclaimed her intention of a military occupation of Macedonia. On October 2 the Russian minister was ordered to leave Sofia.

Italian-Russian Negotiations

While Italy's adherence to the Allies was gained only after long-drawn-out negotiations among Rome, Petrograd, and Paris, this was because for a long period Russia resisted the proposed solution for the various Balkan problems. Sazonov championed Serbian interests and categorically denounced any suggestion of concessions to Italy at Serbia's expense. In April 1915 France was compelled to intervene in order to make clear the danger to the common cause of all the Allies that was being created by the delays in the negotiations. On April 26 the Allies and Italy signed the treaty of London, which gave Italy Dalmatia, Vallona, a protectorate over Albania, and the Dodecanese Islands; on May 16 an Italian-Russian Military convention, signed in the Russians' staff headquarters, stipulated the bases for joint action by the Russian, Italian, and Serbian armies against Austria-Hungary, on which Italy declared war exactly one week later.

Rumanian-Russian Negotiations

Although Rumania was bound to Austria-Hungary by a military convention—which expired in 1916—Russia, which in 1913 had approved Rumania's attack on Bulgaria, had strong grounds for the belief that she could gain the friendship of Bucharest with reasonable ease.

Russian government circles, however, were not in agreement on military participation by Rumania. Sazonov and more especially Izvolsky, who reflected the Allies' views, made every effort to achieve it. The high command, particularly General Aleksyeyev, was opposed to it, on the theory that it would weaken the Russian front in Galicia rather than strengthen it. After her victories in Galicia, Russia offered the Rumanians part of Bukovina, seized from Austria-Hungary; acceptance of this offer would amount in fact to entering the war, and therefore Rumania rejected it. Later, as a result of Russian reverses, Sazonov sought to assure Rumania's benevolent neutrality by offering her all Rumanian territories in the possession of Austria-Hungary, as well as Dobrudzha.

It was not the work of Russian diplomacy itself but rather that of the Allies that at last managed to persuade Rumania to enter the war. After long negotiations, which dealt chiefly with the compensations of every kind that she demanded, Rumania signed a treaty of alliance with Russia, France, England, and Italy on August 17, 1916; it obligated her to join the war no later than August 28. On the same day she signed a military convention with Russia, and on August 28 she ordered mobilization.

Russia's Attitude Toward Greece

Under the provisions of the treaties in force, Greece should have gone to Serbia's assistance; but, in spite of Premier Eleutherios Venizelos, she maintained an armed neutrality. For some time Russian diplomacy took a detached stand: first of all because the Allies, on a number of occasions, were offering Constantinople now to Russia and now to Greece, and also—and this was the controlling fact—because King Constantine of Greece was related to the Russian imperial family.

Not only did the Russian minister in Athens, Demidov, dissociate himself from the Allies' general policy; on more than one occasion Nicholas II opposed their intervention in the internal affairs of Greece and took a position alongside Constantine. This attitude in the Russian court was especially evident when Prince Nicholas of Greece visited Petrograd in July 1916; the tsar went to the extreme of ordering the Russian press to halt all its attacks on Constantine. The Allies were to have to wait for the fall of Nicholas II before they could move forcefully in Greece and compel the king to abdicate.

Russia and the Question of Constantinople and the Straits

Turkey's entrance into the war decided Russian diplomacy to "realize," as the imperial manifesto put it in announcing the declaration of war against Turkey, "the historic mission of Russia on the shores of the Black Sea."

The question of the Straits, which Russia had faced since the eighteenth century, and the political, economic, and strategic importance of which was immeasurable, naturally became one of the Russian government's dominant concerns. But, although to liberal circles, as Miliukov wrote in 1914, "control of the Straits is an end and not a beginning," government quarters, in contrast, regarded it as one phase in a vast plan of territorial acquisitions. Sazonov counseled the Russian high command to carry out military operations against Turkey with more vigor and even suggested that an expeditionary corps be sent against her. But General Aleksyeyev firmly rebuffed this proposal, emphasizing that the German front ought to be the sole objective of the Russian armies and that any secondary undertaking would only weaken their strength.

Sazonov thereupon entered into negotiations with the Allies with a view to obtaining recognition of Russia's rights over Constantinople and the Straits. His ideas were at first received rather coldly in Paris; the key to the situation was in London. On 19 February/4 March 1915 he sent a memorandum to the French and British ambassadors:

The course of recent events leads His Majesty, Tsar Nicholas, to believe that the question of Constantinople and the Straits ought to be finally resolved in accord with the aspirations of Russia through the ages.

Any solution would be both inadequate and fragile if it did not include in the territories of the Russian Empire the city of Constantinople, the eastern shore of the Bosphorus, the Sea of Marmora and of the Dardanelles, and southern Thrace as far as the line from Enos to Midia.

Similarly, and in consequence of strategic necessities, the frontiers of the Russian Empire should embrace that part of the Asian coast between the Bosphorus, the Sakaria River, and the points that will be duly designated on the shore of the Bay of Ismid, as well as the islands in the Sea of Marmora, the islands of Imbros and Tenedos.

The special interests of France and Great Britain in the region above described shall be rigorously respected.

The imperial government is confident that the considerations herein expressed will be received sympathetically by the two Allied governments. These governments may be certain that the realization of plans that they may envisage in other parts of the Ottoman Empire and elsewhere will find equal sympathy on the part of the imperial government.

This program of territorial annexation was approved by the Allies. On March 8, 1915 the French ambassador in Petrograd gave Sazonov a memorandum stating that Russia could rely on the favorable attitude of France in the matter of Constantinople and the Straits. Four days later the British ambassador handed Sazonov the following memorandum (in English):

In the event that the war shall be carried through to a victorious conclusion and that the hopes of Great Britain and France shall be realized in the Ottoman Empire and elsewhere, in accordance with the terms of the Russian document herein above cited, His Majesty's government will remain in agreement with what has been set forth on the subject of Constantinople and the Straits in the memorandum of the imperial government, the text of which was communicated to His Majesty's Ambassador by His Excellency, Mr. Sazonov, on 19 February/4 March of this year.

In addition to this memorandum, in which was expressed the desire that the convention dealing with Constantinople remain secret, the British ambassador submitted a second, which requested a number of privileges for Great Britain, in particular the recognition that the neutral zone established in Persia by the treaty of 1907 become a British sphere.

On 9/22 March Sazonov gave the British and French ambassadors a new memorandum that expressed his gratitude to the Allies for their recognition of Russia's rights over Constantinople and the Straits, and acceded to England's requests, as well as establishing eventual freedom of transit through Constantinople and the free passage of merchant ships through the Straits.

The matter was settled: Russia's rights over Constantinople and the Straits were officially recognized. All that remained was to publish the convention, to which Italy had also adhered. For some time the Allies could not arrive at an agreement on this point. Finally, on 19 November/1 December 1916, Premier Trepov made it public in the Duma.

The Problem of a Separate Peace and Russia's Relations with the Allies

Relations between Russia and the Allies were linked to the problem of a separate peace, which itself was closely dependent on that of Constantinople and the Straits. The extreme internal problems that were besetting Russia and the impotence of her government to resolve the complex difficulties presented by the war led both Russia's friends and her enemies to envisage the possibility of a revolution and a separate peace.

In this respect the Russian reactionaries and the Allies entertained divergent points of view. Pro-Germans in Russia argued that the continuation of the war would inevitably result in revolution, and it was as the means of averting this that they clamored for a separate peace. The Allies, on the other hand, believed that the signature of a separate peace by the autocratic government would bring on a national Russian revolution under the cry of *War to the end*; that was why they believed it worthwhile to disclose the convention on Constantinople and the Straits, in order to excite the patriotism of the Russian people. Germany too was counting on the likelihood of being able to treat separately with Russia, and on several occasions Berlin made proposals to this end. Like the Allies, Germany relied on the bait of Constantinople and the Straits. In March 1915 Princess Vassilchikova, one of the tsarina's ladies in waiting, who was visiting in Austria, sent an initial letter to the tsar to direct his attention to the opportunity for a separate peace. In a second letter she told him that England intended to annex Constantinople but that Germany was prepared to guarantee possession of the city and the Straits to Russia if she was willing to make a separate peace. In May, after a conversation in Berlin with Foreign Minister von Jagow, there was a third letter, the most interesting of all, for it contained a verbatim transcript of the conversation between the princess and von Jagow. "England," he asserted, "in spite of all her promises, will never allow Russia to take" Constantinople. "Germany needs a strong monarchist Russia, and the two neighboring reigning houses have to keep alive the old monarchist and friendly traditions. The prolongation of the war is regarded as a menace to the dynasty. If Your Majesty decides to speak the word *Peace* from the eminence of the throne, you will resolve the destiny of the peoples of the entire universe. If you dispatch a trustworthy person, another reliable individual will be sent from here at the same time with a view to initial negotiations." Princess

Vassilchikova subsequently went back to Russia with letters from the grand duke and the Princess von Hesse—the tsarina's brother and sister—but she was banished from Petrograd and stripped of her rank as lady in waiting.

Among the incidents that gave rise to the conviction in Russia that unauthorized individuals were endeavoring either to initiate peace talks or to make soundings in that direction it is essential to mention the conversations held by Vice Chairman Protopopov of the Imperial Duma in Stockholm. In July 1916 the Russian parliamentary delegation that had left the country and visited the western front went back to Russia by way of Sweden. Without his colleagues' knowledge, Protopopov, who headed the mission, entered into relations in Stockholm with a German agent, one Warburg, who, as Protopopov recounted the story later, assured him that in the event of a separate peace Russia would acquire Constantinople and the Straits. The news of this discussion aroused indignation in Petrograd. Protopopov then insisted that the Russian minister in Stockholm had known of his talks with Warburg. This drew a vigorous denial from the diplomat, who couched it in terms that were personally insulting. Public opinion viewed the whole matter as a trial balloon sent aloft by right-wing circles, and, when Protopopov became minister of the interior, it was believed that his appointment was at least in part the result of his talks in Sweden.

The new Russian foreign minister, Shtyurmer (Stürmer), inspired even less confidence in the Allies. The friendly reaction of the German press to his appointment, as well as the constantly more numerous and more detailed rumors of mysterious conversations, further disquieted the Allies. The situation became so strained that Shtyurmer was compelled, in his dual capacity as premier and foreign minister, to send a telegram to Russia's representatives to the other Allies on 3/16 November:

If only because of their persistence, the Russian government cannot ignore the rumors recently spread by the press in certain countries and dealing with secret negotiations supposedly engaged in between Russia and Germany with a view to the conclusion of a separate peace. The imperial government considers itself obligated to state in the most categorical fashion that these preposterous rumors are merely serving the purposes of the enemy powers. Russia will preserve intact the alliance that binds her to her valiant Allies, and, devoid of all thought of a separate peace, she will fight hand in hand with them against the common enemy without faltering in the slightest and until the hour of final victory.

The documents found in the Russian secret archives and made

public after the war by the Soviet government contain nothing to
indicate that Nicholas II himself had ever thought of a separate
peace. Since the end of the war the question has been clearly resolved:
the tsar kept faith with his commitments to his Allies. But, although
he himself could not be moved, it was nonetheless true, as public
opinion sensed in 1916 and 1917, that the course of events might lead
Russia under the government of a Shtyurmer or a Protopopov to
conclude a separate peace. In any event, such a contingency seemed
likely enough to Russian opinion.

Quite apart from the question of a separate peace, relations between
the Allies and Russia were sometimes influenced by purely technical
problems dealing with such matters as supply and finances. Approximately three weeks before the 1917 revolution an inter-Allied conference was held in Petrograd to discuss current matters of policy and
especially financial questions and the Greek problem. A short time
before the end of the conference the British representative, Lord
Milner, submitted a memorandum to the tsar on February 17, warning
him, in terms that, though discreet, were firm, that the Allies would
assist Russia by supplying her with war materials but only on condition that foreign experts supervise the systematic and orderly utiliza-
tion of these supplies. Similarly, in the most discreet of fashions, the
British minister observed, in discussing certain appointments to the
highest positions in the Empire, that in time of war it was not hierarchic tradition but, rather, personal worth that ought to govern the
choice of men. And the minister's high praise for the public agencies
created by the zemstvo and municipal associations was an indirect
rebuke for the government's indifference.

Russia and the Polish Problem

Ever since the declaration of war the Polish problem had been of
the utmost concern to the Russian government. At the start of hostilities the Cabinet prepared an appeal to the Polish people that was
later signed by Generalissimo Grand Duke Nikolai Nikolayevitch.
This document promised the Poles the future unification of the Polish
nation under the Russian scepter: "Poles. The hour has struck when
the sacred dream of your fathers and grandfathers can be fulfilled. . . .
Let there be an end to the frontiers that have fragmented the Polish
people! Let that people be united under the scepter of the Russian
tsar! Under this scepter Poland will be reborn, free in her religion,
in her language, in her local government . . ."

In spite of this appeal the government took no action to realize the
hopes that might have been aroused in the Polish people. On several

occasions the Cabinet took up the Polish problem, but invariably it collided with the opposition of the reactionary ministers. No longer trusting in Russia's promises, the Poles attempted to act in Paris, where the traditional sympathies for Poland were deeply rooted. The Russian government showed its considerable concern at this, especially after a speech by Léon Bourgeois. Under no conditions could the Russian government afford to let the Polish problem become an international problem. Sazonov alone recognized that it would inevitably become international, whether on the Allies' initiative or on Germany's. Therefore in April of 1916 he presented to the tsar a report in which he developed the idea that it was essential to establish a kingdom of Poland united with Russia. "A political organization must be created in Poland that will preserve the upper hand for Russia and her sovereign over the destinies of the Polish people, while at the same time allowing freedom of action to the Polish national movement, and that, far from contributing to the continuation of the historic disharmony with Russia, will serve to regularize Poland's internal conditions." Although he opposed the grant of complete independence, Sazonov believed that provincial autonomy was not enough, and he recommended the revival of the policy of Alexander I and Nicholas I, who, even after the rising of 1830, continued to govern Poland "according to the Polish laws and with the help of a Polish administration subject to the grand duke residing in Warsaw." He insisted that "to deny the international importance of this matter is to close one's eyes to reality"; that was why he pressed for the adoption of the proposal attached to his report. Its first article was conceived in these terms: "The kingdom of Poland is joined to the Russian state by the indivisibility of the throne and the unity of interest of everything concerning both states. In matters concerning its internal affairs, the kingdom shall be governed by special laws established through special legislation." The other articles provided for the creation of this "special legislation" by the tsar with the concurrence of a Polish Diet, the appointment of a viceroy of the kingdom of Poland, etc.

The proposal was submitted to the tsar. But certain quarters at court and in the bureaucracy launched a furious campaign against it. In July 1916 Sazonov was retired and his successor, Shtyurmer, declared himself in favor of granting Poland only regional autonomy. Once more the examination of the problem was deferred. Finally the government decided to postpone the promulgation of the manifesto on Polish autonomy until Russian troops should once more be in Poland.

The question was thus definitively thrust aside. Henceforth the initiative in the political organization of Poland belonged to the central powers, which, in a public statement, recognized the existence of a Polish state. Russia restricted herself to replying in an official note that she proposed, "after the end of the war, and under the scepter of the Russian sovereign, to establish an autonomous Poland that would include all Polish soil and that, with Russia, would constitute an indivisible state." Thus the tsarist government was unable to resolve the problem. Only Sazonov had grasped the urgency of its solution; possibly his plan would not have satisfied all Polish aspirations, but certainly his was the only attempt to take a realistic view of the matter. It was only after the revolution of 1917 and under the rule of the Russian provisional government that the Polish problem was to be resolved in a broader sense.

III / RUSSIA IN THE FIRST WORLD WAR (1914–1917) [G. DANILOV]

Military and Economic Conditions on the Eve of War

The transition from limited to general mobilization, which was ordered during the night of July 31, 1914, was effected without too much difficulty and almost without disturbance to the population's normal life. But, when war broke out, the Russian forces, which had suffered so much from the disasters in Manchuria and the revolutionary crisis that had immediately followed them, had not yet been sufficiently rehabilitated.

Lacking financial resources and also an adequate war industry, the army and navy had not yet been able to complete their reorganization or to rebuild their reserves. Machine guns and heavy artillery, the importance of which had been made manifest by the war of 1904–1905, had indeed been added to the arsenal, but in far from sufficient number. Supplies of other weapons and munitions were equally far from reaching the proportions that would be demanded by the probable nature of the coming conflict. The reconstruction of the fleet, so sharply reduced by the heavy losses inflicted during the Russian-Japanese War, had barely been begun. In order to counter the constantly growing armaments of its western neighbors, the government had submitted bills to the Duma in 1912 and 1913 for increases in the size of both the army and the navy. These proposals, the execution of which was only just beginning when war came, offered eloquent testimony to the inadequacy of Russia's military preparations.

Great advances, unquestionably, had been made in the economic domain. But there too there were areas of weakness that were unsparingly made apparent by the war from the moment of its onset.

There was first of all the financial situation. Though it was reasonably good, it was soon impaired by the virtually complete elimination of exports and the necessity of placing huge war orders in other countries. It was further aggravated by the fact that Russia had neglected to conclude financial accords in advance with her Allies for the eventualities of war.

Second, there was the inadequacy of the nation's industrial development. In spite of its extremely quick growth, industry even in times of peace was far from capable of meeting the increasing needs of the population. This gap between national output and consumption requirements was specifically and particularly marked in those sectors of industry whose importance becomes crucial in time of war. Russia, moreover, like all the other belligerent states, for that matter, had in no way foreseen or prepared for the adaptation of private enterprises to the exigencies of national defense. These two factors explain why Russian industry was so slow in replacing the exhausted stocks of munitions and why the lack of them was to force the army into a position of extreme jeopardy during the early part of the war.

Finally, there was the paucity of means of transport. The railway network was in no sense proportionate to the immense area of the Empire. In addition, established to meet the Empire's peacetime needs, it was not always adequate for strategic requirements, especially those imposed by mobilization. And it was short of rolling stock. Only a short time before the outbreak of war, in fact, it had been decided to expand the facilities of the railway system with a view to possible military complications in the west, but the lack of funds had delayed the execution of this plan. Usable roads were even less numerous: they were to be found only in Poland and the Transcaucasian region; the use of motor vehicles, which is so vital to modern war, was thus made impossible.

Germany had taken all these circumstances into account in her calculations. She was fully aware that each further year of peace would give her eastern neighbor the opportunity to make notable advances in its preparations and thus create obstacles to her own designs.

The Concentration Plan

The war in which Russia was engaged was a coalition war; the operations of each of the states involved could not be considered separately, but only in terms of the general situation on all the Allied fronts.

Under the provisions of the special military convention concluded between France and Russia for the first time in 1892, it had been agreed that, in the event of an attack by Germany or any other member of the Triple Alliance against one of the Allies, the other would be obligated to go to its defense and to throw all its available resources against Germany. Meticulous analysis of the situation had led the chiefs of the General Staffs of both powers to believe, in the course of their periodic conferences, that there was a strong probability that Germany's major forces would first of all be directed against France, while all or almost all those of Austria-Hungary would inevitably be turned against Russia. On the basis of this hypothesis they had decided that Russia's help to France should take the form of an offensive in East Prussia with forces of sufficient strength to immobilize five or six German army corps there. In addition to this plan of operations, which was regarded as basic, the Russian General Staff had wisely foreseen another for the equally likely possibility that Germany might hurl the bulk of her strength against Russia.

The mobilization was completed without incident, and the total number of reservists who took up arms did not fall below the figure anticipated by the War Ministry. The movement of these troops by rail was also carried out in full conformity with the operational plans. Grand Duke Nikolai Nikolayevitch, the tsar's uncle, was made generalissimo.

When it became obvious in the first days of the war that the German troops were being concentrated in the west, the Russians began to deploy their armies along their own western borders in accord with the original plans of campaign (see map on facing page).

The whole frontier with East Prussia was occupied by the northwestern armies, which consisted of nine army corps constituting the First and Second Armies. Their objective was to launch a swift offensive that would rout the German forces massed in East Prussia and then, when this region had been occupied, to move on to the lower reaches of the Vistula. Thus the composition and the mission of the Russian forces conformed completely to the terms of the French-Russian military agreement.

Four armies comprising sixteen line corps were to operate on the southwestern front against Austria-Hungary, which was able to concentrate her entire forces against Russia. The Russian troops were deployed in the region abutting on Galicia: the Fourth and Fifth Armies inside Russian Poland on the Lublin-Kovel front, and the

OPERATIONS ON THE WESTERN FRONT IN 1914

▨ Russian Forces

Third and Eighth in the Kiev sector, in the region of Rovno and Proskurov. Their objective was to defeat the Austro-Hungarian armies and make it possible to occupy Galicia and the Carpathian passes dominating the Hungarian plain. Russia was anticipating major political consequences from the defeat of Austria-Hungary: on the one hand, the liberation of the smaller Slavic peoples long under the heel of the Dual Monarchy should make the war highly popular with the Russian masses; on the other, penetration by Russian troops into Austro-Hungarian territory should alleviate Serbia's military position, enhance the Allies' prestige in the Balkans, and attract the allegiance of Italy and Rumania, both of which had already defected from the Triple Alliance. Even from the purely military point of view, the defeat of the Austro-Hungarian armies was of capital importance because this alone could make it possible for Russia to undertake a later offensive on a grand scale in German territory that would give her a decisive victory over Germany, the head of the enemy coalition. Once the Russian northwestern armies had attained the lower Vistula and the southwestern armies had beaten the Austro-Hungarians on the left flank of the Russian strategic front, this offensive would in fact have an excellent chance of success.

Two further armies were brought into being: the Sixth, composed of three line corps that were temporarily maintained in the area of Finland and Petrograd against the possible threat of Sweden and a German attack, and the Seventh, made up of several reserve divisions that were to keep watch on the coast of the Black Sea.

As for the Russian fleet, no independent action was possible to it because of its depletion. In the Baltic Sea it would be restricted to the defense of the entrance to the Gulf of Finland; in the Black Sea, where it was reasonably strong in comparison to the naval capacities of the neighboring states, it would uphold the dominance of the Russian flag.

Thus, of the thirty-seven line corps existing in peace time, only twenty-eight could be immediately deployed along the western borders. The nine others, garrisoned in distant regions, had no predetermined assignment, for it would require at least a month to move them to the threatened frontiers. Like the Sixth and Seventh Armies, which served as observation forces, they constituted a kind of reserve in the generalissimo's hands, and their use would be determined only in proportion to their proximity to the front and in accordance with the shifting necessities of the moment.

Besides the thirty-seven peacetime line corps there were thirty-five reserve divisions, created on the first day of the mobilization. The greater part, formed in European Russia, was distributed among the armies—subsequently they were almost all to be assembled into army corps. As for the cavalry, which consisted of thirty-one divisions, it was of course assigned almost *in toto*, with very few exceptions to the various armies from the start.

The Russian Offensive in East Prussia (August–September 1914)

Germany's violation of Belgian neutrality in her preparations for hurling huge masses of troops into the invasion of northeastern and northern France compelled the Russian General Staff, the *Stavka*, to accelerate its own invasion of East Prussia in order to divert as many German corps as possible from the French front (see map on facing page).

By reason of topographical conditions, the Russian First Army, which consisted of four corps under the command of General Rennenkampf, had to initiate its offensive in the direction of the middle part of the Niemen River, north of the Masurian Lakes; the Second Army, commanded by General Samsonov, had to attack on the Narev, rounding the western lakes; the two armies' junction was to be made to the west of the line of lakes. From the military point of view, therefore, the offensive entailed a rather complicated maneuver and required skillfully concerted action. Although the Second Army, whose rear was not well organized, was not yet ready to take the offensive, the high command of the northwestern front officially scheduled the crossing of the border by the First Army for August 17 and by the bulk of the Second Army for August 19. In view of the circumstances of the mobilization and rail transport facilities, this action by the Russian army was precipitate; it was determined by the necessity of countering an increasingly alarming position on the French front and the desire to assist the Allies' armies.

During the evening of August 16 the First Army was deployed along the East Prussian frontier, and on the next day, in the area of Stallupönen, its troops clashed with the Germans and came out the victors.

At this time the Russian command became convinced that the Germans had not left more than four line corps in East Prussia, supported by an equal number of reserve formations, the *Landwehr* and the *Landsturm*. At the same time, the disposition of these troops was a mystery to the Russians; the clash at Stallupönen had merely made it possible to identify some elements of the German First Army Corps.

Carrying on with its attack, the Russian First Army engaged in a savage battle on August 19 in the area of Gumbinnen and continued

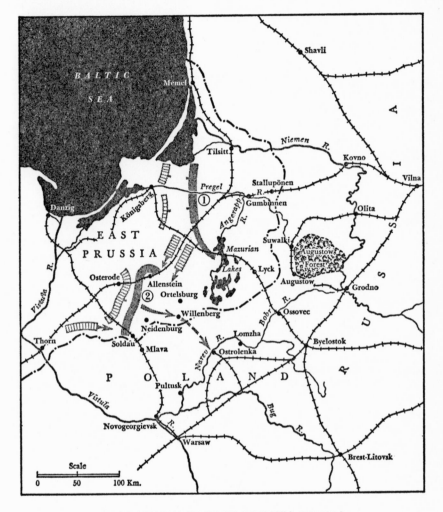

OPERATIONS IN EAST PRUSSIA IN 1914

Russian Forces   ① Gen. Rennenkampf   ② Gen. Samsonov

German Forces

it the next day against three enemy army corps and a reserve division, all striving to go over to the counterattack. In spite of their efforts, the German forces had to retreat westward in the evening of August 20. The Russian First Army's victory below Gumbinnen was so decisive that Baron von Prittwitz-Gaffron, commanding the German Eighth Army, envisaged—as it became known later—the evacuation of East Prussia and the withdrawal of his troops beyond the Vistula.

In order to make the most of a situation that seemed to be highly favorable, General Samsonov, in command of the Second Army, decided to swing his troops westward in a flanking movement in order better to encircle the retreating Germans and prevent them from reaching the Vistula bridges without loss. If this maneuver did not succeed, it was because the First Army did not simultaneously and equally vigorously pursue the retreating enemy. For various reasons General Rennenkampf put off the resumption of his attack until August 23; and afterward, even though he encountered no resistance, he conducted it with a great deal of weakness and hesitation.

This loss of time was decisive for both sides. Defeated and in retreat, the Germans were able to put some distance between themselves and the victors and thus to regain a certain freedom of action. General von Hindenburg, who had succeeded Prittwitz at the head of the German Eighth Army, and his chief of staff, General Ludendorff, had taken full advantage of the respite that had been granted them and completely regrouped their forces. Leaving only a light screening force, made up almost entirely of cavalry, against General Rennenkampf, who was slowly beginning to advance after several days of inactivity, they massed all their available forces, even the garrisons of the major and minor fortifications along the lower Vistula, against Samsonov's army. The Germans managed to concentrate four corps, three divisions, and three special brigades, to say nothing of heavy artillery, in which the Russians were totally lacking, and these were so employed that Samsonov's troops, who, furthermore, were thinned out, soon found themselves in an extremely difficult position.

Between August 23 and 30 a series of important battles occurred in the area where the Russian Second Army was waging its offensive in the direction of Allenstein-Osterode; they resulted in the encirclement of this army, which lost approximately two and a half army corps, captured or missing, in the forests north of the road from Neidenburg to Willenberg; rather than survive such a disaster, Samsonov shot himself. During these operations the Germans had more than once been in a critical position. If, instead of resting on his arms, Rennenkampf had advanced swiftly to complete his junction with Samsonov's army, as the Germans later admitted, the enemy would have been in grave peril of suffering the same fate that overtook the Russian army. In celebration of this vengeance for the defeat inflicted on them in 1410 by the combined forces of the Lithuanians, the Poles, and the Russians, the Germans gave this decisive combat the name of the Battle of Tannenberg. It was an arbitrary label, for the 1914 operations took place far to the east of the village that in the fifteenth century had been the scene of the battle of Tannenberg or Grünwald.

In spite of its serious defeat, the Russian offensive in East Prussia was not useless. Carried out with substantial forces, it had first of all upset the enemy command, filled all Germany with fear, deeply wounded the vanity of Wilhelm II by its initial success—especially when General von Prittwitz made the decision to pull his troops back behind the Vistula—and forced the German command to allay public opinion by immediately developing a plan of campaign that would make it possible to reconquer the territory lost in the east. But above all it had contributed to the alleviation of the Allies' situation on the French front. In fact, in order to reinforce the troops on the eastern front, the German command had been obliged to transfer from the western front two reserve army corps (the Guard and the Eleventh) and the Eighth Cavalry Division. In view of the urgency of this move, it drew these reinforcements from its right wing, which was based on a well-developed railway network.* Thus it weakened its right wing, which was endeavoring to envelop the Anglo-French forces from the north and drive down on Paris, at the very instant when the terrible threat that it posed for the Allies' armies was about to become a reality, and this enfeeblement in itself was of considerable importance. Moreover, the news of the defeats on the eastern front could not fail to have a demoralizing influence on the state of mind of the German leaders, and this too was a factor that must be reckoned with. The great courage of the Allies' troops and the strategic intuition of their commanders took the fullest possible advantage of this situation, but Russia had her part in the preparation for the victory of the Marne that definitively destroyed Germany's initial hope of ending the war by a single blow on the western front.

When the German reinforcements reached the eastern front and the elements of the Russian Second Army that had escaped the disaster fell back on the Narev, General von Hindenburg decided to turn his forces against Rennenkampf's army, which was still holding a fortified line on German soil running from Kurisches Haff to the Masurian

---

*It planned also to shift a third army corps taken from its left flank, but later this plan was dropped.

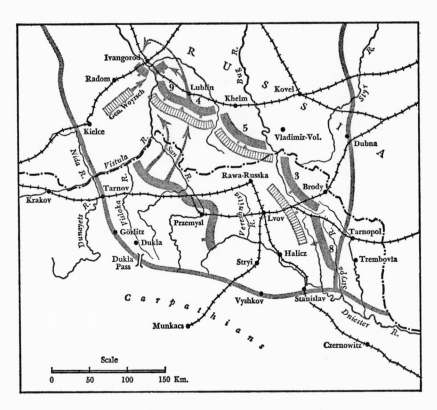

OPERATIONS IN GALICIA IN 1914

Russian Forces   German and Austro-Hungarian Forces

Lakes. Clinging to the methods advocated during peacetime by the German General Staff, Hindenburg strove once more to envelop both flanks of his antagonist, but he did not succeed. Rennenkampf evaded the trap that had been laid for him, and, in mid-September, he managed to fall back to the middle Niemen with heavy losses.

The Russian Offensive in Galicia (August–September 1914)

On the southwestern front the Austro-Hungarians anticipated their opponents' offensive (see map on facing page). Having established a cover force consisting of three to four army corps in front of the city of Lvov, facing east, they deployed almost eight further corps between the Vistula and Rava-Russka and entered Russian Poland. Their attack, especially after the arrival of reinforcements, including a German *Landwehr* corps under General von Woyrsch, from the left bank of the Vistula, created an extremely difficult position for the Russian Fourth and Fifth Armies, which were not yet prepared. This critical period coincided with the most perilous phase of the Russian operations in East Prussia. Nevertheless, thanks to the speedy arrival of Russian reinforcements that made it possible to form a new army, the Ninth, on the right flank of the front between the Vistula and Lublin, and thanks as well to the vigorous counter-offensive by the Russian Third and Eighth Armies, which attacked from the east on the Lvov-Halicz front, the Russian command succeeded in breaking the Austro-Hungarian offensive toward the north. During their counter-offensive the Third and Eighth Armies scored a number of victories that made it possible for them to occupy Halicz on September 2 and, a day later, Lvov, the administrative capital and railway center of Galicia. These smashing successes, as well as the appearance of part of the Russian forces north of Lvov, imperiled the right flank and even the rear of the Austro-Hungarian armies that had thrust deeply into a part of Russian Poland that was lacking in adequate means of communication. In addition, the northern group of the southwestern armies, the Ninth, Fourth, and Fifth Armies, began to press the Austro-Hungarians from the front and from the right.

What ensued was a veritable crisis in the theater of enemy operations. The northern group of the Austro-Hungarians had to give thought to securing its retreat, and, in order to protect this withdrawal, the enemy command decided to reinforce substantially its eastern defense by establishing it along the line of the Vereshnitsa from its mouth in the north to Rava-Russka. This formidable natural defense position, which in addition had been well fortified, was intended to contain the pressure of the Russian Third and Eighth Armies until the bulk of the Austro-Hungarian forces had pulled back across the San River.

The combat that began on September 6 on the Vereshnitsa became a savage battle that went on for five days. It was not until dawn of September 12 that the Austro-Hungarians, fearful lest their defense line be turned in the area of Rava-Russka, began to retreat along the whole front as far as the Dniester. Day for day their withdrawal paced the withdrawal of the German armies in France toward the Aisne after the Battle of the Marne. All the Allied powers could celebrate at the same time their first decisive victory over the collective enemy. Abandoning weapons, vehicles, and the wounded, losing thousands of prisoners every day, the Austro-Hungarian armies fled in disorder beyond the San and the Visloka. More than forty divisions, shattered for the most part into wretched shards, regrouped in the narrow area bounded by the upper Vistula and the Carpathians. The entire western part of Galicia was in Russian hands, and the Russians were at the gates of Hungary and Bukovina. Thus the Russian offensive in Galicia came to a glorious end in mid-September. Millions of men had been thrown into battle on both sides, and along a front of more than 470 versts these massive forces had maneuvered and fought for more than three weeks without a moment's respite.

In direct proportion to the deeper penetration of the five Russian armies into Galicia, their front was necessarily narrowed more and more by reason of the geographical conditions: in the north it was bounded by the course of the Vistula, above the San, and in the south its back was against the Carpathians. Not all these armies were required for the pursuit of the Austro-Hungarians in retreat toward the Visloka; therefore only one of them, the Ninth, was detailed to this mission, and the four others were temporarily halted along the San to await more effective employment elsewhere.

The Battle of the Vistula (September–December 1914)

Sometime in the middle of September a certain quiet came to the French front. The war was becoming one of trenches: French Generalissimo Joffre summed up the situation when he advised his government that henceforth the successes of the troops under his command "will be measured no longer by tens of kilometers but by meters."

Under such conditions the German command might be tempted to take the initiative of operations again by making use of the forces that were being organized in the interior of Germany. In order to prevent

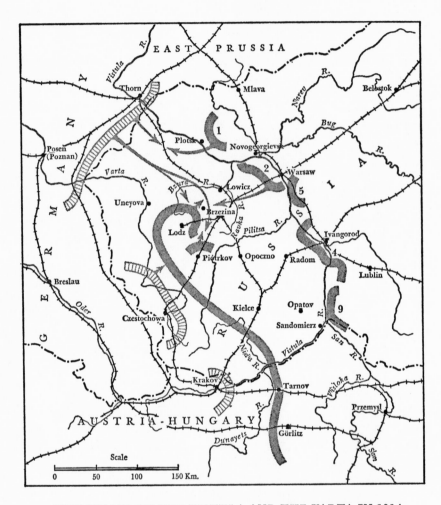

OPERATIONS ON THE VISTULA AND THE VARTA IN 1914

▓▓▓ Russian Forces   ▦▦▦ German and Austro-Hungarian Forces

a new German offensive, the French government approached the Russian Foreign Ministry in mid-September with the request that Russian troops keep up permanent operations on the left bank of the Vistula and thus give the Germans reason to fear a new invasion of their territory. The shift of military operations to the left bank of the Vistula also entered into the calculations of the *Stavka,* which from the start of the war had contemplated the possibility of an invasion of Germany. But, after the Austro-Hungarian withdrawal to the Visloka, the *Stavka* began to receive intelligence of an influx of German troops into Upper Silesia; obviously the German command was in haste to protect its territory against a possible invasion by the Russians and eager at the same time to afford succor to the distressed Austro-Hungarian armies. This information was fully confirmed toward the end of September, when a combined Austrian-German offensive began to take shape between Lodz and the mouth of the Nida. Little by little it was learned that the operation was being carried out by the German Ninth Army, newly constituted and comprising more than six corps; its right flank was the Austro-Hungarian First Army, composed of the least battered units; the whole operation was under the command of Hindenburg and Ludendorff. At the same time there was an Austro-Hungarian offensive on the right bank of the upper Vistula toward the San. Thus the campaign assumed a major scale.

Inasmuch as the sector of the middle Vistula, from the mouth of the San to the Bug and the Narev, was thus laid completely open, so to speak, there was grave danger to Ivangorod and Warsaw, where there were permanent bridges over the Vistula. Furthermore the loss of Warsaw, the political and administrative center of Russian Poland, would be a major blow to Russia. The *Stavka* most successfully remedied this complex and perilous situation by means of a broad behind-the-lines movement that demonstrated the creative qualities of Russian strategy (see map on facing page). It ordered the command of the southwestern front to pull three armies—the Fifth, Fourth, and Ninth, with a strength of nine to ten army corps—out of Galicia and thrust them into the Vistula sector, while the northwest command would concentrate the seven corps of the Second Army in the direction of Warsaw. This plan anticipated that ten army corps—that is, the Second and Fifth Armies in their entirety—in addition to massive cavalry forces, would occupy the sector lying between a point north of the mouth of the Pilitsa and Warsaw in order subsequently to counterattack the German left flank, which was advancing on Warsaw and had no cover.

The troop movements required by this counter-maneuver were made extremely difficult by the destruction of the temporary bridges across the San, the poor state of the roads, and most unfavorable weather conditions. On the whole, however, they were completed within the time specified, and on October 20 the shock forces, the Second and Fifth Armies, which occupied the fortified region of Warsaw, were ordered to move out in a general offensive. But the Germans, overrun by the cavalry that poured out of the Bzura River and enveloped on their left flank by the Russian infantry, recognized the gravity of their position, and during the night of October 20 they began to fall back on the whole front in the sector north of the Pilitsa. Little by little, under the pressure of the attacking Russian armies, their retreat maneuver grew larger and spread to the Austro-Hungarian army as far as the first foothills of the Carpathians.

This success opened broad prospects to the Russian armies. The pursuit of the enemy might easily lead to the invasion of Poznan and, above all, of Silesia, the loss of which would deprive Germany of an area of extreme military and industrial importance. In fact, on the very day when the German troops' retreat began to take shape, the Russian armies were ordered to launch a vigorous attack on the Lodz-Piótrkov-Opoczno-Opatov-Sandomierz front while at the same time continuing to push forward on their right flank. With great skill and speed the Germans made the roads useless behind them as they withdrew; thus they delayed the Russian pursuit and by gaining time succeeded in returning to their own soil. But Silesia still lay under the threat of a Russian invasion: by November 10 the Russian front already ran from Uneyova, on the Varta, to the mouth of the Nida on the south and, beyond, all along the Dunayets.

It was then that the consequences of the disparity in railway facilities came into play. On the left bank of the Vistula the Russians had only a very poor system, and this created great problems for even the smallest troop movements. The Germans, in contrast, by returning to their own soil, were once more in a position to make use of two excellent railways that formed a double circle round the entire Russian border region. The German command on the eastern front, which since the beginning of November had been in the hands of Hindenburg and his inseparable chief of staff, Ludendorff, played this trump; in the region lying between the Vistula and the Varta it quickly concentrated almost six army corps as well as a large force of cavalry, all of which were thrown into an attack against the Russian right flank and strove to envelop it. This avalanche of troops, under the leadership of General von Mackensen, the commander of the Ninth Army, poured on as far as Lodz; its advance guard penetrated even to Piótrkov, infiltrating deeply into the Russian right wing. In spite of the fact that they were outflanked, the Russians showed great tenacity and managed to hold on to the Lodz region. Reinforcements soon reached them from the right bank of the Vistula and compelled the enemy, who had driven too far, to withdraw in haste. On November 22 and 23 one and a half German corps and two cavalry divisions were almost surrounded in the region of Brzezina; it was only at the cost of tremendous sacrifices and superhuman efforts that what was left of them—at the most eight thousand men, on the basis of German sources—managed to cut a passage for themselves and escape in a precipitate retreat.

The Lodz offensive ended with the general withdrawal of the German Ninth Army. Its defeat decided the German command to remove more forces from the western front for use in Russian Poland—the Second and Thirteenth Army Corps of the regular army, the Third and Twenty-fourth Army Corps of reserves, and five cavalry divisions, the Second, Fourth, Fifth, Sixth, and Ninth. This considerable drain prevented the prosecution of the vigorous offensive on the French front that had been waged during the second half of October and in the first part of November on the Yser and at Ypres in the direction of Calais, the British army's base. On the other side, the losses that the Russian troops had taken during four months of almost uninterrupted attack, the shortage of weapons and munitions, mainly rifles and cartridges, the approach of winter, and a military position that had become most delicate compelled the *Stavka* to revise its previous plan of campaign and reduce its scope. Consequently, by the middle of December, the Russian forces were occupying previously prepared positions on the Bzura, Ravka, and Nida Rivers and beginning to fortify them.

The Failure of the Turkish Attack on the Caucasus (October 1914–
January 1915)

Turkey's entry into the war complicated the military situation in Russia. The Turkish fleet, reinforced by the powerful and fast German cruisers, the *Goeben* and the *Breslau*, attacked various points on the shore of the Black Sea on October 29.

Immediately afterward the Turkish Third Army, composed of the three best of the Ottomans' army corps and commanded by Enver Pasha, whose adviser was his chief of staff, Bronsart von Schellendorff, invaded Transcaucasia. This offensive came to a lamentable end. In the early days of January 1915 it was totally shattered below Ardahan and Sarykamysh, and the Turks had to retreat in the utmost haste, pursued by Russian troops. The cold, the depth of the snow, and the mountainous character of the region in which the Turks were fleeing completed their demoralization. The road along which they were retracing their journey was piled with the frozen bodies of men and beasts, with abandoned ammunition, artillery, and transport. The Russians took many prisoners, including an army corps commander and three divisional commanders with their staffs. This catastrophe to the best of Turkey's troops saved the Caucasus from the threat of a new invasion for the rest of the war.

The German Offensive in East Prussia (February 1915)

East Prussia was a standing threat to the right flank of the Russian front (see map facing page 300); by utilizing its excellent railway network the Germans could in effect unleash at any moment an offensive against the middle Niemen, the Bobr, or the Narev, and turn the flank and even the rear of the Russian army, which was still on the left bank of the Vistula. Early in 1915, therefore, the *Stavka* gave new thought to the occupation of the area. It hurled a new army, the Tenth, against East Prussia, and the attack succeeded in recapturing part of it; fortifications were constructed on the Angerapp River and along the eastern outlets from the Masurian Lakes region.

The plan of the *Stavka* consisted first of all in the concentration of a special army, the Twelfth, composed of ten divisions, and its employment for an offensive on the Soldau-Ortelsburg front. This afforded the advantage of allowing the offensive to be begun with currently available forces. Nevertheless the *Stavka* did not believe that it could undertake the execution of the plan before the second half of February—that is, until it had received reinforcements and more munitions.

It was unsuccessful, unfortunately, in keeping the preparations for this offensive secret, and the German command decided to forestall it. At the end of January the Germans abandoned the prosecution of any serious operations on the western front in order to be able to concentrate four new army corps on East Prussia. Three of these, the Thirty-eighth, Thirty-ninth, and Fortieth, had been formed during the winter inside Germany; the fourth, the Twenty-first, was withdrawn from the French front. These troops were ready for action early in February, and their attack against the two wings of the Russian Tenth Army began to become apparent on February 7. In spite of the season and the unfavorable weather, the extremely hard-driving attack forced the Russians back across the middle Niemen and the Bobr; during its retreat the Russian Twentieth Corps was surrounded in the forts of Augustow and, after savage resistance and terrible losses, part of it was made prisoner.

The Russian Advance in the Carpathians (December 1914–May 1915)

During the first half of 1915 the Austrian front was the theater of operations that were to have a decisive influence on the later course of the war: after their advance into the Carpathians the Russians were forced to retreat and to evacuate Galicia and Russian Poland.

At the end of 1914, after the Austrians and the Germans had abandoned the middle Vistula and the San, the Austro-Hungarian troops had fallen back on the Carpathians (see map facing page 303). General Ivanov, commander in chief of the Russian southwestern armies, deemed it necessary to renounce the defensive and launch an attack in order to prevent the enemy's forces from regrouping. He hoped further that, by invading Hungary, he could detach her from Austria and force her to conclude a separate peace. On the other side, General Conrad von Hoetzendorff, chief of the Austro-Hungarian general staff, who was well aware of the seriousness of the situation, decided to pull his best troops out of the Serbian front and send them into the Carpathians. In addition, the Germans were forming a special southern army in the area of Munkács (now called Mukachevo). The Austrians and Germans planned to attack on a front running from the Dukla pass to the Vyshkov pass in order to liberate the Austrian fortress of Przemysl, under siege by the Russian Eleventh Army, and to threaten the Russians' communications with Lvov. Thus, in spite of its being winter, the Carpathian range became the theater of a number of furious battles that inflicted grave losses on both sides. Almost entirely without cartridges and artillery, the exhausted Russian troops scaled the ice-sheathed rocks and made incredible efforts to reach the passes that had been set as their objectives. This merciless task decimated their ranks.

On March 22 Przemysl capitulated with its garrison of more than one hundred twenty thousand men and its nine hundred pieces of artillery. The siege had lasted almost six months; the lack of siege guns and the extreme shortage of ammunition had prevented the besiegers from reducing it earlier.

The city's fall made the Russian Eleventh Army available for other tasks and it was possible to establish a broader objective for the southwestern armies. Specifically, for political reasons, it was now imperative that the axis of Russian efforts be shifted toward the Carpathians. The Dardanelles expedition undertaken by the Allies was intended to knock Turkey out of the war and to resolve the question of the Straits and Constantinople, which was of vital interest to Russia. Since geographical conditions and the weakness of her Black Sea Fleet, which was kept in check by the fortifications of the Bosphorus, prevented her from taking a direct part in this expedition, her troops were striving, and exhausting themselves in the effort, to bring about the definitive defeat of the Austro-Hungarian armies; this would serve to raise the Allies' prestige in the Balkans and persuade Italy and Rumania to join the war on their side. Although, after quite wearing negotiations, the agreement between the Allies and Italy was signed on April 26, 1915, the new ally's active participation did not begin, unfortunately, for another month. As for Rumania, she continued watching and waiting. Toward the end of April Russian troops succeeded in crossing the Carpathian passes and entrenching themselves in a rather broad area of the southern slopes.

The Austrian-German Offensive and the Russian Retreat in Galicia and Russian Poland (May–September 1915)

The Austro-Hungarians were able to hold their positions in the Carpathians only through the help of German troops, mingled with their own in the most seriously threatened sectors. But this was a mere stopgap remedy; in order to prevent the collapse of the Dual Monarchy it was imperative to resort to more vigorous measures and to change the situation drastically. That was why the Germans completely revised their earlier plans. They went over to the defensive in the west in order to concentrate all their efforts on the eastern front, even shifting their General Headquarters to the little town of Pless in Upper Silesia. From this time forth, it was from the western front that they drew the forces and the supplies required for the development of their eastern offensive. They began by requisitioning nine of their best divisions from the west, including the Prussian Guard. With the Austro-Hungarian troops posted on the Dunayets, they were thus able to assemble sixteen to seventeen infantry divisions, real shock troops with good equipment, artillery that included very large-bore cannon, and ample supplies of ammunition.

The Austrian-German offensive began on May 1, 1915 by breaking the Russian front in the sector bounded by the upper Vistula and the foot of the Carpathians, the Görlitz Gap. Not only was the right wing of the Russian southwestern armies engulfed; the rear elements of

THE WESTERN RUSSIAN FRONT IN 1915 AND 1916

▓▓▓▓ Russian Forces 1915   ▒▒▒▒ Russian Forces 1916

their units that had made deep penetrations into the Carpathians and even occupied part of the southern slopes of the main mountain range were also threatened. The lack of rail facilities behind the lines and their inadequate transport equipment prevented the Russians from engaging in any counter-maneuver and compelled them to make a major retreat. Toward the middle of May their troops in Galicia crossed the San again, but in the face of an influx of fresh German forces they could not maintain their positions there. On June 3 Przemysl fell to the enemy, and on June 22 Lvov followed. Everywhere, in the north as in the east, the southwestern armies were withdrawing toward the Russian borders.

Simultaneously with the development of their offensive in Galicia, the Germans were active on the northwestern front (see map on facing page). They took the fullest benefit from the advantage that was theirs in the possession of East Prussia. As a start, at the end of April they launched an attack toward Tilsitt and Memel, on the right bank of the Niemen, by way of Shavli, in the direction of Riga, Dvinsk, and Vilna; then, about the middle of July, their attack spread as well to the Narev front, in the area of Novogeorgievsk-Lomzha (see map facing page 300).

The progress of this attack, which was accompanied by fierce pressure in Galicia against Khelm and Vladimir-Volynsky, exposed the Russian armies that were operating in Poland, and notably those occupying the left bank of the Vistula, to the danger of being outflanked on both sides. Therefore the commander in chief of the southwestern front, General Ivanov, began with the approval of the *Stavka* to disengage his troops in the "Polish pocket." During the night of August 5 the Russians evacuated Warsaw and began to fall back toward the east, while at the same time repulsing enemy attacks and gradually directing part of their forces toward Vilna, Dvinsk, and Riga, where a new front, the northern, was beginning to come into being. Nevertheless it was not until the end of August that they were able to halt the enemy's offensive along a line running through Riga, Dvinsk, and the mouth of the Stryp River, and thence down the Dniester to the Rumanian border. Their withdrawal entailed the loss of all their fortresses in the west. Most, however, had been evacuated in time, because the experience of this war had shown that, reduced to their own unassisted means, fortresses could neither halt the offensive of large massed armies nor withstand the fire of their artillery.

During the four summer months of their retreat from Galicia and Russian Poland, deprived as they were in weapons and ammunition, the Russians had had to resist unaided the pressure of the united enemy forces. Anglo-French troops had indeed attempted a diversionary action in June in order to draw the Germans away from the Russian front, but the limited scope of this effort and its results had not been enough to dull the blow that the Germans had inflicted in the east. On July 7 General Joffre called a council of war in Chantilly in which the Allies examined what steps could be taken to assist Russia, which was being drained. Emphasizing the contributions that Russia had made to the common cause, Joffre concluded that it was essential to plan an offensive by the Allied forces. But such an offensive required lengthy preparation, and it was not until the end of September, when the situation on the eastern front was beginning to become stabilized, that the Anglo-French army was prepared to attempt a new offensive in Artois and Champagne. As for Italy, her operations against Austria-Hungary did not go beyond the Isonzo River and its approaches, and consequently they were powerless to make any radical change in the situation on the main Austro-Hungarian front, which was in Galicia. Hence the Austrians and the Germans were free to concentrate their whole attention and their major forces on the Russian front without abandoning the defensive on all the other fronts—France, Italy, Serbia, the Dardanelles. In September 1915, according to official statistics, they were able to mass 137 infantry divisions and 24 cavalry divisions against Russia in the place of the 50 infantry and 13 cavalry divisions that they had used in the beginning of the war. By giving battle to so numerically strong an enemy Russia had contributed in the largest sense to the success of the Allies' common cause. By drawing the enemy's attention away from the other fronts, the operations of her troops, in short, had guaranteed the Allies a truce of almost a year after their bitter combats in the early part of the war, and the Allies had made extensive use of this respite to prepare themselves for the long and stubborn struggle that was later to carry them to final victory.

The Assumption of the Supreme Command by Nicholas II and the Loss of Vilna (September 1915)

In the face of the Russian armies' difficult situation, compelled as they were to withdraw to the interior of the country after having left in the enemy's hands the vast area of twenty governments of European Russia, the tsar decided that he himself would assume the supreme command of both the army and the navy. On September 5 he arrived at the *Stavka*, which had just been shifted from Baranovichi to

Mogilev, and on the same day he put his plan into practice. The former generalissimo, Grand Duke Nikolai Nikolayevitch, was appointed viceroy and commander of the special army of the Caucasus, with the title and prerogatives of generalissimo. His closest associates left the *Stavka* with him, and Nicholas II appointed General Aleksyeyev as chief of his General Staff.

The tsar's decision to take over the supreme command was approved neither by the majority of the ministers nor by the Duma—nor by the public. Everyone agreed that it was improper for the head of the state to leave the capital and in addition to assume the responsibility for future military operations.

The tsar's decision was criticized all the more because it came only two or three weeks before autumn, when the roads would be impassable, and in the interval there was every reason to expect a new German attack. On September 12/14, in fact, the Germans exerted tremendous pressure on Vilna and Dvinsk. In order to separate the armies of the northern front, formally constituted under the command of General Ruzsky, from those of the western front commanded by General Evert, the Germans sent out their cavalry, some detachments of which thrust as far as the region of Borisov (see map facing page 311). The principal railway lines linking the two capitals with the front were thus temporarily cut. In order to reestablish the broken front the Russian troops had to make a tremendous effort; they did not succeed until the end of September. Nevertheless the region of Vilna, which was so essential to railway communications, was lost. On the whole front from Dvinsk to Pinsk the Russians were reduced to occupying improvised positions that they endeavored to fortify.

Now trench warfare began on the Russian front. The *Stavka* thought to profit by it to completely rehabilitate its forces, exhausted by a bitter year of battle. But events did not give it the time. They compelled it to undertake new offensives in order to help the Allies before it could accumulate the forces and the means essential to their success.

The Russian Offensive in Trembovla (December 1915)

In the autumn of 1915 the Serbian army was seriously defeated by the joint forces of the Austrians, the Germans, and the Bulgarians, Bulgaria having just joined the central powers. All the roads were cut, and the Serbian army was forced to fall back across the mountains to the sea under extremely arduous weather conditions. Specially regrouped for the purpose of affording the Serbians relief, the Russian

Seventh Army attacked at the end of December at the extremity of the left flank of the southwest front, in the region of Trembovla (see map facing page 311). This offensive cost Russia fifty thousand men.

The 1916 Russian Offensives on the Northern and Southwestern Fronts

On December 31, 1915, a new inter-Allied council met in Chantilly with a view to achieving closer coordination of the Allies' efforts in the ensuing year. For the summer of 1916 it envisaged a joint Anglo-French offensive on the Somme and it charged the Russians with creating a diversion by taking the offensive on their front two weeks before the Anglo-French operation. But the Germans forestalled their adversaries. On February 21 they hurled massive forces against Verdun, which was the site of a battle of unprecedented violence and savagery that was to absorb all the forces at their disposal on the western front.

In order to counter the Germans' purposes the Russians unleashed a massive attack on March 18 in the region of Lake Narotch, at the junction of the northern and western fronts (see map facing page 311). Thus they immobilized all the German reserves on the eastern front and indeed, from March 22 to 30, caused the interruption of the enemy's assaults on Verdun. They waged their offensive under frightful conditions, on battlefields thoroughly drenched by the spring thaws and floods, "in mud and blood," as the Germans themselves attested. Their extremely heavy losses ran to a hundred thousand men.

Meanwhile the *Stavka* was preparing for the summer offensive proposed at the Chantilly conference. It decided to concentrate its effort on its western front and to carry out no more than mere diversions on its two other fronts, the northern and the southwestern. In consequence it redistributed its heavy artillery and munitions, both of which were still in very short supply. But the Italian army's reverses undid all the plans. General Cadorna, who was continuing to hold fast with the bulk of his force on the Isonzo, was suddenly flanked by the Austro-Hungarians in the middle of May. Having built up a concentration in the Trentino, they suddenly poured out between the Brenta and the Adige Rivers and placed the Italians in a tragic situation. Even as he hastily regrouped his forces, Cadorna was compelled to appeal to the *Stavka* for emergency help. Russia could offer effective assistance only by drawing the Austro-Hungarian forces away from him. For this purpose she must necessarily redirect all her efforts toward her south-western front, the nearest to the Italian, and assume the offensive as rapidly as possible. Thus the *Stavka* had no choice but to abandon its previously prepared campaign plans and mount an absolutely im-provised offensive.

It was in these unpropitious circumstances that the famous attack by Brusilov, the commander of the southwestern armies, was launched. Begun on June 1, it continued into early September and raged along the whole line running from the Pripyat to the Dniester, almost 375 versts long (see map facing page 311). In the beginning it succeeded in breaking the entire enemy front and driving a breach whose depth ranged from 28 to 75 versts. But the front did not wholly collapse, for it was rapidly reinforced with units drawn from the French, English, and Italian fronts, and even from the newly opened Macedonian front. More than thirty divisions of reinforcements, of which at least twenty-four came from the Anglo-French front and seven from the Italian, were thus thrown in against Brusilov's army. The best among them were turned toward the region of Kovel, the occupation of which enabled the Austrians and the Germans to stop the Russian offensive.

Although it could not achieve a decisive result, Brusilov's offensive had a major influence on the overall situation. It made for a real improvement in the position of the Italian army, it assisted the launch-ing of the Anglo-French offensive on the Somme, and it made up Rumania's mind to join the Allies.

It was at the end of August that Rumania entered the war. Unfor-tunately and most imprudently, she sent her troops into Transylvania and thus opened her right flank and her rear to the attacks of the enemy's combined forces. Russia had to turn to her aid. Russian troops were forced to enter Rumanian territory in order to pull together the remnants of the Rumanian army. The creation of a special Rumanian front imposed a new and onerous burden on Russia. Since the Ruman-ians themselves could provide only six infantry divisions and one caval-ry division, all of which occupied a sector barely 33 versts long, it was Russia that had to defend all the rest of a front that covered 469 versts from the south to the Black Sea (see map facing page 311). In January 1917 she had to transfer thirty-six infantry divisions and six cavalry divisions to this front—in other words, almost a quarter of her forces. The situation on the eastern front was thus considerably worsened, and the Russian armies, spread out beyond their capacities, completely lost their freedom of action.

Operations in the Caucasus and Persia in 1916

On the Caucasian front the Russians scored major gains in 1916. On February 16, after five days of attack, they won control of the fortress of Erzerum, the Turkish rampart. Two months later, on April 19, they occupied Trebizond, and this made it possible for their army to supply all its lacks and pursue its advance. Their operations in a new theater of war, Persia, were still more successful. Toward the end of May a small detachment of Cossacks thrust so far that it made contact with the British staff, which had left the Persian Gulf and was ascending the Tigris.

In sum, at the end of 1916 Russian troops were occupying Erzendjan, Moosh, and Bitlis in Asian Turkey and Hamadan in Persia; the only thought in the mind of the commander of the Caucasian army henceforth was to defend the territory that he had occupied.

The Exhaustion of the Army and the Nation at the End of 1916

A balance sheet of the Allies' achievements in 1916 would show that the chance of victory was slipping farther and farther away from the central powers. The mere fact that by the end of this year Germany was ardently hoping for the end of hostilities and the conclusion of a peace treaty is proof enough.

But these encouraging indications were visible only to those who were in a position to grasp the situation as a whole. They were not apparent to the masses; the masses knew nothing but the cruel life of the trenches, the futility of every attempt to cross barbed wire, the torrents of blood that flowed. The number of men under arms in Russia had already exceeded thirteen million, the number of dead two million, the toll of the wounded not fewer than four or even four and a half million. The officers and noncommissioned officers of some units had been replaced four or even six times. Even though far from all the eligible men in a population reckoned at 170 million had been taken into the armed forces, such a military endeavor in a country that in time of peace never took more than half its conscripts seemed to have reached the breaking point.

In addition, because of the lack of workers, the harvest was beginning to decline. Furthermore, the difficulties of communication with other countries and the inadequacy of the nation's industry were increasingly leading to an industrial crisis and an appalling disorganization in transport. The cost of living was rising rapidly and the population was suffering privations of every kind.

That was why the popular anger could only grow sharper against a government under which living conditions had become so harsh and that had long since ceased, in any case, to inspire confidence. The German command most adroitly exploited the war weariness and the anger against the government, which still stood firm against the execution of the most urgent reforms. During the summer the Germans organized a propaganda campaign and carried it out well enough to shake the Russian soldier's inner discipline and his desire to continue the war.

The Final Russian Offensives in 1917

The thinking element in the Russian army saw a new force for victory in the revolution that overthrew the tsarist system in March 1917. The provisional government shared its view: Russia should launch a new offensive to demonstrate her will to pursue the war to final victory in concert with her Allies.

The organization of this offensive encountered tremendous difficulties: for one thing, the swift demoralization that swept through the army shattered discipline; for another, the internal political situation deprived the provisional government of the power and the authority that it needed. Nevertheless, thanks to the efforts of War Minister Alexander F. Kerensky and the Russian armies, an attack of quite broad proportions was mounted against the Austro-Hungarians on the southwestern front. Begun on July 1,* it raged on both banks of the Dniester. The electrified troops, led by courageous officers at the sacrifice of their lives, succeeded in crushing the enemy, took several thousand prisoners, and pushed as far as the Lomnitsa River after having captured the cities of Halicz and Kalisz (see map facing page 311). But at the first sign of difficulty they fell back toward their own border as quickly as they had advanced, and the people's enthusiasm sank.

Attempts at offensives on the other fronts produced even punier results. A German counterattack early in September in the regions of Riga and Friedrichstadt forced the retreat of the Russian Twelfth Army, which constituted the right wing on the Wenden line, and gave the enemy control of the lower Dvina. In October, without too much effort, the Germans succeeded in occupying the islands of Oesel and Dagö, the possession of which was essential to them for the defense of the Riga region.

Later military events on the Russian front were of even lesser inter-

*It was known in Russia as "the offensive of June 18" (old style).

est. The untrammeled propaganda of the partisans of peace, which was fostered by the Bolshevik government and eagerly accepted by the masses, led to the total disintegration of the Russian army, exhausted by the long ordeals of the war.

On March 3, 1918 peace was signed by four delegates of the Bolshevik government: Sokolnikov, Chicherin, Petrovsky, and Karakhan. On that date eighty divisions of the central powers, more than half of them German, held the eastern front in Europe. This front ran from Narva to Orsha in the center; on the left flank German troops were occupying Finland; on the right, Austrian and German forces were established on the whole territory of the Ukraine, as far as Rostov and the shore of the Black Sea; Turkish troops, who had gone over to the attack, were occupying Transcaucasia.

The conscientious elements in the Russian army had taken no part in the transactions that led to the peace of Brest-Litovsk, and they refused to recognize them. Military experts consulted on the peace terms proposed by Germany had pronounced them unacceptable; furthermore, they had categorically refused to sign any document relative to a cessation of hostilities. The ratification of the peace treaty by the Bolshevik congress forced the most active elements of the Russian army to scatter into the border areas, there to carry on by force of arms the struggle for their fatherland.

CHAPTER 7

Nicholas II (1894–1917): The Reign Concluded

[PAUL MILIUKOV]

------------------◄◙►◦------------------

I / THE FOURTH DUMA AND THE OMENS OF REVOLUTION (1912–1917)

The Elections to the Fourth Duma

The Kokovtsev Cabinet, which had lost faith in the Octobrists, went into the elections in alliance with the nationalists and the extreme right. It was determined to employ every pressure tactic allowed to it by the electoral law of 3/16 June 1907, and particularly the authority enjoyed by the clergy. Inasmuch as the law permitted the government to divide the voters on the basis of their social class, it decided that the clergy should form a separate group and that the Holy Synod and the diocesan bishops should exert pressure on the voting priests. All priests without exception were instructed to take part in the election campaign and to vote for the government's nominees in all polls— that is, for the designation of electors and for that of deputies. In spite of the protests of Metropolitan Anton of Petersburg, the church was thus forced into politics. The priests, a number of whom were chosen as electors of the second degree in the basic electoral assemblies, con- stituted quite a large sector in the provincial electoral colleges, and in certain cases they were the decisive factor in the final selection of dep- uties. Nevertheless the government failed to win the result that it was seeking, first of all because its shameless pressure on the electors often drove them into voting for opposition candidates, and, second, because the priests who became electors were isolated in the electoral colleges of the provinces and were unable to force the election of any large number of clerics as deputies.

The elections resulted in decisive victory for none of the three groups—right, center, and left—that had taken part in them. They were in fact a defeat for the center: having forfeited the support of the government, as well as that of some of the landed proprietors' electors whose sympathies for the opposition had mounted under the third Duma, the Octobrists lost fifty seats, which went to candidates of both the left and the right; the party had only ninety-eight members in the new Duma. But the government was unable to obtain a nationalist reactionary majority that could back it up.

The Parties in the Duma and the Continuation of Reactionary Policy

The composition of the fourth Duma was quite different from that of the third: the center was weak and the two wings were strong; the government parties, which did not command an absolute majority, held 185 seats, while the combined opposition parties held 150; and there were also the 98 Octobrists.* Nevertheless, in spite of their numerical weakness, the Octobrists in the fourth Duma retained the influence that they had had in the third. In fact it was impossible to form a majority without their collaboration. As masters of the situation they maneuvered adroitly between the left and the right; sometimes they joined the right to back the government, sometimes they added their votes to those of the left, as for example at the start of the second session, when they helped to win the adoption of a constitutional motion: "Legislative labors cannot be prosecuted in a normal fashion unless the government and the legislative bodies sincerely cooperate in the realization of the principles set forth in the imperial manifesto of 17/30 October 1905 and in the establishment of strict legality."

The first two sessions took place in an atmosphere of international tension and internal reaction.

While, in foreign affairs, the victory of the Balkan states over Turkey was a diplomatic success for Russia, which had striven so hard to create the Balkan union, the rupture of this union and the war that followed it were a defeat for her. Her hesitations during this crisis, in which she did not intervene militarily, were the result of her unreadiness to support a European war. The military reforms initiated under the influence of the Duma were far from realization; the methods of the War Ministry, which not only the opposition but also the Octobrist center in the third Duma had already castigated, had hardly altered; the war minister himself, General Sukhomlinov, who enjoyed

*Approximately seventeen deputies had no party affiliation.

the special favor of the tsar, was not equal to his responsibilities and was under much criticism.

At home the government was pursuing its reactionary policy. The tsar removed Kokovtsev on 31 January/13 February 1914 and replaced him with Goremykin. This appointment was tantamount to a new pledge to the right and marked a resurgence of reaction. Efforts to restrict the rights of the Duma through arbitrary interpretations of law soon became more frequent, and the rumor was prevalent that the government was planning, through a new *coup d'état*, to convert both legislative Chambers into mere consultative assemblies. At the same time the Ministry of the Interior, now headed by Nikolai Maklakov, was imposing one harassment after another on the nation and paralyzing the operations of the autonomous local governments.

The War and the "Sacred Union" of Parties and Government in 1914

Although isolated groups belonging to the "militarist" party that surrounded the war minister looked with favor on the possibility of armed conflict with Germany, the government, the Duma, and Russian public opinion yearned for peace. In spite of all the omens of its imminence that were visible before August 1, 1914, the outbreak of war caught both public opinion and the government by surprise.

The people looked on it as a war of defense, and the entire press, without regard to political orientation, adjured all parties to unite round the government and to put aside their divergent programs in order to form a solid front against the enemy. The day after Germany's declaration of war the tsar issued a manifesto in which he voiced the hope that "in this terrible year of ordeals internal quarrels will be forgot, that the alliance between the tsar and the people will be strengthened, and that Russia, in total unity, will hurl back the impudent aggression of the enemy." Political parties and certain social organizations endorsed this call for putting aside "internal quarrels." In a manifesto published on the same day as the tsar's, the central committee of the Cadet party asserted:

Whatever our attitude toward the government's internal policy, our first duty is to preserve our country one and indivisible and to defend its position as a world power, which the enemy is challenging. Let us defer for another time our internal discords, let us not give the enemy the slightest pretext for relying on the differences that divide us, and let us resolutely remember that for the moment our primary and single task is to support our soldiers by inspiring them with confidence in our just cause, with serene courage, and with faith in the victory of our arms.

It was most significant that, as soon as the peril of the international situation became known, the strikes that had broken out in the factories of Petersburg during the first half of July, just when President Poincaré of France arrived, were called off at once. But it was in the special session of the Duma on 26 July/8 August that the "sacred union" of the political parties and the government was most impressively demonstrated. After speeches by the president of the Duma, Premier Goremykin, Foreign Minister Sazonov, and Finance Minister Bark, deputies representing the various national minorities—Poles, Latvians, Lithuanians, Jews, Moslems, Germans from the Baltic provinces and the colonies on the Volga—took the floor one after another to proclaim their loyalty, their devotion to the Russian state and nation, and their eagerness to dedicate themselves to the common task, the defense of the fatherland against the invader. Then the representatives of the various parliamentary groups, particularly those of the two major opposition sectors—Efremov in the name of the Progressives* and Miliukov on behalf of the Cadets—arose to state categorically that "the responsible opposition" was offering the government its unqualified support: "We are doing battle to deliver our fatherland from foreign invasion," Miliukov declared, "to liberate Europe and Slavism from Germanic hegemony, to deliver the entire world from the intolerable burden of ever increasing armaments. . . . In this struggle we are united; we set no terms, we demand nothing; we simply cast our resolute will to conquer on the scales of battle."

In the early days of the war the zemstvo and municipality representatives decided to form a Zemstvo Union and a Municipality Union. These organizations turned their efforts at first to help for the sick and wounded; later their activities were expanded to helping to provision the armies. On 12/25 August the government zemstvo representatives met in Moscow and as director general of the Zemstvo Union they elected Prince G. E. Lvov, who had distinguished himself during the Japanese war by his organizational talent.

The proclamation that Grand Duke Nikolai Nikolayevitch as generalissimo addressed to the Poles on 14/27 August heightened the impression that government and people were closely and effectively united. The enthusiasm that took hold of all sectors of Russian society in the first weeks of the war spread even beyond the country's borders. A large number of exiles showed the same spirit of dedication to the cause of a defensive war: in a letter to *The Times* of London, Burtsev asserted that "this war has become a national war for Russia"; another

*The Progressives were a group midway between the Octobrists and the Cadets.

influential exile, Prince P. A. Kropotkin, endorsed the same view, and some Social Democrats such as G. V. Plekhanov also took a resolute position in favor of the war.

During the end of the summer and the whole of the autumn, this state of mind was dominant in the greater part of Russian society, not only among the representatives of the liberal and democratic parties but even among the Revolutionary Socialists and the Social Democrats (Mensheviki). Public enthusiasm could not be shaken, in spite of the terrible defeat inflicted by Hindenburg on Samsonov's army at Tannenberg on 11/24–16/29 August, in spite of the wretched organization of army supply services, in spite of the chaos of the medical services.* The support that public organizations provided to the armies by helping to evacuate the wounded, setting up hospitals, establishing ambulances and canteens in combat zones, proved to soldiers and officers that, whatever the differences of opinion that divided it, the Russian nation was united in its heart with those who at the front were defending it against German invasion.

The Disruption of the "Sacred Union" by Military Defeats and Reactionary Government Policy (1914–1915)

Unhappily, in spite of the tsar's appeal to "put aside internal quarrels," the government's domestic policy did not change. The shortness of the first wartime session of the Duma, convoked for a single sitting, was broadly disillusioning. Satisfied that it had won the support of the left, the Cabinet was in no hurry to summon back the people's representatives; it preferred to take advantage of the circumstances in order to govern alone, generously employing the famous Article LXXXVII of the basic laws authorizing rule by decree. Finances, both as to policy and as to credit circulation, military censorship, help for soldiers' families, changes and additions to military regulations, alterations in tax rates, the creation of new taxes, customs duties, commercial and industrial legislation, and many other legislative functions of the utmost importance were taken out of the Chambers' hands and decided on in feverish haste by the Cabinet, then put into practice, under Article LXXXVII, by mere imperial ukase. In fact the tsar was making laws alone; it was in effect a reversion to autocracy. Nikolai Maklakov, the minister of the interior, was adamant in his attitude of defiance of the nation. He refused to ratify the elections of a large number of members of zemstvo staffs and city councils. He was continually erect-

---

*The wounded, who had to endure long waits to be evacuated, were transported under unhygienic conditions and died by the hundreds on the trains.

ing obstacles to the Zemstvo and Municipality Unions. When Galicia, a Ukrainian-Polish province of the Austrian monarchy, was occupied by the victorious Russian armies, the administrative officials who were dispatched to the area placed an interdict on everything Ukrainian and finally arrested and banished the Uniate Metropolitan Sheptitsky, as well as various other notables. The officials' church policy, which was aimed at the conversion of the Uniates to Orthodoxy, led to deplorable clashes not only with the Uniate clergy but in some areas with the Galician population itself.

Eager to delay the assembly of the Duma as long as possible, the government had decided not to summon it until the autumn of 1915. But public opinion turned uneasy, because there was a growing rumor that reactionary groups had given the tsar a memorandum in which it was argued that the continuation of the war, the tremendous sacrifices that it required, and disorganization at the rear could lead to internal complications and serve to unleash a revolutionary movement; therefore they openly demanded the conclusion of a separate peace with Germany, whose political and social system was much more closely akin to that of the Russian Empire than the democratic society of the western Allies. Under the urgent insistence of the president of the Duma and the representatives of its parties, the government was forced to yield, and the assembly's return was scheduled for the end of January/middle of February 1915. This session lasted three days, two of which were devoted to the study of the budget. Although the budget committee allowed the subject to be discussed as fully as was required, although it directed debate not only toward the financial law itself but also toward the government's general policy, the Duma itself, which was short of time and could allow only fifteen minutes to each group's spokesman, was obliged by force of circumstances to cut matters short. In a public sitting the "sacred union" between government and assembly was maintained. It was only in the closed hearings of the national defense committee that government policy was subjected to criticism. After they had listened to statements by Foreign Minister Sazonov and War Minister Sukhomlinov—the general insisted that the army was adequately supplied with ammunition, food, and equipment—Miliukov and Shingarev attacked the government's position toward the national minorities and reproached it for its infringement of the "sacred union," the preservation of which was essential to the success of the war; they concentrated much of their fire on the work of Maklakov as minister of the interior and called for his resignation.

In the spring the shortage of ammunition, especially of artillery shells, the lack of which had already made itself painfully apparent during the bloody winter fighting in the Carpathians, created a threatening situation. When the Germans launched their offensive in Galicia, the rear and the front alike acknowledged that the Russian armies owed their defeat to the inadequacies of their supply system. Parliamentary quarters and public opinion embarked on a savage campaign against Sukhomlinov, whose reassuring statements before the national defense committee during the winter had "betrayed" the confidence of the Duma.

The Growth of Discontent and the Disorganization of the Economy (1915)

Under the influence of the military defeats there was an unmistakable shift in public opinion. Little by little the "sacred union" was supplanted by a sentiment of growing anger against the criminal indifference of the government, which was leaving the Russian army without ammunition and other war material in the face of a formidable adversary. This resentment spread through all sectors of society. The wounded, sent home on brief furloughs after their hospital stays, revealed the cruel conditions under which the army was fighting, and they declared that it had been betrayed by the government. The trial of Colonel Myasoyedov,* on charges of supplying information to the enemy, corroborated the rumor, which had raged through the whole country, that treason had penetrated into the very heart of the army. In Moscow, toward the end of May/middle of June, popular indignation culminated in the looting of shops and stores belonging to persons with German or other non-Russian names, and, thanks to the connivance of the police, which looked on this as a useful diversion for the people's resentment, the pillage was on a very large scale. The floods of refugees fleeing before the enemy's advance seeped little by little into the interior of the country, carrying with them the tales of the privations that they had suffered, spreading disease, and congesting the cities. The high command having ordered the evacuation of all villagers from areas abandoned to the enemy, most of them had had to give up their homes; the Treasury was compelled to assist them, and this was a grievous burden on it.

Public apprehension and anger were aggravated in direct proportion to the mounting evidences of the increasing disorganization of the national economy, especially in the field of transport. Since the

*An officer of the secret intelligence service.

railway system could not meet the needs of moving the huge quantities of material required for the supply of the armies, the Ministry of Communications was forced to impose more and more curbs on individual travel and commercial shipments by rail. The home market was adversely affected by this, and various items vanished from commerce. The high cost of living created hardship in the large cities. Both inflation and the curbs on transport contributed to raising the prices of all basic goods. The mobilization of several million workers and peasants in the prime of life had deprived industry, commerce, and agriculture of their indispensable labor force at the very moment when war imposed on them the utmost efforts to keep the army supplied with arms and ammunition, equipment, and food.

The disorganization of the economy disturbed not only public opinion, which had long insisted on the necessity of correcting it through methodical action, but also the government. Under the influence of military defeats primarily caused by the disorganization at home, the Cabinet decided to meet the nation's wishes by summoning the Duma for 19 July/1 August and modifying the administration of economic affairs: a Cabinet decision of 7/20 June 1915, which the tsar approved, established a "special council for the coordination of measures to assure the material and military supply of the army."

The congress of industrial and trade representatives, the city councils of Moscow and Petrograd, the joint conference of the directors of the Zemstvo and Municipality Unions, the similar conference of mayors and zemstvo delegates—all were clear manifestations of the same view in public opinion. Under this pressure the government decided not only to convene the Duma but also to oust avowed partisans of reactionary policy from the Cabinet. Maklakov, Sukhomlinov, Sabler (attorney general of the Holy Synod), and Justice Minister Shcheglovitov were forced to resign even before the Duma met; those whom public opinion justly held responsible with Sukhomlinov for the Russian armies' reverses were stripped of all their posts. But the names of the new ministers showed that the government was not genuinely concerned with altering its policy. Although General Polivanov, who succeeded Sukhomlinov, was popular in the army and Parliament—Count P. N. Ignatyev, a liberal, did not become minister of public education until the winter of 1916, after Kasso's death—Prince Shcherbatov as minister of the interior, A. Khvostov as minister of justice, and A. Samarin as attorney general of the Holy Synod were not the men who could make it easier for the government to be reconciled with the Duma and public opinion.

The Offers of the Duma to the Government and the Creation of the "Progressive Bloc" (1915)

When the Duma reconvened on 19 July/1 August, it found itself confronting a partly revised Cabinet, but the premier was still old Goremykin, who did not have the assembly's sympathies and who was incapable of putting a policy of conciliation into practice.

After the government had presented its statements, a large majority in the Duma—the whole of the opposition, the Octobrist center, and even the moderate groups on the right—adopted a resolution that declared the necessity of changing the course of domestic policy and forming "a ministry enjoying the confidence of the country"; it also listed the essential internal reforms and stated that union between the government and the country was necessary in order to support the army and achieve victory. Only some of the nationalists joined the extreme right in the negative vote. This marked the creation of a large and stable majority held together by the desire to assist the government in organizing the material support of the army and achieving a "ministry of public trust" and a program of liberal reforms. The Duma began by adopting bills for the creation of special committees assigned to directing military supply services and combatting the country's economic disorganization. The law of 17/30 August, following the model of the special council of 7/20 June, established four "special committees" for national defense, for fuel supply to transport, public institutions and enterprises engaged in national defense, for rations, and for the transport of fuel and food required for the armies' needs; it later added a fifth committee for "help to refugees." Presided over by the appropriate ministers, their memberships consisted not only of representatives of the government but also of elected representatives of the Duma and the Imperial Council; thus both Chambers were enlisted in the work of maintaining military supplies and the battle against the economic problems created by the war.

During this summer session, which coincided with the loss of Galicia, Poland, and Lithuania by the Russian army, parliamentary circles evinced more and more interest in preserving the party union and the majority achieved in the first sitting. Put forward by the opposition, the concept of establishing a stable parliamentary majority was warmly received by the center and some of the nationalists. Only the remainder of the nationalists, part of the extreme right, and the Social Democrats and the Workers, who had a different conception not only of general policy but even of the war, refused to give their allegiance to it. The negotiations conducted by the representatives of the opposition, the center, and two of the right-wing groups that had voted for the establishment of a "ministry of public confidence" resulted, in spite of the obstacles encountered in the course of drawing up a joint program, in the creation of a solid parliamentary bloc that became known as the "Progressive bloc." Its program, made public on 26 August/8 September, embraced two principles of general policy: first, the formation of a homogeneous government composed of leaders enjoying the country's confidence and resolved to carry out as expeditiously as possible a program framed in agreement with the two Chambers; second, the radical alteration of administrative procedures based on suspicion toward every independent public activity; in particular: strict adherence to legality by the government, the elimination of interference by military and civil authorities in matters not bearing directly on military operations; the replacement of local governmental personnel and the adoption of a reasonable and logical policy that could safeguard internal order and avert conflicts of social class and national minority. It also listed a whole series of measures to be taken for its execution; first of all those of an administrative nature: a general amnesty for political and religious crimes and misdemeanors, the recall of political exiles, the end of religious persecutions, the grant of autonomy to Poland, the abrogation of the legal restrictions imposed on the Jews, the prohibition of persecution of Ukrainians in Russia and Galicia, the reestablishment of the professional trade unions. Then there were legislative proposals, which included the grant of completely equal rights to the peasants, the creation of the cantonal zemstvo, and municipal and zemstvo reforms. The example of the Duma was followed by the Imperial Council. In that Chamber an established majority adopted the program of the "Progressive bloc." Weaker than the majority in the Duma, it was adequate nevertheless to assure the approval of bills already passed by the Duma.

The reactionary right was of course made anxious by the creation of the "Progressive bloc." The council of the Union of the Nobility, which feared some change in governmental policy, called on Goremykin by letter to remain faithful to the principles of the reactionaries. To demand a new domestic policy, it argued, was to seek to profit by the difficult circumstances of the war in order to attempt to achieve a program of liberal reforms that "may lead to new disorders with the purpose of changing the political system in Russia." The government itself was divided as to the policy to be adopted. Premier Goremykin, who was frightened by the emergence of the "Progressive bloc" in the

Duma, made every effort to seduce the right wing of the parliamentary majority away from the opposition, and he strove to establish a right-wing majority prepared to back him. On the other hand, several ministers, including Sazonov, Krivosheyin, minister of agriculture, and Kharitonov, the state comptroller, announced their readiness to seek the support of a moderate liberal majority. The result was a crisis within the Cabinet itself; only some of Goremykin's right-wing colleagues went along with him, while the majority of the ministers tended toward a willingness to satisfy the wishes of the Duma and make certain of government collaboration with the parliamentary majority by changing the composition of the Cabinet.

The Tsar's Commitment to Intransigence under the Influence of the Tsarina and Rasputin (1915)

At this point Tsarina Alexandra Fyodorovna appeared on the stage. She was under the domination of a man who played a major political part for a few years before the war and even during it. He was a Siberian peasant of obscure antecedents who had given himself the title of *starets* (man of God) and who was known everywhere by the nickname of Rasputin ("the libertine"), which had been bestowed on him by the people of his own region. He was one of the blackest figures in the history of modern Russia. Thanks to the relations that he had been able to form in court circles, he had managed to make his way into the tsarina's confidence and to assure himself of her respect and her devotion by his charlatan's prophecies and the clever employment of his "magnetic influence." The tsarina followed his counsels blindly, not only in her family life—Rasputin exploited the illness of Tsarevitch Alexis Nikolayevitch to enhance his own influence—but also in the domain of politics generally. The ascendancy that this miserable fraud exercised over her and, through her, over the tsar was a powerful weapon that was used by the clique of courtiers to influence appointments to posts at top government levels and thus to affect the fate of the country as a whole. Those who were currying favor at court without discomfort over the means to be chosen were certain to succeed if the all-powerful *starets* condescended to lend them his support, and candidates for Cabinet posts crowded his reception room, for his goodwill was the *sine qua non* of the attainment of power. The correspondence between the tsar and the tsarina, made public after 1917, showed that the tsar, who became ever more amenable to his wife's counsels, consulted her on every aspect of foreign and domestic policy and that Alexandra Fyodorovna made every effort to direct her husband's feeble will. It was in fact under the influence of the tsarina, herself inspired by Rasputin and a convert to the most extreme conservatism, that in the autumn of 1915 Nicholas II made two decisions whose consequences changed the destiny of his country.

The first of these was the rescript of 24 August/6 September 1915, which relieved Grand Duke Nikolai Nikolayevitch of his post as generalissimo, and by which the tsar appointed himself to the supreme command of the armed forces. After the summer defeats the grand duke had lost the confidence of both the country and the army, and his removal was a necessity. But the tsar declared that "the duty of serving my country that God has laid on me requires me, now that the enemy has penetrated within the borders of the Empire, to assume the command of the armies . . ."

The second fatal decision was the ukase of 3/16 September of the same year, which suspended the powers of the Duma and, for the first time in Russia's constitutional history, did not, in spite of the basic laws, fix a date for the next session of the legislature. This ukase, which Goremykin had procured after a visit to the tsar at his military headquarters, ratified the triumph of the right-wing minority in the Cabinet and was taken as a challenge by Parliament and public opinion. Like the rescript of 24 August/6 September, it proved that the tsarina was making every effort to imbue the tsar with the mysticism that had taken hold of the entire imperial family and that was cleverly fostered by Rasputin and his backers. It marked the beginning of a new period in the history of the war: thereafter the tsar and the government abandoned any attempt at agreement with the majority of the Duma and of public opinion and made their final commitment to the fatal course that would lead to revolution.

The Rupture Between the Nation and the Government and the Assassination of Rasputin (1915–1916)

The suspension of the Duma entailed the successive retirements of those ministers who had favored an accord with the parliamentary majority and announced their opposition to the tsar's assumption of the functions of supreme commander. One after another they departed: Prince Shcherbatov, minister of the interior; Samarin, attorney general of the Holy Synod; Krivosheyin, minister of agriculture; then, a few months later, Polivanov, the popular minister of war, and Foreign Minister Sazonov, whose removal undermined the influence of Russia in the Allied states, where he enjoyed a great standing. They were replaced with candidates chosen by the tsarina and Rasputin, resolute advocates of a policy of reaction like A. N. Khvostov, a member of the extreme right in the Duma, who became minister of the interior. That Goremykin himself had to yield as premier to Shtyurmer (Stürmer) was not because he was considered inappropriate to head the new Cabinet but because Rasputin's group was insistent on having one of its own men as premier. Shtyurmer was the former deputy minister of the interior who had dissolved the zemstvo of Tver. The tsar and the tsarina, who looked on him as one of the most faithful servitors of the imperial family and a reliable defender of the throne, placed all their trust in him.

The appointment of so avowed a reactionary made any accord with the Duma impossible. When he also took over the Foreign Ministry after Sazonov's removal, parliamentary quarters were torn by the deepest anxiety. For the whole fate of Russian foreign policy was at stake. The new foreign minister was in fact so profoundly ignorant of the complicated problems of international affairs and even of the language of diplomacy that he had to restrict himself to sitting in silence while his deputy foreign minister, Neratov, dealt with the Allies' ambassadors. The whole year of 1916 was cloaked in an atmosphere of discord between Parliament and government. The Duma was summoned for only cursory sessions, during which the parliamentary majority attempted to realize the legislative program of the "Progressive bloc" and bitterly criticized Shtyurmer's reactionary domestic policy. The membership of the Cabinet was constantly being revised; it was like a game of ministerial leapfrog. This was one of the characteristic aspects of the period; the nearer the revolution approached, the more often the ministers were changed, but none of them made the slightest alteration in the basic spirit of government policy, as was proved by the appointment of A. D. Protopopov as minister of the interior to replace Khvostov, who had fallen into disgrace. Vice President of the Duma—it was in this capacity that he had taken part in the journey of Duma and Imperial Council members to the Allied countries and the western front—a member of the Octobrist party and the "Progressive bloc," Protopopov deserted his former friends when he became a minister and delivered himself into the hands of reaction. He owed his appointment to Rasputin's influence, and he brought to the performance of his ministerial duties the proverbial zeal of the convert.

The abyss that had opened between the whole nation and the government grew deeper and deeper. Even court figures saw the perils in the course to which the nation was being driven by the irresponsible individuals who dominated the tsar through the intermediary of his wife. Some members of the imperial family tendered a memorandum to Nicholas II in an attempt to call his attention to the mistakes in his government's policy and the necessity of making concessions to the Duma. The conflict between the government and the nation reached its peak in the autumn of 1916, during the sittings of the Duma. These began on 1/14 November in a climate of mutual irritation. This time the anger of the Duma, which was manifest in the deputies' speeches, burst out not only against the government but also against the individuals who were the true culprits in the rupture between the government and the Chambers. From the floor of the Duma, P. N. Miliukov enumerated one by one the members of the camarilla that surrounded the tsarina as the chief instigators of the policy of reaction. When he had catalogued all the reactionary steps taken by the government in contravention of the will of the parliamentary majority and public opinion, he concluded: "What is this? imbecility or treason?" Shulgin, a nationalist from the right wing of the "Progressive bloc," who spoke next, seconded his denunciations. The government made the enormous error of taking advantage of its right of military censorship to forbid the publication of the speeches delivered on the opening day of the Duma. Readers who turned to the next day's newspapers for the news of the session found only empty white space. This only further excited their curiosity; and so, in spite of the censorship, the texts of the banned speeches were circulated not only within Russia but at the front with the speed of lightning, and the whole nation knew the charges that had been made on the floor of the Duma.

Shtyurmer paid for the errors of his government by his downfall. But the new premier, A. Trepov, who belonged to the closed circle of top officialdom, was no better suited to please the majority in Parliament and the public. Every effort that he made to curry favor with the Duma and the press was a fiasco. The deputies received him frigidly; the members of the Socialist opposition made a ritual of continually interrupting his speech, and even the news, which he announced in the middle of it, that the Allies had assented to Russian possession of Constantinople and the Straits did not produce the effect on which he had counted. The session ended on 17/30 December in an atmosphere of general anxiety and disorder, for the rupture between the government and the Duma had been only made worse.

That night there was an orgy in the palace of Prince Felix Yusupov. During the debauchery potassium cyanide was mixed with the cakes and wine served to the inspiration of the reaction, Rasputin, the man of God, but he was too strong for it. He was then shot to death. The assassins—Prince Yusupov and Deputy Purishkevitch, whose accomplice was Grand Duke Dmitri Pavlovitch—put the corpse into a car, drove to the Petrovsky Park, and threw it into the water. The news of the assassination spread at once, and the entire country greeted the death of Rasputin as a supreme warning to the camarilla and the leaders of the government.

The Shadow of Revolution (1917)

A *coup d'état* at any moment was rumored; it was whispered that the conspirators, among whom were officers in the frontline armies— one of those mentioned was General Krymov, another was Aleksyeyev, both of whom were regarded as capable of taking such an initiative— sought to compel Nicholas II to abdicate in favor of the tsarevitch and appoint the tsar's brother, Grand Duke Mikhail Aleksandrovitch, as regent. The plan for a regency by the grand duke was discussed in those parliamentary circles from which a few weeks later the provisional government was drawn. In addition every means was resorted to in the effort to make some impression on the tsar, who had deliberately insulated himself from the realities of politics and stubbornly confined himself to the mystical atmosphere of his intimate circle. Early in January 1917, Sir George Buchanan, the British ambassador, in violation of all the rules of diplomatic propriety, broached the subject of Russian domestic policy during an imperial audience at Tsarskoye Selo and asserted that this policy must be changed by seeking alliance with the Duma and public opinion. But no argument could move the tsar. Far from even contemplating the concessions that were required, the reactionary camarilla that surrounded the tsarina sought on the contrary to take advantage of the parliamentary vacation to strengthen the right wing of the Cabinet, which was led by Protopopov. Premier Trepov was compelled to resign on 27 December 1916/9 January 1917 because he had attempted to reach an understanding with the majority in the Duma by getting rid of Protopopov and the other ministers opposed to the "Progressive bloc." Trepov was succeeded by old Prince Golitsyn, whose busy participation in the charitable endeavors sponsored by the tsarina had determined his appointment. This change was sufficient to demonstrate that the tsar and the tsarina were firmly resolved to proceed with their policy of reaction. There could be no further doubt after the tsar authorized Golitsyn to postpone the return of the Duma from 12/25 January to 14/27 February.

The resentment aroused by this policy and by the tsarina's interference not only in domestic but also in foreign affairs fired the entire nation, the army as much as all the classes of civilian society. From the grand dukes, who wrote to Nicholas II in protest against the influence wielded over Russian policy by irresponsible individuals, down to the merest frontline private, who felt that he was being betrayed, the whole nation was convinced that the court and the reactionary camarilla were inevitably dragging Russia down to catastrophe. In February the evidences of the anger of the masses were unmistakable. A demonstration had been organized in Petrograd for the day when the Duma was to reconvene, 14/27 February; a procession of workers was supposed to parade through the city, present itself at the Duma, and, in the name of the working class, submit a series of political demands, particularly one for a government answerable to the Lower House. That the demonstration did not take place was the result of the success of the leaders of the "Progressive bloc" in persuading the workers to call it off; the progressives had every reason to believe that in actuality the idea of this demonstration, which might have led to grave clashes, had been originated by the political police department of the Ministry of the Interior.

But what they had been able to avert on 14/27 February erupted a few days later. The workers' disorders, which began on 24 February/ 9 March and which were brought on by the lack of food in the capital, were transformed into a formidable revolutionary movement that was joined by the regiments of the Petrograd garrison.

II / THE FEBRUARY/MARCH REVOLUTION (27 FEBRUARY/12 MARCH–25 OCTOBER/7 NOVEMBER 1917)

The history of the February Revolution can be divided with considerable accuracy into four periods of two months each.

In the first period, under the provisional government that was set up on the fifth day of the revolution, 3/16 March, and that remained in office until 5/18 May, the representatives of the bourgeois party and those of the entire Socialist bloc were locked in a deathgrip struggle, principally over the issue of war or peace.

The second period, under the second provisional government or first coalition government, from 6/19 May to 2/15 July, was taken up by the struggle between the moderate Socialist parties, which, by agreement with the Soviet of Workers' and Soldiers' Deputies, supported the government, and the Bolsheviki, who launched an armed revolt in Petrograd from 3/16 to 5/18 July.

The third phase, which began with a long Cabinet crisis, resolved only on 24 July/6 August, was marked by the formation of the second coalition government (24 July/6 August–26 August/8 September) and by that government's vacillations as it was buffeted by the winds of the right and the left; although the rightist parties reacted against the July phase and initially gained the upper hand, they lost their influence when Kornilov launched his insurrection.

The fourth period began with the third Cabinet crisis, which was also the longest, lasting until the formation of the third and final coalition government on 27 September/7 October. Under this government, which endured exactly one month, until the Bolshevik revolution of 25 October/7 November, the Bolsheviki built up an unchallengeable superiority in the capital's garrison and the Soviet of Workers' and Soldiers' Deputies, succeeded in thoroughly discrediting the moderate Socialists among the masses, and organized their victory.

Thus the political conflict that was carried on under the four governments born of the February Revolution led, after the ouster of a middle-class Cabinet, to the successive rises to power of a bourgeois-democratic coalition, the Socialists, and the Bolsheviki, while the revolution, as it spread among the masses, led to the collapse of the army and the progressive disintegration of the country.

The February/March Revolution and the Abdication of the Tsar

During the morning of 27 February/12 March, while the members of the Imperial Duma were meeting in the Tauride Palace to be officially apprised of the tsar's ukase suspending their labors, a mutiny that was totally unrelated to this ukase broke out in the barracks of the Petrograd regiments, first in the Volynsky and Litovsky Regiments and then in the Pavlovsky and Preobrazhensky Regiments of the guard. The soldiers seized control of the arsenal, occupied the Fortress of SS. Peter and Paul, liberated all political and common-law prisoners alike, set fire to the Palace of Justice and the headquarters of the political police, etc. As soon as they learned what had happened, the members of the Duma in a private meeting elected a provisional committee of their own colleagues "to restore order and establish contact with the persons and organizations that have taken part in the rising." But toward evening, when the sweep of the revolutionary movement became known, this provisional committee felt obliged to take into its own hands the power that the tsarist government, which had completely lost its head, had allowed to get out of its hands. That evening a meeting was held in the Tauride Palace, hastily organized by the Socialist and worker groups of the Soviet of Workers' Deputies. They decided to enlarge their ranks with the Soldiers' Deputies from the rebellious regiments. Even though it was thrust into the background by the motley crowd that swiftly overran the premises of the Duma, the provisional committee continued to make its arrangements and sent its emissaries to all departments.

The Cabinet and the tsar's brother, Grand Duke Mikhail, sent a telegram to General Headquarters to persuade Nicholas II to appoint some leading figure enjoying universal confidence to form a parliamentary ministry. Meekly yielding to the tsarina's advice and paying no attention to the arguments advanced by General Aleksyeyev, Nicholas refused, ordered the execution of "decisive measures to crush the revolutionary movement," and sent General Ivanov to Petrograd with dictatorial powers. With the same obstinacy, in spite of the most urgent counsel that he remain with the army, the tsar decided to go to Tsarskoye Selo, where he wanted to rejoin his wife and his ailing children.

Meanwhile the movement in Petrograd was becoming better organized. On 28 February/13 March the mutinous regiments, led by their officers, presented themselves before the Duma to announce their allegiance to the revolution; food supplies for the capital were assured; steps were taken to prevent the imperial train from reaching Tsarskoye Selo, and at the Dno station the tsar had to turn back toward Pskov. Moscow also joined the movement. The leaders of the armies recognized that it would be impossible to withdraw troops from the front without disrupting the defense. It was under these conditions that on 1/14 March the provisional committee proceeded to form a revolutionary provisional government. The unchallenged leader of the municipal and zemstvo organizations, Prince G. E. Lvov, was chosen as premier; the majority of his ministers consisted of the most prominent spokesmen of the Duma parties that had constituted the "Progressive bloc": V. L. Lvov (right wing), Godnev (Octobrist), Monovalov (Progressive), Miliukov and Shingarev (Cadets), Nekrasov (left Cadet). One among them, Kerensky, was a member of the Workers' party and a Revolutionary Socialist who had agreed to accept the Ministry of Justice in spite of the Socialists' refusal to take part in a bourgeois government; the other ministers, chosen outside the Duma, were Gutchkov, a member of the Imperial Council (Octobrist), Tereshchenko (independent), a young member of the clandestine conferences that had preceded the revolution, and Professor Manuilov of Moscow (Cadet). That evening the provisional committee of the Duma and the men chosen to form the new government entered into talks with the representatives of the Soviet of Workers' and Soldiers' Deputies in order to gain their support for the revolutionary government. The Socialists, who were still not at all certain of the support of the masses and who had been taken by surprise by the revolution, were conciliatory enough. They accepted an agreement on the basis of a radical social and political program that at the same time acknowledged the special rights of the army in general and of the rebel troops of the Petrograd garrison in particular. Thus the most active element in the initial stages of the revolution demanded and obtained its reward.

The creation of the first revolutionary government was hailed with general enthusiasm. But the fate of the tsar and the dynasty had still to be decided. On 2/15 March the Duma committee assigned Gutchkov and Shulgin to demand the abdication of Nicholas II and the accession of Tsarevitch Alexis under the regency of Grand Duke Mikhail. Generals Aleksyeyev, chief of the general staff, and Ruzsky, commander in chief of the northern front, announced their support for abdication; the commanders of the western and southwestern fronts, Generals Brusilov and Evert, and then Grand Duke Nikolai Nikolay-evitch, who was in the Caucasus, followed their example. In the face of such unanimity in the high command, the tsar could only submit. Nevertheless at the last moment he amended the provisions of the act of abdication by keeping the throne from his son, in violation of the law, and designating his brother Mikhail as his successor. This change, as the tsarina's letters later showed, concealed an ulterior motive; it was intended to make it possible later, when circumstances had turned more favorable, to declare the abdication null and void and to restore the legitimate heir to his rights and to unlimited power.

Meanwhile the intention of demanding the establishment of a republic was rapidly growing among the parties of the left in Petrograd. The tsar's decision effectively robbed the advocates of a constitutional monarchy of their last support. During the night of 2/15–3/16 March the Duma committee decided to submit both points of view to Mikhail: that of the republicans, backed by Kerensky and Nekrasov, and that of the constitutional monarchists, supported by Miliukov. During a conference held the next morning, Mikhail followed the counsel of Rodzyanko, president of the Duma, who told him that he could not guarantee the safety of the grand duke's life if Mikhail assumed the power renounced by the tsar; Mikhail deferred a decision until the Constituent Assembly should have determined what Russia's political system should be. In effect this postponement amounted to a renunciation and a decision in favor of a republic.

On the same day, 4/17 March, the tsar's abdication and Mikhail's renunciation were made public, and the provisional government, indirectly recognized by Mikhail's renunciation, assumed its duties.

The First Provisional Government (3/16 March–5/18 May)

On 6/19 March the provisional government announced its program. First of all, in conformity to the state of mind that had determined the adherence of the Duma and the army to the revolution, it promised to provide the troops with everything that they required for carrying on the war to final victory, and it pledged itself to "maintain the alliances and fulfill the treaties" already in force; consequently it was recognized on March 22 by the United States, two days later by France, England, and Italy, and on April 4 by Belgium, Serbia, Rumania, and Portugal. Next it promised to convoke a Constituent Assembly as soon as possible, to give the nation firm guarantees of freedom and equality, to prepare elections to local self-government assemblies on the basis of universal suffrage, and to "recall with honor" the political exiles. At the same time it proclaimed a general political amnesty.

Its first actions corresponded with its promises. On 4/17 March, having abolished all the ordinances that violated the Constitution of Finland, it appointed a commission to investigate the illegalities perpetrated by officials of the old government. On 7/20 March, under the influence of the Soviet of Workers' and Soldiers' Deputies, it decided to deprive Nicholas II, who had gone back to General Headquarters, of his liberty and to intern him and his wife under house arrest at Tsarskoye Selo. On 12/25 it abolished the death penalty. Four days later it issued an appeal to the Poles asserting the necessity of creating "an independent Polish state composed of all territories populated in the majority by Poles," united with Russia "in a free military union," and invited to "express its wishes through the agency of a Constituent Assembly convoked in the capital of Poland." In the earliest days it unseated the old local government officials and replaced them with the heads of the permanent district and government zemstvo commissions; it conferred on the local population the mission of defining the relations between these representatives of the central government and all the "public committees," soviets, etc., that had sprung up spontaneously everywhere; it then took steps to establish the eight-hour day and to transfer the crown estates and the appanages to the state. On 17/30 March it issued an appeal to the peasants to promise to refrain from seizing land until it had prepared the documentation that would enable the Constituent Assembly to resolve the agrarian problem. On 20 March/2 April it abolished all restrictions of religion and nationality by decree. On 26 March/8 April it decided to float a "liberty loan" at 5 per cent. On 27 April/10 May, the anniversary of the meeting of the first Duma, the Premier declared: "We may regard ourselves as the most fortunate of men: our generation has found itself in the happiest period of Russian history." He concluded his address with a poetic quotation: "Freedom, let others despair: never will I lose faith in you!" The speech reflected the sentiments of many of his associates.

The Soviet and the Socialist parties, in contrast, were far from content with the first results of the revolution. Long before its outbreak the defeatist movement of the western Socialists had spread into Russia. From the start of the war the extreme left had stood against the patriotic Socialists and affirmed, in the Congresses of Zimmerwald (September 5–12, 1915) and Kienthal (February 5–9, 1916) the necessity for struggle "by every possible means for immediate peace without annexations." In Zimmerwald the extreme left had also appealed for the union of the world proletariat in an implacable class struggle against "capitalist and imperialist governments" side by side with the fight for peace. It was the leading spirits in the Zimmerwald decisions— the exiled Russian Socialists, Lenin, Trotsky, Martov, and others—who had announced in Berne, at the outbreak of the February Revolution, the principle that they would carry back into Russia: "Either the revolution will smash the war or the war will smash the revolution." On 28 February/13 March—the second day of the revolution—the Bolshevik central committee in Petrograd had declared that "the immediate and direct task of the revolutionary provisional government is to establish contacts with the proletariat of the belligerent countries with a view to a revolutionary struggle by the peoples of all countries against their oppressors." On 7/10 March it had laid down the measures that should be taken by the Soviet of Workers' and Soldiers' Deputies for the accomplishment of this purpose: "Free access to the front and the immediate rear in order to convert the front into a revolutionary army organized on the basis of democratic principles; the necessity of sending emissaries of the Soviet to the front and allowing free passage for the party's propagandists." In addition, it urged the Soviet to "call on the proletariat, through the intermediary of the Socialist parties in all countries, to launch a revolutionary struggle against its oppressors and to fraternize on all fronts with the revolutionary armies of Russian democracy." No government could follow such a course. Hence an immediate conflict on the question of war and peace began between the provisional government and the "Zimmerwaldians," who were supported by the moderate Socialists.

The Zimmerwaldians soon gained the advantage. At the end of March they succeeded in overcoming the rather weak resistance of the government and establishing regular contact not only with the front but also with Socialists in other countries. On 14/27 March the press published two documents voted by the Soviet of Workers' and Soldiers' Deputies: one was the draft for a *Declaration on the Soldier's Rights*, which was immediately treated by the front as a law even before it had been discussed by the special committee set up by War Minister Gutchkov and headed by General Polivanov; the other, an *Appeal to the Peoples of the Whole World*, proclaimed that the time had come to launch a decisive battle against the "annexationist aims of the governments" and that "the moment is at hand for the peoples to take control of the question of war and peace."

The effects of the Socialist propaganda were not slow in manifesting themselves. The disorganization of the army at the front, symptoms of which had appeared even before the revolution, spread rapidly; it had already gone so far by the beginning of April that General Lukomsky asserted: "It is currently no longer possible to carry out the offensive operations planned for the spring" in agreement with the Allies. While the British and French, in consonance with that accord, were launching their spring offensive in the middle of April, General Aleksyeyev was compelled to postpone the Russian army's "offensive operations" at first until mid-May and then until July, and it was this postponement alone, according to General Ludendorff's statement in his autobiography, that saved the German army.

The Allied governments were of course deeply apprehensive at the increasing influence of the soviets in Russia, and they dispatched three moderate Socialist ministers—Albert Thomas of France, Henderson of Britain, and Vanderwelde of Belgium—to Russia in order to hasten the initiation of the promised offensive.

During this time, while pursuing its campaign against the war minister, the Soviet also attacked Foreign Minister P. N. Miliukov, demanding that in conformance with the appeal of 14/27 March he issue a proclamation on the aims of the war that would include the formula of "peace without annexations or reparations." Miliukov was ready to do only what was consonant with the interests of Russia and the Allies. On 27 March/9 April, instead of a diplomatic note, he published a call to the country in which he set forth the libertarian ideology of the world war, which was identical with Russian revolutionary ideology but different from that of Zimmerwald: instead of adopting the formula of "without annexations or reparations" he asserted: "The aim of free Russia is not to dominate other peoples or to seize their national patrimony or to annex foreign soil by force, but to assure a strong peace based on the right of all peoples to self-determination." This declaration, though it was perfectly clear, was not enough to stop the propaganda of the Zimmerwaldians, who promptly demanded that "the next step" be taken: that is, to insist that the Allies issue an identical statement and take the first steps on "the road to peace talks." Miliukov categorically refused. Kerensky, who freely let it be known that he was "democracy's hostage" in the Cabinet, broke away from the other members of the government on this issue, as he officially announced on 6/19 April at a formal reception for the foreign Socialists who had just arrived in Russia. He appealed to the Soviet, to which the visiting Socialists also turned because at that time they deemed it necessary to gain the favor of Russian democracy. The position of the Zimmerwaldians was reinforced, especially when Thomas, arriving in Petrograd on 9/22 April, took a firm stand against Miliukov and for Kerensky and the Soviet, in which at that time the leader of the government majority was a Georgian Socialist named Tsereteli, a former member of the second Duma who had been brought back from his exile in Siberia. Within the government, Tereshchenko aligned himself with Kerensky. Thereafter Kerensky, Tereshchenko, and Tsereteli entered into direct relations with Thomas and the British ambassador, Sir George Buchanan. In these circumstances Miliukov thought it feasible not to demand that the Allies open preliminary peace talks but to communicate to them his "appeal" of 27 March/9 April with an explanatory note, the text of which, approved unanimously by the government, gave the lie to the rumors that attributed to Russia the intention of concluding a separate peace, and—on the request of Thomas—pointed out the necessity of establishing "guaranties and sanctions" against the recurrence of new and bloodier wars.

This statement was not yet enough for the Zimmerwaldians. On the same day when the note was sent—18 April/1 May—Lenin, in his newspaper, *Pravda,* called for the fraternization of troops at the front—which in fact had already begun—and the workers in the factories adopted a resolution demanding the public disclosure of all treaties and the convocation of an international conference for the purpose of evolving peace terms and initiating negotiations. The extremists used the publication of the note as the occasion to organize an armed demonstration on 20 April/3 May against the government and in particular against Miliukov, and the demonstration continued into the next day; this disorder was exploited by the Bolsheviki to provoke shooting in the streets—the first since the start of the revolution. Meanwhile, as a result of some limited amendments made in the note and agreed to by Miliukov, Tsereteli prevailed on the Soviet to declare itself satisfied by the government's explanations, and on the evening of 21 April/4 May there was a street demonstration in support of the government. Nonetheless the Soviet had endeavored during these days to impose its direct authority for the first time on the armed forces of the Petrograd garrison. Prince Lvov, Kerensky, and Tereshchenko concluded, therefore, that the sole means of restoring unity to the government was by including representatives of the Soviet in it. During the same evening of 21 April/4 May, in a meeting with Soviet's executive committee, Lvov raised the question of confidence. On 26 April/9 May the government posed the same question to the country as a whole, explaining what it had done "to rebuild political life on freedom and law" and what obstacles it had encountered since the "process of disorganization" had outrun that of "the creation of new social relationships." On the same day Kerensky precipitated a Cabinet crisis by presenting the provisional committee of the Duma and the party organizations with a written statement that henceforth "he could not assume the burden of power unless he was directly elected and mandated by his party." The Soviet was taken by surprise by this crisis, for it anticipated the Soviet's criticisms, and initially, on 29 April/12 May, it declared against the entrance of the Socialists into the government solely because the leaders of its majority, which supported the government, feared that by accepting power for which they would be answerable to the Soviet they themselves would be laid open to attack by their rivals on the left, the Bolsheviki, and thus would gradually lose their influence over their followers. But, when War Minister Gutchkov resigned the next day, on the ground that he was placed in a position of inability to function "under the conditions that have been imposed on the government's authority" and that "threaten fatal consequences to the defense, the freedom, and the very existence of Russia," a new government coalition arranged with the help of the Allied Socialist representatives became inevitable. On 1/14 May the executive committee of the Soviet approved the Socialists' participation in a coalition ministry with the bourgeois parties.

After five days of bargaining over the allocations of portfolios the first coalition government was formed on 6/19 May. It retained nine members of the previous government, including the former premier, and five Socialists, including Tsereteli, the leader of the government majority in the Soviet, and Chernov, the head of the Revolutionary

Socialists. In order to make certain of the new government's primary task, which was the organization of an offensive, Kerensky assumed the Ministries of War and the Navy. Miliukov, who had refused to accept the Ministry of Public Education in this coalition government, was succeeded as foreign minister by Tereshchenko. Inasmuch as the Soviet accused Miliukov of being an "imperialist," his departure emphasized the political significance of the change of government, which was a concession to the demands of the Soviet.

The First Coalition Government (6/19 May–2/15 July)

The program of the second provisional government or first coalition government, issued on 6/19 May, implicitly revealed the arduously achieved compromise of viewpoints almost impossible of reconciliation. On the issue that had led to the conflict with the foreign minister, that of a "democratic" peace, it offered only the vague promise "to undertake preparatory steps toward an understanding with the Allies." On the problem that had brought about Gutchkov's resignation, the army, it was visibly influenced by the Socialists sent by the Allies: in fact, although it pledged to "reinforce the democratization of the army," it also adopted as its positive goal the "reestablishment of its military power" not only with a view to "the defensive" but also with a view to "offensive" action, which was unacceptable to the Zimmerwaldians. In the economic domain it gave the Socialists not only "the control of the state and the public control of production" but also "the organization of production by the state in the event of need." On the other hand, it made only the most discreet of references to the land problem, citing "maximum wheat production" and "regulations for the use of land." Finally it announced the institution of heavy direct taxation and, once more, "the speedy convocation of the Constituent Assembly" as soon as a "democratic self-government" had been established.

After he had signed the "soldier's charter" on 11/24 May—it had just been approved by Polivanov's committee but it had already been a major contributor to the disorganization of the army—Kerensky immediately went to the front, in pursuance of his pledges to the Allies, in order to "persuade" the troops to take the offensive. He visited Helsingfors, Kamenets-Podolsk, Odessa, Sebastopol, Riga, and many other cities. He made speeches to the soliders about freedom, enthusiasm, the republic, peace, "the fairy tales of the great French Revolution," but he told them as well that liberty entailed obligation —*"liberté oblige"*—and that the "elimination of external discipline

344 / HISTORY OF RUSSIA, VOLUME THREE

creates the duty of inner discipline." The soldiers listened and cheered, but, as soon as he had gone, they relapsed into their pacifist sentiments; it was only among a few shock units that it was possible to further the idea of an offensive with the help of the officers. Moreover, Bolshevism had definitely won the allegiance of the sailors of Kronstadt and made inroads in Sebastopol, where it rapidly disorganized the Black Sea naval forces and compelled Admiral Kolchak to resign as commander in chief. Finland demanded new concessions. The Ukraine, which had thus far obtained nothing, decided to move on its own initiative and set up a provisional Ukrainian government, the "central *Rada*." In spite of Kerensky's prohibition, it proceeded to create national regiments, and on 10/23 June, in Saint Sofia Square in Kiev, the *Rada* staged a public reading of its first *universal*,* which, although it was put in cautious terms, nonetheless prescribed in fact that local government and taxation be wholly Ukrainian.

In practice Tereshchenko had no choice but to carry on with Miliukov's foreign policy. The Allies' replies (24–26 May) to the Russian proposals for the revision of the war aims were so unencouraging that the government could not bring itself to make them public. As for the international conference planned for Stockholm by the Socialists, the Allies rejected it until a preliminary agreement should have been reached in Paris; the American note was especially sharp. The Soviet press was angry: since agreement was impossible, why not force "the French and English bourgeoisie" to accept the ideas of the Russian revolution and, if there was a final refusal, break completely with both nations? The Soviet could not arrive at an understanding even with Albert Thomas, although he was more than ready to make concessions. In the note that he transmitted to the French minister when Thomas left Russia on 31 May/13 June, Tereshchenko indicated the government's particular concept in veiled phraseology. But on the same day he was compelled to make public the intercepted correspondence between Robert Grimm, the leader of the Zimmerwaldians, who was then in Petrograd, and Federal Councilor Hoffmann of Switzerland on the subject of peace terms with Germany. The Socialists in the government, who thereupon stopped speaking of themselves as Zimmerwaldians, had to agree to the drastic step of ordering Grimm's expulsion.

The disharmony that prevailed in the coalition government on diplomatic and military matters could be disguised, but two other

*The ancient term in the Ukraine for a government manifesto.

issues set the Socialist and bourgeois ministers at odds on labor and land problems. Although the disorganization of transport and the drop in labor productivity had led to a grave industrial crisis, the workers' demands had substantially increased. The Socialist ministers wanted to settle the mounting conflict between capital and labor through state intervention, control of industry, and high taxes on "war profits." The executive committee of the Soviet went further: on 16/29 May it approved the completely Bolshevik proposal to place the nation's entire economic life under "the direct management of the state," giving it even the monopoly over trade and cartels and the right to allocate labor, which was made compulsory. Confronted with this decision, Minister of Commerce Konovalov submitted his resignation, and no one would consent to replace him. As for the land problem, it made opponents of Prince Lvov and Minister of Agriculture Chernov, who, through his agents, encouraged the peasants to seize the landowners' estates without waiting for legislative action.

Not only were the ministers divided, but the Socialist ministers themselves were the targets of vehement criticism from the left minority in the Soviet. As they gained more and more direct experience in government, they could not help learning how complex and difficult its task was, and they were forced to revise in a more moderate direction their notions of the means of carrying out that task. This served the Bolsheviki as the pretext for engaging during May and June in a tremendous demagogic propaganda campaign in the factories of Moscow and Petrograd, going to the extreme of accusing the Socialist ministers of having "sold out to the millionnaire, Tereshchenko." On his arrival in Russia on 4/17 April, Lenin—who had crossed Germany in a "sealed train"—announced that the bourgeois democratic revolution had ended and that it must be transformed into a Socialist revolution. His slogan was *All power to the Soviets*, and he now called his group *Communist* and no longer *Socialist*. In the beginning his backers had been amazed by this change and had publicly protested against it in *Pravda*. But Lenin soon forced them to accept his thinking. It was the Communists' purpose to win a majority in the Petrograd Soviet and to raise the masses in revolt by means of vigorous propaganda in the factories and the garrisons against the moderate and Revolutionary Socialists and the Mensheviki, who under the leadership of Chernov and Tsereteli, were supporting the coalition government. The results of this propaganda were encouraging enough to cause the Bolsheviki to decide to attempt an armed demonstration in the streets of Petrograd on 10/23 June, the intention of which, if it succeeded, was to make the government its prisoner. But the Soviet had got wind of the plan and on its vigorous insistence the demonstration was countermanded.

From 3/16 June to 24 June/7 July the All-Russian Congress of Soviets was held in Petrograd. Its 1090 members had been elected by 305 Soviets and 53 similar organizations. The two largest groups in the Congress were the Revolutionary Socialists (285) and the Mensheviki (248): there were only 105 Bolsheviki and 32 internationalists. But it had no authority in Petrograd. The same thing was true of the Central Executive Committee *(Tsik)* that it elected and vested with full powers; but, made up of three hundred members, of whom one hundred had to be provincial residents in order to represent the revolutionary authority in the interior, it was still under the control of the "star chamber"—the name given popularly to the government group led by Tsereteli and Shkheidze, the irremovable president of the Soviet. In fact the working masses and the troops in the capital were going over increasingly to the Bolsheviki. On 18 June/1 July, when the Soviet organized a peaceful demonstration by way of compensation to the Bolsheviki for the countermanding of the armed demonstration of 10/23 June, the government was already so far out of favor that, instead of the slogan, *Support the coalition government*, the demonstrators' banners bore the inscription, *Faith in the Soviets*. Moreover, the major banners in the parades consisted of those that had been prepared for the earlier demonstration with the Bolshevik slogan, *All power to the Soviets*, or *Down with the ten capitalist ministers* (including Kerensky), or *Long live the control and organization of industry!* and, above all, *It is time to end the war* and *Bread, peace, freedom!* On the following day, the news that the long-awaited offensive had begun on the day of the demonstration provoked a new and enthusiastic manifestation, with other participants and other slogans. But this was only a "bourgeois" demonstration in honor of the Russian army and the Allies—the last of its kind, because the expectations to which the offensive had given rise were soon shattered.

Konovalov's resignation had led to a limited Cabinet crisis; the stand of the Socialist ministers brought on a full crisis. The triumvirate of Kerensky, Tereshchenko, and Nekrasov in fact dominated the government; through Tsereteli as its intermediary, it established agreement with the Soviet and took no account of the other ministers, the representatives of "bourgeois" democracy. Thus it attempted on its own to resolve the Ukrainian problem. Without consulting their colleagues, four ministers went to Kiev, where they evolved an agreement with the Ukrainians that did not recognize the unity of the Russian state or the fundamental principles of constitutional law. On 2/15 these ministers demanded that their colleagues ratify this agreement without the slightest modification. The Cadet ministers—Shingarev, Shakhovskoy, Manuilov, and Stepanov—refused and resigned. Just when the coalition created on 6/19 May was about to disintegrate, other events occurred that were to produce major repercussions on the course of the revolution and that prolonged the government crisis for three weeks.

The Cabinet Crisis and the July Days

The government crisis gave the Bolsheviki a useful pretext for a formal demand for the dissolution of the coalition with the middle class and the surrender of all power to the Soviets. Their propaganda in the factories and garrisons had been so effective that several regiments and tens of thousands of workers spontaneously decided to act on 3/16 July. As soon as they became convinced of the impossibility of holding them back, the Bolsheviki agreed to take over the leadership of their movement; in the event of success Lenin was ready, it seemed, to have the ministers arrested and seize power. Actually the Bolsheviki were not yet certain what they would do if they were victorious; in addition, they were afraid that the provinces were not yet ready for the *coup d'état* and that the soldiers at the front might turn against the Petrograd garrison. All these factors made them hesitate. During the morning of 4/17 July twenty thousand sailors arrived from Kronstadt on their own initiative to help the workers and soldiers. They were conducted to the Tauride Palace to call on the Soviets to seize power; this demand was reiterated by tens of thousands of workers from the Putilov factory, as well as the First Machine-Gun Regiment and a grenadier regiment.

But the moderate majority in the Soviet, which was still supporting the government, had not the slightest desire to assume power. Having failed to achieve the purpose for which the masses had been brought out, the revolt gradually subsided; a torrent of rain at the critical moment also played a large part. The sailors went back to Kronstadt. During the same night, furthermore, troops from the front who had remained loyal and had been summoned by the government arrived to add their strength to that of the Cossacks who had withstood the attack of the rebellious workers and soldiers. At the same time, the disclosure of documents by the press revealed Lenin's dealing with the Germans and sowed confusion among the garrison troops. Public opinion turned violently against the Bolsheviki. Tsereteli had no difficulty in obtaining a decision not to resolve the government's fate immediately and in winning the Soviet's acceptance of a proposal that saved the basis of the coalition: to retain the government as it stood—that is, incomplete—until the Soviet in a plenary session attended by its provincial members should decide the government's fate. This gave the coalition two more weeks of life.

Anti-Bolshevik sentiments grew more pronounced when during the following night, 6/19–7/20 July, Petrograd learned that Kerensky's offensive had failed and that the army was fleeing in disorder. Everyone felt at once that the Bolsheviki were responsible for the disintegration of the army, and the leaders of the Soviet, in accord with the government, spoke of vigorous repressions and even of "military dictatorship." Lenin, on the other side, dropped the mask when he asserted: "On 4/17 July a peaceful transfer of power to the Soviets was still possible. . . . As of this moment the Soviets in fact turned over power to the counterrevolution. . . . At present the peaceful growth of the revolution is impossible in Russia, and this is the question posed by history: either the total victory of the counterrevolution or else a new revolution."

The anti-Bolshevik reaction that followed the July revolt was managed by Kerensky. In order to apply the required repressive measures, he decided that he himself would assume the leadership of the revised coalition. After Prince Lvov, to whom deliberately unacceptable conditions had been presented, had yielded his post to Kerensky, the latter hastily filled out his government with members of the "Radical Democratic Party," especially established for this purpose. The bourgeois parties immediately protested against these appointments. But Kerensky demanded—and obtained—the Soviet executive committee's recognition of his government as a "government of revolutionary safety." At the same time he was invested with "unlimited powers for the restoration of order and discipline in the army and the resolute struggle against any counterrevolutionary and anarchist manifestations." Although Lenin and Zinovyev had time to escape, two other Bolshevik leaders, Trotsky and Kamenev, were arrested. The sailors of Kronstadt were forced to hand over their principal leaders. Many of the rank and file were imprisoned. The population was ordered to turn in its weapons. The distribution of Bolshevik newspapers in the army was prohibited. For the first time the right-wing political organizations, such as the Union of Officers and the Union of Merchants and Industrialists, openly revealed themselves. Petrograd could observe a spectacle that had long been forgot: religious funerals, in which Kerensky took part, for the Cossacks killed by the Bolsheviki. Tsereteli's original plan was amended: the Soviet's plenary session in Moscow—Moscow having been chosen because of the disorganization of Petrograd by Bolshevik propaganda—was supplanted by a "state conference" composed of representatives, in almost equal numbers, of not only Socialist but also bourgeois organizations. The mood was such that Tsereteli himself was prepared to go into eclipse in the face of Kerensky's dictatorship, and he told the Soviet: "The revolution's adolescence, in which everything was a rose-colored dream, is over. . . . One cannot combat anarchy with ideas."

But the fundamental contradiction that still persisted between the demands of the Cadet party, which he had invited to join his government, and the program approved by the Soviet on 8/21 July confronted Kerensky with major obstacles to the final establishment of a new coalition government. The Cadets demanded a strong ministry independent of the Soviets and the party organizations, while the Soviet's program clung to utopian proposals that had previously forced the Cadets' representatives to leave the government and that they could not accept. As a way out of this dead end and of obtaining the resources for the formation of a new ministry to his taste, Kerensky suddenly announced on 21 July/3 August that, given the impossibility of forming a government invested with sufficient authority in the eyes of the whole country, he was resigning. On the same day, in the Malachite Hall of the Winter Palace, where he had just established residence, there was a gathering of representatives of the parties and of influential organizations; at dawn the next day, after an entire night of lively debate, they entrusted him with full powers to form a new government. Kerensky had reached the peak of power, and the manner that he assumed, the authoritarian tone of his speeches, his imperious voice, his theatrical gestures, his solemn, chopped way of speaking, seemed to confirm this impression. But the capital's masses had already turned away from him; at the front, after the failure of the offensive, he had lost his former authority, and the army was already looking for another candidate for dictatorship, a man whose support could be relied on from all those who could not accept a government ostensibly strong but in actuality the vassal of the Soviet. Confronted by the poorest masses of the capital converted to Bolshevism, the Soviet too began to diminish. As the political center, which Kerensky sought to represent, declined, the two extreme wings grew stronger. Nevertheless Kerensky could not resolve himself to making a choice. His endless vacillations between right and left threatened finally to make him equally useless to both.

The Formation of the Second Coalition Government
(25 July/7 August)

The second coalition government was finally set up on 25 July/7 August.* Kerensky held not only the premiership but also the portfolios of War and the Navy, with Savinkov as deputy war minster; Tsereteli, who deemed it necessary to strengthen his influence in the Soviet, was not a member of the government; it was joined by four new members of the Cadet party, but, apart from his rival, Chernov, a member of the same party, Kerensky had no powerful competitors. Instead of making public a program, on the formulation of which it was impossible to arrive at agreement, the government confined itself to issuing an "appeal" to the country over Kerensky's signature alone. It dealt with nothing but the problems of the moment, which required the "renunciation of debate in the face of the enemy," and, given the "implacable military necessities," the establishment of an "iron rule" in order to "save the fatherland by heroic effort."

The "state conference," which was held in Moscow from 12/25 to 15/28 August, was dramatically illustrative of the basic contradiction inherent in the second coalition, which, for all its ambitions for strength and the show of its power, could find support in neither of the two camps, the Socialist or the bourgeois, whose antagonism was becoming more and more violent. In spite of the absence of the Bolsheviki—who were not represented in the conference but who provided evidence of their power by organizing strikes in the city during the conference and depriving its members of water, light, and restaurant meals—it was indeed two opposing parties that met in the Great Theater of Moscow with virtually equal representation among the two thousand delegates: when one side applauded, the other hooted. The salient features of this conference, in which there were neither votes nor decisions, were, first of all, the oratorical tournament between the ministers, whose speeches in sum were very moderate— Chernov did not speak—and the party leaders. Then, on 14/27 August, there was the reading of the moderate Socialists' program by Shkheidze, the chairman of the Soviet; accepted by very many of the left-wing organizations but still unacceptable to the non-Socialist democrats, it undeniably but unsuccessfully sought to moderate and make

*This does not take into account the hasty revision of the Cabinet immediately after the July days.

more practical the demands of the program of 8/21 July; finally there were the speeches of Generals Kornilov—now generalissimo in place of Brusilov—Aleksyeyev, and Kaledin, all of whom urgently demanded that the harshest disciplinary measures be adopted at the front, that the death penalty be restored not only at the front but also in the rear, that the powers of the elected military committees be restricted, etc. Before he presented these demands General Kornilov had taken precautions: he had arrived in Moscow with an armed guard and all the visible apparatus of the dictator. He was expecting to be removed and in that event he was prepared to engage in open combat against Kerensky. The premier himself was fearful of an attempt at a military *coup d'état;* but he did not decide to remove the general. Nevertheless he was not successful in concealing his apprehensions. Nothing could better illustrate the contrast between word and act, between the claim to unlimited power and manifest impotence, between a vaunted iron will and a visible paralysis, than the speeches that teemed with threats and with allusions to conspirators whom he did not identify, but whom he claimed to know, and that ended in virtual attacks of hysteria. If no conflict erupted, it was obviously only postponed.

Kornilov's Insurrection (28 August/10 September)

The two weeks that elapsed between Kornilov's speech in Moscow and his insurrection were spent in dickering between the generalissimo, whose staff headquarters was at Mogilev, and Kerensky. Twice, on 3/16 and 10/23 August, Kornilov went to Petrograd to try to reach an understanding with Kerensky. Their discussions covered not only needed military reforms but also the possibility, in the event of Kornilov's resignation, of a military *coup d'état,* for which the pretext could be found in the armed demonstration by the Bolsheviki that was expected in the capital for mid-September. Inasmuch as the Petrograd regiments had clearly been demoralized by Bolshevik propaganda, Kerensky had called in the Third Division to protect the city against a larger-scale repetition of the July disorders. Negotiations with Kornilov were carried on through the agency of Savinkov until the actual day of the general's insurrection. Both Savinkov and Kornilov wanted to destroy the Soviets and expedite the realization of military reforms. But, under the influence of second-rank politicians, real adventurers like Zavoiko, Aladyin, Dobrinsky, and others, Kornilov conceived the notion of changing the composition of the government at the same time in order to remove it from the Soviet's influence.

Since there could be no thought of removing Kerensky altogether, Kornilov thought in terms of retaining him but making him minister of justice, as he had been in the first provisional government. There was a great deal of sympathy for Kornilov, but the men around him and his methods antagonized the most important political quarters. Having prepared a series of proclamations and scheduled his *coup d'état* for 27 August/9 September in Petrograd, he was ingenuous enough to disclose his plans to Kerensky on the evening before the deadline through a former member of the provisional government, V. L. Lvov. Kerensky telephoned and promised to go to staff headquarters, but this was a mere maneuver intended more effectively to unmask the general's plot. In spite of the view of a large number of the ministers, who on the eve of the *coup* either resigned or turned over all authority to the premier and a "directorate" of five members, Kerensky hastily proclaimed Kornilov a traitor and ordered him to resign his post as generalissimo. From this Kornilov deduced that Kerensky was completely in the power of the soviets, and he decided, as he had warned Kerensky that he might, to disobey, to raise the army in open revolt, and to compel the government to reform itself by shaking off the soviets' domination. The troops that he sent against the capital were under orders to destroy the Soviet, to butcher its members without quarter, especially the most influential of them. Thus Kornilov expected to "assure the country of a firm and strong government."

But in this battlefield it was an uneven combat for a general without political experience. He lessened his chances still further by remaining in his headquarters instead of going with his troops. When they came near to Petrograd, Kerensky at first lost his head. He spent the day of 28 August/10 September and the ensuing night in mounting terror, shared by his associates, and a number of attempts was made to effect a reconciliation between the generalissimo and the premier. Only the Bolsheviki, for whom Kornilov's victory would be tantamount to a death sentence, retained their composure. They formed a "combat council" and established a network of "revolutionary war committees" everywhere as quickly as they could; these put an end to Kerensky's hesitations and at once organized resistance to Kornilov. They resorted to their old methods, the effectiveness of which had been proved: destruction of railway trackage, disorganization of railway communications, propaganda missions to Kornilov's troops, etc. The officers gathered by the generalissimo in Petrograd in expectation of the armed rising proved utterly incompetent and fled at the crucial moment. By 29 August/11 September Kornilov's defeat was beyond question.

A day later, General Krymov, who was in command of the corps dispatched against the capital, was compelled to submit to Kerensky's order to present himself in Petrograd; greeted by the premier with the utmost brutality, he went to the War Ministry and killed himself. On 31 August/13 September Kornilov and his collaborators were formally charged with mutiny. Kerensky appointed himself generalissimo and General Aleksyeyev chief of his General Staff in order to rid himself of Kornilov more easily. Kornilov refused to surrender and once again attempted from his headquarters to dictate conditions; then, on 1/14 September, he resigned himself to submission and was arrested with such other generals as Denikin, Markov, and Erdeli.

The liquidation of Kornilov's insurrection dissipated the last hope of reinforcing the revolutionary government through an alliance between Kerensky and military quarters: it was no longer possible to rely on the generals' help. At the same time there was an end to the period of anti-Bolshevik reaction aroused by the July disorders. Now all the trumps were in the Bolsheviki's hands, and the political pendulum swung as quickly to the left as it had at first to the right. Kerensky's impotence against the Communist group of the Soviet became obvious when, in his ordinance of 4/17 September, he sought to put an end to the direct action of the "revolutionary war committees" by dismissing them; instead of obeying, they announced that they would continue their operations. On the demand of the Petrograd Soviet, Savinkov, who had become war minister when Kerensky assumed the post of generalissimo, was at once thrown out and replaced by General Verkhovsky, who was thus rewarded for having refused to put the Moscow garrison under Kornilov's orders. Verkhovsky revoked all the measures previously adopted at Kornilov's suggestion for the restoration of discipline in the army; he went back to the methods of persuasion and "democratization."

The Final Government Crisis and the Creation of the Third Coalition Ministry (25 August/8 September–24 September/7 October)

The resignation of a large number of ministers on 26 August/8 September had set off the Cabinet crisis. After Kornilov's insurrection there was open conflict between Tsereteli's policy, which was founded on the idea of coalition and sought to end the revolution by gaining the recognition of a bourgeois republic, and Lenin's, which was striving to transfer power to the Communist party by way of the soviets and to achieve a Socialist system in Russia. On 31 August/13 September Tsereteli's policy was formally rejected by the Petrograd Soviet, which, by 279 votes against 115 and 51 abstentions, adopted a Bolshevik resolution: the withdrawal of power not only from the Cadets, who were accused of having maintained relations with Kornilov, but in general from all "qualified-voter elements" (the bourgeois), and the creation of a government composed of revolutionary proletarians and peasants, which would propose a democratic peace to all the warring nations, publish the secret treaties, abolish the death penalty at the front, grant freedom of propaganda in the army, abolish private property in land, etc. Tsereteli and Shkheidze remarked that this vote implied a complete change in the soviets' former policy and that, if it was not the product of sheer chance, the existing staff would have to resign; they threatened the Soviet with a new danger, the enmity of the right, and they predicted that it would be isolated from the rest of the country if it officially adopted the Bolshevik tactic. In vain: on 9/22 September they were beaten again, by 619 votes against 41 and 67 abstentions, and they resigned their posts. Nevertheless Tsereteli remained in control of the executive committee of the All-Russian Soviet. There he succeeded in winning a new reprieve: the fate of the government would be resolved by a special "democratic conference"; if the principle of coalition, especially with the Cadets, was officially doomed in advance, Tsereteli compelled the admission that the future government would be responsible to "revolutionary democracy." As a result of these flexible conditions, which applied to all democrats, Socialist or other, he in fact rescued the concept of coalition once again.

The "democratic conference," which convened on 14/27 September, was actually enlarged to such an extent that it embraced, if not the "qualified-voter elements" directly, at least those of the moderate Socialists and democrats, chosen among members of cooperatives, peasants, members of the newly formed democratic municipal and zemstvo assemblies, military and economic organizations, etc. So, when at last, after long discussions, its more than 1400 members got down to voting, it fell into confusion: first, by 766 votes to 688, it adopted the principle of coalition; then, by 739 votes against 139 and 196 abstentions, it approved participation by certain "qualified-voter elements" in the coalition; finally, by 813 votes to 183, it refused to approve such an alliance, and Tsereteli, voicing the unanimous opinion of the staff, was in a position to announce that "organized democracy has no practicable, feasible uniform plan." On 20 September/3 October a special committee of 110 members decided to drop the much discussed principle of coalition—it was favored by 50 members and opposed by 60—but to obligate the future government, whatever its composition, to a specific program: namely, that of 14/27 August, and to declare its responsibility to a representative body composed of members of the "democratic conference" and enlarged by "qualified-voter elements." It then entrusted the task of forming a government to a staff of five members made up of backers of the Soviet's old majority.

In order to be able to arrive at an agreement with the candidates already proposed by Kerensky, who belonged in part to the Cadet group and in part to Moscow industrial and commercial circles, it was necessary to eliminate the two conditions imposed by the "democratic conference": the program of 14/27 August and responsibility to a representative body. This was accomplished during the negotiations carried on between 21 September/4 October and 24 September/7 October: to the representative body of 367 members of parties and Socialist organizations created by the "democratic conference" the government added 156 members of the "qualified-voter" groups, chosen by itself; both were regarded as having been "summoned" by the government, which was not answerable to them. The new representative body was entitled the "Council of the Republic" and its powers were to expire six weeks after the inception of its sessions—in other words, when the Constituent Assembly convened. On 25 September/8 October the membership of the last coalition government was announced: the "directorate" of five members set up on 27 August/9 September was increased by three Cadets—Konovalov as vice premier, Kishkin, and Smirnov; five Socialists—Gvozdev, Malyantovitch, Liverovsky, Bernadsky, and S. Maslov—and one member of the industrial and commercial group, S. Tretyakov. On the same day Trotsky was elected chairman of the Petrograd Soviet, replacing Shkheidze. Tsereteli having departed for the Caucasus, the function of intermediary between the government and the executive committee of the Soviet was assumed by Dan, a Menshevik, and Gots, a Revolutionary Socialist, both of whom showed less flexibility and compliance than their predecessor in their dealings with Kerensky; furthermore, during this last phase of the revolution, the former government members of the Soviet were leaning more and more toward the left, and this was certain to influence the work of the Council of the Republic.

The Final Conflict (24 September/7 October–25 October/7 November)

In the first session of the Council of the Republic, denominated the Pre-Parliament, the Bolsheviki ostentatiously left the hall in order to go "to the barricades." They were no longer concealing their intentions, and Trotsky frankly announced that the new government was "a civil-war government." Taking advantage of the existence of "double authority"—the government's and the Soviet's—as a result of which a special rule of "revolutionary legality" was made possible, publicly violating the law and harassing the government, the Bolsheviki were almost overtly preparing for the overthrow of the government. Only the date of action remained to be settled. The scheduling of the start of the second All-Russian Congress of Soviets for 25 October/7 November determined the date of the revolt: the Bolsheviki planned to propose formally to the congress that power be transferred to the workers and peasants. Since this involved a peaceful means of transfer, so to speak, it could be discussed with the other Socialist parties, and, in the end, Kerensky himself was brought into the negotiations; he was thinking of replacing his coalition Cabinet with a purely Socialist government. In actuality, as Trotsky later said, these negotiations "were a mere game"; the Bolsheviki were systematically planning an act of force and were determined to carry it out before the Congress of the Soviets opened in order to confront it with an accomplished fact.

Their preparations were pushed forward without concealment. Unquestionably the session of their committee that was attended by Lenin, emerging from his hiding place, and in which only two votes —those of Zinovyev and Kamenev—marred the unanimity of the decision to attempt a *coup d'état* was kept secret, but the consequences of the decision were disclosed in the most apparent fashion. There was first of all the rebellion by the regiments of the Petrograd garrison, which refused to leave the capital and go to the front after the German army and navy had captured both shores of the Gulf of Riga. This was followed on 12/25 October, with full public knowledge, by the creation of a "revolutionary war committee" and the appointment of Soviet commissars assigned to maintain communication between this committee and the regiments. Finally, on 17/30 and 18/31 October and 21 October/3 November, there were the conferences with the representatives of the garrison, which provided public assurance that the state of mind of the military was in harmony with the end in view: namely, the overthrow of the government—the Bolsheviki themselves regarded 21 October/3 November as "the official start of the revolt." All these measures were taken on the pretext of defending the proletariat against possible "counterrevolutionary" attacks. This was the meaning that was ascribed as well to the indecisive defense measures to which the government finally made up its mind. Until the very end Kerensky wavered between the urgent demands of his non-Socialist colleagues, who requested immediate measures for the protection of the government against the imminent revolt, and those of the Socialists, who proposed a final and peaceful solution through the creation of a Socialist government. Kerensky thought that he could rely on the Pre-Parliament, in which, however, it proved impossible to establish a government majority. In actuality there was in the Pre-Parliament the same conflict that had had raged in the democratic conference in Moscow between the same two antagonists, chiefly on the two major questions of the moment: war and peace, the army and diplomacy. The new War and Navy ministers, General Verkhovsky and Admiral Verderevsky, owed their appointments to the Soviets, and hence there was no occasion for surprise in the fact that a majority could not be assembled in the Pre-Parliament on the problem of preserving discipline in the army. General Verkhovsky went as far as to attempt direct negotiations with the parties in the intention of propounding the principle of a separate peace, but, confronted by the opposition of Kerensky and Tereshchenko, he had as a result to resign. Tereshchenko's speeches on diplomatic matters went constantly round and round in the same vicious circle: beneath their radical language what lay hidden was pure impotence; they so angered the Socialists that there was talk of replacing the foreign minister, but on this point too the Pre-Parliament was incapable of arriving at any formula that could effect union among the parties. Finally, just before the revolt, in the face of the impossibility of continuing to hold his peace on the *coup d'état* being planned by the Bolsheviki, Kerensky delivered a veritable indictment before the Pre-Parliament, "demonstrating, with documentary evidence in hand, the existence of a state of revolt" and demanding "the support of this high assembly." But in spite of the danger the Socialists denied him this support, and, while the Bolsheviki, even as they were dispatching armed detachments to occupy predetermined strategic points in Petersburg, dangled the hope of an agreement before Dan and Gots, the Socialists continued to insist on a peaceful resolution of the revolt.

At dawn on 25 October/7 November Kerensky could see for himself not only that revolt had just broken out but that the military staff had taken no steps for the defense of Petrograd. For this he blamed those officers who had falsely reassured him. He assigned Kishkin, a civilian minister, to command the women's battalion, which was called a "shock battalion," as well as the detachments composed of cadets from the military academies assembled before the Winter Palace—a measure that further cooled the enthusiasm of the military authorities;

then he hastily left the capital under the protection of a car belonging to the United States embassy, which preceded his own under the American flag, and set out to lead the troops called back from the front. By noon, meanwhile, the rebellious Petrograd regiments had dispersed the Pre-Parliament. Toward the end of the afternoon the Winter Palace was cut off from all communication with the city. In vain the provisional government waited for Kerensky's return with troops. In the evening the cruiser *Aurora*, which had gone over to the Bolsheviki after her arrival from Kronstadt, shelled the palace. Although some of its defenders deserted it when they became convinced of the futility of resistance, the government, on the belief that until the convocation of the Constituent Assembly it remained the repository of supreme authority and could be dispossessed only by force, refused to surrender. Learning how matters stood at the palace, a delegation composed of members of the city council and leading political figures meeting in the city hall decided to go to the palace in order to set the government free "or die with it," but the Bolshevik patrols would not let the delegation pass. Returning to the city hall, the delegates and those deputies who had just left the Congress of Soviets and opposed the *coup d'état* formed a "committee for the safety of the fatherland and the republic." A group of student officers, encouraged by the delegation's arrival, drove the Bolsheviki out of the Winter Palace. This victory was only fleeting, for a new mass of sailors, soldiers, and workers of the Red Guard forced its way into the palace, whose commanders surrendered on condition that the lives of the student officers be spared. The members of the provisional government were arrested, transported at the risk of their lives to the far bank of the Neva, and imprisoned in the Fortress of SS. Peter and Paul, where they were reunited with the ministers of the old autocracy overthrown by the February Revolution.

Fate's irony decreed as well that Kerensky should turn for succor to the same troops who had marched on Petrograd in September in pursuance of Kornilov's *coup d'état*. What had happened to Kornilov was repeated without change, but even more swiftly. The troops, consisting largely of Cossacks, had no desire to do battle, especially for Kerensky, and they scattered. General Krasnov succeeded, however, in regrouping several hundred Cossacks and tried to stage a march on Petrograd in spite of the opposition of the commander in chief of the northern front, General Cheremisov, who had already entered into negotiations with the local Soviet. He managed to reach Gatchina from Pskov. Kerensky made every effort to encourage this detachment's advance in the hope that the units summoned back from the front would arrive at any moment and that Petrograd would rise against the revolution. But these recalled units too were blocked by the obstacles created by the railway workers' union. The Cossacks, seeing no sign of the expected infantry and entertaining nothing but antipathy toward Kerensky, showed even less inclination to give battle. Kerensky urged them nevertheless to advance on Tsarskoye Selo. Krasnov and his four to six hundred Cossacks, who were beginning to clamor for Kerensky's removal, hesitated. On 30 October/12 November, near Pulkovo, five hundred Cossacks launched a "battle" against fifteen to thirty times as many opponents under the command of a German Lieutenant Bauer; they held until nightfall, when Krasnov fell back on Gatchina. The day before, the Bolsheviki had mercilessly crushed the premature attempt at attack staged by the cadets of the Petrograd military academies. In the interim the emissaries sent out by the Bolsheviki had shaken the resolve of both the officers and the soldiers at the front. The railway workers were increasingly successful in blocking troop movements toward Petrograd. After the retreat to Gatchina, they called on Kerensky to enter into negotiations with the Bolsheviki for an armistice. The Cossacks, despairing of ever seeing the infantry arrive, had already launched talks of their own with the Bolsheviki. The Bolsheviki replied from Krasnoye Selo with the demand that Kerensky be delivered to them, and they sent Dybenko, a sailor, to Gatchina. During 1/14 November the talks culminated in an agreement, but, ten minutes after his arrest, Kerensky succeeded in fleeing, dressed as a sailor and wearing motoring goggles. General Dukhonin, who assumed the duties of generalissimo after Kerensky's disappearance, officially ordered a halt to the troops' march on Petrograd. On 3/16 November, by proclamation, he called on all democrats to unite for the salvation of the country and to elect a government recognized by the entire nation. The Bolsheviki ordered him to initiate peace talks with the Germans. When he refused, they sent an expedition commanded by Second Lieutenant Krylenko, with the title of supreme commander of the Russian armies, against his quarters in Mogilev, and on 20 November/3 December Dukhonin was killed by a sailor. Just before his death he had ordered the release of all the generals arrested after Kornilov's insurrection—that is, Kornilov himself, Denikin, Markov, and others, who soon assumed the leadership of the anti-Bolshevik campaign in the Don Cossack regions.

In Moscow an attempt to restore the fallen government also failed. At the news of the *coup d'état* in Petrograd, the Moscow city council gathered around it the representatives of the democratic organizations, who formed a "safety committee" but remained neutral. The garrison commander, Ryabtsev, adjured the population "not to engage in civil war." The Bolsheviki proved more energetic. Against the safety committee they set up a revolutionary war committee charged with the duty of "supporting" that in Petrograd. They held the majority—four of its seven members—and soon they were alone in the committee, for the Menshevik and Revolutionary Socialists members walked out "because of the Bolshevik tendency to stifle the will of the minority and act behind its back." This committee set about the vigorous organization of revolt: it prohibited the publication of bourgeois newspapers, won over the larger part of the garrison, and occupied the Kremlin. The officers, the cadets of the military academies, and the students, meeting in the Alexander Military Academy, called on the Bolsheviki to evacuate the Kremlin. This they did on 28 October/ 11 November, and the student officers took over the center of the city, cutting off the revolutionary committee's communications with distant parts of the city. But this victory was anything but lasting, for the defenders of Moscow were divided, and the resoluteness of the officers and student officers did not have the approval of the democratic parties. Under pressure from the railway workers, the safety committee demanded the establishment of a Socialist government and agreed to a twelve-hour armistice with the Bolsheviki for 29–30 October/12– 13 November. Far from respecting this truce, the Bolsheviki took advantage of it to make sure of reinforcements. On 1/14 November they called on their opponents to surrender unconditionally. The population was passive, the left wing in public opinion was opposed to the struggle, no reinforcements arrived to strengthen the government's supporters, the student officers categorically refused to fight for a Socialist government; besides, there were only five thousand of them, whereas their adversaries had tens of thousands of men already available and were continually being reinforced from the districts in the vicinity of Moscow. The Bolsheviki fiercely shelled the student officers' assembly points, the Kremlin and the Alexandra Military Academy. On the evening of 1/14 November the "White Guard" resolved to embark on negotiations; on the following day it laid down its arms; those of its members who could not resign themselves to defeat fled one by one to the Don, where an army of volunteers was brought into being.

Russia had entered on a new phase of her existence, a period of disorganization and decay, during which a series of large and small "republics" was formed and arbitrarily assumed the prerogatives of the sovereign power. This disintegration had begun under the provisional government. In the summer of 1917 the peasants had started on their own initiative to take over the estates of the large landowners and to destroy the nobles' country houses. Demoralization had already infiltrated the army, weary of war; crowds of soldiers, still carrying their weapons, had invaded cities and villages and set up tyrannical rule everywhere; deserters, the number of whom had grown to inconceivable dimensions, had set off homeward for their villages, pillaging entire districts and igniting pogroms along the way. The disorganization of transportation brought on a food crisis: famine had begun in many areas and the peasants refused to sell their wheat at the price fixed by the government, because inflation had led to a rise in living costs that was to assume terrifying proportions later under the Bolsheviki. The "control" of industry by the workers had also borne its fruits: in spite of the powerful backing that the state had afforded to all sectors of war industry, the employers had been unable to contend with the rises in wages and the incessant strikes; they had abandoned their factories and one after another had closed. All these symptoms already foreshadowed, of course on a much smaller scale, those that have been customarily regarded as characteristic of the advent of the Soviet system. The disorganization created by an inordinate military effort, the extreme exhaustion of the army, the economic collapse—in a certain sense all these things had prepared Russia for Bolshevism. The soldiers had stopped fighting of their own will, while the peasants had taken over the land and the workers had seized the factories. Lenin had only to put his seal on the accomplished fact in order to be certain of the support of the soldiers, the peasants, and the workers.

CHAPTER 8

Russia Under Soviet Rule

[P A U L   M I L I U K O V]

The latest stage in Russia's history, which began on 25 October/7 November, is not yet over. Its results are unknown and unpredictable. Hence it is extremely difficult to attempt an impartial historical account of it. But this book would remain unfinished if it ignored the social experiment that for fifteen years* has endeavored to lead not only Russia but also the entire world into new avenues. We shall confine ourselves, however, to dealing with the most important facts, and, as much as possible, only with those that are impossible of challenge.

The first fifteen years of the Soviet system may be divided into three periods of five years each, every one of them marked by modification, if not in essential tendencies and aims, which remained unchanged, at least in the tactics of the Communist party.

In the first period (25 October/7 November 1917–1922), in which it established all its instrumentalities, the Soviet state was gravely hindered not only by the effects of the First World War, which imposed a major burden on the population, but also by domestic problems, above all civil war that did not end until 1921. This was the period of "war Communism," as it was called by the Communists themselves in order to emphasize the fact that, if they were unable to accomplish their goal, it was because of the difficulties of war time.

The second period, the origins of which, specifically, lay in the extreme desolation of the country and the frightful famine of 1921–1922, was also regarded by the Bolsheviki as a temporary "retreat," a "respite," during which, through a most fainthearted reversion to the principles of the "bourgeois" system, they hoped to be able to give the country the opportunity to remedy the evils that they ascribed to the war and for which their antagonists blamed their own social

*It is important to recall that this history was written before 1935.—Translator.

experiment. This period of "restoration" or NEP* phase continued for the next five years—1923–1928; in fact it both began and ended somewhat earlier. This return to a certain economic freedom rapidly brought about the revival of the country's economic forces, the improvement of its finances, the reorganization of its communications.

The third period, which began in 1928, was one of Socialist "reconstruction." In conformity with revised Communist doctrine, the Soviet government returned to its original task and, by exploiting the achievements of the NEP, it undertook to transform Russia immediately into a "Socialist" state. The most characteristic event of this period was the Five-Year Plan, which was intended to create state industry that could "catch up with and outstrip" western Europe and the United States and to accomplish the "collectivization" of agriculture. At the time of writing, it would appear from certain indications that this period was close to its end.

I / "WAR COMMUNISM" AND LENIN (1917–1922)

The Oligarchical Organization of the Communist Party

At the time when the Bolsheviki seized power, their political and economic program was far from completed and their number was very small. The Communist party still counted only about fifty thousand members, including some ten thousand old revolutionaries (the *podpolshchiki*, accustomed to illegal "underground" activity) and thirty-five thousand new members who had joined only in 1917, during the conflicts with the provisional government. Although in ten years the number of party members multiplied tenfold—in other words, to a half-million—the ruling elite, the *verkhushka*,† embraced only about fifteen thousand men, among whom 100 in the central organizations in Moscow and 225 in the central organizations of the other regions played the dominant part. Thus the system was essentially oligarchic, as Lenin acknowledged in 1920: "The party," he said, "is led by a central committee of nineteen members elected by the congress, but the day-to-day work in Moscow has to be entrusted to even more restricted groups, the *Orgbyuro,* or 'organization bureau,' and the *Politbyuro,* or 'political bureau,' to each of which five members are elected by the central committee meeting in plenary session. As a consequence, this is the most genuine of oligarchies." Lenin expressed

Novaya ekonomicheskaya politika, or New Economic Policy.
†Literally, "the summit."

himself clearly and curtly on the function of these central party organizations in the management of the affairs of the state: "In our republic no important question of policy or organization is resolved by any state agency whatever without instructions from the party's central committee."

The First Steps

It was natural that the new government should have shown a certain hesitation when it was confronted with the problem of governing so vast a country with forces that were so minuscule. When he was asked before the October revolution whether the Bolsheviki would be able to remain in power, Lenin replied by employing all the rhetoric of Bolshevik demagogy without disguise:

When the last worker, the last man without a job, the lowest cook, every ruined peasant sees that the proletarian government . . . is stripping the parasites of their surplus wealth, establishing the homeless by force in the houses of the rich, putting the land into the hands of its workers and giving control of the factories and the banks to the workers, that millionnaires who have concealed their wealth are being immediately and severely punished, then . . . millions of fighters will arise . . . and the capitalists and the *kulaki* will not be strong enough to overcome the people's revolution.

That was why the first governmental program of the Bolsheviki—the program that brought them victory—expressed not so much the aims of their doctrine as the desire to satisfy the most urgent and imperative needs of the masses.

On 25 October/7 November—the very first day of their revolution —the Bolsheviki authorized the peasants to seize the lands of the rich without waiting for decisions by the Constituent Assembly. The decree of 28 October/10 November called on the exhausted troops to con-clude an immediate armistice with the German soldiers, regardless of risk, on every part of the front. The decree of 1/14 November gave the workers the right of general management of the factories in which they labored. That of 2/15 November left the various national minorities in the country free to decide their own destinies, "even to the point of detaching themselves" from Russia.

In the realm of economics the Bolsheviki at first manifested greater caution. Their decrees of 26 October/8 November, which "nationalized" the banks and turned over the large farming estates to local peasant committees, certainly settled the fate of big capital, but they did not even threaten the basic principle of private property, moderate or small in size, or of individual ownership of land. Similarly they were content at the start to subject private industry only to the control of the workers; it was only when this control had completely disorganized the management of the factories that they began little by little—the operation was not completed until the end of 1919—to nationalize all industrial enterprises. It was only on October 21, 1918* that they nationalized all internal business and took it on themselves to control the distribution of industrial and farm products among the cities and the rural areas. Of course the execution of this vast enterprise was totally inadequate, and clandestine private business did not go out of existence. Foreign trade, which was obviously easier to nationalize, was not interfered with, however, until May 4, 1918; besides, by that time it was reduced virtually to zero.

The Dissolution of the Constituent Assembly

In the beginning the Bolsheviki offered no opposition to participation by the other Socialist parties in the government. Among the Social Democrats, as among the Revolutionary Socialists, there were extreme-left groups that considered it possible to collaborate with the Soviet authorities, and indeed many of their members were included in the government. But this did not last long. Relations became strained with the election of deputies to the Constituent Assembly, which the provisional government had scheduled for November. Although the Bolsheviki had long since substituted their slogan, *All power to the Soviets,* for that of the Russian Radicals, *The Constituent Assembly,* they were nonetheless waiting for the results of the elections before establishing a definitive stand toward the Assembly, that "idol" of the democrats. Contrary to their expectations, they did not obtain a majority in it. According to incomplete election statistics, they received only 9.5 million votes among 36 million electors, or slightly more than one-quarter, against 20.9 million, amounting to an absolute majority, for the Revolutionary Socialist party and 4.6 million for the bourgeois parties, including 1.9 million for the Cadets, 1.7 million for the candidates of the various national-minority parties, only 300,000 for the monarchists, and 200,000 for the landowners. Therefore, the Bolsheviki had only 175 deputies against 417 Revolutionary Socialists, 34 Social Democrats of various shadings, and 64 bourgeois and national-minority delegates. A Constituent Assembly thus distributed was unacceptable to them. After having proclaimed the Cadet party an "enemy of the people" and postponed the convocation

*Starting with January 1918, the old style having been abolished, all dates are given in the new style.

of the Assembly until January 18, 1918, they decided to move by force against the popular representative body, which they accused of no longer standing for the voters' wishes. On January 18, the very day of their first session, after a long series of fiery but useless speeches, the deputies were dispersed at dawn by Zheleznyakov, the leader of the sailors' guard, on the pretext that "the guard is tired." Bukharin, the ideologist of Bolshevism, speaking from the floor, declared "war to the death against the bourgeois parliamentary republic" and cried: "The question of power will be settled by civil war."

The First Soviet Constitution

The first Soviet Constitution of the Russian Socialist Federated Soviet Republic (RSFSR) was promulgated on July 10, 1918. According to the doctrine of Marx and Lenin, the state was the expression of the class struggle and the Constitution in any given society expressed the relation of forces among the classes. The proletariat having conquered on 25 October/7 November, the state should assume the form of the "dictatorship of the proletariat."

The basic organs of the state were the Soviets, for which the Bolsheviki saw a precedent in the Paris Commune of 1871. To Lenin the soviet form of government had huge advantages over all others by reason of the fact that the Soviets possessed everything that was necessary for domination: "the armed force of the workers and peasants, in close alliance with the masses, and the means of keeping this force in the hands" of the victorious party; "a form of organization of the vanguard" of the proletariat,* and, finally, "the possibility of combining the advantages of parliamentarianism with those of immediate and direct democracy—that is, the functions of both the legislative and the executive power."

It was on these bases that the Constitution was founded. It opened with a "declaration of the rights of the oppressed working masses," in which it proclaimed the abolition of private ownership of land; the ratification of the law on worker management "as the first step in the complete transfer of factories, workshops, railways . . . to ownership by the workers' and peasants' Soviet republic"; the repudiation of the debts contracted by the tsarist government; the nationalization of the banks; "compulsory labor service for all"; the disarmament of the bourgeoisie and the creation of a "Socialist Red Army of workers and peasants"; the abolition of secret treaties; "fraternization among the soldiers and peasants of the armies currently at war";

*Compare the doctrine of Georges Sorel.

the conclusion, "at any cost," of a "peace without annexations or reparations"; the liberation of colonies; and the transfer of all power to the Soviets alone.

It then stipulated the "general principles" and methods of operation of the government. The supreme authority of the RSFSR was the All-Russian Congress of Soviets and, when it was not in session, the All-Russian Central Executive Committee,* which appointed a Council of People's Commissars† for the "general management of business," with eighteen sections, or "People's Commissariats" for "the management of the various branches of the administration." The same pattern of organization was repeated in the federated regions, in which, of course, the jurisdiction of the local bodies was limited by that of the All-Russian central bodies. The right of voting was granted *de facto* only to the workers, the soldiers, and "peasants employing no labor"; the other classes were excluded from participation in the direction of the country under penalty of prosecution. Freedom of opinion—in other words, freedom of the press, of assembly, and of association—also became the monopoly of the "workers." In reality all power was completely dependent on the party, as Lenin emphasized: "We ought to know and remember that the establishment of the Soviets' power, *de jure* and *de facto,* rests on the party, which governs, appoints, and organizes on the basis of one single principle. . . . The party commands, it governs the entire state, it dominates and ought to dominate the apparatus of the state."

But the troubled years of the first phase of the Soviet system made it impossible to observe the provisions of this Constitution. The result was a simplification of the operations of the machinery of government. An official report on party activity acknowledged that "the exceptional circumstances of 1919, 1920, and part of 1921" had exerted a major influence, that "mobilizations for the transport of troops and food had succeeded one another without interruption . . ."; that "the party as a whole resembled a disciplined army on a war footing . . ." This was why all the opponents of the Communist system and even certain members of the party soon began to demand observance of the Constitution of July 10 as a minimum program.

The End of the War and the Treaty of Brest-Litovsk

The first urgent problem that called for resolution by the victors of 25 October/7 November 1917 was the earliest possible end of

---

Vserossysky tsentralny ispolnitelny Komitet, abbreviated as *Tsik.*

†*Sovyet narodnykh Komissarov,* abbreviated as *Sovnarkom.*

the war. On 28 October/10 November they informed the entire world by radio of their order for peace. They then made a direct appeal to the Allies. Without waiting for an answer, they ordered Generalissimo Dukhonin to embark directly on peace talks with the Germans. When he refused, as we have seen, Dukhonin was killed by a sailor. His successor, Krylenko, made a wireless request for an armistice, the truce was signed on 2/15 December, and the peace negotiations began a week later at Brest-Litovsk.

In order to understand the progress of these negotiations it must not be forgot that the Bolsheviki, when they seized power in Russia, set themselves a more important goal: the creation of revolution in Europe and the whole world. Even before they knew whether their power in Russia was solid, they hastened to pursue this international objective, which they were convinced that they would achieve in very short order. They had had Germany's backing in their struggle for power. Their first concern was to destroy her morale. They were convinced that the German diplomats' and generals' refusal to conclude a "democratic peace" at once would be the best means of furthering revolution in Germany. Therefore they made every effort to obtain the greatest publicity for the peace talks and—in vain—they requested that these be moved to Stockholm. There was no measure of their amazement when, on their proposal that all nationalities be given the right of self-determination, the Germans suggested that the Soviets give up Poland, Lithuania, Kurland, and part of Livonia and Estonia. On two occasions the talks were broken off, but, since the Germans stood fast on their positions and the German proletariat said nothing, Trotsky decided on February 4, 1918 to make a "gesture unique in the world's history": "neither peace nor war"; he offered to demobilize the Russian army and "put the Russian front under the protection of the German workers." The Germans' retort was a general offensive on February 18 and an ultimatum three days later that increased their demands. After much discussion the party's Central Committee had to capitulate. On March 3, 1918 a treaty for a separate peace was signed: it included independence for Finland and the Ukraine; the separation of Poland, Lithuania, and Kurland; German occupation of Estonia and Livonia; the cession of Batum and Kars to Turkey; and a prohibition on Bolshevik propaganda in Germany.

The Allies and the Start of the Civil War

Russia's Allies had long hoped that the new government would continue the war against the central powers. After the peace of

Brest-Litovsk their sole hope was placed in civil war, which was already beginning against the Bolsheviki. The Allies' diplomats left Petrograd for the north at the very moment when the Soviet government, in fear of the German offensive, was moving to Moscow.

In the territory of the Don Cossacks and at Rostov on the Don, where Russian officers who had escaped persecution by the Bolsheviki had joined a group of generals, including Kornilov, Denikin, and the former generalissimo, Aleksyeyev, a Russian army of "volunteers" had begun to form as early as November 1917. In January 1918 it amounted to three thousand men, but it could not hold its positions in Rostov and Novocherkassk in the face of the strong Soviet forces that were advancing from all sides. On February 11 General Kaledin, the ataman of the Don, committed suicide, and twelve days later the "volunteers" and their leaders set out for the steppes beneath the foothills of the Caucasus. This extremely bitter campaign, known as the "ice campaign," during which their number rose to nine thousand, attested to their vigor. They tried unsuccessfully to seize control of Ekaterinodar. On April 13 Kornilov was killed by a bomb, and his successor, General Denikin, had great difficulty in leading the army back to Rostov. At this time the Bolshevik power of resistance had been somewhat weakened. The Austrians and Germans, who had made a separate peace with the Ukraine on February 9 at Brest-Litovsk, occupied Little Russia and the Don. In Kiev they organized a government under the "hetman" Skoropadsky and on the Don they contributed to the election of General Krasnov as ataman of the Cossacks.

Although Kransov and Skoropadsky had been willing to bow to the wishes of the German emperor, the "volunteers," in contrast, had remained loyal to the Allies and counted on their help against the Germans and the Bolsheviki. Fearing the creation of a German front in Russia, the Allies began to show some interest in Denikin's army and to attempt to help him within certain limits. They were already supporting those Russian political parties that were combatting the Bolsheviki in order to create an "eastern front" against the Germans in Russia. They were interested too in another group suitable to the development of this front, the Czechs, who, under the tsarist government, had formed a "legion" against the Austro-Hungarians and then striven to fight their way back into Europe as quickly as possible in order to continue the battle on the French front. Along the lengthy route that they had elected—by way of Siberia and Vladivostok—the Czechs battled the Bolsheviki and helped Russian officers to drive them away from the Trans-Siberian. These successes induced the Allies to change the Czechs' destination and authorize them to set up an "anti-German front" in Siberia, while at the same time calling on them to ally themselves with the "Russian people" against the Bolsheviki. Consequently they halted their movement toward the Pacific and turned their forces toward the Ural. On July 25, 1918 they captured Ekaterinburg. Before evacuating this city, in which they had interned the imperial family, the Bolsheviki assassinated the tsar, the tsarina, and all their children on July 16; two days later in Alapayevsk, which the Czechs and the "Whites" did not take until September 28, the Bolsheviki also assassinated Grand Dukes Sergey Mikhailovitch, Ivan, Konstantin, and Yegor Konstantinovitch, as well as the tsarina's sister Elizabeth, who had become a nun.

The Allies' Intervention

Now the Allies decided to intervene directly. Influenced by the Treaty of Brest-Litovsk, the British had landed a force at Murmansk on March 11, and in July they sent further troops to Arkhangelsk. Their purpose was not only to safeguard the munitions and other war material delivered on credit by the Allies but also to create an "independent Russian army." On August 2 Russian officers drove the Bolsheviki out of the government of Arkhangelsk and, with British help, set up a government under the leadership of N. Chaikovsky, an old exiled revolutionary who was very popular in England.

At Samara on the Volga, which was captured with the help of the Czechs on June 8, a group of Revolutionary Socialist deputies from the dissolved Constituent Assembly established a "Committee of Members of the Constituent Assembly" and introduced it as the "embryo of pan-Russian power." On August 1 the "people's army" that it was able to rally numbered eighty-five hundred volunteers and twenty-two hundred soldiers mobilized among the local populations.* The Allies promised to back up this army in order to establish a "Volga front" from Samara to Kazan. This "front," which was in fact created at the end of July and the beginning of August of 1918, was too distant from the northern regions for Allied help to reach it; hence it had to be abandoned in September and October—Kazan was taken on August 7 and then evacuated on September 10, Samara on October 8.

*Theoretical calculations as of September 1 estimated the potential military population embraced within the jurisdiction of the Samara government as one hundred twenty-one thousand men; but on August 19 only twenty-one thousand had yet been mobilized.

Russian and Allied operations against the Bolsheviki were more successful in Siberia. The British dispatched Admiral Kolchak there with the task of assembling an army in the Far East. In addition the French and the Czechs were insistently demanding the organization of a single "all-Russian" government. After long negotiations this government was established by the congress that was held in Ufa on September 23, 1918 by the political parties and the various Russian governments.* It was headed by a moderate Revolutionary Socialist, N. Avksentyev, and its seat was in Omsk, in western Siberia. But it could not impose its authority. On December 1 it was overthrown by right-wing officers with secret assistance from the British, and it was replaced by the personal government of Admiral Kolchak, who assumed the title of "supreme chief."

It was, naturally, the fertile regions of the south closest to the Moscow center that were the most fought over between the Bolsheviki and the "Whites." But it was also just in this area that help from the Allies was slowest in arriving and lowest in effectiveness. In fact, they gave no serious thought to intervention there until after the capitulation of the central powers on November 11, 1918—in other words, when there was no longer any need to create an "eastern front."

Since they foresaw a victorious Bolshevik offensive in the south as soon as it should have been evacuated by the Austrians and the Germans, the anti-Bolshevik military leaders and Russian political parties strove to accelerate the Allies' help. General Berthelot, the commander of the Allies' forces on the Rumanian front, promised to dispatch one hundred fifty thousand men (twelve divisions) who would be landed at Odessa; it was agreed that the abundant supplies of the former Rumanian front would be made available to the Russians and that they would be handsomely provided with war materials. On December 19, 1918 a French division landed at Odessa, where General d'Anselme assumed command in mid-January 1919. As for the British, who had incorporated the Caucasus into their "sphere of influence," they had had a division at Batum since November 1918.

The Bolshevik Peace Proposal

General Berthelot's plans came into collision with the resistance of the Allies' delegates meeting in Paris for the peace conference. While

*The Samara government (*Komuch*), the provisional government of Siberia, the Cossacks of the Ural and Orenburg, the local government of Ekaterinburg, the Kirghizi, and the Bashkiri.

Pichon and Orlando announced their endorsement of them, Lloyd George, Wilson, and Clemenceau opposed them in the sessions of January 1 and 21, 1919, arguing that one hundred fifty thousand men were too few to be of any practical value and that no one was going to send any more men into a country where, in addition to everything else, there was the danger of the demoralization of the troops. Military assistance was supplanted by the plan, suggested by Lloyd George and approved by Wilson, to call together the representatives of "all sectors of the Russian people" on the island of Prinkipo in order to arrive at an agreement.

On February 4 the Bolsheviki eagerly accepted this proposal and agreed to make all kinds of concessions to the Allies. But the representatives of the anti-Bolshevik governments refused on February 19 to have any dealings with the "criminal usurpers," and the projected conference collapsed. Three days later, with Lloyd George's knowledge, Wilson sent William Bullitt, a young assistant to the American delegation at the peace conference, to Soviet Russia in order to work out peace terms on the basis of the Bolshevik proposals. On March 14 a draft peace treaty rich in alluring concessions was drawn up in Moscow: all the governments of Russia would retain their territories, the economic blockade would be lifted, a general amnesty would be proclaimed, the troops would be brought home and disarmed, etc. But Europe's state of mind had already shifted, because the "White" armies were beginning to score victories and the Bolsheviki were too obvious in their determination to bring on "world revolution." Hence the Soviet government's offers were futile.

The Third International

The day after the Soviets received the invitation to go to Prinkipo (January 22, 1919), Lenin invited all the world's Communist parties to meet in Moscow and organize the "Third International" in final form. This project had been prepared during the war by the left Socialists' congresses in Zimmerwald (September 5–12, 1915) and Kienthal (February 5–9, 1916), at which the Russian Bolsheviki, in spite of the "social patriots" of the Second International, had won acceptance for their formula of "immediate peace without annexations." The Third International was created by the Moscow Congress of March 2–6, 1919 in spite of the paucity of delegations and the absence of the most important parties, those of England, the United States, etc. The manifesto of the Congress, issued on March 10, asserted the feasibility of an immediate overthrow of the capitalist system and stated that a "new revolutionary era" had begun. The consequence was the evolution of a plan for revolution in all central Europe, beginning with Germany, where in fact three risings were attempted and all were stamped out by Noske, and Hungary, where, in agreement with Lenin, Bela Kun seized power. The documents captured in Radek's office in Wilmersdorf (Berlin) proved that the Bolshevik plans went far beyond what was actually achieved. It was at this same time that their activity in Asia—Afghanistan, India, etc.—became known.

The Defeat of Allied Intervention

The Allies' intervention was neither sufficiently coordinated nor sufficiently sizable to be effective.

In Odessa the French had only twelve thousand men, of whom six thousand were Greeks and Poles. They could not hold out against the Soviet forces. When they were not succored, as they had relied on being, by the Ukrainians under Petlyura, the leader of the Ukrainian separatists who had just driven out the "hetman" Skoropadsky and who were themselves to be routed a few days later by the Bolsheviki, the French fell back toward Odessa after having been defeated at Nikolayev and Kherson. Confronted with a wave of protests in the Chamber of Deputies, the French government issued orders for the evacuation of Odessa within three days of April 1.*

The British were no better able to maintain their positions in the Caucasus. They evacuated Baku in June and July 1919, Tiflis in July and August 1919, and Batum a year later, on July 9–10, 1920.

Another British effort in the Baltic area was no more successful. The "White" Russians had established a "northern corps" of thirty-five hundred men there, and since the end of 1918 it and the Estonian army commanded by General Laidoner had been fighting the Bolsheviki. Under pressure from a Briton, General March, a "democratic Russian government" was set up in Reval; it recognized the independence of Estonia and won the Estonians' support for a march on Petrograd. After he had recruited an army of twenty thousand men and been assured of backing by the British, General Yudenitch took the offensive on October 4, 1919. In the next two weeks he advanced as far as Gatchina, Pavlovsk, and Krasnoye Selo. On October 20 he was only a few miles outside Petrograd; but at this critical moment

---

*Carried out in haste, the evacuation order spread panic through the city, which contained one million residents. General d'Anselme was able to embark ten thousand volunteers—the others set out overland for Rumania—and about thirty thousand civilians.

the Estonians refused to give him help. The Bolsheviki, led by Trotsky, the creator of the Red Army, turned his flank; the British fleet, sailing out of Kronstadt for Riga, did not support his drive, and he was forced into a precipitate retreat (November 2–14). On December 1 he resigned his command and four days later the "democratic government" was dissolved.

Kolchak's Defeat in Siberia

In Omsk, Admiral Kolchak, whom General Denikin had acknowledged as the "supreme chief," enjoyed the assistance of an extremely brilliant diplomatic staff, including Generals Janin of France and Knox of England. After the capture of Perm on December 24, 1918 by the Czech General Gayda and the Russian General Pepelyayev, Kolchak evolved a plan of campaign against Moscow in January. His three armies, which totaled almost one hundred thirty thousand men, captured Ufa on March 13 and advanced as far as Novo-Uzensk, Bugulma, Elabuga, Glazov, and Vyatka in April.

But all the weak points in the campaign became manifest in May. Gayda had a row with Kolchak and resigned, the Siberian peasants refused to fight, and, under the influence of Bolshevik propaganda, they instigated several risings in the rear. The Siberian administration was as bad as it could be; the abuses of its officials and officers angered the population. Conspiracies were begun around Kolchak himself, and, becoming more and more nervous, he was incapable of exerting any authority but absolutely refused to share power with anyone. Nevertheless the Allies were still prepared to back him up on condition that he make democratic commitments. This he agreed to do on June 4. But his army was in full retreat. On October 14 Omsk itself was threatened by the Bolsheviki, who captured it on November 14. At Irkutsk, to which it had fled, Kolchak's government found itself in the midst of left-wing parties that were sympathetic to the Bolsheviki, and whatever was left of its authority vanished. Since the Trans-Siberian right of way was under the protection of the Czechs, whose government had urged them to observe neutrality, Kolchak's troops had to carry out their retreat across the *taiga* through a terrible freeze and suffered abominably.

Leaving Omsk with seven trains, which he was compelled to abandon one by one along the way, Kolchak himself was finally compelled to board the Czechs' train. He had not yet reached Irkutsk when the city was gripped by a revolt fomented by the Revolutionary Socialists. On the demand of his ministers he resigned his post on January 4, 1920 and implored the protection of the Allies' representatives, to whom he turned over the stock of gold that he had brought with him. The Czechs allowed him to be arrested in the Irkutsk railway station on January 14 when the insurgents threatened to block the passage of the train. Kolchak was tried by the Bolsheviki, to whom the Revolutionary Socialists had yielded their authority on January 22, and on February 7 he was shot as his retreating army was approaching the city.

Subsequently this army went on to the Far East, which was under Japanese occupation from the mouth of the Amur to northern Sakhalin. In Vladivostok, under Japanese protection, another "White" government was established, but it was able to remain in office only until October 25, 1922; in fact, as soon as the Japanese left the city, it was occupied by the Bolsheviki.

Denikin's and Wrangel's Defeats in Southern Russia

After General Aleksyeyev's death on October 8, 1918, General Denikin assumed the command of the "armed forces of southern Russia" and established his headquarters in Ekaterinodar in the northern Caucasus. Increased between May and October, through the mobilization of soldiers locally and the enlistments of Cossacks, from sixty-four thousand to one hundred fifty thousand men, his army at first achieved a number of victories. It captured Kharkov and Tsaritsyn on the Volga on June 24 and 30, entered Kiev on August 30, advanced toward the north in the direction of Moscow, and seized Kursk on September 20 and Voronezh ten days later.

But, after the capture of Orel on October 13, its problems began. The Cossacks, who constituted the largest part of its forces, refused to go farther; they were reluctant to move into the desolated northern areas and abandon the rich reserves of the south, which indeed were of especial attraction to the Bolsheviki. The population, which had received the "Whites" as liberators, was soon undeceived and began to look on them as no more than the agents of the great landed proprietors seeking to recover the lands seized by the peasants. Tyranny and violence were the characteristic means of government in these occupied territories. General Wrangel wrote to Denikin: "The war has become a source of profits." Denikin was incapable of remedying the situation. The officers, most of whom were monarchists, regarded him as too far "left" and the "left" criticized his government because it was too far "right." The failure of his offensive was made final by the retreat of the Cossacks, who were in haste to return to their own lands. Almost without resistance they reached, first, Rostov, early in

January of 1920, and then, after the evacuation of that city on January 9, Ekaterinodar on March 4, arriving finally at Novorossysk on the shore of the Black Sea. At the end of March some of them were evacuated to the Crimea by sea; the rest, Don and Kuban Cossacks who constituted the majority of the force, surrendered. Denikin tendered his resignation and went abroad after he had appointed his rival, General Wrangel, who enjoyed the support of the officers, to succeed him on April 4, 1920.

Wrangel could only postpone the inevitable evacuation. He led what was left of the army—about twenty thousand volunteers and twelve thousand Cossacks—into the Crimea. Once he had restored his men's morale and discipline, he undertook three successive operations in the direction of the Dnieper and the Kuban between June and September 1920. When he refused to cease his activities, the British government was no longer willing to support him. The French government, on the other hand, encouraged him, and even officially recognized his government on August 10. But the Bolsheviki, having hastily ended their war against Poland,* threw all their forces against him beginning on November 3. His army, which had lost almost 60 per cent of its effectives, was demoralized, abandoned its equipment, and fell back in disorder. The enemy, having forced the Isthmus of Perekop on November 8–9, pursued him into the Crimea. Unable to hold out longer, Wrangel assembled 126 boats in the ports and on November 13–14 they took aboard some 135,000 persons, including 70,000 soldiers, and, after a most difficult voyage, landed them at Constantinople.

Wrangel, however, did not regard his army as having been dissolved, and he abandoned neither his power nor the idea of resuming the battle abainst the Bolsheviki. France, which had assisted him during the evacuation, refused to continue her support, and on April 17, 1921 she announced that she no longer recognized the existence of his army. From August 4 to December 14 the fugitive soldiers were kept in military camps on the peninsula of Gallipoli and the island of Lemnos, whence later they were removed to Bulgaria and Yugoslavia.

The Exiles

The emigration that had begun in November 1917 assumed much greater proportions with the two evacuations from Novorossysk and the Crimea. In addition to the soldiers, the officers, and the Cossacks of the "White" armies, a vast mass of persons left Russia: members of all

*See page 378.

classes deprived of their civic rights by the Bolsheviki and exposed to the persecutions of the *Cheka**—landowners, industrialists, bankers, scholars, writers, politicians, journalists, lawyers, physicians, artists, actors, musicians. . . . This emigration, a unique phenomenon in the world by reason both of its size and of its social components, was reckoned at a minimum of one million persons by the most conservative estimates. The statistics of a special committeee of the League of Nations set the number of Russian refugees in 1932 at approximately 844,000, of whom almost half (about 400,000) had settled in France, about 150,000 in Slavic countries, 120,000 in countries bordering on Russia, and 100,000 in China and Manchuria.

The exiles adapted themselves to their new situation. Those who belonged to the liberal professions pursued their former activities as much as possible, and they included writers, scholars, and artists of high repute. But the greater number was forced to seek a livelihood through manual labor, in industry or agriculture. Politically they remained divided into many parties that ranged from Socialist to extreme-right monarchist.

The Reasons for the Failure of the "Whites"

There were at least four categories of reasons for the failure of the "Whites."

The first category was military: the talents of the Russian generals who went over to the Bolsheviki, the ardor of the young Soviet "Partisans," the strategic advantage enjoyed by the "Reds" through their possession of internal lines of communication, while their opponents had to operate at isolated points on the periphery.

The second was economic: the natural wealth of the south, which attracted the "Reds," and the poverty of the northern territories, where the supply problem of the "Whites" became increasingly difficult in direct ratio to their gains.

**Verkhovnaya Chrezvychaynaya Komissya*, abbreviated as *Vecheka* or *Cheka*, an extraordinary commission created in December 1917. The police force of the revolution, it was the replica of the tsarist *Okhrana*. It made itself famous through the terrorist campaign that it waged against "class enemies"—that is, the middle class, the intellectuals, the "White" officers, and the members of non-Communist parties.

Abolished on February 6, 1922, it was replaced by the *Obyedinennoye gosudarstvennoye politicheskoye upravlenye* (the OGPU or GPU). This organization was invested with broad powers: a decree of October 16 empowered it to shoot bandits caught in the act; another secret decree of November 15, 1923 endowed it with a court that could impose the death penalty on "counterrevolutionaries," "*saboteurs*," etc. Thereafter the terror was turned against workers, peasants, and everyone who was accused of having "harmed" the interests of the proletariat.

The third and major class was social: the popular masses, to whom the Bolsheviki made the most alluring promises, and above all the peasants, who had taken over all the properties of the former land-owners, could not trust the presence of so many members of the privileged classes, the victims of the revolution, in the ranks of the "Whites."

The fourth category was political: the suspicion of the various national minorities of the old Empire toward the "Whites," whom they regarded as centralists and enemies of autonomy; the behavior of the "Whites," who despoiled the local populations of everything, and the abuses of their officials in the areas that they occupied; the delays and the inadequacies in assistance from the Allies, who, as a result of their lack of agreement on the struggle against the Soviets and because of the intervention of political parties for or against the "Whites" and the "Reds," let slip the opportune moment when the Bolsheviki had as yet neither consolidated their authority nor completely organized the Red Army.

The War Against Poland

The Polish campaign began in April 1920 with the entry of Polish troops into the Ukraine and their occupation of Kiev. In May an offensive by the "Reds" forced the invaders to retreat. In June the Poles regained the advantage. In July a second drive by the "Reds" carried them to the very gates of Warsaw. In August, the regrouped Polish army relieved its capital and inflicted a severe defeat on the "Reds." The Soviets had to negotiate, and they signed the preliminary peace terms of Riga on October 12, 1920. Under the final treaty, also concluded in Riga, on March 18, 1921, Russia gave up a population of 4.25 million White Russians, Ukrainians, and Great Russians, and lost a territorial area of approximately 39,000 square miles that separated Russia from Lithuania.

Soviet Foreign Relations: the First International Treaties and Conferences

The first foreign agreements were made with the nationalities detached from Russia. These were the peace and trade treaties of 1920: with Estonia on February 2, with Lithuania on July 12, with Latvia on August 11, with Finland on October 14. Under these treaties Russia lost 18,360 square miles and 1.11 million inhabitants in Estonia, almost 20,000 square miles and 2.258 million inhabitants in Lithuania,

25,400 square miles and 1,850,662 inhabitants in Latvia, and almost 150,000 square miles and 3,336,940 inhabitants in Finland—in short, a total of more than 213,000 square miles and 8,555,562 persons. With the addition of the 100,000 square miles and 15.8 million Russians surrendered to Polish jurisdiction, the more than 15,000 square miles and 2.75 million inhabitants of Bessarabia annexed by Rumania, and the 6800 square miles and 492,000 inhabitants of the Kars district ceded to Turkey in March 1921, the amputations inflicted on Russia reached a grand total of 335, 469 square miles and 27,597,562 persons.

Soon afterward the Soviets began negotiating also with the great powers, toward which their attitude altered in proportion to the consolidation of their successes. Lloyd George, who had been convinced of their triumph from the start, insisted that direct relations with them be established. It was on his initiative that a Soviet delegation headed by an engineer named Krasin arrived in London on May 31, 1920. But the Bolsheviki were not willing either to acknowledge imperial Russia's debts or to abandon their revolutionary propaganda in the British colonies. Suspended as a result of the war against Poland, which Lloyd George vainly endeavored to halt by proposing his own services as mediator, and resumed after the preliminary peace talks in Riga, the negotiations led to the first trade treaty with Britain on March 16, 1921.

Other trade treaties were subsequently concluded by the RSFSR with Germany on May 6, with Norway on September 2, with Austria on December 8, with Italy on December 26—all in 1921—and, in 1922, with Sweden on March 1 and with Czechoslovakia on June 5.

Lloyd George continued to press for the growth of relations with Soviet Russia. At the Conference of Cannes (January 6, 1922), when it was examining means of restoring the economic prosperity of the countries damaged by the war, the Allies' Supreme Council was thinking above all of Russia, and therefore the Soviets were invited to the Conference of Genoa, which ran from April 10 to May 17, 1922. While the Moscow delegates were absolutely immovable, the Allies could not reach agreement among themselves. In fact, whereas Lloyd George was prepared to make serious compromises with the Soviets, France and Belgium insisted that they recognize foreigners' title to property in Russia. As for the Bolsheviki, they demanded credits with which to rebuild their country's economy.

In order to find a way out of the deadlock at which the negotiations had arrived, it was decided to convene a group of experts in The Hague (June 15–July 26, 1922). There both sides proved to be farther apart than in Genoa. Litvinov, who had replaced Chicherin at the head of the Soviet delegation, refused to discuss either the tsarist debts or compensation to foreign owners of nationalized enterprises until credits had been granted to the new Russia. The conference broke up without result.

While they were engaged in public discussion in Genoa with the Allies, the Soviets were secretly concluding with Germany, which recognized them *de jure*, the Treaty of Rapallo of April 16, 1922. Because German policy was at that time vacillating between east and west, this treaty was significant of Soviet diplomacy's tendency to set eastern and western countries against each other. In 1921, in fact, Russia had already signed treaties of friendship with Persia on February 26, with Afghanistan on February 28, and with Turkey on March 18, and all these, like the Treaty of Rapallo, included *de jure* recognition of the Soviet government.

In the international Conference of Lausanne (December 4, 1922–February 5, 1923 and April 23–July 27, 1923), where the Soviets were invited "to be represented in the discussion of the question of the Straits," Chicherin, with no success whatever, defended the Turkish point of view, which in part coincided with the Russian. Although the agreement on the Straits was unfavorable to their country, the Bolsheviki agreed to sign it.

Before the end of the Lausanne Conference a serious conflict arose between Russia and Britain. Some British fishing vessels had been seized in the waters off Murmansk, and a note from Lord Curzon on May 8, 1923 protested and demanded "full and entire satisfaction." This was granted on June 11.

The Domestic Situation: the System of "War Communism"

Until 1920 the internal situation in Russia was extremely difficult. The necessity of centralizing all the country's resources against the "White" armies, which were attacking on all sides, compelled the Bolsheviki to an inordinate expansion of the state's jurisdiction and to the creation of a system that essentially was nothing but "state capitalism," even though Lenin, in order to give it the appearance of a transition to the Socialist system, denominated its actions by names borrowed from the terminology of "Socialist" doctrine.

As soon as they had got rid of the civil war and concentrated in the hands of a few agencies the whole management of a country in the process of disintegration, the Bolsheviki began to apply the system that they themselves called "war communism." The ideal of this system was the complete elimination of all business, that "bourgeois" exchange of products, and of the medium of that exchange, money, in order to attain to the "exchange in kind" of industrial for agricultural products. Since the workers in the factories were already wholly within the power of the state and even completely militarized, what remained to be done was to seize from the peasants the wheat required for the feeding of the army, the workers, both industrial and clerical, and all the residents of cities—in other words, in 1920, some thirty-five million men.

This mission was entrusted to "brigades" of workers dispatched to the villages, and also to the poor peasants themselves, the *byednyaki,* who were organized into special detachments. On December 22, 1920 Lenin noted with satisfaction that wheat supplies were adequate:

Three hundred twenty million poods before the revolution: this was approximately the minimum without which nothing could be accomplished. The first year of the revolution produced fifty million poods: this meant famine, tremendous misery. The second year produced a hundred million . . . the third year [1919–1920] two hundred million. . . . The figure has doubled every year. . . . For the first time we are on our feet: we shall have available a supply of about three hundred million . . . Without a reserve of this kind it is impossible to rebuild the country's industry, it is impossible to think of reorganizing transportation, it is impossible even to embark on the great task of the electrification of Russia.

In 1920–1921, as a result of forced requisitions, the Commissariat of Supply succeeded in stockpiling 350 million poods. But it could do so only by confiscating all the reserves that the peasants vainly strove to conceal.

The Consequences of "War Communism"

This economic system led to a rapid decline in production. The peasants gave up intensive cultivation; then they began to sow less; in 1920 the area under cultivation had diminished by almost half. Livestock was equally reduced. Inflation saw to the deficits in the budget, and the value of money depreciated steadily. At the same time, wages were decreasing in purchasing power and the workers were abandoning the factories for the farms. In 1921 the output of nationalized industry was only 14 per cent of the prewar figure. The abolition of business had given rise to clandestine markets where it was possible to obtain everything, but at exorbitant prices. The workers stole the products manufactured in the factories and went off with them to buy wheat in the agricultural governments.

With the first poor harvest, in 1921 and 1922, famine began. The population of the southern governments and the Volga left the countryside and marched on the cities. "Holding detachments" had to bar their way. The roads were congested with caravans of vehicles of all kinds; people wandered about at random, in areas unknown to them, to "the king of India," as they put it. On the basis of official figures, this famine, the extent of which was unprecedented in Russia, claimed approximately five million victims; but this official statistic falls short of the truth. In 1920 and 1921 the peasants' anger was manifested in a number of risings in eastern Siberia, on the Volga, in the governments of Tambov and Ryazan, etc.; even the sailors of Kronstadt mutinied, and their rising made a profound impression on the Bolsheviki.

The "Retreat"

Lenin had to admit that he had been wrong. "Experience shows that the immediate conversion to purely Socialist methods is beyond our capacities," he wrote. ". . . The peasant is no longer willing to tolerate the relations that have come into being among us. . . . We have to take into account the wishes of enormous masses of the population . . ." Therefore he decided to begin "a major retreat"—in other words, as he openly asserted, to abandon requisitions and "go back to taxation, to freedom of trade, and this in large measure presupposes the restoration of capitalism."

In July and August 1921 the government issued a number of decrees that signified a major change. This was the "New Economic Policy," the NEP. Lenin and the party found consolation for this change by calling it a step backward in order to be able to leap higher. Nonetheless, the "step backward" did not please all the Communists, and Lenin, who, furthermore, was soon to become gravely ill, lost much of his authority. Hence the NEP was not to last long.

II / THE NEP AND THE STRUGGLE FOR SUCCESSION TO LENIN (1923–1927)

The USSR and the Constitution of July 6, 1923

The Soviet government inaugurated the second period of its existence by adopting a new federal Constitution and a new name, the Union of Soviet Socialist Republics, from which two words that appeared in the former name of the RSFSR were absent: *Russian* and *Federated*.

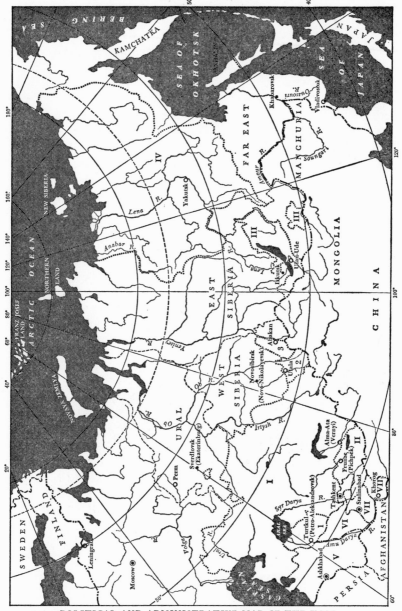

POLITICAL AND ADMINISTRATIVE MAP OF THE U.S.S.R.

▬▬▬ **·** ▬▬	Boundaries of the U.S.S.R.
▬ **·** ▬ **·** ▬	Boundaries of Federated Republics
··················	Boundaries of Autonomous Territories (A. T.) or Republics (A. R.)
▬ ▬ ▬ ▬	Boundaries of Regions (*oblast* or *krazh*)

◉	Capitals of Federated or Soviet Republics (S. R.)
○	Capitals of Autonomous Territories (A. T.) or Republics (A. R.)
•	Regional Capitals

The Autonomous Republics of the Kazaki (I), the Kirghiz (II), the Buryat Mongols (III), and the Yakuti (IV), and the Autonomous Territories of the Karakalpaki (1), the Oirati (2), and the Khakassi (3) are part of the R.S.F.S.R. The three republics of Central Asia are the Socialist Soviet Republics of Turmenistan (V), Uzbekistan (VI), and Tadzhikistan (VII), from which the Autonomous Territory of Badakhchan (VII₁) was separated.

POLITICAL AND ADMINISTRATIVE MAP OF THE U.S.S.R.

—··—··— Boundaries of the U.S.S.R.
—·—·—· Boundaries of Federated Republics
·················· Boundaries of Autonomous Territories (A. T.)
    or Republics (A. R.)
— — — — Boundaries of Regions (*oblast* or *krazh*)

⊙ Capitals of Federated or Soviet Republics (S. R.)
○ Capitals of Autonomous Territories (A. T.)
    or Republics (A. R.)
• Regional Capitals

The Autonomous Republics (AR) of Karelia (I), the Chuvachi (II), the Tartars (III), the Bashkiri (IV), the Volga Germans (V), the Kazaki (VI), the Crimea (VII), and Daghestan (VIII), and the Autonomous Territories (AT) of the Komi-Zyriani (1), the Votyaki (2), the Mari or Cheremissi (3), the Mordvinians (4), the Kalmuki (5), the Adigs (6), the Circassians (7), the Karatchayevians (8), the Kabard-Balkari (9), the Northern Ossetians (10), the Ingush (11), and the Chechens (12) are all members of the Russian Socialist Federated Soviet Republic (R.S.F.S.R.).

The Autonomous Republic of Moldavia (IX) is a dependency of the Ukrainian S.S.R.

The Soviet Republic of Georgia (X), with the Autonomous Republics of Abkhazy (X_1) and Adzhary (X_2) and the Autonomous Territory of the Southern Ossetians (X_3); the Armenian Soviet Republic (XI); and the Soviet Republic of Azerbaijan (XII), with the Autonomous Republic of Nakhitchevan (XII_1) and the Autonomous Territory of Karabakh (XII_2) are all part of the Transcaucasian S.F.S.R.

Under a treaty signed on December 30, 1922, the four major "independent" republics—the RSFSR, White Russia, the Ukraine, and Transcaucasia (which included Azerbaidjan, Georgia, and Armenia, gathered into a federation after December 13, 1922)—created the USSR properly so called. At the end of 1924, two "independent" republics, Uzbekistan and Turkmenistan, entered the Union, which then embraced fifteen "autonomous territories"—this was the term applied to the least numerous or least advanced national minorities—and fifteen "autonomous republics." Of these thirty "territories" and "republics," twenty-three were members of the USSR.

On December 5, 1929 they were to be joined by a seventh republic, Tadjikistan, which until then had been an autonomous territory and then an autonomous republic within Uzbekistan. After 1930 the Union consisted of fifteen "autonomous republics" and eighteen "autonomous territories"; twenty-four of the "republics" and "territories" were included in the RSFSR.

The census of 1926 gave the following figures for the areas and populations of the seven republics in the Union:

REPUBLIC	SQUARE MILES	POPULATION
RSFSR	7,628,563	100,800,000
Ukraine	174,517	29,020,000
White Russia	48,957	4,983,900
Transcaucasia	82,447	5,872,741
Uzbekistan	71,930	4,447,600
Tadjikistan	59,498	827,400
Turkmenistan	189,652	992,000
Total	8,255,564	146,943,641*

*According to the statistics available on January 1, 1931, the population had risen to 161 million.

The instrumentalities of government in the Soviet Union were: the Congress of Soviets, the method of election of which favored the cities and hence the working class; the Union's Central Executive Committee, elected by the Congress to govern when the Congress was not in session and composed of two Chambers: the Soviet of the Union and the Soviet of Nationalities, both of which had the same legislative and administrative rights, although the former represented the population of the USSR as a whole and the second represented the respective national minorities; the Presidium of the Central Executive Committee, which exercised power between the Committee's sessions and the composition of which consisted, for two thirds, of the officers of the two Chambers, to whom were added nine members elected by those Chambers jointly; and, finally, the Council of People's Commissars, which included the heads of "Union commissariats" and of what were called "unified" commissariats.

The "People's Commissariats" were divided into "commissariats of the USSR," "unified commissariats," and "autonomous commissariats." Those of the first category—Foreign Affairs, the Army and Navy, Foreign Trade, Communications, Transport—were the same for all the federated republics, which in these areas had only "agents of authority" completely subordinated to the federal commissars. Those of the second group—National Economy, Food and Supply, Labor, Finance, Labor and Peasant Regulation—coexisted in the central government and in the republics of the Union; those of the third group—the Interior, Justice, Agriculture, Public Education, Health, and Social Security—functioned only within the republics. It would therefore seem that these preserved a certain autonomy. But such was not the fact, because the local "unified commissariats" and the "autonomous commissariats" were not sovereign within their jurisdictions; they were more or less subordinated to the Union, which controlled internal commerce, owned all the large industrial enterprises, held full power over local budgets, set the conditions for the cultivation of land and the disposition of crops, established the bases for colonization, laid down the basic principles of law, procedure, and the Civil and Criminal Codes, and directed public education and health. The Presidium of the Central Executive Committee could invalidate any ordinance whatever enacted by the local authorities. On the other hand, decrees issued by the central government were automatically applicable in all parts of the USSR. The independence of the individual republics was the more illusory in that all their institutions were subject to the direction of the Communist party and all problems between central and regional authorities could be resolved by the mere transfer of the respective officials. The Soviet of Nationalities, a kind of "second Chamber," did indeed represent the national minorities to which in 1917 the Bolsheviki had promised freedom "even to the point of secession," but the majority in this Soviet was held by the delegates of the RSFSR, 73.5 per cent of whose population consisted of Great Russians; and since, in addition, the minorities' representatives were lost in the Congress of Soviets, it could exert no influence on the general policy of the Soviet Union.

According to the Constitution, the USSR was freely open to any "Socialist republic" in any country anywhere, because, in harmony with its basic principle, it could and should become a worldwide union as a result of successive adhesions to it. Similarly the Constitution declared that each of the republics of the Soviet Union had the right to withdraw from it. In practice, Soviet jurists found that this right had only a "declarative" validity and that any effort to convert the "theoretical sovereignty" of a republic into actual sovereignty should be regarded "as the inception of a national and counterrevolutionary movement." The statement that formed the preamble to the Constitution asserted that the USSR, in contrast to those countries still in "the camp of capitalism," had guaranteed "the liberty of nations and the equality, peaceful coexistence, and fraternal collaboration of peoples"; but neither the text of the Constitution nor the method of its application justified this assertion.

In short, the Soviet Union was federal only in appearance. The republics that constituted it were in fact subject to its rule, just as the Union itself was subject to the dictatorship of the Communist party, whose central committee and political bureau—in the last analysis, the secretary general—alone made policy decisions.

The NEP and the "Rehabilitation"

The end of the civil war and the start of the NEP fostered the rehabilitation of Russia's productive capacities now that she had regained her economic unity—for the Soviets now had available the whole economic complex that embraced the coal of the Donets, the oil of the Caucasus, the wheat of the Ukraine, the Volga, and western Siberia, the iron of the Urals, and the livestock of the steppes.

The elimination of unregulated requisitions of wheat in favor of a regular tax in kind, as well as the pledge of their right of enjoyment of their holdings, induced the peasants to increase their sowing and to build up their livestock resources. Big industry was reorganized on commercial principles and the workers went back to the factories that they had abandoned. Small industry was in part turned back to private enterprise. The restoration of the free market in consumer goods made it possible for private capital to reappear and quickly gain control of a large part of the wholesale trade. The renascence of internal commerce was also encouraged by the stabilization of the currency; the Soviet ruble, which had lost all its value in 1924, was withdrawn from circulation and replaced by a new monetary unit, the *chervonets*,* whose soundness was initially assured by reserves of gold and foreign currency. Taxation, which had been completely eliminated during the

*Its nominal value, nine rubles and ninety-two kopecks, was virtually the same as that of the pound sterling.

period of "war Communism," was reinstituted and in 1923 an attempt was made to prepare the first regular budget. The population, which had been seriously depleted according to the 1920 census (which was incomplete), began to rise rapidly.* Foreign trade, which had virtually disappeared, increased from year to year, side by side with those sectors of the national economy that had suffered the most and were now steadily raising their productivity.

Dissensions Within the Party and the First "Discussion"

The NEP was an unending source of anxiety to some members of the Communist party. Zinovyev, the dictator of Petrograd, was the first to voice his alarm at the creation of a "new middle class." Trotsky foresaw the threatening growth of private capital and the opening of the frontiers to foreign products. Stalin, the secretary general of the party, observed in 1925 that a new atmosphere filled with confidence prevailed among the workers who had gone back to the factories and among the peasants, who no longer feared the return of the former owners of the land. The formation of commercial, industrial, and cooperative agencies, as a result of the NEP, gave rise to tens of thousands of new specialists whose real knowledge overwhelmed the party's old dabblers. The Communist party itself was being altered as the militants of the "old guard," the veterans of the days of "underground" combat, disappeared and a new generation arose and neglected the task that had once been made paramount: world revolution and the Socialization of Russia.

In order to soothe the malcontents, the government began, some eighteen months after the start of the NEP, to harass the *nepman*, the representative of capital who had come back in the form of the speculator. Driven out of commerce, capital fled to the villages, where it took over the purchase of wheat and raw materials. Driven next from the villages, it sought to engage in small homework industry and credit operations. What delayed its ultimate elimination was the conflicts among the leaders of the party.

From 1923 on, Lenin, whose authority had hitherto been enough to cut off internal discussions, had been confined to his bed. The struggle for his succession began before he died. The antagonists were Trotsky, on whom the dying leader relied completely and who regarded himself as the legitimate heir, and Stalin, the secretary general of the party, who already held power *de facto* and distributed posts of authority, and who was supported by Zinovyev and Kamenev.

*The annual rate of growth was 2.5 per cent.

It was in the autumn of 1923 that Trotsky brought on the first public "discussion." The opposition, which had taken shape in 1922 against the policy of the party's central committee and political bureau, and of which he emerged as the leader, criticized the ruling circle for sacrificing the workers to the peasants so that the workers were no longer anything but "puppets." The opposition blamed the party leadership for the fact that the best workers were deserting the party, whose ranks had indeed been seriously reduced, both by the "purge" that had eliminated one hundred ninety thousand members in 1921 and by the withdrawals of the old members and the reluctance of the young men to take their places. The opposition called for the application of "democratic principles" within the party—a phrase on which Trotsky seized for a major demagogic campaign that was addressed principally to the young and the military "cells." It demanded the right to form an independent "fraction," insisted that officials be chosen by election and not by appointment, that the post-revolutionary generation be entrusted with power in preference to the "old guard," and that the central committee be subject to reelection.

An attempt at compromise failed. Then for the first time Stalin displayed his power by having Trotsky sent to the Caucasus "for reasons of health."

The Death of Lenin and the Struggle Between Trotsky and Stalin

Lenin died on January 21, 1924. He left a "political testament" in which, after a warning that division among the leaders could lead to schism, he warned of Stalin's "coarseness" and the danger to the unity of the party that was represented by his presence as its secretary general, whereas he declared Trotsky "the more able," although "too much in love with himself."

Trotsky exploited this document, which the central committee endeavored to keep secret, to mount a new and open attack against Stalin. In his book, *The Lessons of October*,* he elaborated his theory of permanent revolution, claimed the credit for the Bolshevik victory over the provisional government, and denounced the cowardice of Zinovyev and Kamenev, who, with Stalin, constituted a "triumvirate" or, as he called it, a troika (a three-horse team). Stalin's retort was action. He solidified his position in the party by bringing into it some two hundred thousand "Lenin recruitment" workers, all totally loyal to him personally, and by manipulating the elections for the Thirteenth Party Congress to his best advantage, so that his opponents

*That is, the revolution of 25 October/7 November 1917.

were made to appear virtually as criminal suspects. But it was not until January 1925 that the party's central committee decided to issue a formal condemnation of Trotsky; it accepted his resignation as chairman of the "revolutionary military council" and thus removed him from the leadership of the Red Army; further, it warned him that, in the event of fresh resistance to the party's orders, he would be ousted from the Politburo and the central committee.

With Trotsky out of the way, Stalin had now to defend himself against his allies of yesterday, Zinovyev and Kamenev; Zinovyev had a very high estimate of his own strength because he had the support of the Communist party of Leningrad. The conflict appeared to be one of doctrine: Stalin supported the new thesis that Socialism could be "built" in Russia, however backward the country might be, without waiting for revolution in western Europe, whereas Zinovyev, the chairman of the Third International, insisted that a world revolution must first be carried through. At bottom this conflict was above all personal; Stalin's opponents wanted to remove him as secretary general. They did not succeed, in spite of the reputations of Zinovyev and Kamenev, who, as "the closest disciples" of Lenin, held themselves out as the authentic interpreters of "Leninism." When the Leningrad Communists suggested to the Fourteenth Party Congress in December 1925 that the secretary general be made subordinate to a political bureau invested with full powers, they were answered with acclamation for Stalin. Kuibyshev, a creature of the secretary general and chairman of the party's basic organism, the "central control commission," stated categorically: "Comrade Stalin has been able to surround himself with the finest elements in the party." Thus, for the first time, Stalin openly emerged as the true "chief" of the party.

The Fourteenth Congress marked the end of the "triumvirate": Zinovyev lost his position as "viceroy" of Leningrad and his organization was dissolved; Kamenev was removed from his post as commissar of trade. But the opposition regrouped, bringing Zinovyev and Kamenev together with Trotsky and some other groups of malcontents. This *Nop* (new opposition) found a basis for agreement in denouncing the concessions made to the NEP and rejecting Stalin's new theory on the possibility of building "Socialism in one country." By resorting to clandestine meetings and pamphlets, the opposition organized a real conspiracy against "Stalin's fraction." The central committee responded by first expelling Zinovyev from the Politburo. Then it ousted all the backers of the opposition from the party. On October 16, 1926 the leaders of the *Nop* were compelled to make a public apology before the central committee and beseech it to readmit those whom it had ousted. At this evidence of weakness, Stalin, who asserted that "the opposition is retreating because it has no army," intensified his repression: Zinovyev was stripped of the chairmanship of the Third International, Trotsky was removed from membership in the Politburo and Kamenev was ousted as a probationary member.

In spite of the leaders' surrender, the "farthest left" fraction of the *Nop*, under Sapronov and Smirnov, continued its fight against the central committee in 1927. Even the penitent former leaders rejoined the opposition about midway through the year. The publication of clandestine propaganda was shifted to Berlin. A program signed by eighty-three members of the opposition and later by fifteen hundred more was transmitted to the Politburo; because of international problems that will be dealt with presently, Stalin's policy was very sharply criticized; furthermore, Trotsky publicly accused the group of preparing a *Themidor*. Stalin sought to end the conflict through compromise. The opposition, which in addition felt that it enjoyed the backing of certain groups in the party itself, merely increased its activity; in the words of Rudzutak, a backer of Stalin, it reiterated "at every street corner that the economic system was falling apart, that the situation of the working class was growing worse, that the kulak peril was rising, that the worker was gagged, that militarism and Fascism were mounting within the party." This propaganda was especially intense in the Young Communist League and among the young workers and the soldiers of the Red Army. Leaflets distributed everywhere changed that "the dictator, Stalin, is moving farther and farther right and becoming the defender of the capitalist and the kulak."

There were other broadsides as well: "Long live freedom of speech and the press! Down with the power of the Soviets!" Anastos Mikoyan, one of Stalin's new acolytes, declared: "The men of the opposition have their program, their central committee, their regional committees; they accept those who do not belong to our party as well as those who have been expelled from it; they have their own treasury, their own press; they organize demonstrations and evolve special slogans for the nonparty masses. . . . The most important fact of this year is that the opposition is no longer a fraction but a party." Now the opposition had an "army," and the hostility between the contesting groups became so acute that they threatened each other with acts of terrorism.

In the face of this danger Stalin resorted to extreme measures: on October 28, 1927 the central committee and the central control commission, meeting in plenary session, decided to exclude Trotsky and Zinovyev from the party's central committee. On November 12, furthermore, they were expelled from the party itself for having "undermined the dictatorship of the proletariat"; in December seventy-five other leading members of the opposition, including Kamenev and Rakovsky, the former ambassador in Paris, were similarly expelled by the Fifteenth Congress.

De Jure *Recognition of the Soviet Union by England and France*

For a long time nothing of these internal dissensions was known abroad. On the contrary, Lenin's "step backward" and the good results of the NEP gave rise among foreigners to the hope that the "Russian experiment" might finally succeed. The visits to Russia by Édouard Herriot in 1922 and Anatole de Monzie in 1923 confirmed this impression in France. In England, Lloyd George's attitude and the Labor party's opinion also favored the Soviets. The victories of the left in both countries in the elections of December 1923 and May 1924 brought about a decisive reversal in favor of the Soviet government, *de jure* recognition of which was a part of the left's program in both countries.

At its first meeting the new British Cabinet under Ramsay MacDonald decided to recognize the Soviets *de jure*, as Germany had done in 1922. This recognition, which was formalized on February 1, 1924, was hedged by certain reservations on the subject of the obligations of imperial Russia and on that of propaganda against the interests and the political system of Great Britain. On February 9 Chicherin rejected these reservations, and the Communist International continued to demand independence for Ireland, Egypt, and India.

On July 14, 1925 an Anglo-Soviet conference began in London for the settlement of all outstanding matters in dispute. While the British insisted on acknowledgment of the tsarist debts, the Bolsheviki demanded credits. Agreement seemed impossible. On the urging of Labor members of the House of Commons, MacDonald confined himself to signing the agreement of August 8, which, while it deferred the solution of all unsettled questions, recognized the Soviet government's monopoly over foreign trade and the diplomatic immunity of members of the Bolshevik trade mission. MacDonald's government fell shortly afterward and on November 21 Stanley Baldwin's Conservative Cabinet refused to ratify the August agreement. Nevertheless the *de jure* recognition was not rescinded, and the trade treaty of 1921 remained in force.

Herriot's government in France, which came to power as the result of the elections of May 11, granted *de jure* recognition to the Soviet government as of October 28, 1924; but it intended to "reserve expressly the rights inhering to French citizens under the obligations contracted by Russia or her nationals under former governments" and to apply "the same reservations to the responsibilities assumed since 1914 by Russia toward the French state and its nationals"; moreover, "nonintervention in domestic affairs" was to be reciprocally obligatory.

A French-Soviet conference scheduled for January 10, 1925 was adjourned *sine die* because Communist propaganda in the factories, the army, the navy, and the French colonies prevented the restoration of normal relations and also because no agreement could be arrived at on the acknowledgment of the debts and the compensation to be paid to the owners of French businesses in Russia. In September 1925 Soviet Ambassador Krasin offered proposals that Joseph Caillaux rejected as inadequate. In December Chicherin himself went to France to suggest to Aristide Briand that the negotiations be resumed on a broader base. As a result a conference was begun on February 26, 1926 under the leadership of Soviet Ambassador Rakovsky and French Minister of Public Works de Monzie, and this time it set about a detailed examination of the problems of debts and credits. On April 14 the Soviet delegation suggested a contractual settlement of the prewar debts on the basis of sixty-two annual installments of 40 million gold francs each, but only on condition that credits in money and goods be granted. This offer was found unacceptable and the talks were broken off on July 10. Almost a year later, on June 30, 1927, Rakovsky asked that they be resumed, and on September 21, after a visit to Moscow for consultations, he presented new suggestions: the payment of sixty-two annual installments of 60 million gold francs and the grant of most-favored-nation status to France, but still on the condition that credits be granted equivalent to 120 million dollars over six years. The discussions continued, notably on methods of guaranteeing the annual payments by means of Russian goods and oil imported into France. The recall of Rakovsky, who was criticized by the French press for remarks that he had made during his consultations in Moscow and who was attacked by the Communist party for having taken part in the opposition to Stalin, once more interrupted the negotiations.

The Soviet Union won recognition *de jure* from other states as well: Italy (February 7, 1924), then Austria, Denmark, Greece, Norway, Sweden, Mexico, China (May 21, 1924), Hedjaz, and Japan (January 20, 1925).

Among all the great powers only the United States remained hostile to the resumption of normal relations. It had been the last to agree to Allied intervention in 1918–1919 and the first to abandon it. On August 10, 1920, in a note signed by Secretary of State Bainbridge Colby, it had declared its desire to abstain from any action affecting "the vital interests of Russia" as long as she was not in the hands of a "government recognized by the civilized world" and capable of "making itself heard." On May 31, 1921 a note signed by Secretary of State Charles Evans Hughes had condemned "the protracted occupation of the strategic centers of eastern Siberia" by Japan and declared that "America would never recognize the legitimacy of the claims" arising out of that occupation. In its note of September 19, 1921 in the Washington Conference it had declared it "inadmissible to take decisions injurious to legitimate Russian interests." After 1923, while the United States did not prevent its residents from entering into private commercial relations, which became more and more extensive, with the Soviet Union, it continued officially to ignore the Soviet government.

The Activities of the Communist International and Diplomatic Defeats

The Communist International was a major obstacle to the establishment of normal and durable diplomatic relations with the government of the Soviet Union. It was of no avail for that government to insist that it was wholly independent of the International; it was common knowledge that the Communist parties of Europe received substantial subsidies from the Soviet Union and that the management of the International was in the hands of the Russian Communist party's Politburo. And besides did not the Soviet government itself, in the voices of its own representatives, unceasingly proclaim that it would never stop helping the working classes of all countries to achieve the world revolution?

The Third International's activity was especially great in England, where it was supported by a large minority in the trade unions. In an attempt to paralyze Bolshevik propaganda, Baldwin's government arrested the Communist leaders in their headquarters in King's Street in London. Publication of the documents seized in this raid made clear the influence of the Bolsheviki in the British colonies, the International's propaganda instructions, and the source of funds. The sentencing of the Communists on November 24, 1925 to one year in prison for "inciting to revolution" did not prevent the Bolsheviki from taking a very active part in the miners' strike of 1926, in which their press claimed to see the beginning of civil war in England and of revolution in the world. But all these events considerably weakened the Communists' influence in the trade unions.

In the Far East, on the other hand, they were at first dramatically successful. Their propaganda found fertile soil in the xenophobic Chinese nationalist movement. Sun Yat-sen, the nationalist leader, entered into an alliance with them and took over the direction of the party that was created with their support, the Kuomintang, which set up a government in Canton. With this as their base, the nationalists and Communists conquered all southern China between 1925 and 1927 and moved their seat of government to Nanking. But the class conflict that erupted between the nationalists and the moderate leader, Chiang Kai-shek, after the death of Sun Yat-sen broke the alliance with the Bolsheviki and the Soviet representatives were expelled from China on December 14, 1927.

Bolshevik participation in the Chinese revolution chilled the ardor of British backers of a reconciliation with the Soviet Union. The Conservatives demanded the abrogation of the 1921 trade treaty and of the official recognition granted in 1924, as well as the expulsion of the Bolsheviki. Sir Austen Chamberlain leashed his party's impatience for a time, but on February 23, 1927 he warned Rosenholz, the Soviet representative, that the continuation of Bolshevik propaganda would mean a rupture. On May 12 the government ordered a search made in the premises of Arcos, the Soviet trade delegation, and on May 26 it suspended diplomatic relations with the USSR.

In every way 1927 was a difficult year for the Soviet Union. On April 6 the Soviet consulate in Peking was sacked. In June the Soviet representative in Poland, Voikov, was assassinated in Warsaw. All these events corroborated the Bolshevik belief that the "capitalists and imperialists" of the entire world were preparing to attack. Stalin was already interpreting the murder of Voikov as "a second Sarajevo." Although it was the general impression in Moscow that war was imminent, the anticipated world revolution did not break out.

After Zinovyev, whose projects had failed one after another, had been removed as chairman of the Third International, Moscow seemed to recognize that the International's aggressive tactics were incompatible with the maintenance of normal diplomatic relations. The star of Chicherin, who had never enjoyed any real influence among the Bolshevik leaders, began to wane, and Litvinov, who had thus far remained behind the scenes, moved more and more into a major position. More effective measures than propaganda and agitation in every country of the world were required in the face of the threats of war. Hence Soviet diplomacy began to follow other avenues: on the one hand, in anticipation of war, it strove to consolidate its relations with those powers most favorably disposed toward Russia; on the other, it sought to reduce the danger of attack by taking part in the general movement in favor of peace, offering its own program of pacifism and disarmament although without interrupting the prosecution of the plan for the militarization of the Soviet Union.

The Treaties of Alliance with the Eastern States

The idea of forming an association to counter the League of Nations, which Moscow regarded as the chief organizer of the future war against the Soviet Union, was not new. Since 1921, as we have seen, the Soviet Union had gone in search of Oriental allies against the West and concluded treaties of friendship with Turkey, Persia, and Afghanistan. These assets had now to be exploited. In the Near East, as in China, the chief trump held by the Bolsheviki was the renunciation of all the conquests of tsarist diplomacy and the contrast between this generous move and the "imperialism" of the European powers. The Soviets were in direct contact with the Moslem world by way of Turkmenistan, Uzbekistan, and Kazakstan, all of which became republics in 1924 and were allowed—under the control of the party, of course—broad scope for the development of their national civilizations.

The first treaty of alliance between Russia and an eastern nation was that with Turkey: signed in Paris on December 17, 1925* by Chicherin during his journey abroad, it imposed on each party the renunciation of any agreement, alliance, or hostile act directed against the other, including financial and economic accords, and this implied the exclusion of membership by these allies in the League of Nations.

Two other, similar treaties were concluded with Afghanistan and Persia. The revolution in Afghanistan and the accession of Amanullah, the little "Afghan Peter the Great," to the throne brought together the governments of Moscow and Kabul, which on August 31, 1926 formally pledged themselves, without reservations relative to the League of Nations, to "oppose hostile actions by a third power." †

*It was renewed in 1929.

†Amanullah, who was solemnly welcomed to Russia in 1928, was dethroned in 1929, and no assistance was offered to him by the Bolsheviki; but his successor, Nadir Khan, continued the policy of friendship with Moscow.

The treaty with Persia (October 1, 1927) replicated the terms of the Turkish-Soviet agreement but with reservations for Persia's obligations as a member of the League.

Soviet diplomacy did not confine itself to dealing singly with each of these three eastern countries; it also helped them to arrive at similar agreements among themselves on the model of the Little Entente in Europe. Such was the origin of the Turkish-Persian and Persian-Afghan treaties of April 22, 1926 and November 28, 1927 respectively. In November 1927 delegations from Mongolia, Afghanistan, and Turkey attended the ceremonies celebrating the eighth anniversary of the Communist revolution. Moscow could hail its own "anti-Locarno."

The Treaty of Neutrality and Nonaggression with Germany

In Europe the Soviets succeeded in strengthening their relations with Germany. She was the first nation—in 1921—to obtain economic concessions in the USSR. Since 1922 she had been helping in the organization of the Red Army and had transferred part of her own armaments to Russia. In June of 1922 she sent Graf von Brockdorff-Rantzau as her representative to Moscow. But Zinovyev's attempts to launch a revolution in Germany in 1923 had somewhat cooled the friendship. As a result of the search made on May 3, 1924 by the Prussian police in the premises of the Soviet mission—a search that did not have the approval of the national government—Soviet Ambassador Krestinsky temporarily left Berlin. But the rift was of brief duration. The German delegation to Locarno wanted to arrive with some document in its pockets that would resemble the Treaty of Rapallo, and on October 12, 1925 a new Soviet-German trade agreement was signed, to take effect on March 12, 1926.*

At the same time, however, Gustav Stresemann's policy was orienting Germany toward the West and preparing her membership in the League of Nations. Chicherin having told Berlin that such membership would be tantamount to Germany's entrance into a coalition hostile to the USSR, Stresemann promised him, by way of reassurance, that Germany would not accept Articles XVI and XVII of the League of Nations Covenant: that is, she would refuse to obligate herself to allow passage across Germany for armies that might be sent against the Soviet Union. The treaty of April 24, 1926 brought the two countries still closer, each pledging itself to maintain neutrality in the event

---

*An annex to this treaty, more advantageous to German industrialists, was to be signed on December 21, 1928.

of aggression by a third power and to refuse to join any coalition aimed at financial or economic boycott of the other.

Litvinov's "Pacifism"

The other road taken by Soviet diplomacy, that of pacifism, was not a new one either. The Soviets had scouted it out in 1922 and 1923. At Genoa in April 1922 Chicherin had announced the submission of a proposal for disarmament, which, at the instigation of Louis Barthou of France, the conference had refused to entertain on the ground that this was beyond its competence. On June 12, when the Soviet army had just been decreased, Litvinov called on Poland, Latvia, Estonia, and Finland to reach an understanding with the Soviet government for the execution of a proportionate reduction in armaments. In the Moscow Conference that began on December 2 he had suggested to them a reduction of 75 per cent to be carried out within eighteen to twenty-four months, but, in spite of lengthy discussion, he had been unable to obtain any response. In the Conference of Rome in 1923 he had also raised the question of naval disarmament without any greater success.

After 1926 and 1927, when Moscow changed its policy, he carried on a twofold pacifist activity—on the one hand with the Soviet Union's neighbor states and on the other in Geneva.

In March 1926 he once more suggested to Latvia, Estonia, and Finland that they conclude treaties of neutrality and nonaggression "on the model of the pacts concluded by the USSR with Turkey and Germany." These countries were still eager to reach an understanding, as they had attempted to do in 1923 before the Moscow Conference, not separately but "collectively," and to bring Poland and Rumania into the negotiations. But, in spite of lengthy endeavors, the diversities in their interests had made it impossible for them to establish an "eastern Locarno," a bloc of all the Baltic countries except Lithuania, which would not forgive Poland for her annexation of Vilna. On August 20 Finland, Latvia, and Estonia agreed to embark separately on negotiations with the USSR though without losing contact with one another meanwhile. But Poland, to which on August 27 Moscow proposed the conclusion of a treaty of neutrality and nonaggression, implored the others once more to reach a prior understanding with her in Geneva. The talks dragged out. Only Lithuania, on September 28, signed a pact with the USSR, which, by emphasizing that it did not recognize Poland's annexation of Vilna, finally alienated that country. Finland, Latvia, and Estonia in their turn suspended the negotiations on November 27 and 28. Finally broken off by the assassination of Voikov, the Soviet representative, in Warsaw in June 1927, the talks were not resumed until the third period of the history of the USSR.

Invited by the League of Nations on December 12, 1925 to take part in the disarmament conference and to send his delegates to the preparatory commission, Chicherin at first refused on the ground that he had no wish to go to Switzerland, where Vorovsky, a Soviet representative, had been assassinated on May 13, 1923. But at this time Stalin was interested in taking part in international conferences. The dispute with Switzerland having been settled by the Berlin agreement of April 14, 1927, the Soviets sent a delegation to the international economic conference in May and then announced their readiness to be represented in the November session of the preliminary commission for the disarmament conference.

In the first meeting of this fourth session, on November 30, Litvinov submitted a radical proposal and made no secret of his propaganda purpose: the immediate and total abolition of all land, sea, and air armed forces. The commission courteously deferred the study of this proposal for its next session.

This was the fifth, which began in March 1928.* After vehement and sarcastic retorts to the opponents of his "major" project, Litvinov offered a second plan for limited disarmament, which would obligate the most powerful countries to reduce their armaments by a half, the less powerful by a third, and the weakest by a quarter! In spite of his protests, analysis of this was put off for the sixth session. Meanwhile the Soviet government was invited to sign the Briand-Kellogg Pact after all the other powers had already been asked to do so. Litvinov, who demanded equality of treatment, strove in vain to offer amendments to it; he had to sign it without reservations on August 31, 1928.

In the April 1929 session, his second disarmament proposal having been rejected after three days of debate—rejected for procedural reasons in spite of his futile efforts to obtain a vote on its substantive merits—he engaged in extremely sharp criticism of the preparatory commission's work, denounced its sterility, and demanded the urgent convocation of the general conference in the hope that, under pressure by the popular masses, the governments would be "compelled there to adopt an attitude more in harmony with the demands of the peoples."

---

*Chronologically, this and the ensuing sessions belong to the third phase of the history of the USSR, but we did not wish to break up the recital of Soviet action in the preparatory commission for the disarmament conference.

At the November 1930 session, which finally managed to draft a disarmament convention, Litvinov allowed himself to be replaced by a second-rank functionary, Lunacharsky, who reiterated all his predecessor's criticisms in the final meeting on December 9.

The Militarization of the Soviet Union

Basically, it was not so much on peace treaties as on the militarization of the entire population that the Soviets relied for a guaranty against the eventual attack of the "imperialists."

In their view the Red Army was the army of "the whole world" and entrance into it was open "to the workers and toilers of all countries." They carefully kept all unreliable elements out of it. Disarm the bourgeoisie and arm the proletariat: this was the foundation of the Soviet Union's class army.

According to the decree of September 18, 1925, which established compulsory five-year military service, young men eligible to bear arms were assigned to the regular army or the territorial units, or else "classified in the category of surplus members of the classes under arms." The regular army, having attained its maximum strength of 5.3 million men during the civil war (on January 1, 1921), had successively been reduced to 1.6 million later in 1921, to 800,000 in 1922, and to 520,000 in 1924–1925, mainly for budgetary reasons. The territorial units comprised 430,000 men. In both the reserves and the regular army, the men had to put in two years of active duty—three years in the navy—and undergo periodic refresher courses for the next three years. The category of "surplus members of the classes under arms" was required only to undergo periodic training for five years. At the end of the fifth year of service, men of all categories were assigned for thirteen years to the reserve, which totaled as many as 9.5 million men capable of bearing arms.

Apart from the army there were societies of "volunteers" who collaborated in the national defense: for example, the *Osoaviakhim*, or Society of Chemical and Aerial National Defense, which in 1927 had 2.9 million members,* and the *Avtodor*, or Automobile Society, which had 1.2 million. In all schools, furthermore, from the elementary to the highest, there were courses in military instruction that included physical exercises and maneuvers. The press never stopped citing the perils of war, and thus it maintained a warlike climate in the country.

*It was to rise to 5.1 million in 1929, and the Five-Year Plan provided for its growth to 17 million.

*Socialist Reconstruction in Rural Areas and Stalin's Victory over
His Opponents*

Two phenomena, superficially contradictory but actually comple-
mentary, became clear toward the end of the period with which we are
dealing. In the first place, industry, trade, and agriculture, stimulated
by the NEP, were approaching the prewar level of 1913, which was
taken as the base year for the comparisons made by Soviet economists
In the second place, Stalin, who was to allow himself to embark on
experiments the audacity of which had deterred even Lenin, finally
succeeded in ridding himself of his political adversaries, surrounding
himself with dedicated collaborators, and winning over all the party
and state officials. This gave him a feeling of confidence in himself
and in his power, a feeling that never deserted him even when the
opponents of his system abandoned themselves to a panic dread of the
collapse of the Communist system.

Under the influence of Lenin, who feared the peasants' reactions,
the party had adopted the slogan, *To the villages!* First it granted the
peasants a new land law in 1922, enlarging their rights to lease and
convey their lands—in other words, virtually reviving the right of
private ownership of land. After the poor harvest of 1924, when there
was great fear of peasant revolts and Zinovyev in alarm raised again
Lenin's question, "Who will win?" new and major concessions were
again made to the peasants. In 1924 the powers of the autonomous
village administrative authorities had been considerably broadened.
In May 1925, when the elections to the rural soviets had been relatively
free, the voters had turned out in greater number, themselves chosen
"nonparty" candidates, and slashed the proportion of Communists
elected by almost half. Agricultural taxes had been reduced and
measures adapted to increasing the output of the rural economy had
been taken under study. Some time earlier, in 1923–1924, the government had extended itself to bring down the prices of industrial products while at the same time raising those of farm products; thus it
had closed the "scissors" * that had hitherto been so widely apart to
the disadvantage of the peasants.

Beginning in mid-1925, after it had been able to ascertain that there
would be a good harvest, the government changed its tactics toward
the peasants. By way of a start the party decided to dispatch some three

*Drawn on a single graph, the two curves of industrial and agricultural price
levels between July 1922 and October 1923 had the appearance of a pair of widely
opened scissors, in the words of Trotsky, who said: "The scissors must be closed."

thousand propagandists (two thousand Young Communists and one thousand instructors) to the rural areas in order to strengthen its influence there. Then Stalin issued a new policy keynote: the NEP having accomplished its aim and the period of "rehabilitation" having come to an end, the nation must resume the task interrupted by the "backward step" and dedicate itself to "reconstruction"—in other words, complete the task of building Socialism. If personal rivalries are left out of consideration, it was essentially this policy that created a division between the majority of the party's central committee, which stood with Stalin, and the opposition. The latter invoked one after another of the views of Lenin, the twenty volumes of whose works, obviously, could serve as a rich source of arguments on behalf of both sides. Stalin's partisans contended that Lenin had not waited to introduce Socialism into Russia and that only the necessity for retreat in the face of the country's disintegration had forced him temporarily to postpone the experiment without definitely abandoning it. They declared that, instead of tolerating the parallel existence of two sectors in the economy, the "Socialist sector" (the workers and industry) and the "private sector" (private retail trade and agriculture), as had thus far been the practice, the nation must build up the public sector at the expense of the private in order to make certain of the victory of Socialism. Trotsky and his friends also fell back on Lenin as the source for their arguments that, on the contrary, Russia was not yet ripe for Socialism and that Socialism could not be gradually constructed in that country until the social revolution had triumphed in the more industrialized countries. They insisted that it was impossible to make Socialists out of Russian farm workers, that the "private sector," instead of being abolished, should be exploited by means of high taxation for the benefit of the "Socialist sector," that it was impossible to fulfill Stalin's dream of "building Socialism in one country," and that hence the party must not direct its energies toward the national reconstruction of Russia but continue, as before, to assist the international proletariat.

This left-wing opposition, which charged Stalin with flirtation with the "bourgeoisie" in the cities and the kulaks in the villages, and with deserting the principle of international revolution, was joined by a right-wing opposition that believed that he was not yet making enough concessions to the "private sector" and that the best course, since the "Trotskyites" denied the possibility of building Socialism in Russia, was to give up any experiment in Socialism. These two opposition movements, so different in their essence, concurred in their rejection of Stalin's project for "Socialist reconstruction."

Stalin himself, having removed and, often, eliminated the "cowardly" leaders of the opposition, intended to demonstrate to their many left-wing partisans that he himself was offering the farthest left program of all. In his view the best means of disarming Trotsky's backers, of proving his own "leftism," of opening new prospects of victory for the revolution, of reviving enthusiasm, of restoring confidence in the party "apparatus," especially among the new generation that had half forgot the origins of the revolution, was the inception of the Five-Year Plan, which was a logical sequel to his idea of absorbing the "private sector" in the "Socialist sector." The curious aspect of the matter was the fact that the executors of this plan were to be not the major representatives of the "old guard," whom Stalin had either exiled or restricted to minor posts, but just those men of the new generation, men between thirty and forty, in whose name Trotsky claimed to speak. The ambitions of the most talented among them—Vyacheslav Molotov, Andreyev, Lazar Kaganovitch, Kuibyshev, Rudzutak, Ordzhonikidze, Mikoyan—who became members of the central committee or the control commission, would thus be satisfied and Stalin would find loyal and powerful allies in them.

III / THE FIVE-YEAR PLAN AND "STALINISM" (1928–1932)

The third phase in the Soviets' history was characterized by a new social experiment undertaken on Stalin's personal responsibility. Far outstripping Lenin's in its boldness, it was no longer based on "Leninism," which itself had already supplanted Marxism in 1917, but on "Stalinism"—in other words, on the belief in the feasibility of building Socialism in a single country. In domestic policy the new doctrine was made manifest in the conflict with the peasants, the "socialization" and "collectivization" of private agriculture; in foreign policy, by virtue of the fact that the USSR stood more and more in need of foreign help and had to expand its foreign commerce, it entailed a certain decrease in the activity of the Third International.

The Five-Year Plan for Super-Industrialization

In all honesty there was nothing new in the idea of a "plan." Once the state assumed the responsibility for the production and distribution of goods, the "plan" made itself necessary, and with it arose the necessity of a budget and a stabilized currency. In 1923, as we have seen, an initial budget, which was naturally still far from complete, had been prepared, and in 1924 the currency had been reformed. In 1925–1926 a special commission "on state planning" had been ordered to establish what were called "control figures," which were to be published annually and, after the verification of the bases of the annual budget, were to determine the state economy's planning for the future. What was new was the preparation (at the end of 1927) and the ratification (in 1929) of a Five-Year Plan *(pyatilyetka)* covering the next five years—1928–1929 to 1932–1933;* in particular it was the fact that, after the final revision of this plan and the start of its application, the pace of its accomplishment was forced to the extreme. Thus the goal of the plan became the quick and total absorption of the "private sector" by the "Socialist sector," as a result of the considerable expansion of industry at the expense of agriculture. It was decided that over five years 64.6 billion rubles would be invested in the national economy: 16.4 billion in industry, 3.1 billion in electrification, 10 billion in transportation, and 23.2 billion† in agriculture.

The Soviets could no longer count on loans from abroad. Who then would provide such huge sums? The population itself. Having calculated that the national income, which was reckoned at 70.2 billion rubles in 1927–1928, should reach 128 billion—a rise of 82 per cent—in 1932–1933, the plan called for the allocation of approximately 40 per cent of it (whereas Germany, before the depression, could similarly allocate only about 14 per cent of hers) to development, and of this sum only a quarter would come from peasant enterprises while the rest would be produced by taxation and forced loans. The basic task of the budget would be to divert the money raised from the peasantry to industrialization. The plan's theoretical calculations also included the income that would be produced by the sale of the products of nationalized industry; it assumed in fact that the costs of industrial production would decline by 35 per cent, that part (24 per cent) of this reduction would make it possible to lower the selling prices of the products, and that the rest (11 per cent) would be net profit that would be invested in industry. Finally, it forecast a rise in gross industrial output from 18.3 to 43.2 billion rubles in five years—in other words, a growth of 136 per cent, of which 35 per cent would come from new enterprises.

It was less optimistic for agriculture, counting on an increase of only 21.6 per cent in the area under cultivation and 55 per cent in

*At this time the fiscal year began on October 1 and ended on the following September 30. As we shall see presently, this was to be changed at the end of 1930.

†Of this sum, only 5.8 billion was to be provided by the state; the rest was to come from the peasants themselves.

output—on the supposition that productivity would grow by 25 per cent—so that the money value would rise from 16.7 to 25.8 billion rubles.

The Conditions of the Plan's Execution

The framers of the plan expressly anticipated that its application would subject the population to the most severe sacrifices and reduce its own consumption to the minimum. On the other hand, they promised a considerable future improvement, in particular an increase of 47 per cent in the face value of wages and a rise of 71 per cent, with due allowance for reductions in the cost of goods, in real value. Furthermore, since there was no question of developing "light industry" for the production of ordinary consumer goods, but only "heavy industry"—that is, the production of capital goods such as machine tools, blast furnaces, factories, etc.—it was obvious that Russia was incapable of pulling herself up unassisted to the industrial level set by the plan. Foreign help was essential to her. It was to other nations that she had to turn for the engineers, the architects, the skilled labor that she lacked, and she hired at least twenty thousand "specialists" in Germany and the United States. It was also from other nations that she had to buy the mechanical equipment for the new factories. All this required money, and in foreign currencies. In order to acquire these currencies she had to increase her exports, which, after their total disappearance in 1919, had thus far returned to only 40 per cent of their pre-revolutionary figure, particularly for Russia's major product, wheat. But, as a consequence of the distribution of landed property in the early years of the revolution, the peasants' holdings had become too small and in most instances produced only enough wheat for personal consumption. Only the more prosperous peasants, the kulaks, could sell their wheat and buy manufactured goods; but they were suspect from the political point of view and harried by the government as "bourgeois." This situation led the Soviets to evolve an idea that, at the inception of their government, had induced them to preserve the large estates of the old landowners and turn them into "soviet economies," the *sovyetskaya khozyaistva,* abbreviated as *sovkhoz.* These model agricultural operations had been converted into "grain factories," which, in all honesty, returned only a very modest output in unskilled hands. Inasmuch as he now had a more powerful bureaucratic organization, Stalin decided to turn all Russian agriculture into a "grain factory"—in other words, to "socialize" and "collectivize" the small individual holdings. This confiscation of private owners' land and equipment was to destroy the usefulness of the kulak class, which would then in its turn, like the old class of large landowners, be "liquidated."

Thus the original intentions of the Five-Year Plan were little by little outrun. Its original authors were indeed to be accused of "moderatism," persecuted, and, for the most part, exiled. The same fate was to befall the former economic and statistical experts: they were to be officially accused of "sabotage" and the Statistical Institute, their operational headquarters, was to be abolished.*

The Slogan of Industry: "Catch Up with America"

The Five-Year Plan marked the start of a new social revolution, a new change in the Soviets' domestic and foreign-trade policies: they intended not only to develop the working class and reinforce Socialism in Russia but also to assure their country's complete economic independence. Everything in the state was supposed to contribute to a single end: "Catch up with America and outstrip her." In order to encourage and arouse the workers under the plan, its execution was accelerated under another slogan: "The Five-Year Plan in four years!" Enterprises were called on to engage in competition with one another on the basis of the principle of "Socialist rivalry." *Udarnik* groups (members of shock brigades) and "heroes" of the Five-Year Plan were designated to galvanize the mass of the workers and encourage them to work harder. In order completely to convince the population of the necessity of a faster pace, the government exploited the atmosphere of panic created by the alleged threats of attack by the world "bourgeoisie" against the "Socialist fatherland of the workers." From the very outset, preparation for war was one of the basic purposes of the plan. That was why, with German cooperation, it particularly emphasized the development of the chemical industry and the manufacture of arms and airplanes.

What was especially important was the creation of heavy industry, which had to manufacture the tools of production. Vast undertakings were launched under the direction of the finest foreign technicians. With the collaboration of Hugh L. Cooper, the American engineer who built the Wilson Dam on the Niagara River, Europe's largest hydroelectric generator, the Dnyeprostroy, was constructed on the Dnieper. Eleven engineers of the Arthur G. McKee Company of Cleveland

*After this action, published statistics were to be generally quite incomplete and hardly reliable.

built Magnitostroy, one of the world's greatest steel mills, in the Ural steppes at the foot of Mount Magnitnaya, where in addition they created a whole city, Magnitogorsk, out of nothing. More than a thousand miles from the southern Urals, in the heart of Siberia, a vast coal-mining development was undertaken in the Kuznetsk Basin at the same time to supply fuel for the huge furnaces of Magnitogorsk. With the help of Henry Ford and the Austin Company of Ohio and New York, a large automobile factory and a big city were created near Nizhni-Novgorod. At Stalingrad (formerly Tsaritsyn) on the lower Volga, under the direction of John K. Calder of Detroit, a large tractor factory was built. Factories of every kind, power stations, steel mills, machine-tool industries began to spring out of the earth everywhere. Imaginations were captured by a kind of intoxication of the colossal. Not only did Russia want to create "giants of industry" that could smash all production records; in the building of them she strove to smash all speed records.

Obstacles to the Accomplishment of the Plan

The achievement of the plan encountered major difficulties. The extreme haste with which construction was initiated even before plans were completed, the lack of skilled labor, the unreliability of workers recruited from everywhere who could not endure the frightful housing, food, and health conditions, the inadequacy of the railway system and its equipment, the delays in the deliveries of the raw materials essential to the construction and regular operation of the improved new machinery . . . all these factors combined to cause a remarkable increase in the cost of building the new industrial enterprises and to impair the productive capacity that had been scheduled for them.

As for the older enterprises, which were now given only secondary consideration, they at once encountered difficulties that would threaten the new undertakings later when they had been completed. First of all, the reductions in product prices, which were supposed to bring about the expected rise in both production and consumption, did not materialize. In actuality, though factories were ordered to increase their output—and to provide statistical documentation of these increases—they could do so only by substantially lowering the quality of their products, and prices, far from dropping at the rate that had been anticipated, often rose. If the sales of the products of nationalized industry did not bring the government the income on which it had counted, it was chiefly because the responsible officials had neglected to make the strictly commercial calculations that had assured the success of industrial operations during the NEP. According to the decree of January 31, 1930, all credits requested by industrial enterprises had to be granted directly by the State Bank. Obviously the bank had no way of ascertaining whether the requests were well founded; it granted them automatically and the directors of the industries had no reason to concern themselves with their costs of production.

The tremendous growth of production and consumption that had also been envisaged in the plan equally failed to materialize. On the contrary, there was very soon a "famine of goods," which meant a lack of products that were basic necessities. In the first year of the plan (1928–1929) it had to be officially acknowledged that there were "deficits" in the supply of cotton and woollen goods, leather products and shoes, metal products, and glass; in the second year, sugar, vegetable oats, and tobacco were added to the list. In the spring of 1929 the insufficiency and irregularity of food shipments to the cities forced the revival of the system of ration cards for the distribution of bread and other food products to the privileged elements of the urban population. In July 1930 Finance Commissar Bryukhanov admitted that Moscow and other cities were short of bread, sugar, vegetables, meat, butter, and cloth. The population was reduced to living on cabbage and potatoes. The rise in wages did not match that in food prices: between 1928 and 1931 wages went up 38 per cent and food prices increased 90.6 per cent. Thus the worker's purchasing power was diminished.

It was above all in the most important sectors of production, the mineral and metallurgical, that production fell below estimates. In order to conceal the gap, the government was compelled to extend the second year of the plan by a quarter, from October to December 1930, and hence to revise the fiscal year to begin on January 1 instead of October 1. It threw all the responsibility for these failures on the managers of the enterprises; it accused them of deliberate "sabotage" and even of collusion with foreigners. A number of "show" trials, which ended in sentences of death or exile, deterred qualified Russian experts from any desire to hold important positions and show any evidence of initiative.

These failures in production were caused not only by the bureaucratic character of the institutions but also by the migrations of the labor force and the total disorganization of transportation.

Already short of food and then increasingly badly housed—each individual was restricted to about sixty square feet in 1927–1928 and to somewhat less in the following year—the workers abandoned their jobs, as they had done during the years of "war Communism," to go elsewhere in search of better living conditions, or even deserted industry altogether and went back to their villages. Certain enterprises, chiefly the new factories and the mines, had personnel turnovers of almost 100 per cent in a single year. In vain the government strove to attach the worker to his job by official prohibitions on labor migrations; the workers paid no attention.

The execution of the plan and the creation of direct connections between producers and consumers imposed far greater burdens on transportation than those of the free-market system. Having been singularly overlooked by the authors of the plan, transport was by far unequal to its tasks. On April 15, 1930 *Ekonomicheskaya Zhizn (The Economic World)* admitted in an editorial that "no transport organization is told the timetables, the number, or the kinds of shipments for which it will be responsible in the ensuing months," and it denounced "the criminal levity that governs the management of the communications system." The disorganization was so great that shipments were delivered only after inordinate delays and with utter confusion: while goods were piling up and deteriorating in one place, they were totally lacking in others. When a factory did not receive needed items on time, it had to suspend all its operations. Some of the errors were ludicrous: a group of Bashkiri employed in the woodworking industry suddenly received five thousand dog muzzles; Berezov, in remote Siberia, was presented with a large shipment of French dictionaries; adults got children's clothing, peasants received perfumes and silk stockings, etc.

And the plan could not succeed without a stable monetary system. That was why, in order to maintain the stability of the currency, it provided for only infrequent *chervonets* issues, at the maximum in the equivalent of 250 million rubles a year. But, as a result of the extravagances of factory managements and the startling rise in construction costs, these modest provisions were soon seen to be inadequate. In 1928–1929 there had to be an issue of 671 million rubles; in 1929–1930 it was 1.602 billion; on January 1, 1931 the total of bank notes in circulation had reached 4.355 billion rubles and by June 1, 1932 it was 5.786 billion. On what was left of the private market in 1930 the ruble had lost three-quarters of its face value for the purchase of manufactured goods. Later it was to lose 90 per cent and even more.

The "Liquidation" of the Kulaks

It was above all Stalin's peasant policy that had a serious effect on the plan.

The Sixteenth Party Conference declared in a resolution that "Socialist construction is developed not by the absorption and destruction of private undertakings but by their technical operation and their economic revival." That was why the plan at first estimated that by the end of the fifth year only 23 per cent of the wheat would be supplied by sovietized and collective farms and 77 per cent would come from individually owned farms—thus admitting the existence of 121 million "individual" peasants against 14 million "socialized" peasants. But, in proportion to the increases in the rate of execution of the plan, the government envisaged the "collectivization" of the 22 million individual peasant farms in order to "motorize" agricultural production more easily through the use of tractors. It was hoped in this way to increase the productivity of the land and to produce enough wheat not only to feed the cities and the army but to export abroad. Naturally the class argument was used to reinforce the economic argument. On December 27, 1929 Stalin declared: "The government is moving from a policy of limiting the tendency to the exploitation of others manifested by the kulaks to the policy of liquidating the kulaks as a class."

Against the kulaks and what might be called the subkulaks—the less prosperous peasants, those who owned two cows rather than one and employed a hired worker at harvest time in addition to the members of their families, a group that represented no longer 4 per cent but 10 per cent of all the peasants—it was therefore proposed to resort to the violent methods formerly used against the old land-owners. In actuality, the new measures were more cruel. According to a confidential party bulletin of January 6, 1930, special detachments comprising altogether twenty-five thousand proved Communists were ordered to "dekulakize" a certain number of families in each village, designated in advance; this meant that they would be shot or sent into exile and forced labor—in the forests of the northern regions—or else left where they were but stripped of all means of support. The order was carried out at night by armed groups that drove men, women, and children out of their houses into glacial cold, confiscated all their belongings, and forbade the other peasants to give them any help. Many of the kulaks died of cold and hunger; others, crammed virtually without food into freezing freight cars that crossed the whole of Russia from the south to the north, died on the trains; still others perished of exhaustion brought on by their harsh labors and cruel treatment in the northern forests. The expropriated kulaks must be counted by the hundreds of thousands, even by the millions. The only class in Russia that was self-supporting was thus annihilated.

Agricultural Collectivization and Its Consequences

The decree of January 6, 1930 called for the conversion of the holdings of "poor" and "average" peasants (*byednyak and serednyak*) into "collective economies"—*kollektivnoye khozyaistvo,* abbreviated as *kolkhoz**—during the spring of that year in the regions producing wheat for the market—the Ukraine, the Caucasus, and the lower Volga—and in the spring of 1931 in all other areas. The terrorized peasants were compelled to enter a *kolkhoz*: in two months the number of collectivized families rose from 5 million to 9.5 million; by the end of the spring it had reached 50 per cent of the total. These exceptional measures, which drastically changed the age-old system of the rural areas, led the peasants to kill their livestock and consume their reserves before they joined the *kolkhoz*. There was reason to fear that the fields would be left to lie fallow. Assassinations of Communists increased in the villages, and in many instances the peasants revolted.

Thereupon Stalin ordered the publication (March 2, 1930) of his famous article, *The Vertigo of Success,* in which he harshly criticized the excesses of zeal in which the executants of his will had engaged. The decree of March 15, 1930 allowed the collectivized peasants to leave the *kolkhoz* and regain possession of their tools, and it authorized those who remained in the *kolkhoz* to retain private ownership of one cow each, of small animals, of poultry, and of a garden. On the other side, the decree of April 5 granted large credits and various privileges to the *kolkhoz*. In the interval between these two decrees, almost 9 million families left the *kolkhoz;* in the wheat-producing areas, however, some 40 per cent to 45 per cent of the peasants remained collectivized.

Nevertheless the campaign for collectivization was resumed in the autumn of 1930. Again trains filled with kulak families set out for the north. On the whole, the peasants' resistance was weaker, and in January 1933 Stalin could point out that 80 per cent of all peasant families were collectivized. In the Ukrainian steppes the ratio reached 82 per cent, in the lower Volga 81.9 per cent, in the middle Volga 86 per cent, and among the Volga Germans 95 per cent.

It did not take long for the consequences of collectivization to

*This term covered three different forms of "collective economy": groups whose members helped one another to work their respective holdings but in which the parcels remained privately owned and the crops were not collectivized; associations in which only product was collectivized; and complete "communes" in which everything was common property.

become apparent. First of all there was a considerable decline in livestock, which made the feeding of the cities more difficult; according to official figures, between 1928 and 1930 the number of horses dropped 8.3 per cent, cattle 29.4 per cent, sheep and lambs 22.6 per cent and pigs 48.7 per cent. Although subsequently, as a result of the use of tractors, the total area under cultivation was increased—from 284.38 million acres in 1929 to 330.17 million in 1931—the quality of seed and especially of the harvests left much to be desired. The peasants felt that they were working for others and they took no interest in the crop because it was confiscated by the state; sowing and harvesting were carried out with great delays.

While in 1930 these consequences were hidden by the abundance of the harvest—a very high figure of 22.5 million tons, of which almost 6 million were exported during the winter—they showed themselves unmistakably in the ensuing, less fortunate years. In order to make certain of its export capacities, the government increased its appropriations of the peasants' wheat harvest to half the gross crop, and sometimes more. In 1931, in spite of a poor harvest, it seized 6 per cent more than in the previous year; as in 1920, this was tantamount to stripping the peasants of part of their own food and even of their seed. Naturally the situation turned much worse in 1932: reduced to famine, the peasants of the southern regions and the Volga showed less willingness than ever to sow and reap; they resorted to every possible method to delay their deliveries to the state and to conceal part of their crops for their own use. The government went to the extreme of promulgating a decree on August 7, 1932 that threatened the death penalty for anyone who stole the state's share of his own field's output. Thus the country fell back into a condition that recalled 1921 and the eve of the NEP.

Stalin's "Admissions"

The leaders of the USSR could conceal neither from themselves nor from others the obvious causes of their failures. In the speech that he delivered to industrial managers on June 23, 1931 Stalin listed some of them, such as the lack of a labor force, and offered remedies: the necessity of increasing the wages of skilled workers—which amounted on this point to the abandonment of "equalization"; the renunciation of "anonymous" labor and the revival of individual responsibility in each task; the elimination of the "unbroken work week"* wherever it obtained and the resumption of the conventional week of six days at work and one day off; the rebuilding of confidence in directors of factories and/or experts, even those who were not party members and who had thus far been treated as "saboteurs"; and, finally, a return to a strict commercial accounting system, with the replacement of remote management "on paper" by immediate decentralized management in every enterprise. Of course Stalin did not attack the basic principle of "building Socialism" and he said absolutely nothing of the much more serious failures that have already been discussed, but the remedies that he proposed showed that he had embarked on a period of concessions.

Soviet "Dumping"

The success of the Five-Year Plan implied a favorable balance of trade. Before its adoption, when imports were beginning to exceed exports, the *Vnyeshtorg* (Foreign Trade Office) restored the balance by reducing its purchases abroad. But now this method was no longer feasible because it was impossible to decrease the imports of machinery. There was thus no choice but to increase exports as much as possible by setting extremely low prices.

This "Soviet dumping,"† as it was called abroad, was sometimes imputed to the desire to sabotage the industry and trade of other states, as in the end it could not ultimately fail to do. But its basic purpose was to enable the USSR to pay its bills abroad. Unfortunately for Russia, it coincided with a worldwide drop in the prices of raw materials, which represented the bulk of Soviet exportation.

In vain it was attempted to increase the number of export items; in vain it was sought to enlarge the shipments of wood and oil in order to compensate for the inadequate production of certain raw materials; receipts were far from matching the expanded volume of exports. The foreign-trade deficit rose from 22 million rubles in 1930

*Prescribed by the decree of August 27, 1929, which divided the working year into seventy-two weeks of five days each, plus five revolutionary holidays for all. Workers who were supposed to work for four days and rest on the fifth were divided in each factory into five equal groups so that the machinery continued to function without interruption for 360 days.

†In order to understand the low prices of Soviet export products, it must be remembered that Stalin's system did not make it possible to calculate production costs with precision and that in the absence of true economic planning no one could take into account either the waste in domestic expenditures or the losses in foreign trade.

to 294 million in 1931 and fell back to 142 million for the first seven months of 1932. In order to supplement the income from this trade the Soviets were compelled to resort to the expansion of foreign credits. But these were granted only on the most disadvantageous terms (interest ran as high as 25 per cent, or even more). The British, German, and Italian governments guaranteed their nationals' sales in Russia; in Germany, where the guaranty reached 90 per cent— 65 per cent from the state and 25 per cent from the seller's city—the vendor's risk was only 10 per cent, and this risk was largely covered by an increase (sometimes as much as 25 per cent) in the price of the items offered. Such a system could not survive indefinitely. Early in 1932 the Soviet Union's debt in Germany was 1.2 billion marks. The Soviets could not go beyond this. It became more and more difficult for them to pay for their purchases of machinery abroad: they were granted extensions on arrearages of unpaid interest, but new credits were refused. It was precisely at this time that their budget was seriously threatened by the consequences of agricultural collectivization.

The Inadequacy of Wheat Stockpiling and the Palliatives

By assuming, as it had done in the period of "war Communism," the task of direct distribution of farm and factory products, the government had also imposed on itself the obligation of gathering enough wheat to feed the numberless army of soldiers and workers and also to cover exports. Although the wheat reserve rose from 576 million poods in 1927–1928—the last year of the NEP—to 660 million in 1929, 1.25 billion in 1930, and 1.4 billion in 1931, this was not the result of an increase in the productivity of the land; nor was it a the result of the seizure of all the peasants' reserves. In the beginning of 1932, therefore, the government was anxiously wondering whether there would be enough wheat for even the spring sowings. Its fears were confirmed when spring came and sowing was carried out extremely late and carelessly, especially by *sovkhoz* peasants but also by those of the *kolkhoz*.

In order to remedy the serious consequences of this situation, the government adopted a whole series of measures. Acknowledging first of all that "motorization" had been insufficient, it demanded "the return to the horse." Then, after the party's central committee, in the Seventeenth Congress of February 1932, had emphasized the problems of an overaccelerated collectivization and pointed out that "good figures do not always attest to good quality," it decided to restore the cows to the peasants; it slightly reduced the farm tax, decreased the stockpile figure by 264 million poods, and on May 6, 1932 authorized the *kolkhoz* peasants to sell their surplus crops on the markets. But this attempted return to a free market revived speculation: since free-market prices were infinitely higher than official prices,* the middleman reappeared in the markets and the members of the *kolkhoz* began to sell the collective property. The local authorities responded by setting prices for the markets and prosecuting the merchants for "speculation," etc. Their arbitrary measures caused the government to issue a decree on "revolutionary legality" in a vain attempt to protect "Socialist property." Among the peasants, furthermore, the right to sell wheat had "reinforced their resistance to the delivery of their crops to the state";† hence this right was restricted by being reserved only to a *kolkhoz* that had fully met its obligations to the stockpile.

If the government had created markets, it had done so only in order to escape in part the responsibility for the food supplies of the cities. In addition it was seeking to reduce the number of mouths that it had to feed. On November 15, 1932 it decreed that any worker who was absent from his job, even for one day, without valid reason would be discharged and deprived of his food card. On December 10 it decided to carry out a new "purge" of the party, which it regarded as too large,‡ as well as encumbered with members suspected of collusion with the taxpayers. Seventeen days later, in order to thin out the population of the cities—which were so difficult to feed—it revived the system of the domestic passport that had been so much abused by the imperial police and that was employed now against the peasants who had fled to the cities to escape famine or collectivization and against anyone assumed to be a counterrevolutionary. Whoever could not obtain a passport was driven out of the cities: according to Kirov's estimate, eighty thousand persons had to leave Leningrad and no doubt as many more were expelled from Moscow.

*During the Five-Year Plan (from 1927 to the summer of 1932) free-market prices soared from .87 kopeck to 13 kopecks for a kilogram (2.2 pounds) of meat, .20 kopeck to 3.5 kopecks a kilo for flour, .1 kopeck to 2.5 kopecks a kilo for potatoes, 2 to 35 kopecks a kilo for butter, .4 kopecks to 9 kopecks for ten eggs, .2 kopeck to 2.7 kopecks a liter (slightly more than a quart) for milk, etc.

†On October 15, 1932 the stockpile figure was more than 5 per cent below that of the same date in the previous year.

‡On July 1, 1932 the party had 3.13 million members. Such a party, Bukharin said, was no longer a party; it was a "society," which took back its freedom and its independence.

To reduce the number of consumers whose support was the obligation of the state was not enough. The peasants must still be compelled to produce enough grain to assure that support. The government seemed determined, regardless of the cost, to overcome the passive resistance of the rural areas, notably that of the most productive, which were also the least docile. It felt strong enough, if Bukharin is to be believed, to be able to reduce the recalcitrant peasants "to bits."* Nevertheless the fact remained—and Stalin admitted it—that farm collectivization had failed and that this failure made it impossible to sustain the "rhythm" of industrialization. The optimistic statements of the official newspapers and the defenders of Stalin's "general line" became less and less convincing.

The Resurgence of Opposition to Stalin

At the same time as the problems were mounting, the opposition came back to life on the left as well as on the right. At the plenary session of the party's central committee (September 28–October 3, 1932), Stalin ran into serious resistance. The resolutions that were adopted were of course carefully polished, but to overcome his opponents he had once more to resort to his old method of conjuring up a "conspiracy."

On October 9 the central committee's officers decided to expel the "plotters." In addition to the young "counterrevolutionaries" (Ryutin, Maretsky, Ptashny, etc.) , these included Zinovyev and Kamenev, who had earlier been readmitted into the party after suitable penances. All were officially accused of having attempted to set up a secret bourgeois organization with a view to restoring the capitalist system, and in particular the kulak class, in the USSR. *Pravda,* to which the opposition members were "corrupt liberals and conciliators, products of bourgeois degeneracy, etc.," asserted that their program included the restoration of their lands to the kulaks, the elimination of all farm collectives, and the restitution of Socialist enterprises to Capitalist concessionnaires.†

*In the "penitential" speech in which, in January 1933, he confessed his errors and called for harsh penalties against the "opportunists" of the right whom he had supported, Bukharin used the word *utrambovat*. This picturesque word really means not "to level" but "to shatter," as a road roller smashes pebbles.

†Early in January 1933 new "plotters," accused of urging the renunciation of industrialization and the restoration of kulak private capitalism, were denounced. Supply Commissar Eismont and Tolmachev were thrown out of the party and Smirnov was expelled from the central committee. Rykov, Tomsky, and Schmidt, members of the central committee who had "encouraged" the conspirators, were bidden to make drastic changes in their behavior under the threat of severe punishment.

Soviet Diplomatic Concessions in the Chinese-Japanese Conflict

In foreign policy there was now a danger of war that was no longer theoretical but real. But, even while it vigorously pursued the militarization of the country, the Soviet government made every effort to postpone hostilities and followed a very cautious policy, as for example in the growth of the Chinese-Japanese conflict that arose out of the Japanese occupation of Manchuria.

Initially Soviet circles, especially in Manchuria, showed a high degree of bellicosity. When in February 1932 the Japanese asked permission to use the Chinese Eastern Railway to move troops to Kharbin, the local authorities at first refused, but soon Moscow granted its approval and the Japanese took the fullest advantage of it. At the same time the Soviets increased their forces in the Far East; they enlarged their army there from seventy thousand to one hundred seventy thousand men, moved in concentrations of tanks and planes, etc., and, to justify these precautions, published documents in which "responsible" Japanese military figures set forth a program for the annexation of Siberia as far west as Lake Baikal. The Soviets' attitude compelled the Japanese to keep their troops at some distance from the Russian borders, but it created a climate of diplomatic strain. In both Moscow and Kharbin armed conflict was believed to be imminent in April and May, but Japan offered reassuring declarations and the tension abated.

The proclamation of Manchuria's independence at first revived the strain. Then, in October 1932, the Soviets agreed to accept Manchurian consuls in their country and even in Moscow, and, although the Soviet Union refrained from openly recognizing the independence of the Manchurian state, it was only in order to avoid compromising its own relations with the United States. On December 31, 1931 Litvinov had proposed a treaty of nonaggression to Japan. A year later the Japanese government rejected the proposal, though at the same time stating its readiness to examine the creation of a Japanese-Soviet-Manchurian committee to prevent border incidents.

The Negotiation of Nonaggression Treaties

Litvinov's pacifist policy, too, changed its character. Although he still preserved an intransigent position in the disarmament conference that opened in Geneva on February 2, 1932 and though he endeavored without success to push through his two disarmament plans, on the other hand he followed a busy practical policy of negotiating nonaggression treaties with countries bordering on the USSR.

This time the initiative came from France. At the end of 1931 the French press disclosed that on August 21 a French-Soviet pact had been initialed and that its ratification was dependent on the conclusion of similar treaties by the USSR with France's allies, Poland and Rumania. On January 25, 1932 a Polish-Soviet treaty was approved. Once again its ratification was made subject to the signature of similar accords with other countries abutting the Soviet Union. Litvinov, who had already talked with the Finns on January 21, negotiated with Estonia on February 8 and with Latvia the next day. But Rumania refused to enter into any agreement unless the Soviets recognized her annexation of Bessarabia. When the Rumanian-Soviet talks dragged out, Poland signed separately in July. The negotiations with Rumania were resumed more actively in October under pressure from Herriot, who did not wish to allow the USSR to continue forming a bloc with Germany. The Rumanian government under Vaida-Voevoda was favorably inclined toward an agreement that would lay aside the Bessarabian question, but a violent protest by its minister in London, Titulesco, followed by his resignation, forced it to retreat. Although Rumania did not resume the negotiations, France ratified her own nonaggression treaty with the Soviet Union on November 29, 1932.*

The Denunciation of the Anglo-Soviet Trade Treaty

In contrast to the Soviet Union's relations with France, its ties with England were seriously impaired in 1932. On January 27 the Anglo-Soviet talks on the acknowledgment of the tsarist debts were broken off because the USSR once more tried to make this dependent on the grant of long-term credits. The British coalition government then reduced the scope of the government guaranty offered to Britons selling to Russia and the term of the credits already allowed to Soviet trade, both of which, under the Labor government, had far exceeded their original limits, established respectively at 1.6 million pounds and twelve months. It was publicly known that England's imports from Russia were four to five times as large as her exports to Russia, that the Russians were taking advantage of this fact to pay for their purchases in Germany and the United States with British credits, and that in addition their low prices had unsettled Britain's home market; the British public was particularly critical of the importation of Russian wood cut by the forced labor of the kulak exiles in the

*Nevertheless she allowed talks with a view toward a trade treaty to be dragged out.

northern forests—a fact that contributed to its low price; therefore British opinion demanded the denunciation of the 1930 agreement. Moreover, in conformity with the decision of the empire conference in Ottawa, England could no longer allow the Soviet Union the benefits of most-favored-nation status. On October 17 she denounced the 1930 treaty while at the same time offering to engage in preliminary talks for the negotiation of a new treaty on different bases.

IV / THE "CULTURAL REVOLUTION"

Religion

Article XIII of the Constitution of July 10, 1918, which declared that, "with the object of guaranteeing the workers true freedom of conscience, the church is separated from the state and the school is separated from the church," and that "freedom of religious and antireligious propaganda is recognized for all citizens," fulfilled the long expressed aspirations of the Russian liberals. In fact the Soviets could not remain neutral toward the church, since Article XIII of the Communist program declared that "the party should contribute to the liberation of the working masses from the bondage of religion." The fight against religion, to the Communists, was part of the class struggle against the bourgeoisie. Therefore they made it their business to set up all kinds of legal barriers to the Orthodox religion, to abolish the entire church administration, to eliminate all religious schools, and to permit religious instruction only on a private basis and only for persons over the age of eighteen.

On 5/18 November 1917, at the same time when the Bolshevik revolution was achieving its triumph, a council that had been sitting since 15/28 August to reestablish the patriarchate abolished by Peter the Great elected Bishop Tikhon as patriarch and created a Synod and an "ecclesiastical administration," which included laymen, to assist him. The council and the patriarch vigorously protested against the "persecutions" that were beginning, and they endeavored to resist the Soviet decrees directed against the church; in an appeal to the Orthodox the council went to the extreme of calling on them to "go up to Golgotha" and to resist openly, even if it meant martyrdom.

The Soviets retaliated with terror, which led Tikhon to publish, on October 26, 1918, a "pastoral letter" to the people in which he overtly attacked the "internationalist" government and vehemently protested against the executions of priests and bishops and the confiscations of church properties. The government, which was still re-fraining from decisive steps, decided to set up in opposition to the dominant church a more radical, and opportunist, religious party, which it assisted in founding a "renewed" or "living" church. The struggle turned more bitter when on February 23, 1922 the government promulgated a decree ordering the confiscation of all church wealth for the relief of the famine victims. On February 28 the patriarch threatened to excommunicate any layman or priest who obeyed this decree. On May 12 he was arrested, and the management of church affairs was taken over by the leaders of the "living church," who had officially recognized the Bolsheviki.

In May 1923 the "living church" summoned a council, deposed Tikhon, pronounced capitalism a "mortal sin," and engaged the faithful to combat it under the aegis of the Soviet government. This attitude and the religious reforms—modest though they were—that it introduced alienated the majority of the Orthodox from it. Tikhon thereupon understood that he must make concessions; first, on June 15, 1923, he acknowledged that he had been wrong in resisting the government and he declared that "he was henceforth no longer the enemy of the authority of the Soviets"; he was then set at liberty and resumed the leadership of the church. When he died on April 7, 1925, he left an "appeal" to exhort the faithful to "loyalty to the Soviet power" and the priests "to countenance no resistance to the government."

After the patriarch's death the Soviets did not permit the convoca-tion of a new council to choose his successor, and the leadership of the church devolved on a "custodian of the patriarchal throne," Metropolitan Peter. Since he refused to bow to the government, the Soviets helped the leaders of the "living church," which assumed the less discredited name of "new church," to convene a second council in October 1925, attended by the bishops and priests who stood with them. This council accused Peter of having maintained relations with the exiled monarchists and supplanted him with a "supreme church leadership." Peter and his supporters were arrested in December 1925 and later deported to Siberia and the Solovki Islands.

The majority of the believers and the bishops remained loyal to him nevertheless. The successor whom he had designated, Metro-politan Sergey, proclaimed, following Tikhon's example, that the "old church" would remain loyal to the government and would not meddle in politics. The bishops deported to the Solovki Islands announced that they too were prepared to submit, provided that, in accord with the Constitution, the church be permitted to exist. The Soviets first arrested Sergey, then negotiated with him, set him free, and authorized him on May 18, 1927 to organize a "provisional Synod." By officially "legalizing" the "old church," they made certain, as they had to do, that they would exercise a direct influence on its religious leadership. This situation led to opposition to Sergey among the more stubborn bishops and priests. In a pastoral letter of July 27, 1927 Sergey justified his compromise and, furthermore, called on the priests in exile to take a "loyal position" toward the Soviet government. This demand was not well received, and a schism arose in the Orthodox communities abroad; there was already a monarchist church under Metropolitan Anton in Karlovici, Yugoslavia, as well as Metropolitan Evlog's non-political church in Paris; Bishop Seraphim led a new church out of the Paris congregation and placed it under Sergey's orders. In addition, branches of the "new church" were also established, notably in America.

The Soviets did not confine themselves to taking the entire ecclesiastical organization into their grip. The law of April 8, 1929 and the amendment to Article XIII of the Constitution promulgated on May 22 prohibited all "religious propaganda" and forbade the church to engage in teaching and charity; worship became so difficult that it called for the greatest spirit of sacrifice on the part of priests and communicants alike. Moreover, the Bolsheviki organized antireligious propaganda on a grand scale, beginning in the schools. The League of the Godless, created in 1925, lowered its admission age to fourteen and in addition enlisted children between six and fourteen as "pioneers"; its membership, which totaled only 128,000 in 1928, had risen by 1930 to 2.5 million, "pioneers" included. In order, they said, to meet the people's "demand," the Bolsheviki removed the bells from the churches, closed and demolished others, and converted still others into cinemas, theaters, schools, and cooperatives. All resistance to these actions was put down. Such churches and priests as survived were placed under crushing fiscal obligations; persons who gave asylum to priests were heavily fined; clerics themselves were forbidden to live in their own parishes. Thanks to Sergey's concessions, the "old church" was able to preserve 30,000 parishes, 163 bishops, and tens of millions of believers.* Its position was nonetheless extremely precarious after the closure or conversion of many of its churches. A great number of its priests was compelled to obey the orders of the Bolsheviki, who looked on the bishops as their own functionaries. For lack of a theological school a new generation of priests could not

*In 1927 the "new church" had 6245 parishes and 140 bishops.

be trained, while the old generation was gradually dying out; in 1930 half the priests were more than fifty years old.

Although the religious spirit persisted more vigorously in the villages and among the peasants in the Red Army, it was necessary everywhere to hide one's beliefs and to conduct religious services in secret. Stimulated by their successes, the Soviets issued a decree on May 15, 1932 that established a "five-year plan for atheism" in order to eliminate religion completely. In its first year the religious schools of all faiths still in existence were closed and the clerics of these faiths were deprived of their ration cards—in other words, of any chance at food. On May 1, 1934 all houses of worship of all religions were to be closed in the capitals of all the republics and in the major cities, "religious shrines" in family residences were to be finally liquidated, and the publication of religious books and the manufacture of religious articles was to be prohibited. In the third year, all priests who had not yet abandoned their robes were to be expelled from the Soviet Union. "On May 1, 1937 not a single house of prayer shall still stand in all the territory of the Soviet Union, and the very notion of God shall be banished from the Soviet Union as a survival of the Middle Ages and a tool for the oppression of the toiling masses."*

Schools

In the realm of education, as in other domains, the Soviets began by introducing the most modern principles. But they soon recognized that these principles, borrowed from European and American pedagogues by a teaching staff of very radical tendencies, could be applied only in a small number of "model" schools. Now, according to the program laid down by the Communist party in March 1919, the purpose of the elementary school was "to educate a generation capable of definitively establishing Communism." Hence the curriculum ought to be "polytechnical"—that is, it ought to teach all branches of production—and, according to the doctrine of Marx and Engels, it should "develop all the abilities of the members of the Communist society."

The task that the Soviets were setting themselves was not simple. First of all they were lacking both in schools and in Communist teachers. Just before the revolution, thanks to the action of the Duma, Russia was on the point of making the schools accessible to all: according to 1911 statistics, there were 154,177 teachers of both sexes

*Events subsequent to the completion of this book proved that the "five-year plan for atheism" was never carried out.—Translator.

with 8,146,637 pupils, and by 1915 there were already 122,123 elementary schools. Completely abandoned during the civil war, many of these schools had been destroyed; in 1921 their number had declined to seventy-six thousand with only six million pupils. Over the next two years the situation continued to deteriorate; the number of "first-degree" schools, corresponding to the old elementary schools, and their pupils had fallen respectively from seventy-six thousand to forty-three thousand—a decline of 41 percent to 47 per cent in terms of 1915—and from six million to three million. The number of "second-degree" schools, analogous to the former middle schools, and of their pupils had dropped respectively from 3700 to 866 and from 410,000 to 210,000. The teaching corps itself made no secret of its hostility to the Soviets. The All-Russian Union of Teachers frankly declared against them and was dissolved, and "suspect" teachers were discharged. It was only after the NEP that the teachers shifted from open hostility to "neutrality," and, through the intermediary of a new All-Russian Union of Workers in Public Education, to submission to the government. Even by 1927, however, the number of those who were affiliated with the Communist party was only 4.8 per cent in the villages and 5.6 per cent in the cities.

Moreover, the Soviets had to create a new curriculum. The statute of 1918 sought to apply the single school accessible to all in its three degrees—elementary, middle, and upper. But soon, instead of providing a general education for everyone, the school had to concern itself primarily with practical and technical vocational training, and the principle of the single school was abandoned. Giving up the democratic illusions of 1918, a new statute, issued on December 18, 1923, revised the scholastic system. It provided for three kinds of schools, each of which would prepare its students for a certain category of occupations, and the maintenance of which was the responsibility of the local population: the first-degree school, which embraced four years, led to the lower trade school; in the second-degree school, the three-year first cycle led to the *technicum* and "vocational courses," while the second cycle of two years* prepared the student for the higher professional schools. The maximum age for general education was set at fifteen—in other words, the completion of the first cycle of the second-degree school; as Education Commissar Lunacharsky sarcastically observed, this was something that "only the most savage and the most impoverished countries can permit themselves." Thus only

---

*Thus the student who entered the first cycle of the second-degree school had seven years of study (four, then three), while those who went on to the second cycle had nine years (four, then three, then two).

the first-degree schools and the first cycle of the second-degree schools, intended for the masses, still aimed at providing a general education.

In order to prevent this education from contravening the program of "social education," it resorted to the "complex" method: classes were taught not by subject (spelling, arithmetic, geography, etc.) but by "packages" on current topics familiar to the peasant, such as a cow, a mouse, a river, a dragon-fly, etc., and, if possible, the classes were held in a garden or an orchard or a field and not inside the school—the fruit of this method was to be a considerable decline in the capacity to read, write, and calculate. In order to save education from collapsing into chaos, official programs classified the "complexes" by headings: "work," "nature," and "society." In the first year of the first-degree school the central theme was "the family"; the next year it was "the countryside" or "the urban neighborhood"; in the third year it was "the regional economy"; in the last year it was "the economy of the RSFSR and other countries." But these programs were practical neither for the teachers, who had no textbooks, nor for the pupils, who were taken out of the schools into the streets and obliged to engage in some "social activity." In addition, the employment of the system of "collective groups" of pupils who enforced their own discipline undermined the authority of the teacher, who was still further hampered by the interference of the party, which established "cells" of its "pioneers"* in the schools. New curricula were issued in 1927; although they were less radical, their application did not much improve the teaching conditions.

Beginning with the NEP, the Soviet school gained more popular support. The number of schools of all degrees increased with the rise in government credits; it went from about 44,000 in 1923 to 122,000 in 1928–1929, while the number of pupils rose from 3.21 million to 12 million. Once again there was talk of making the schools available to all by 1933–1934. But this project was too costly, and the number of schools did not mount so quickly as the number of school-age children.

Vocational concerns were predominant in the schools: the two cycles of the second-degree school tended in fact to provide a specialized technical training. Technical schools for adults were also formed in every factory; there were two thousand of them in 1921 and one hundred thousand in 1927. The higher schooling was enlarged with "technical institutes" for the textile, electrical, and chemical industries, the agricultural sciences, etc.; the existing establishments were ex-

*Created in 1922, this organization already had more than six hundred thousand members in 1924 and about two million in 1928.

panded to include "workers' schools," direct access to which, on the party's recommendation, was available to "the worker out of the shop or the peasant behind the plow" who, in Trotsky's striking phrase, showed a taste for "biting into the granite of knowledge"—and of course the result was a decline in the level of education.

According to the school census of 1927 there were 6309 trade schools with 838,968 students at the time when the Five-Year Plan had already been evolved. Now the framers of the plan had estimated that its fulfillment would require 176,000 engineers and 260,000 technicians, to say nothing of the 450,000 experts—90,000 of them with higher education and 360,000 with ordinary training—necessary for the collectivization of agriculture. Since the vocational schools could provide only a minimal proportion of those needed, the whole system of education then in force must be recast if the government wanted to "guarantee production" and, in particular, to "purge" the schools of persons "alien" to Communism. The accomplishment of this mission was entrusted to young General Bubnov, who, in September 1929, succeeded Lunacharsky as commissar of public education and spoke only in the military terminology so characteristic of Stalinist domination: "the adoption of a combat cadence," "the mobilization of the troops of public education," "the cultural campaign," "breach" . . . these were the new watchwords.

In pursuance of the Five-Year Plan's program, a major effort was concentrated on increasing the number of schools. On the strength of official statements, the student body grew in 1930–1931 from 13.5 million to 20 million members, of whom 14 million were in the elementary schools, 3.7 million in preschool institutions, 600,000 in technical institutes, 300,000 in higher institutions, etc. Since the number of schools, teachers, and textbooks did not rise in proportion, it was necessary to fall back on expedients: in whatever premises were available—some were still being used by other public services— the pupils were distributed into three groups who succeeded one another on successive days; in the first-degree schools the pupils who had completed their four-year course were enrolled by force as teachers, and in the second-degree schools the sixth- and seventh-year students were made professors. The 1927 curricula were branded "kulak programs" and their authors were treated as "Menshevik opportunists." The curricula were modified on the basis of a new theory that had gained official acceptance, V. Shulgin's concept of the school as "the cultural training-ground for the factory." Moreover, much time was allotted to military exercises, which accounted for one-fifth to one-third of the school hours.

The reform of 1930–1931 immediately debased the level of education. The government, which recognized the fact, endeavored in 1932 to correct its excesses; among other measures, it ordered the abandonment of the various experimental methods and the return to general cultural subject matter.

In the field of higher learning, the universities were "purged" by the expulsion of the majority of their old professors, above all the most learned, and they were divided into separate schools (technology, pedagogy, Soviet law, social sciences, medicine), the cost of which was met by the economic organizations. The Academy of Sciences was reformed on a Marxist line, and, though the new members admitted to it might have had only minimal scientific background, they were veterans of real apprenticeship in the party. The number of "workers' schools" and their successors (night schools and accelerated courses) rose from 177 in 1928–1929 to 694 in 1930–1931, and the number of students of worker origin mounted from 30 per cent to 55 per cent. As for the number of institutions of general higher learning, they increased from 151 to 537 and their student bodies grew from 191,000 to 272,000. But here again quantity was achieved only at the cost of quality: the workers who were increasingly being sent to school were poorly prepared for the pursuit of education; real scientific preparation gave ground before "class" teaching and military preparation.

In 1932 the Commissariat of Public Education acknowledged these faults and denounced "the simplistic conception of the problem of the relations between science and production and the limitation of the tasks of learning to mere day-to-day problems." Under the decree of September 19 the universities' libraries were returned to them. In addition, entrance and promotion examinations were brought back; access was made easier for the children of educated parents; once more the professors were empowered to train "aspirants" to their profession. . . . But at the time of writing it was still too early to assess the results of these new measures.

Literature

A number of Russian writers of great talent—Ivan Bunin, Dmitri Merezhkovsky, Alexander Kuprin, I. Shmelev, B. Zaitsev, Balmont, the poet, and many others—had left Russia at the start of the Bolshevik revolution. Those who remained in the country, like Bryusov and Alexander Blok, or who returned to it, like Alexey Tolstoy and Andrey Byely, had to adapt themselves willy-nilly to the new system.

Here again Bolshevik sympathies tended first of all toward extremes, such as futurism, which, in the person of the poet Vladimir Mayakovsky announced itself as "the art of the proletariat." Soon futurism had a competitor in the organization called *Proletkult* (Proletarian Culture), which was aiming for a monopoly on literature and pledged itself to set to work at once on the development of Socialist forms of thinking and feeling. But the new government did not propose to tolerate any monopoly aside from itself, and a third group also sought its favors: this was the organization of worker and peasant authors, filled with enthusiasm for the great works of triumphant Communism but too lacking in talent and literary practice.

The NEP restored a relative freedom that benefited the writers whose training was of the old sort. A young group, which had already attracted notice but concealed its intellectual independence under the name of the "Brothers of Serapion," which was derived from the German romantic, Hofmann, produced writers of talent such as Zoshchenko, the humorist, and Fedin, Slonimsky, and Tikhonov, the novelists. Other writers, who had embraced silence, now spoke out: these were the men known as *poputchiki* ("fellow-travelers") : Boris Pilnyak, Isaak Babel, Leonid Leonov, backed up by authors of the earlier generation such as Alexey Tolstoy, V. Veresayev, and Ilya Ehrenburg. They were immediately attacked by the "proletarian" authors. But the "proletarians" did not enjoy the government's support; Trotsky and Lunacharsky demanded tolerance for nonproletarian talent, which more or less included some of the worker and peasant writers such as the founders of the group called *Pereval* (The Transit). This was the period of the best works in Soviet literature, which turned aside from military themes in favor of psychological subjects: such novels as Fadeyev's *Razgrom (The Defeat)*, published in 1925–1926, and Leonov's *Barsuki (The Badgers)* and especially Gladkov's *Cement*, both of which appeared in 1926 and enjoyed great success.

The tolerance practiced during the NEP did not survive it. After 1928 the government exerted constantly increasing pressure on literature, which, like the school, it compelled to serve only the task of "building Socialism." More and more radical literary groups were created, and each new one accused the others of betraying the cause of the proletariat. Thus the *Rossyskaya assotsiatsya proletarskikh* (abbreviated as RAPP—the Russian Association of Proletarian Writers) declared war on the *Vserossysky soyuz pisateley* (All-Russian Writers' Union) and was itself attacked by its left-wing members, such as E. Lebedinsky, and they in their turn were denounced in 1928 by the extreme left, which held that literature should abandon the description of the "living man" and "psychological refinements" in order merely to execute Stalin's "Socialist orders." The broadly developed novel gave way to the short "essay," which glorified the Five-Year Plan, the *kolkhoz,* and other triumphs of the proletarian revolution. An outstanding success in this domain was Bezymensky, who also, however, was very quickly excommunicated. This atmosphere of round-robin denunciation degraded the level of literature. Nevertheless, probably because of Maxim Gorky's influence over Stalin, the government seemed later to be relaxing its tutelage over the art of letters; on April 23, 1932 the RAPP was dissolved because of its intransigence and its excesses.

The Press and Posters

The daily press and posters were even more effective than books in influencing thought.

"Our press and our party are inseparable," a Bolshevik author wrote. "The names of the newspapers were synonyms of the party; the party itself has been formed on its press organs." Only the official press, of course, could publish in the USSR. *Izvestia* was the organ of the Soviet government and *Pravda* was that of the party. In addition to these two publications, which were much too heavy reading for the ordinary newspaper buyer, the party issued a number of special journals for the peasants, the workers, the Red Army, the young, women, etc., and in each the editors clung to the language familiar to the reader group. During the NEP the newspapers gave up abstract commentary, which was difficult for the popular masses to comprehend, in favor of appeals to the readers' feelings and interests. In order to establish a bond between the newspapers and their readers, the party created the "worker correspondent" *(rabkor)* and the "peasant correspondent" *(selkor),* who became the government's eyes and ears in the farthest corners of the country. With the inception of the Five-Year Plan the tone of the newspapers changed once more. Henceforth they were under instructions not to inform or to please but to "lead" the public by acquainting it with the government's decrees. This was when they began to rely so heavily on military terminology: this was their method of transmitting the capital's instructions to the various "fronts" that were established; a front for the purchase of wheat, a front for spring and autumn sowing, etc.; it was also the means of reprimanding "breakdowns" in production and demanding faster output rates, "shock" production pace and "Socialist competition" among factories, villages, institutions; designated targets were set by the press for its readers to "take by storm";

the newspapers "ripped off the masks" of "saboteurs" and foreign "imperialists"; they paraded the specter of war and called for more armaments and the fulfillment of the "Five-Year Plan in four years."

The poster was the favorite tool of Soviet propaganda. No great inspiration was required for its success; it was enough to find the most vivid images to illustrate a slogan—*Everything for the defense of the country!* or *Who is for the Soviets?* or *Soviet Russia is a besieged fortress.* Initially these, with caricatures of the tsar, the pope, and the bourgeois, were the usual subjects for the cartoonists. The best posters were those of D. Moor (Orlov) and V. Denisov, who had already made reputations as caricaturists before the revolution. Somewhat neglected after 1922, the poster returned to fashion after 1928, and its dominant themes were the stockpiling of wheat, state bond issues, industrialization, and collectivization.

Cinema and Theater

The theater and in particular the cinema were intended to supplement the work of the press and the poster.

The cinema became a state monopoly in 1923. As Eisenstein, the Soviet director, wrote, it "is not a mere entertainment; it is intended for the propaganda of the Soviet state and its ideas among the people. . . . To us, art . . . is one of our weapons on the front of the class struggle." That was why, after having translated novels like *Cement* into film, he specialized thereafter in executing "the social commands of the time." According to Léon Moussinac, on April 1, 1927, there were more than 5000 film theaters in the RSFSR, including 1491 in actual theaters built for the purpose, 1780 in clubs, 232 in villages, 1498 mobile auditoriums in the rural areas, and 142 similar ones in the Red Army; in the Ukrainian SSR there were 2020; in the other federated republics there were approximately 1000—in other words, more than 8000 in the USSR as a whole.

In the field of theater the methods of the old "academic" stage, including Stanislavsky's famous Moscow Art Theater, were abandoned. A new doctrine took over: that of the "theatrical October," * whose prime pioneer, Meyerhold, a director from the old days, decided to employ "cubist-futurist construction in three dimensions," which eliminated stage sets and replaced the dance with acrobatic gymnastic exercises. The theater passed through the same conflicts of doctrine that harried literature: it moved from the concept of "art independent of class" to that of collaboration in "building Socialism"; psychological

*So-called in honor of the revolution of 25 October/7 November 1917.

drama was condemned and the proletarian playwrights brought forth "class dramas" that dealt with "economic phenomena" and not with "living man." But the reaction against "class" themes sprang up sooner in the theater than in literature. The public stopped going to propaganda plays and crowded other kinds as soon as the theaters began again to offer pre-revolutionary works. If the theater wanted to work for propaganda purposes, it had above all to go back to being believable; "to move hearts" required the living human voice, not the gymnastics of acrobats, as the Soviet government seemed in the early 1930s to have grasped.

Art

The most famous Russian artists, such as Shukhayev, Yakovlev, Sorin, Chagall, Byenois, Somov, Korovin, Grigoryev, and so many others, left the country. Those who remained in the Soviet Union turned chiefly toward futurism and cubism. In the beginning the state demanded above all that they demonstrate a feeling for the "monumental," portraying the "collective man," the "machine man." They erected colossal statues—though in stucco—in the public squares, depicting heroes of revolution from Styenka Razhin to Marx and Engels. On Soviet ceremonial occasions they lavished bright colors over the fronts of buildings and the lawns and trees and flowers in the parks and squares. But this playfulness did not last long. Under the NEP state subsidies ended, the "supply and demand" system began to function again, and the old artistic tendencies reappeared. The portrayal of machines and the "collective man" was dropped by artists, who turned to the depiction of subjects familiar to everyone and treated them in a realistic manner. Naturally these subjects were selected, preferably, from episodes of the Communist revolution, but they also included once more, to the great delight of visitors to art exhibits, genre painting and even landscape and still life.

In 1928 art began to reflect the new political orientation. It was ordered to become "class art" and to take a direct part in "building Socialism." The "material object" became the type of proletarian art, and the ideal manner of treating this "object," in architecture and furniture, was that of "constructivism," as preached by Le Corbusier. Even the mass of the people was invited to collaborate in artistic production. "Naturalist" realism had to give way to so-called "proletarian" realism. Since no one quite knew in what this new style consisted, its practitioners fell back on an "engineer's esthetic" in architecture and an "esthetic of social adaptation" for all objects of daily use such as furniture, dress, fabrics, etc.; in this area the "standardization of the business office" was the type of Soviet artistic achievement.

Music

The two Russian composers who enjoyed worldwide renown, Igor Stravinsky and Sergey Prokofiev, lived and worked abroad, as did the representatives of the older generation—Glazunov, Cherepnin, Gretchaninov, Medtner, and Rakhmaninov. Hence the Soviet Union's musical output was particularly poor.

The attempts made to introduce the newest "sounds" and musical "futurism" were deplorable failures. What was required for the masses was the simplification, not the complication, of music; that was why the commissions for "monumental" works intended to celebrate revolutionary "heroism" lured chiefly the professional musicians who executed them in the conventional style of which alone they were capable.

The real artists withdrew into themselves and composed without thought of being heard. Myaskovsky, who had written eight symphonies, continued the old traditions of the Conservatory of St. Petersburg; Feinberg carried Skryabin's mysticism to the point of musical pathology; Aleksandrov was extremely academic; none of them fell under the influence of the Communist revolution.

Among the younger men, A. Mosolov, who composed imitations of the thumping and hissing of machinery, and A. Kreyin, who was commissioned to write a symphony on "Marx-Lenin-Stalin," were exceptions; but the others—Lobachev, Korchmarev, Bugay, and the rest—merely turned out triumphal marches, were in no way innovators, and followed in the footsteps of their masters of the older generation.

Science

Although a number of scholars, like the writers and the artists, left Russia in order to carry on their work abroad, many remained in the Soviet Union. Those who were not supplanted by "Red" professors and scholars continued their labors in the Academy of Sciences, the special institutes, and the universities. Many of them—some with worldwide reputations—were unable to endure the cold and hunger of the period of "war Communism." Others—historians like Platonov, Tarle, the Moscow group, and the disciples of Klyuchevsky, accused of being monarchists and maintaining relations with foreign countries —were deported to the provinces or imprisoned. There were many more, "specialists" employed in various industries, who could not prevent the failures made inevitable by the government's exigencies and who were accused of counterrevolutionary "sabotage" and made to expiate the flaws of "Socialist construction" through arrest, exile, or condemnation to forced labor during the period of Stalinist domination.

Some scientific disciplines, however, were more fortunate than literature. The social, political, economic, legal, and humanist disciplines, of course, could not go against Marxist doctrine. The more fortunate were principally the pure sciences, such as mathematics, physics, chemistry, and biology, or the sciences adaptable to practical application, such as geography, which prepared an inventory of the country's natural resources, or archeology and linguistics, which studied above all the various national minorities in the Soviet Union, or statistics, at least until Stalin shut down the Central Statistical Office and the Institute of "Probabilities" *(Konyunkturny Institut)*. Undoubtedly they too suffered from the disorganization of the universities, but they were not short of financial help from the government. They had larger sums than before with which to equip special institutes and organize explorations of areas of Russia that were virtually or wholly unknown, especially those inhabited by the autonomous minorities.

In the domain of history the study of the revolutionary movement and, thanks to the disclosure of unpublished documents, of the last years of tsarism made great advances. Interesting works, too, appeared in the field of Russian art, particularly religious art (the ikon and the fresco). But it was mainly in the sciences whose findings had no political aspect that there was a rise in new publication and that the most important results were achieved.

Conclusion

At the date at which this narrative ends—December 1932—it was licit to believe that the third phase in Soviet history, that of the Five-Year Plan and the dictatorship of the party's secretariat general, should be nearing its end. If the second Five-Year Plan, which Soviet experts were then preparing, but which had been temporarily postponed, was to be achieved, this would take place in a completely changed political environment.

In these past five years, as we have seen, the Russian revolution had become quite seriously "nationalized"—in other words, it had in part lost its "international" aspect. The very grave problems with which it had to cope were specifically Russian problems. The major problem was the contradiction between the agricultural character of the country, with its disproportionate development, and the excessively rapid rate of its industrialization. The effort undertaken to overcome this obstacle through the socialization and collectivization of agriculture had undeniably failed.* It was this failure that should mark the end of the Stalinist period. It proved that the country was not in a position to support an industrial structure that was burdensome because it lacked a national market sufficient to absorb its output and it could not continue exporting abroad at a loss. This had been completely understood by the opposition to the Stalinist system, by the representatives of the older generation (the "old guard"), who had been thrust out of the management of business, and also by the younger men, who were not wholly the captives of the official doctrine and who, as they observed the course of events, must have recognized the existence of a gulf between that doctrine and the possibility of a normal life for the mass of the people that was being sacrificed to it.

Undoubtedly the existence of a huge bureaucracy—which was intermingled with the Communist party†—could keep the current system in being by preventing radical and quick reforms. But it was essential to take into account the deterioration in the economic situation of the officials, the hatred that they inspired in the masses, and, finally, the bonds that united these masses with the young men enrolled in the Red Army. All these factors might allow us to foresee changes, the partisans of which were becoming more and more numerous. In appearance the two oppositions seemed to derive diametrically opposed conclusions from the same facts: the "right" opposition more and more sharply demanded the restoration of living conditions better suited to Russia, while the "left" opposition insisted on a return to Trotsky's idea of "permanent revolution" and the renewal of international action in its original totality and simplicity. At bottom both were in accord in their call to the nation to retrace its steps and return to the road abandoned by the Russian revolution on 25 October/7 November 1917. But history does not move backward. Whatever the possible change may be, it will open a new era in the history of Russia. To predict its character is not the task of the historian.

*In his report to the plenary assembly of the party's central committee in January 1933 Stalin acknowledged that the great majority of the *kolkhoz* and the *sovkhoz* was not yet profitable.

†On July 1, 1932, as we have seen, the membership of this party totaled 3.13 million in spite of the series of "purges."

Index

DATE DUE

13 Jan 77			